Working and building in this busy
immigrants coming to where so man
men – although there were some w
ideas, of chancers and enthusiasts as
ation, with many
largely a world of
a world of bright
which managed to
consume a phenomenal amount of alcohol. It was a world where the nascent gas industry
was just one element among all the innovation and ideas to which young men flocked –
and where some others came with more dishonest intentions. It was a very beguiling time
– and one whose legacy remains with us today.

I must apologise in advance for constant mention of streets and neighbourhoods which
will be unfamiliar to many readers. Most will be on the current street atlas and *The Horwood
Plan*, a contemporary street map, is available online and in the form of a printed book. I
agree however that it takes a lifetime to understand the cultural significance of these streets
– the difference between, say, Haggerston and Hoxton, or Stepney and Wapping. London
was, and remains, an area of small quirky neighbourhoods, housing a population of
amazing ethnic and cultural diversity.

Sadly, most people will not see old gas works as an attractive subject. In the early twenty-
first century they are thought of as dangerous, polluted sites and a cause for public
concern. This book is not a treatise on the dangers but an exercise in historical detective
work. The intention is to identify some of the early gas works their promoters and
locations and at the same time to describe how the industry was set up and developed in
industrial east London. It also looks at the use of the 'waste' products of coal gas
manufacture, those who bought them and what they tried to do, or actually, did with them.

It is necessary to be quite clear that, although it is usually thought that 'gas works' and 'gas
lighting' used inflammable gas made from coal, this is not necessarily always the case. This
study also looks at one major alternative.

The technology of coal gas lighting was developed initially for use in single buildings, in
France and the English Midlands, and installations to light individual industrial buildings
with 'gas light' are recorded as early as 1805/6. Gas lighting was developed at the height of
the 'industrial revolution' and made a major contribution to that process although
historians examining industrialisation have rarely discussed it in any depth.

The first recognisable gas works in the sense of a gas factory which made and supplied gas
to the public was in London and introduced issues concerning business and technology
which are not discussed here. However the idea of a gas works for public supply was in
itself new and introduced issues of ownership and control, not resolved for over a century.

5

In order to examine these issues we need to know more about this new industry. All that this book can do is to describe what it can and maybe throw a few ideas into the mix.

In the mid-1950s E.G. Stewart collated a list of gasworks sites, past and present, in what was then the area of North Thames Gas. Stewart was a process engineer, employed by the Gas Light and Coke Company, the forerunner of the nationalised North Thames Gas Board and his career was associated with gas manufacture in that area. His book therefore is solely concerned with gas works sites north of the Thames and so South London was omitted. Stewart provided a huge and diverse collection of gas works sites – his list includes huge modern works, together with tiny, short-lived experimental plants and some purely conjectural private gas works.

The River – the Thames – is a barrier across the metropolis and 'the other side of the river' remains a foreign country to both north and south. Both before and after nationalisation in the 1940s it has provided a seemingly unbridgeable barrier between gas companies. A guide to gasworks south of the river has never been produced.

In the early 1990s Friends of the Earth (FOE) published, with much publicity, a list of old gas works sites with the message that here lay pollution, both undiscovered and unrecorded. It emerged that FOE, unaware of the existence of Stewart's book, had used a list drawn up by the then defunct Greater London Council.

This book attempts only to identify gas works sites in east London before 1850 and it must be admitted that the definition of 'east' London is fairly eccentric. For good historical reasons it has been stretched west far enough to include the very first gas works at Westminster and to the east to include one early works in Woolwich in the South East, but only as far as the banks of the river Lea on the north side of the Thames.

Not all the gas works listed are 'gas factories' providing coal gas for lighting to the public. Some early industrial plants for factory lighting are included, together with some for scientific research and demonstration. It is hoped that this will show some of the inter-relationships between commerce and the scientific establishment.

Some of the narratives included here were originally used in a series of articles on early gas work sites in the *Newsletter* of the *Greater London Industrial Archaeology Society* and the articles about the Greenwich and Woolwich sites have appeared in *Bygone Kent*. I would also like to thank Brian Sturt, a historian who has specialised in the early gas industry, for his comments, which appear throughout this text.

There are many ways in which the influence of the gas industry could be examined in regard to its place in the history of the environment - I hope this work can demonstrate some of the ways in which this happened, but I would not claim to do more than indicate some of the milestones. I have attempted to describe some of the connections between the gas and other industries through the sale and exploitation of gas-making by-products and to look at how, for example, the 19th century chemical industry in east London grew because of the gas industry. Detailed research might reveal numerous industrial processes that were enabled either by a process or a substance that emerged because the gas industry was able to provide it. Industries grow and feed off each other - how important was the gas industry in the process of industrial growth?

INFLAMMABLE GAS MADE FROM COAL

The first "gas works" opened in London from 1811. Other works soon followed and the production of gas from coal quickly became a major industry throughout Britain -and, ultimately, the world. It seems reasonable to argue, that this industry had an enormous potential to effect change in the world around it. In terms of timing it should be seen as an important industry of the 'Industrial Revolution'.

It is with surprise, or resignation, that the historian of the gas industry turns to general histories of that period and finds gas hardly mentioned. Typically there will be a sentence that links it to industrial growth in Midlands towns with a comment on the lines that factories were able to work longer hours because of improved lighting, or something similar. With luck, there will be additional remarks about safety at night in an urban environment.

Gas manufacture was a major industry - there were working sites throughout the country and they used a lot of raw materials, influenced transportation, and employed many people. It would seem reasonable to suggest that its influence must have been greater than the, very obvious, end result of improved lighting. What was its relationship to the surrounding industrial world? Was lighting what was initially intended?

One aspect might be the influence of the London gas industry on coal mining areas and the growth, in particular, of the Durham and Northumberland coal fields and communities during the early 19th century. This should include the business links, which grew up between investors and owners in both London and the North East. Something else might be the impact on shipping and river trades, for example in the 'coal trade' where coal came by ship from the North East ports to London. This might take in, for instance, ship design, the spread of wharves and wharfage regulation on both Thames, and Tyne, development of wharf machinery, and so on. There are also other extractive industries, which developed through the need for return cargoes of ballast. This need for transport extends into railway development and transhipment methods - and continues into questions on the location and design of communities.

While this book examines the London industry it is also important to understand the wider European input into the development of gases for lighting purposes. Many of the researchers who came to London were from the Continent or had been educated there. There were also parallel developments in some European countries.

This is a vast field for research – and this work will take a brief look at the influence of the waste products of the coal gas industry on the chemical industry in particular.

COAL GAS
BEFORE IT WAS USED FOR LIGHTING

GAS FOR BALLOONS

By the late 18th Century research into inflammable gas made from coal and its properties had been undertaken for some time. Many of its earliest applications appear to have had either military uses or for amusement, and much of the research took place in mainland Europe. There have been a number of studies into 'Lighter than air gases' and the development of their use in works, for instance, by Paul Austerfield and Leslie Tomory.

Some of the earliest experimenters were those who wanted a gas, which had to be lighter than air, for use in balloons. It is often very unclear what gases were used in particular instances of balloon flights – although some of the enthusiasts are known to have experimented with coal gas. One such was Professor Jean Pierre Minkelers who set up a small gas lighting scheme as part of research into ballooning at Louvain University, in what is now Belgium, in the early 1780s.

In 1785 a lecture was advertised at the Museum of Natural History in Oxford by the Professor of Natural Philosophy on 'Inflammable Air – Theory of Balloons'. It was a subject under some discussion. Research into suitable gases for ballooning was a serious business and it is very likely that such research would have also have been of interest to the British military authorities

Machinery to make gas for this purpose would need to be portable, so it could be taken to the site of the proposed flight, so it is not suggested that anything like a gas works was involved. Gas industry historian Brian Sturt has commented to me '*The early use of coal gas* [in balloons] *must have been fraught with many problems ... and unless it had high hydrogen content also had poor lifting power. Later, when it was possible to purchase a holder full it could be arranged to beef up the hydrogen content to partially overcome this. It was bad enough in the 1820s - imagine what it was like 40 years earlier!*'

Flights which definitely used coal gas to lift the balloon took place well into the 19th century. A letter from Charles Green, perhaps the best-known British balloonist, said that coal gas was first used for the Coronation Balloon on 19th July 1821. Well ...maybe!

Gas -making for balloons was to be become part of the London gas companies' work in the 19th century - but it was only a sideline. Indeed in 1824 Phoenix Gas Co. had what

9

appears to be a price list and a set of rules which balloonists must agree to and observe while balloons were being filled. Some of the rules sound suspiciously like the result of past exasperation, since they include strictures that balloonists were forbidden to speak to gas company staff or to touch gas company equipment. In 1831 the Phoenix engineer was particularly thanked for his efforts in regard to a balloon. The Phoenix Company, based in inner South London was particularly near some 'gardens' – entertainment sites which were often used by early balloonists.

Some sites used for balloon flights are mentioned in the text and there is a short list included in the section on scientists.

In all probability there were many attempts and experiments which will remain unknown – and many will have hoped to have found useful applications for gas made from coal. Coal gas used for lighting appears to have emerged as the leading application – it had a very obvious use, was reasonably simple to set up, and, as we will see could be used commercially for widespread use.

Most histories of the gas industry begin by describing the period before coal gas for lighting was 'invented' - they run through a standard list of researchers and then go on to describe the first attempts to use coal gas for lighting. Many of the researchers were clergymen, who, presumably, had time on their hands, were educated and in a position to make 'scientific' enquiries. By the 1780s the possibility of using coal gas, or other inflammable gases, for lighting had been around for some time and had been taken up by those who thought they could put them to practical effect. They were part of a body of European research in France, and also parts of Germany and Bohemia. Many historians have written only about developments in England and concentrated on applications developed in the Midlands for use as lighting equipment for factories.

So – we should look at what was happening in London.

10

A DEMONSTRATION OF GAS LIGHTING IN PIMLICO

The first traceable London site associated with the development of coal gas for lighting, of which I am aware, was experimental. It took place before gas lighting became a commercial possibility but had a prospective customer in the Corporation of Trinity House This was, and is, the body responsible for lighthouses around the much of the coast of the British Isles. In the late 18th Century they were clearly interested in finding a means of powering their lights, and which should be one capable of independence from links to the shore for considerable periods and suitably bright.

On 24th May 1828 a letter appeared in the *Mirror of Literature, Amusement & Instruction*, a popular magazine, telling the story of an experimental gas lighting scheme in London in 1789. The writer of the letter was a 'T. Hatchard' and he described how, in 1783, he had been employed to write a '*fair copy*' of Lord Dundonald's patent for tar manufacture. The text of this patent gives plenty of hints on how to make gas from coal. Archibald Cochrane 9th Earl of Dundonald had indeed been looking for industrial applications for his various researches – and we will look at him, his good ideas and his persistent failures, and those of his son, later.

Hatchard said that in 1789 his neighbour was '*an elderly man called Campion who had lost large sums in Bristol making mixed metals*'. 'Campion' can be firmly identified as John Champion one of a family involved in a number of industrial activities but mainly known for the manufacture of brass in Bristol and Anglesey. John Champion's son had, like Dundonald, experimented with tar manufacture. '*Mr. Campion*', said Hatchard, was very elderly but, as a Quaker, had a '*comfortable annuity allowed by his society*'. It also seems more than likely that Champion would have been looking for industrial applications for this new technology.

Both Hatchard and Champion can be found in street directories of the day. Hatchard's address was '*Brewer Street, Pimlico*' and Champion's was *5 New Buildings, Princes Row, or Warwick Row*. This street is at right angles to Brewer Street, so their homes were adjacent, but not actually next door to each other. Warwick Row is still there. It is an area we would now describe as 'Victoria'. Brewer Street is now Bressenden Place – which in the 18th Century led to Elliott & Co.'s massive Stag Brewery. The brewery later became Watneys, closed in 1959 and is now the site of a supermarket. The area was then very different with no Victoria Station, no tourists, and near open space in parks and gardens. At the back of the houses were extensive garden areas. The street layout though is essentially the same.

11

Hatchard and Champion discussed the Dundonald patent. They then set up '*a fire place and chimney*' in Hatchard's garden. Hatchard said '*over the fire I placed an iron pot ... which held about a half-bushel of coals .... to which I attached a tin cylinder .. The smoke when lighted produced a column of bright flame .. which burned for six or seven hours*'.

Champion then wrote to the Corporation of Trinity House to ask if they were interested in using the process for their lighthouses. An entry in their minute book records how a delegation of Elder Brethren visited and saw the '*light by means of vapour issuing from coal*'. They granted Champion 20 guineas in thanks but the idea was not taken up. Hatchard said that this was because it might '*injure the (whale) oil trade which was considered a nursery for seamen*' - a common fear at the time.

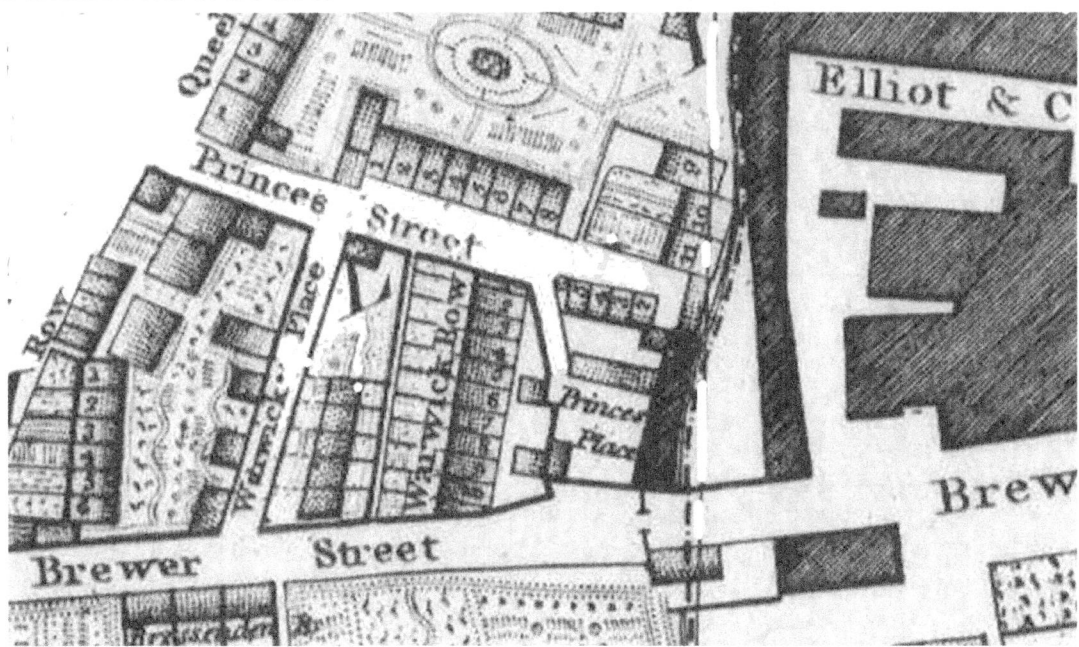

Champion also approached a '*Birmingham manufacturer*' who wanted a share of the process but this time Champion himself broke off negotiations for fear of '*the effect of former failures*'. That 'manufacturer' was Matthew Boulton of the Boulton and Watt Partnership, better known for their development of steam engine technology. This correspondence, which is preserved in the Birmingham Reference Library, tells a rather different story. It shows that Champion told Boulton about the '*trial made by Trinity Corporation at their expense*' and offered a half share for £300 pounds – clearly showing that he saw this as a technology which could be exploited. He met Boulton to discuss the matter and then heard no more, although he wrote again offering to explain further.

12

It should be pointed out that Matthew Boulton was William Murdoch's employer and this episode demonstrates that Boulton knew about the methodology of gas lighting and its possible application two years before Murdoch's famous experiments in Cornwall.

Several others knew about this gas lighting demonstration of the 1780s. John Champion told his nephews, Nehemiah and Charles Lloyd, both prominent and wealthy industrialists in Bristol. A number of Trinity House brethren also witnessed it. None of them seem to have been particularly surprised - which suggests that the possibility of lighting by gas was well known in the late 1700s. Some of the earliest applications for the industrial use of gas lighting in London were undertaken by men, like Joseph Huddart with connections to Trinity House, as we will see.

To return to Hatchard and Champion. It seems '*Mr. Campion being about four score*' the matter was dropped. Champion died in Pimlico, in 1794.

SO WHAT IS THIS ABOUT – IF ANYTHING?

Hatchard wrote his letter to the press in 1828 – about forty years after the event. No one came to his defence to verify his story. *The Mirror* printed a tactful note from a John Davy, which pointed out that many people had demonstrated gas lighting before Murdoch. *The Mirror's* editor added a note to say that they had declined to print a letter from 'Verax', which was '*impugning the veracity of Mr. H's statements on every point*'.

Despite many suspicions I think we have to accept that this story of experiments in Brewer Street is true – in that the verification from the Trinity House minutes makes it a really an uncontestable source. Trinity House is just too respectable and well funded to get it wrong.

A number of historians have noted and speculated on the letters to Matthew Boulton in the Birmingham archive. Hatchard's account fits neatly in almost every respect with what they say. Perhaps too neatly for comfort, although how could he, writing in 1828, have known the contents of the Boulton and Watt correspondence books let alone the Trinity House Minutes?

The conclusion is that several people knew about Champion's and Hatchard's experiments. Matthew Boulton is shown as knowing about a gas lighting scheme which took place two years before those of his employee, Murdoch's, experiments. In Bristol, Nehemiah and Charles Lloyd with numerous contacts were aware of it.

In *The Mirror* both replies pointed out that the roots of gas lighting went back a very long way indeed. This account was too long ago to profit any importunate inventors who might hope for a share in, what was by 1828, a source of very considerable profits. It was probably felt that Hatchard needed to be shut up before he made too many claims. He had, after all, by his own account stolen the ideas himself from the Earl of Dundonald's patent. The old Earl was still alive in 1828, although financial acumen never was his strong point – but he had numerous sons who were a lot sharper.

WHO WAS HATCHARD?
– AND WHAT HAS HE TO DO WITH LAMPOSTS?

Mr. Hatchard was soon forgotten. Why was he so quickly shut up when he made claims, apparently for the first time, about an invention some forty years earlier? Why did he wait so long before he wrote to *The Mirror*? Who was he? His identity has not been particularly easy to unravel.

A family called Hatchard lived in the Westminster area in the late 18th century. One of them, John, born of '*respectable and devout*' Thomas and Sarah in 1768, was about the same age as our Mr. Hatchard. Apprenticed to a bookseller he later founded the famous bookshop in Piccadilly. His father, Thomas, was probably a carpenter and in 1821, a generation later, a Henry Hatchard was a carpenter and undertaker on Millbank - then an industrialised riverside area within easy walking distance of Westminster and Pimlico. He might have been the Henry Hatchard thrown out of St. Margaret's Church in 1821 '*for brawling*'. So, the Hatchard family were established, and probably, well known in the area, if only for fighting in church.

In the 1840s several Hatchards in the Westminster area were described as '*sculptors*' - which, I think, is a euphemism for '*monumental mason*'. Henry Hatchard was a carpenter, and carpenters make coffins and so perhaps the family was in the undertaking business. In 1820 a James Hatchard who lived in Brewer Street was a member of the Royal Society - perhaps 'T' is a misprint for 'J' in the signature of the letter in the *Mirror*.

There is another twist. In 1794 Henry Hatchard, the Millbank undertaker, adopted a baby who was distantly related to his wife, Sarah. The child, also Henry, was the actual son of Thomas Sugg, an ironmonger of Hoxton whose firm were to become manufacturers of gas lighting appliances and it has been claimed that Thomas Sugg laid the first ever gas main in Pall Mall in 1807. In 1989 Sugg Lighting Ltd. installed lights in Trafalgar Square, which replicated those of the original Sugg patent and today's Sugg family are understandably keen to draw attention to their connection to the earliest days of gas lighting, describing themselves on their web site as 'World Leaders in Heritage Lighting'.

In the 19th century Sugg's engineering works was handily adjacent to the Westminster Gas Works in Marsham Street but such gas appliances were not their only trade. In the 1840s Hatchard and Sugg were undertakers of York Street, Westminster. Perhaps William Sugg had a line in coffin handles while his Hatchard cousins supplied coffins and monumental masonry.

Does this relationship with a well known supplier of gas lighting appliances make T. Hatchard's 1828 letter more or less suspect? Certainly, there appear to be relationships here that are not apparent at first sight. Later in the 19th century Sugg family members were often deeply embroiled in the internal politics of the gas industry.

15

COAL GAS FOR LIGHTING - HOW DID IT GET GOING? WHAT IS THE LONDON 'SPIN' ON IT?

We need to move forward very fast from 1789. Histories describing the earliest years of the development of coal gas for lighting will generally start with unverified stories of William Murdoch's work in Cornwall and continue with descriptions of development work at the Soho works of Boulton and Watt in Birmingham. It takes a long time before they get to London – but perhaps we need to look at London first see how this connects to Murdoch and Birmingham.

FREDERICK ALBERT WINSOR

This section gives some details – and guesses – about the life and work of one of the most influential figures in the early London gas industry. The next few pages, while being biographical, also describe much of the promotional work which was undertaken before the launch of the first public gas works. A process that, in Winsor's case, seems to have been far in excess of what was needed.

Gregory Watt, son of James Watt and in the Boulton and Watt Partnership, had witnessed a demonstration of street lighting in Paris by Phillipe Lebon using gas made from wood. He reported back on what he had seen and thus seems to have initiated work on gas lighting in Birmingham. Someone else who saw the demonstration was a German London resident who returned from Paris with very different ideas about gas supply to those of Boulton and Watt. Frederick Albert Winsor was someone who was, well, eccentric, but did have some very good ideas. One of them was the revolutionary notion of a gas works as a central factory where gas for lighting could be made and then distributed to customers. Other people were aware of the nascent water supply industry using a distribution network and the need for a legislative framework for its operation.

SO WHO WAS FREDERICK ALBERT WINSOR?

Winsor's antecedents are unclear - a number of identities have been ascribed to him. It seems likely that he had some undisclosed influence since those in powerful positions – including members of the Royal Family – gave him more help than could reasonably be expected. What remains of him and his work is a large body of pamphlets. What we know about him is largely derived from them.

Most of the histories of gas manufacture mentioned here have attempted to identify Winsor. For example, it has been said that he was:

...   'A strange German Moravian' (McKenzie in 'Vital Flame)..... or .... 'a German Professor of Commerce'.... or ....'born in Brunswick' (Stewart, Town Gas)......or .... 'an attentive foreigner from Moravia.... born in Znaim' .... (Everard) or .... ' born in Brunswick in 1763, though he is sometimes said to have been a Tsech a native of Moravia. He changed his name from Friedrich Albert Winzer to Frederic Albert Winsor when he settled down in England ' (Elton) .... or .... 'Hofrath Friedrich Albert Winzer '(Cotterell)

('*Hofrath*', by the way, means 'court advisor')

Almost none of that is true

CONFUSION – THREE WINSORS??

He has been confused with other people. The references to 'Moravia' and 'Znaim' are confusing him with one, Zachaus Andreas Winzler. In parts of Central Europe it is 'Winzler' not 'Winsor' who is seen as the inventor of lighting gas and as such he has been well researched. Arthur Elton picked up on him from German sources, Leslie Tomory in '*Progressive Enlightenment*' devotes several pages to him and there is also a biography in Czech.

Zachaus Winzler was born in 1750 in Swabia. He was a theologian and chemist – with considerable and sophisticated chemical skills. He travelled widely and had an important role in Austria on saltpetre production. He knew about Lebon's work in Paris and published a book in 1802· which described his 'thermolampe', derived from Lebon's. He demonstrated its use in cookery at Znaim, which is presumably the reason he has been identified as Czech.

Archduke Charles of Austria used Winzler's expertise in a gas lighting scheme for Vienna in 1803 and this was described to Joseph Banks in England in 1803. Archduke Charles's brother, Archduke John of Austria, visited the Gas Light and Coke Company's Westminster Works in 1816. Arthur Elton saw these letters in one of the envelopes of the Woodcraft collection at the Patent Office Library in the 1940s. When I checked the collection in the late 1980s the letters were not in the envelope. There was, however, a

17

letter from Elton to the effect that the letters were very valuable and would soon be stolen if they remained where they were. Enquiries to the library staff as to their whereabouts met with silence.

Elton also notes a Johannes Wenzler who designed a 'thermolampe', in 1802, in Passau, and he is also noted by Leslie Tomory, and elsewhere. Tomory comments that *'a longstanding source of confusion .... is the existence of three people with similar surnames'*. I would add that - personally - it is also the source of some suspicion. The names are all slightly different and they appear to have come from different areas of central Europe. But surely this is beyond a coincidence? Did they know each other?

These other researches, and the strange similarity of the names should make it quite clear that the invention of gas for lighting was not uniquely British – but proceeded in many parts of Europe at around the same time and that this was known in British scientific circles. However Leslie Tomory in discussing this issue has pointed out that in different countries there were different outcomes – hence in Germany research on coal gas 'led to an industry which produced synthetic chemicals from wood derivatives'. In Britain research led to the establishment of the gas manufacturing industry - but the initial response in London was very different to that of English provincial areas.

SO – FREDERICK ALBERT WINSOR

The instigator of the gas industry in London was initially Frederick Albert Winsor. So, what do we know about him? He was born in Germany in 1763 as Friedrich Albrecht Winzer to Henry Otto and Caroline Winzer - but exactly where is not clear. His naturalisation papers give his birthplace as 'Meuden, Kingdom of Prussia' which I am unable to trace. From his own account he was a 'merchant' or a 'Professor of Commerce'. He later claimed to have dealt with the banking house of Bloxham, Wilkinson and Taylor since 1787 and that they had held a cash account for him of £100,000 pa. - which does seem to be a great deal of money and implies investment in something rather more ambitious than the promotion of gas lighting. He is said to have worked for Weinholdt & Co. This may be the Bremen firm of John Wienholt who were importing Turkish goods into London in this period – including ammoniac and opium. In 'Notice Historique' he mentions property in Holland and speculation in corn from Hungary - but what else? Winsor's real business and connections are far from clear but they are presumably the reason he originally came to London.

18

WINSOR ARRIVES IN LONDON

Winsor seems to have arrived in England in the early 1790s, and claimed that in 1792 he spoke no English at all. He received British Citizenship in 1795. He may, however, have had another reason for arriving since the marriage registers of St. Peter, Cornhill, record the marriage of an F.A.Winzer to Harriet Wilkinson on 15th January 1791. Was she perhaps also a daughter of the banking house of Bloxham, Wilkinson and Taylor? His son, also Frederick Albert, was born in 1797 and his wife may have died around the same time, perhaps in Hamburg. Frederick Albert Jnr. may not have been Winsor's only child. Records show two children born in the 1820s to a 'Frederick Albert Winsor' - who could, of course, have been either the gas light promoter, or his son. These are Harriet Susanna christened 31st July 1822, and Frederick William Hodsoll Winsor christened 7th May 1824. In 1908 a history of 'St Mary's Lodge No 63', a Masonic Lodge was published written by Bro. Frederick Albert Winsor Jnr. who had died in 1874. The forward pays tribute to the work of Winsor *'and his brother'*.

Whatever Winsor's business interests were, he soon began a career as a pamphleteer. He began with a translation of poetry but soon turned to contemporary politics. He published a number of pamphlets. These were: *'The sympathy of souls'* published in 1795. *Memorial delivered at Rastadt by Frederick Louis de Berlepsch against his British Majesty as Elector of Hanover'*. Published in Brunswick in 1798. He began to use the pseudonym 'Obadiah Prim', the *'a hypocritical Quaker'* in Susannah Centlivre's 1717 play *'A Bold Stroke for a Wife'*. There may have been three other publications, none of which have been traced. They were: *History of some great Mandarins. Political Review of the present and future state of Europe; Energetic Address of the Rev. Mr.Lavater;* and *Oh My Country. Political Confessions of a true Briton.* He also seems to have changed his name to 'Winsor' and published *'Address to the sovereigns of Europe', by Obadiah Prim. Published in London.*

His next leaflet was more identifiably British and with an economic, rather than a political, theme - it was published however, using the German version of his name. It is dedicated to the Light Horse Volunteers of the City of London and Westminster- a local militia with an interest in smart uniforms, swordplay, field days and cold collations. They were based in the building, which later became the Royal Free Hospital in Grays Inn Road and which still stands as the Eastman Dental Hospital. As a member Winsor would have been on social terms with a membership drawn from the innermost circles of City finance. The leaflet was: *'The Prosperity of England midst the clamours of ruin' by a Merchant of London published London. Preface by F.A.Winzer.*

WINSOR AND GAS LIGHTING

Winsor claimed to have been interested in the possibilities of gas light and to have experimented from around 1784, despite his stream of leaflets on political subjects. He said he had been prevented by pressure of work from continuing with this interest. In this he was probably no different to many young men with an enthusiasm. It must be presumed that his experiments were carried out in wherever it was that he came from. There were a number of experimenters in gas lighting throughout Europe before 1784 and it is assumed that the young Winsor had heard of one of these – and, as is speculated above, he may even have been related to them.

It was around this time that Winsor became aware of Lebon's work in France and he went to Paris to persuade Lebon to sell him some gas lighting equipment. He was unable to meet Lebon himself and had to negotiate via a M. Charles Pougens of the Institut Nationale. Lebon refused to sell without a bulk order and so Winsor went back to England to experiment for himself.

Having decided to make the necessary equipment himself and, having done so, took his ideas to the Duke of Brunswick, who, as father in law to the British Prince of Wales, would have seemed a useful contact – although of course the Prince's relationship with his wife, Caroline was not good, to put it mildly! That Winsor went to the Duke implies that he did not as yet have access to political circles in England but that he did have contact at that level in Brunswick itself.

Next he published a translation of Lebon's publicity material:

'Description of the Thermolampe invented by Lebon of Paris', published, with remarks in French, English and German, by F.A.W. of London. Braunschweig.

It is perhaps worth noting that in the same year Zachaus Andreas Winzler had published a booklet in Brno with almost the same title. This of course fuels the suspicions that they somehow knew each other, added to which that they both used the word *'thermolampe'* to describe the apparatus. Frederick Albert Winsor then returned to London and set up an experimental plant in one of the most affluent London suburbs - at the 'Rhedarium', just off Park Lane.

THE RHEDARIUM

Apart from Winsor's attempts to contact Lebon in France, and his own vague references to youthful experiments, nothing has emerged about Winsor's technical experience in making gas. His knowledge, on the evidence of his pamphlets seems to have been sketchy, to say the least. There is just one contemporary comment in Repertory of Patents in 1826 which suggests that he was responsible for some small-scale gas making plants. He is however known to have had two bases for experimental work, the earliest in this complex of buildings once associated with balloon ascents.

One of the few clues, which we have about the earliest gas making plant in London, comes from William Matthews. He was an early gas enthusiast who wrote down what he saw going on at the time. He said that Winsor was backed by a 'Mr. Kenzie' who lent him space in his premises. This 'Kenzie' was, he said, a retired coach builder who 'lived near Green Park'. This story is backed by one of Winsor's young assistants whose name was Stephen Hutchinson. Hutchinson claimed in Mechanics Magazine in 1836 to have invented a gas purification system himself while working for Winsor in 'Green Street'. In fact Winsor's Plain Questions and Answer gives an address of 41 Green Street.

On *Horwood Plan,* 41 Green Street is shown as the entrance to a very large open space, which seems to fill up an entire block at the back of the street. It is marked 'Rhedarium' - and this is described in the relevant volume of the '*Survey of London*' whose anonymous researcher has also picked up the connection with Winsor and his experiments with coal gas. The Rhedarium had been built as military stables in 1738 and then sold, in 1784, to be used as a coach manufactory by a Mr. Murdoch MacKenzie. The pictorial title shows an auction of horse-drawn vehicles in progress, while the plates illustrate a variety of dilapidated wagons, carts and carriages. The street layout remains the same today.

There are yet more tantalising connections – since, on 30th November 1784, it had been the site of departure for one of Blanchard's balloon flights. That balloon had used hydrogen gas prepared by Argand (the Swiss inventor of the oil burner) himself. Of such interest was the flight that Matthew Boulton, William Murdoch's employer, was kept informed of events throughout as L.T.Rolt recorded in The Aeronauts.

So, who was Murdoch MacKenzie? What, and who, did he know? What was his interest? Why did he support Winsor? Who were his associates and backers? Unfortunately, it has not been possible to answer these questions. There is however, another co-incidence in Green Street – nearby was the home of the future naval hero and adventurer, Thomas Cochrane. He was the son of the Earl of Dundonald, who was one of the earliest demonstrators of gas lighting. Thomas was himself an inventor of lighting systems based

21

on coal oils. This was done in his spare time from being a naval captain and commander, who, among numerous other things, pioneered the use of Congreve's rockets in the battle of Aix Roads in 1809.

As with so much else in the early gas industry it is tempting to ask 'what was *really* going on?' The Rhedarium was demolished in 1914 and the block of buildings which surrounded it is now full of diplomats and the road abuts directly onto Park Lane. 41 Green Street has been rebuilt and the old entrance blocked up. To the rear is Wood Mews where Renaissance Court', bearing the date of 1887, appears as a pastiche of an earlier stable block. Inside the block is a big, inaccessible garden laid out on the footprint of the older buildings. It is full of large mature trees, some of which could well date from Winsor's day. It is a garden which could yet hold a lot of secrets.

What did Winsor's work in Green Street amount to? Probably just a small demonstration plant – 'simple and informal' – consisting of two retorts, one on each side of a kitchen fire. Gas made was led to a condenser and taken by pipe to the parlour above. It generated enough gas to light four candlesticks and a glass globe which served to heat, or to boil water or warm dishes - thus *'inflammable air may.... be led from the kitchen to any room to be applied for cooking, heating and lighting at the same time'*. This small scale and domestic arrangement was the forerunner, not only of massive gas work, but of many small gas lighting plants, designed to heat and light a house and which represent a popular, but almost totally unresearched, field in which the gas industry grew.

FREDERICK ALBERT WINSOR AND THE PROMOTION OF GAS LIGHTING IN LONDON

In 1804 Winsor took out his first patent:

18th May 1804 Patent 2764 Oven, stove, or apparatus for extracting inflammable air, oil, pitch, tar and acids from all kinds of fuel and reducing the same into coke and charcoal.

It is not difficult to see that this patent is rather more detailed than it needed to be if it was only for making gas for lighting. Furthermore, the detailed specification describes how the gas can be conducted through *'tubes of silk, paper, earth, wood, or metal to any distance'* and that gas could be applied to produce light and heat *'in all public or private illuminations, lighthouses, telegraphs and making signals on steeples, hills, towers, mountains, houses, ships and seacoasts'* as well as producing by-products *'charcoal for gunpowder, pitch and tar for preserving wood, wood or vegetable acid for making alum, vitriol and copperas, for dyeing and tanning, ammonia for many purposes, including purifying the foul pestilential infections of the air'*. It is, however, rather vague about how all of this was to be done.

At around the same time as the patent application Winsor began to publicise his ideas through public lectures. Elton noted the earliest one which was advertised at the Lyceum Theatre in *The Times* of 21st September 1804. Soon another pamphlet appeared:

'The superiority of the new patent coke, over the use of coals, in all family concerns, displayed every evening, at the large theatre, Lyceum, Strand .... addressed to all the enlightened inhabitants of London and the British Empire'. London.

This, his next publication, points to something very important about Winsor. This is which that, unlike Boulton and Watt, his plans were not restricted to making gas for lighting. In fact by this stage, it appears that the manufacture of coke, not gas, was his main aim. This is something which will be discussed later in the chapter on coke. Coke remained important and, as gas companies grew, they all sold it and generally called themselves *'gas light and coke'* companies. Of course, by 1804, 'Coke' had been known and used in manufacturing for well over a century but Winsor was now claiming an improved version.

Gas historian Brian Sturt has commented 'coke had been in use well before a hundred years before 1804. The brewing industry was using coke in the 17th century and no doubt others preceded them. The modern coking industry was established in the mid-18th century, producing coke for metallurgical processes – the main requirement was a hard, uncrushable product suitable for blast furnaces, etc. When coke was produced from coal carbonisation – like that produced by Winsor – this was in effect a low temperature coke.

Compared with that from coke ovens it has a higher volatile content and consequently improved combustion characteristics which were especially suited for use in a domestic grate – hence the hype about patent coke, etc." It sometimes appears as if Winsor's first intention was to start a coke company, to which 'gas' was added as an afterthought.

Nearly fourteen years later, in 1818, 'coke' was included as an entry in Abraham Rees' *Encyclopaedia*. Here, Rees highlighted a patent held by *'Mr. Winsor ... for the manufacture of a superior kind of coke'* - showing that Winsor was seen as the purveyor of something new and exciting. One of the surviving copies of this pamphlet, which I saw in the old Patent Office collection, also demonstrates Winsor's wider knowledge of the subject, since it is inscribed to *'The Rev. Watson, Bishop of Landaff with greatest respects from the Author'*. Dr Watson was also Professor of Chemistry at Cambridge and an acknowledged authority on coke.

In 1804 Winsor was not the only person to produce something to be called 'patent coke'. He himself mentioned *'that celebrated haacter* (sic) *Doctor Clarke' who set up a patent coke company in 1804.'* This is quoted in the Gas Light & Coke Co. Minutes in June 1812 in a letter from Winsor. There he describes Clarke as *'a Newton in theory'* saying that he *'persuaded the Committee of the intended coke company and the subscribers that he could construct a large stove to answer all the purposes required, and thus he spent £1000 of the coke company's money'*. Clarke has not otherwise been traced.

In 'Nicholson's Attack' Winsor described a *'phantasmagory celebrity'*, a Mr. Philipstall *'who subscribed to a patent coke company'*. Patent coke seems to have been a feature of the period. Paul de Phillipstall (aka Paul Philidor) lectured on chemical subjects at the Lyceum during the early years of the 19th century and had demonstrated the use of coal gas for lighting in Dublin in 1804. Winsor also detailed how Phillipstall had left London to erect a lighthouse in Dublin and then went to Scotland with *'a ghastly puppet show'*. He has been studied by historians of illusion and presented his version of the Phantasmagoria at the Lyceum Theatre in 1801.

Winsor published two more pamphlets in 1804.

'The New Patriotic Imperial and National Patent Company, for establishing sundry manufactories to make and extract for home consumption and exportation, coke, charcoal, ammonia, acids, oil, tar, chemical salts, &c. From all the combustibles in nature; and for applying the inflammable air obtained from the raw fuel to the purposes of heating, boiling, smelting, lighting, illuminating, &c'. Anon. London

and

'Account of the most ingenious and important national discovery for some ages. British Imperial patent light ovens and stoves, by which above 1,000 per cent, are saved and gained in light, heat, and some valuable products for British manufactures, commerce and navigation as proved by an exact account of profit and loss affixed ... London

Perhaps in these titles too we can see that to use coal gas for lighting was not Winsor's only idea - perhaps not even his main idea, since lighting is buried in the titles among proposed applications for the products of the distillation of coal.

In '*Account of the most ingenious*' he describes a gas making plant for domestic use and makes some astonishing claims for the use of what might result from the distillation of coal. One of these claims was about what he described as 'pyroligneous (i.e. 'specifically from wood') and coal acids' – knowledge of such products of coal and wood carbonisation was still very rudimentary. However, around this time, Charles Mackintosh was researching the use of related substances in Scotland, and it is possible that Winsor knew him.

Winsor also discussed the use of the by products of gas making in tanning. This included the waterproofing of leather, and, more alarmingly, the curing of ham and beef. He said that it was '*valuable in the fabrication of white lead, copperas and alum*' and '*fixes dyes strongly*'. Note the title is '*for establishing sundry manufactories to make and extract for home consumption and exportation, coke, charcoal, ammonia, acids, oil, tar, chemical salts, &c.*' . At this stage Winsor was not actually discussing the setting up of a gas company but of something more general which would exploit all these things, including, of course, coke. Much of what he had to say in these early leaflets was about the all-embracing nature of what could be done, to use the products of the distillation of coal in sorts of ways.

It is however in the appendix of the second leaflet, called the '*Account Current of Profit and Loss*', that Winsor reveals both his current thoughts on the use of gas and some of his wilder speculations. He provides a detailed balance sheet for a domestic gas-making stove. There is no need to go into a lot of details about his calculations, although some authors have describing this in detail Suffice it to say that Winsor reckoned that for every £6 spent on domestic heat and light using his method, the grateful householder could expect to make a profit of £64. 10s. He also hinted, at the very end, that a company might be set up to realise this good fortune.

Meanwhile he continued with his lecture series at the Lyceum and at Green Street. Inevitably, he attracted those who wished to claim his ideas as their own.

ENTHUSIASTS AND DEMONSTRATIONS

While Winsor was drawing attention to the possibilities of gas lighting through lectures, demonstrations, and pamphlets a number of others were experimenting with this exciting new medium. Some were scientists, some were entrepreneurs, some enthusiasts; among them were many charlatans. All sorts of enthusiasts were experimenting with setting equipment themselves to make inflammable gas and lighting apparatus. We know odd bits and pieces about some of them. There must have been many more.

Some gas lighting schemes were set up as demonstrations:

TOTTENHAM COURT ROAD

This is a mysterious early gas making plant. The only information about it is a chance remark by someone known to be deceitful! If it existed it was in a residential area at the bottom end of Tottenham Court Road which stood opposite a massive brewery complex. There is no indication as to the date except that it was likely to be before 1811. The word 'works' is probably a massive overstatement —much more likely it was something makeshift in a shed at the back of the shop.

This is a mystery unlikely to be solved. In copies of *Mechanics Magazine* from the 1830s a

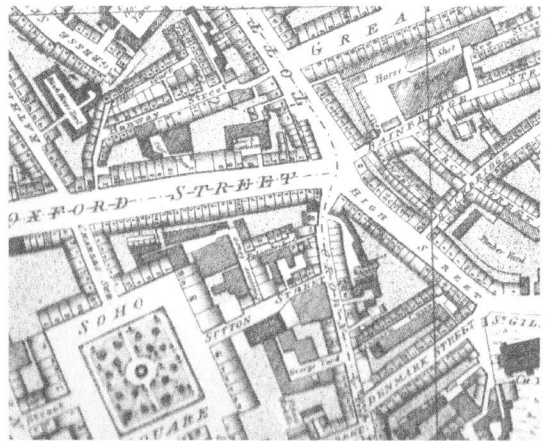

certain Clovis recalled how one Stephen Hutchinson had worked with Frederick Albert Winsor in his first experiments at Green Street. He said that Hutchinson had also been involved in the building of a gas works *'for a West India Merchant ..... opposite the Meux Brewhouse in Tottenham Court Road'*. The Meux Brewhouse was the vast Horseshoe Brewery on the corner of Tottenham Court Road the site of which is now partly covered by the Dominion Theatre. As a very large building sited on a corner, this brewery was 'opposite' numerous small works and businesses; any one of which could have been a *'West India Merchant'*. However there was no other large works in the area which would be an obvious candidate and which could account for Hutchinson's statement.

Soon after this item was published Clovis was unmasked by *Mechanics Magazine*. Many of his letters had been about Stephen Hutchinson and had pointed out that Hutchinson was responsible for almost every invention of significance in gas manufacture and that he, Clovis, had personally witnessed them all. At the same time Hutchinson was applying for patents on all of these inventions. Eventually *Mechanics Magazine* was able to report that they had discovered that 'Clovis' was the *non-de plume* of Stephen's father, Joseph Hutchinson, former manager of the Liverpool Gas Works. We are left to make up our own minds on the truth of the Tottenham Court Road installation, or indeed about Stephen's numerous alleged inventions.

Stephen Hutchinson was to continue with a varied and interesting career, working for the London Gas Company which lost a lot of money under him. *Gas Engineering* commented, '*a worse arranged works never came to our notice*'. He eventually died in 1881 as the result of a bite from his pet eagle.

LARDNER'S CHEMIST SHOP

A demonstration apparatus set up in a shop in a fashionable part of London - and installed by someone who had had access to Winsor's ideas. It shows some of the excitement and novelty value which lighting by gas was beginning to acquire.

In June 1805 the *Morning Post* described the shop window at Lardner's Chemist Shop in Piccadilly. Each evening it was '*brilliantly illuminated with Carbonated Hydrogen Gas from the decomposition of coals*'. Who was responsible for this? It appears that one of Frederick Albert Winsor's assistants had decided to go freelance!

This resulted from Winsor's lecture programme. Winsor's English was not good and he needed English speaking assistants as help as interpreters. He therefore recruited a number of young men for this task – he described them as '*bungling smiths and low tinkers*'. Naturally, they learnt a lot about gas lighting in the process.

One day one of these demonstration assistants, Edward Heard, failed to turn up at a lecture. He had, he said, been '*dining with friends*'. This excuse was too much for Winsor. He saw it not just as a dereliction of duty but thought that Heard thought himself too refined to lower himself to work in the lecture room. Winsor castigated Edward, who he called 'Isaac' Heard. (The real Isaac Heard was a prominent dignitary of the times,

27

currently Garter King at Arms - so perhaps Winsor was indulging in a sarcastic point vis a vis Edward Heard's pretensions!)

Edward Heard had been working at Lardner's Chemists in Piccadilly situated on the corner of Albany. He advertised himself as a 'chemical assistant'. Winsor said, in Nicolson's Attack that he had taken him in *'clothed and fed him'* but non-attendance at a lecture was too much, and Winsor sacked him.

Heard departed with the script of Winsor's lecture still in his pocket and went off to his

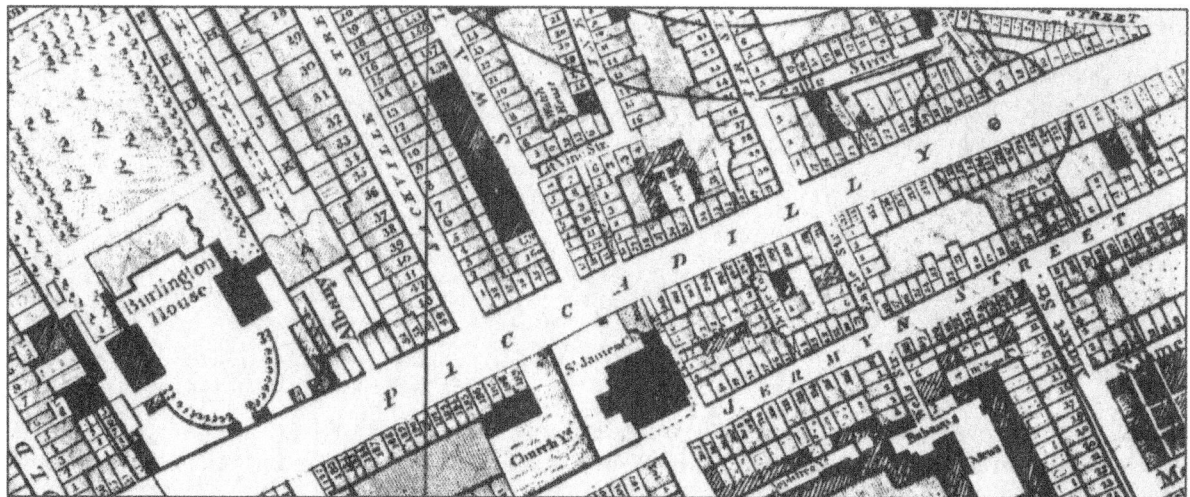

former employers where he arranged the shop window demonstration based on what he had learnt from Winsor.

He was to go a lot further than Lardner's in Piccadilly. He went to Bristol, and maybe elsewhere, to advertise his system and demonstrate gas lights. He later worked with David Gordon on the first Portable Gas scheme and developed a gas purifying system.

Thirty years later he hit hard times and applied for charitable relief. After his death in 1858 the gas industry of the day opened a subscription fund towards support for his widow and children and in recognition to the contribution he had made to the earliest years of the industry.

GREGORY'S SHOP

Norton Folgate was, in due course, to be one of the earliest local authority areas to contract with a gas company, the Chartered Gas Light and Coke Company, for gas lighting in their streets. Earlier, however, a local shop keeper seems to have set up a gas making display of his own.

Nothing is known about Mr. Gregory's shop window beyond a single comment by William Matthews in his *Historical Sketch*. It might also be conjectured that there is a connection with Mr Desanges, mentioned below, whose premises was very near Norton Folgate.

Gregory himself joined the Gas Light and Coke Company Board in the early 1820s. He had a shop in Norton Folgate, the small 'Liberty' just north of the City Boundary and an extension of Bishopsgate Street. As a local authority Norton Folgate was an early buyer of gas for street lighting. Mr. Gregory was a local enthusiast also able to advertise the wonders of gas lighting for himself, and at the same time persuade local vestryman of the desirability of using it for street lighting.

While the nature of Mr. Gregory's shop is not known it might be noted that a later Gregory family were potato merchants in the area and that Norton Folgate backs onto Spitalfields Fruit and Vegetable Market. It might also be noted that Thomas Livesey, the Gas Light & Coke Company's Deputy Governor, had a brother who had married into the Spitalfields potato trade so perhaps the gas light was being used to illuminate a display of potatoes. Family history research on the Liveseys reveals that Thomas's brother James (grandfather of the 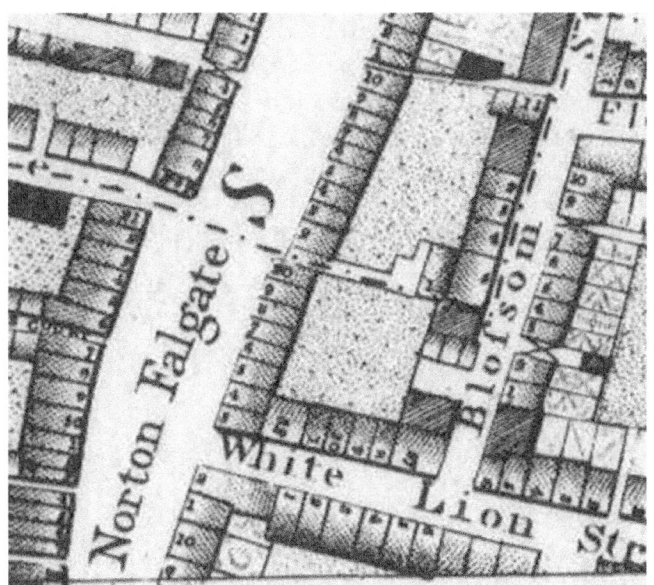 more famous George) had a greengrocer's shop in Bethnal Green Road and had married a Miss Hewes, from a Lincolnshire potato growing family.

DUKE OF RICHMOND

In his reply to 'Mr. Nicholson's Attack' Frederick Albert Winsor said a few things about Edward Heard's behaviour and defection. One of them was that Heard had gone to the Duke of Richmond who had opened a gas works with Heard's expertise. It is assumed that this is Charles Lennox the fourth Duke of Richmond who had succeeded to the title only in 1806. He was a soldier and politician, a member of the Privy Council and was, in 1815, to give the great ball in Brussels before the Battle of Waterloo.

Richmond had already supported the new gas company and his name was given as one of the sponsors of 'Considerations ... .on the Intended Heat and Light Co.'. This document which was intended to reflect the more sensible aspirations of the organising committee as against the views of Frederick Albert Winsor.

But, where was the Duke's gas works? It could have been on any of his extensive properties which included a London house in Portland Place, Goodwood in Sussex, Gordon Castle near Fochabers and Glenfiddick Lodge, Dufftown.

There is however another of the strange coincidences which continue to haunt this narrative. The town house of the Dukes of Richmond had been Richmond House, burnt down in 1791. In its place Richmond Terrace was built but not until after the fifth Duke had succeeded in 1819. What was on the site in the intervening twenty-eight years? The *Survey of London* does not comment. The southern boundary of the Duke's property was Cannon Row, site of the first gas works of the Gas Light and Coke Co. So did the Duke perhaps have something to do with the Cannon Row site?

THE FIRST GAS COMPANY IN THE WORLD

As time went on Winsor began to gather a body of supporters and backers around him. They launched a company to be known initially as the National Heat and Light Co. How were potential backers to know if his claims about gas lighting were rooted in reality? Since much of what he said in his pamphlets must have seemed like fantasy.

In 1806 he published:

"To be sanctioned by an Act of Parliament. A National Light and Heat Company for providing our streets and houses with light and heat, on similar principles, as they are now supplied with water, demonstrated with the patentee's authority and instructions by Professor Hardie at the Theatre of Sciences, No.98 Pall Mall. London.

This clearly promotes a new set of ideas. It is based on the concept of a gas supply available to the public made by a central gas factory. He still claimed that the vast profits, already noted in his previous speculation on domestic supplies, were still there. He estimated that he could supply gas light and heat to the entire country and still make a profit of £114,845, 294.

Winsor had taken premises in Pall Mall and this became his base for demonstrations and the first offices of the new company. It has some claim to be described as a permanent gas works in that although what was installed was a small demonstration plant, it nevertheless provided gas for lighting on a regular basis for some time.

97 PALL MALL

Winsor seems to have given public exhibitions at 97 Pall Mall from 1806, although any gas making plant there must have been very small. That Winsor was able to take offices in an expensive part of the West End implies that he was gathering support and finance.

He published a new pamphlet announcing '*A National Light and Heat Company*'. This noted that information could be obtained from '*that well known scientific experimenter and lecturer, Mr F.Hardie, Surgeon and Professor of Philosophical Chemistry, at The Theatre of Science, 98 Pall Mall*'. Invitation tickets to demonstrations in the Pall Mall building are in some archives and were described in some detail by Arthur Elton in '*The Triumph of Gas Lights*' from tickets in the Woodcraft collection and his private collection.

Hardie was one of several lecturers on what was a very popular circuit in the early 19th century who held demonstrations on a number of scientific subjects in Pall Mall. Winsor's liaison with him did not last very long however, since in some copies of Winsor's pamphlet his name has been crossed out and the address changed to number 97.

The location of these addresses in Pall Mall can easily be worked out from the *Horwood Plan* which helpfully provides street numbers. No. 97 was on the south side with a long garden backing onto the gardens of Marlborough House. Winsor himself said that it had once been the Star and Garter Inn. There had been two such inns in Pall Mall and this one, on the south side, was probably the least important. It was nevertheless very well known at the time. The fact that it was so near to Carlton House, home of the Prince Regent, raises questions about Winsor's relationship with the Crown and governing circles.

Winsor's pamphlets also describe the extent of the premises, which comprised a lecture room, a saloon with a chandelier, committee room with an atlas supporting a globe and other lights, drawing and dining rooms, a passage and stairs, a yard and entrance - all lit by gas.

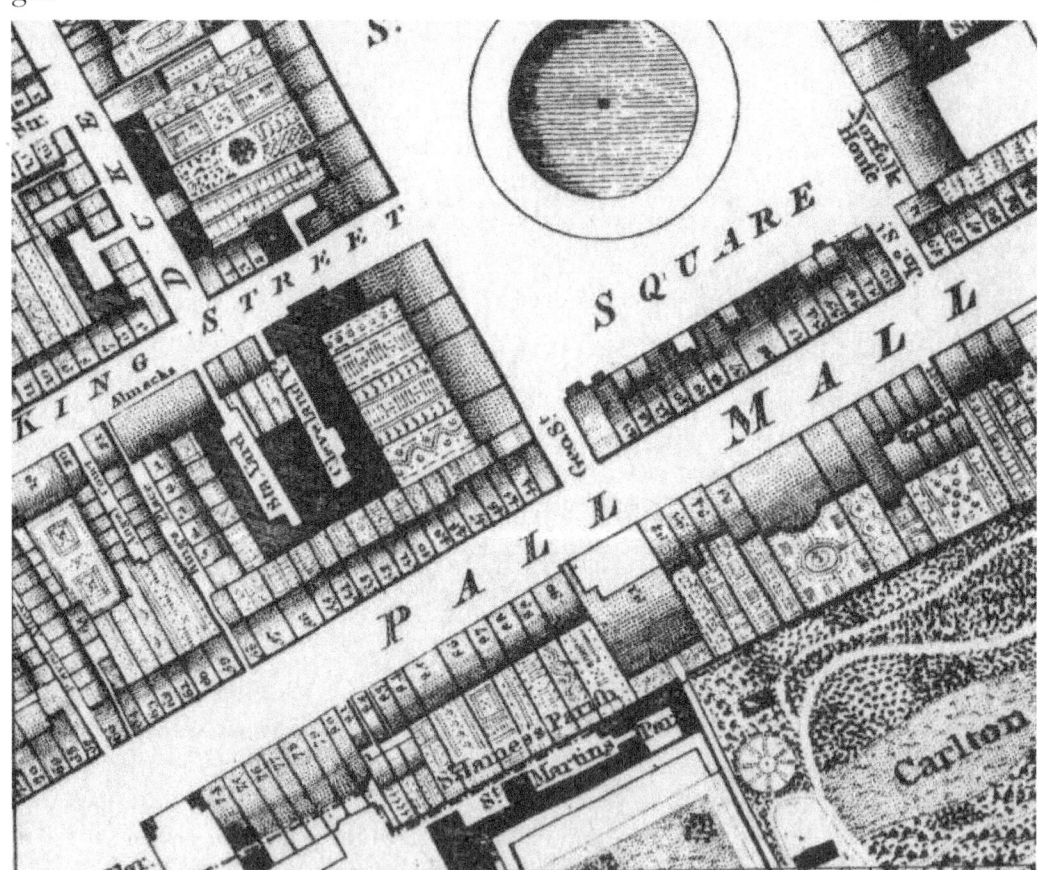

The Pall Mall building became the first offices of the new gas company. Once Winsor had parted company with the new directors they bought a lease on next-door, no.96. The Gas Light and Coke Co retained the building as offices until 1814. It then became clear that it was likely to be part of the area to be cleared for new buildings planned by William Nash in what became Lower Regent Street. The remainder of the lease was sold for £500 and the site now lies under London's clubland. Almost the last occupant of the site was Winsor's fifteen-year-old son, also Frederick Albert. He had been commissioned by the new Gas Light and Coke Company to work out how the new gas company was to dispose of its waste products. With his enforced departure an era closed.

WINSOR
PUBLIC RECOGNITION & SUPPORT

As early as the 1st January 1807 Winsor was publicly attacked in the scientific press. It is a measure of his ignorance about the scientific establishment in England that he had not heard of the '*Journal of Natural Philosophy*', called *Nicholson's*, and had some difficulty buying a copy to see what had been written about him.

Nicholson's was a most respectable publication which had, in the previous few years, published articles about the gas made from coal and its constituents from several of the leading chemists of the time. They included William Henry, Boulton and Watt's consultant; William Cruickshank of the Royal Military Academy and William Brande of the Royal Institution. It is not difficult to imagine what they thought of Winsor. This episode marks the beginning of what was to become a campaign against Winsor but something that at that stage could not have been clear. It shows that people who already had a stake in gas lighting were beginning to take Winsor's skills as a publicist seriously and did not intend that he should get in their way.

Winsor eventually got hold of *Nicholson's Journal*. He had not been able to find it in any bookseller and had had to call at Nicholson's 'Scientific Establishment' at 10 Soho Square. He found that he was mentioned in an editorial comment on a letter from 'a correspondent'. The anonymous contributor had written to ask if Winsor's claims were worthy of encouragement and the editor had replied that they were '*worthless*'. This drew from Winsor a whole flurry of pamphlets. First of all a spirited reply to *Nicholsons* in which he defended himself and described much of his past. Indeed much of the biographical information which we have about Winsor comes from this pamphlet, which he called '*Nicholson's Attack*'. He said that *Nicholson's* '*laboured insinuations, to raise if possible, public suspicion against my private character, conscious honour and rectitude promoted me to overlook with a smile ..but*' he goes on, '*I'll shame by silence or by satire joke*'. This is just what he continued to do.

Winsor produced four, or possibly five, more publications during the course of 1807:

Ludicrous debate among the Gods and Goddesses in a Grand Council assembled on the proposed destruction of the notorious London smoke by the use of Gas Lights. by Obadiah Prim, MD, BA, FRS, FAS.

A copy of 'Ludicrous Debate' has not been found. Information about it came from Arthur Elton's MS. He saw a copy in 1949 at the then Gas Light and Coke Company HQ in Horseferry Road. I saw what was presumably the same copy in the 1990s, fleetingly in a cardboard box. It was together with other books at the now defunct Bromley by Bow Gas Museum where it was being packed away for removal. I was not allowed to look at it. Its present location is not known but it is most likely in the National Gas Museum at Leicester.

Elton said that 'Ludicrous Debate' claimed that the introduction of gas lighting would 'purify all' and get rid of 'vapours most vile ... clouds of black smoke' by which 'the sky of Great Britain, my favourite isle, is shamefully obscured'. Smoke pollution was a subject of growing public concern and one in which a number of scientists were actively involved at the time.

Analogy between animal and vegetable life. Demonstrating the beneficial application of the patent light stoves to all green and hot houses. This deals with the topic of heat and light to the forcing of plants This was currently a fashionable subject in scientific circles of the day.

National Deposit Bank: or the bulwark of British Security, credit and commerce, in all times of difficulty changes and revolutions. This is about the need for new mechanisms to raise the large sums of capital, necessary if a gas company were to be set up.

Plain Questions and answers refuting every possible objection against the beneficial introduction of coke and gas lights. This includes the answers to what must have been common questions about gas. Winsor stated, for instance, that gas would not catch fire without a spark to 'inflame' it, and that a room full of gas would not catch even if a candle were brought in. He also said that it *'is more congenial to our lungs than vital air'.*

Cowpox and gas lights contra malice and ignorance of life, health and fortune against death and poverty. A simple dialogue between Messrs. Life & Co. and Death & Co. Published by a friend of truth for the uninformed. This attacks a number of (unnamed) learned professors and pontificates on the subject of vaccination. Elton thought that the 'Professor' attacked was a Mr. Hyde who had demonstrated the effects of asphyxiation on birds. He also felt that it was this leaflet, which finally exhausted the patience of Winsor's body of supporters.

34

In these leaflets the emphasis had clearly changed and show how Winsor had begun to defend himself against critics while publicising a wider range of uses for coal gas.

A provisional committee of Winsor's supporters had already been formed. On 4th June 1807 he gave a public demonstration of gas lighting to co-incide with the celebrations for the birthday of George III. The display was arranged along the wall of Carlton House, residence of the Prince Regent. It would thus have needed permission from him. This fact alone implies some sponsorship from the Royal Family.

There were thirty-two burners along the wall between Carlton House and the Mall. At a door into the gardens was a device made to resemble the Prince of Wales feathers and at the back gate of Carlton House was a *'grand transparency over the gateway, consisting of … cut glass stars … with gas lights behind besetting the crown and the letters GR.'*

Unfortunately, in 1807 there was also the suggestion of some sabotage to the central device. Elton quotes a report in a contemporary journal in which Winsor complained that 'liquid asafoetida' had been poured along the wall. It has been claimed that the ironmongers, Sugg, supplied the hardware for this demonstration. Suggs were relations of Hatchard described above earlier and later major supplies of gas appliances whose publicity in the 20th century takes care to describe their links to this early demonstration.

Today there is a green plaque on 100 Pall Mall to say that the first use of gas street lighting in the world was demonstrated, by Frederick Winsor in June 1807. This was installed here in 2007 by the Institution of Gas Engineers and Managers to commemorate the demonstration. The brief ceremony was enlivened by members of the gas lighting section of Westminster Council in appropriate clothing for such workers in 1807 and the plaque was unveiled by the Mayor of Westminster to a small but appreciative audience of gas historians.

On 24th July 1807 a meeting was held at the Crown and Anchor Tavern in the Strand to consolidate support to petition Parliament for a Charter and turn the provisional committee into the 'National Light and Heat Company'. Details of these first supporters are given below.

Most famously, Winsor lit part of the south side of Pall Mall, opposite Carlton House at the end of the year. This consisted of thirteen hollow iron lampposts, each twenty-four paces apart, and each supporting three glass globes. He had good reason to feel pleased with himself and on 22nd December 1807 he advertised the company in *The Morning Chronicle* and at the same time warned the public against *'impostors who … ignorantly assert, that Gas is pernicious to inhale, whereas every Apothecary's apprentice knows the contrary'*. Winsor, his supporters and the cause of gas lighting were on their way!

WINSOR'S BACKERS

Who were Winsor's first backers? Some rough details in this chart with more detail below.

They were a far more diverse group of men than those who subscribed to later gas companies. There are actual aristocrats like the Duke of Athol as well as enthusiasts like John Williams. There are a number of people who were, or whose relatives were close to the Throne. There are a number of medical doctors, lawyers, brewers and some close to the City Corporation. Perhaps they were all actually enthusiasts – why else would they be involved in this untested project.

Below is a short chart showing names and backgrounds. There are more details about these men when we get to the National Heat and Light Company

James Ludovic Grant (for detailed biography see below)	Aristocrat Royal connections	Career Sailor Royal Navy & East India Co	Home, Farnborough
James Hargreaves		Possible doctor	Ruthin, North Wales
John Murray, 4th Duke of Athol	Aristocrat	Scientific interests	Blair Athol Great George Street,
Viscount Anson	Aristocrat Ex MP	Horticultural interests	Shugborough
Christopher Baynes Baronet	Chair, London Docks Co.	Militia officer	Kilburn, Thirsk Harefield, Middlesex
Charles Cockerell	Member, family of architects MP. East India Co.	Banker	Sezincote, Broadway
John Turton	Royal doctor	Doctor	Brasted Place, Kent
Isaac Oliphant		Doctor	Chelsea
Matthew Bloxham	MP	Banker Partner of the Foudriners	Gracechurch Street Birchin Lane

William Devaynes	Chair East India Co. MP	Banker	Pall Mall Dover Street Highbury Cheltenham
Arthur Noble		Banker	London
Edmund Cobb Hurry .	Family of Yarmouth Ship owners	Banker Chair P'tsmouth Railway	
Joseph Garland	Director Imperial Gas Co	Businessman	Newfoundland?
William Paxton		Banker	Middleton Hall Carmarthen
John William Henry White		Magistrate	Parliament Place
Joseph Cooper		Merchant	Bishopsgate Street Clapham
Francis Cloust		Barrister	.
Leyon Levi		Merchant	
Joseph Ricci		Merchant	
George Cooper Ridge		Merchant	Morden Park, Mitcham
Thomas Saunders	Common Councillor City of London	Solicitor	
John Thompson		Merchant	
John Ambrose Tickell		Merchant	
Baron Wolffe	Baron Holy Roman Empire		Woodbine Cottage, Tunbridge Wells
William Holmes	MP Tory party whip. Irish, brewing		
William Belcher Parfitt		Brewer	Eversley Southampton
James White Barlow		Merchant	Tokenhouse Yard Bowes, Chipping Ongar

AND MEANWHILE ....

Other people were busy setting up coal gas lighting systems of their own. While Winsor was working on this scheme in Westminster something different was set up on the northern edge of the City

EARLY GAS MAKING PLANT
SET UP TO LIGHT
INDIVIDUAL BUSINESS PREMISES

The following accounts are of gas making plants installed, normally to provide lighting to industrial premises. It is not suggested that these were the only ones – just the ones we know about. Some have been taken from information in the archive of the Birmingham based Boulton and Watt Partnership, others from Winsor's pamphlets and elsewhere. Some of them are associated with 'improver' within the City of London Corporation, some are Government bodies, and some are business like Golden Lane and Huddart who were attempting something new. Others like Desanges and Ackerman are clearly enthusiasts. Ackerman's attempt to use gas clearly seems to have failed and it may be a sign that - before public supply gas works - that these gas making plants were best in a heavier industrial setting. Theatre lighting is a more complex subject and I understand a specialist work may be in production.

GOLDEN LANE BREWERY CO
GAS WORKS

The gas making plant erected for the Golden Lane Brewery was the first known in London to provide a supply of gas for a purpose other than for demonstration and experiment. It was sited to the immediate north of the City of London in an area historically rich in industry. It is also particularly of note that the company which had taken it up was one interested in applying new technologies to a traditional product and at the same time challenging a hugely successful sector with new methods of working. It is also important to note the interest in it taken by City politicians seeking to modernise. This is London's first gas works serving industry.

This first traceable gas lighting installation in a London factory does not seem to have been installed by either Boulton or Watt or by Winsor. However it may be the first commercial plant sited in London, which could make coal gas to use for lighting purposes.

Devotees of real ale should note that, even in the early 1800a, people thought that big breweries were ruining the beer. On the *Horwood Plan* a *'Genuine Beer Brewery'* is shown on the east side of Golden Lane in an area then known as 'St. Luke's'. Some writers have assumed that 'the Golden Lane Brewery' was something to do with the famous Whitbread Brewery, which stood a hundred yards away in Chiswell Street. Whitbread was a big commercial porter brewer and the deadliest rivals of the Golden Lane Company and later they also they had a gas making plant of their own. The Golden Lane Brewery was set up on co-operative principles. They were supported by publicans to provide a traditional product which they thought was under threat because of the factory-scale manufacture and sale of porter. Porter was made by large scale brewers like Whitbread. A description of the brewery is in *Peter Mathias, The Brewing Industry*.

The Athenaeum reported in August 1807 that the Golden Lane Brewery had installed a carbonising furnace and seven lamps in Golden Lane and four in nearby Beech Street. These lamps were supplied by pipes branching at right angles from a main source. Each pipe terminated in a lantern where the gas was burnt, via three small holes pierced in the end of the pipe. These lamps were about twenty yards apart and gave a 'very brilliant' light. It was thought that that seven hundred feet might be the optimum length of main through which gas could be conducted from its source. It was also said that the smell was disagreeable, particularly when the lamps were first lighted, although people would get used to it.

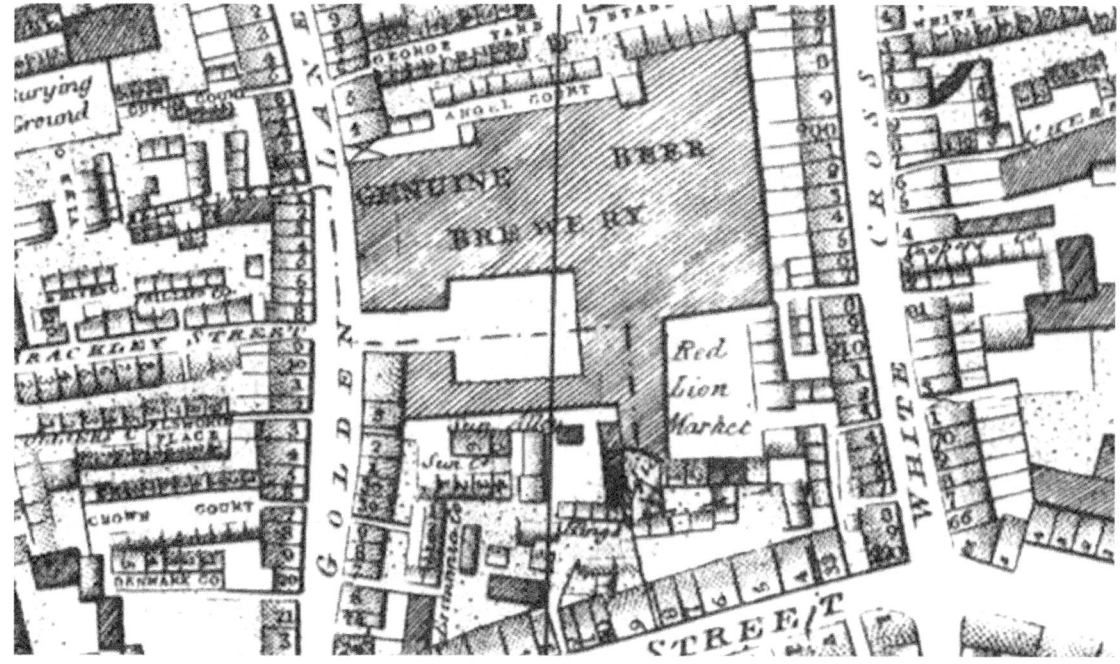

One of the most interesting and important things about this little gas making plant is that it was used for a demonstration of street lighting. The local Alderman, Matthew Wood, a City of London 'improver', arranged this, and indeed, he may also have had an interest in the brewery. Later, he supported a number of other, more commercial, gas companies. This interest from within the governing circles of the City of London can be noted elsewhere.

It is not known who installed this plant. It does not appear in the list of Boulton and Watt's customers and Winsor disclaimed it publicly. Sir Arthur Elton speculated that it might have been a freelance effort by Boulton and Watt's engineer, William Murdoch, who was involved with an isinglass manufacturer opposite the brewery in Golden Lane. It seems likely that the brewery owners had taken over a Boulton and Watt steam engine installed by the previous occupant, which implies that they were in touch with them. E. G. Stewart ascribed the installation to Josiah Pemberton who had some connections with Boulton and Watt. The fact is however, that there are no records.

The locals were not impressed. The booklet 'Heroic Epistle' tells us that: "the flame issuing from the chimneys has afforded nightly amusement to the frequenters of the neighbouring alehouse'. The point is however that the public was beginning to be aware of this new way of providing light. The Athenaeum was quick to comment about the 'length of time' that they waited to see such a demonstration undertaken. Gas was fast becoming a desirable commodity - something which people knew would be of use to them, rather than just having a laugh about in the pub.

Today the Golden Lane Brewery site is covered with housing managed by the Peabody Trust and owned by the City of London. It is however actually sited in the London Borough of Islington.

MR. DESANGES

This was a small gas making plant about which almost nothing appears to be known. It raises the question of how many more similar projects were undertaken by enthusiasts. It may in fact have been the first gas making installation in London which was in an industrial setting.

The sole source of information on this gas making plant is Winsor's comment in his reply to *'Nicholson's Attack'* where he says that a *'Mr. Desanges of Spitalfields'* had attended his lectures and had since built himself a gas making plant.

Who exactly Mr. Desanges was is not made clear, but there was a certainly a family of that name living in the Spitalfields area in the early 19th century. A William Desanges died there in 1807 who had a son was named Francis. In 1839 Francis Desanges & Co were at 22 Chicksand Street as silk dyers as well as drysalters and oil pressers; they had earlier been in Wheler Street. (often written as 'Wheeler' Street).

Francis Desanges, was Willam's third son. He was a prominent figure in City of

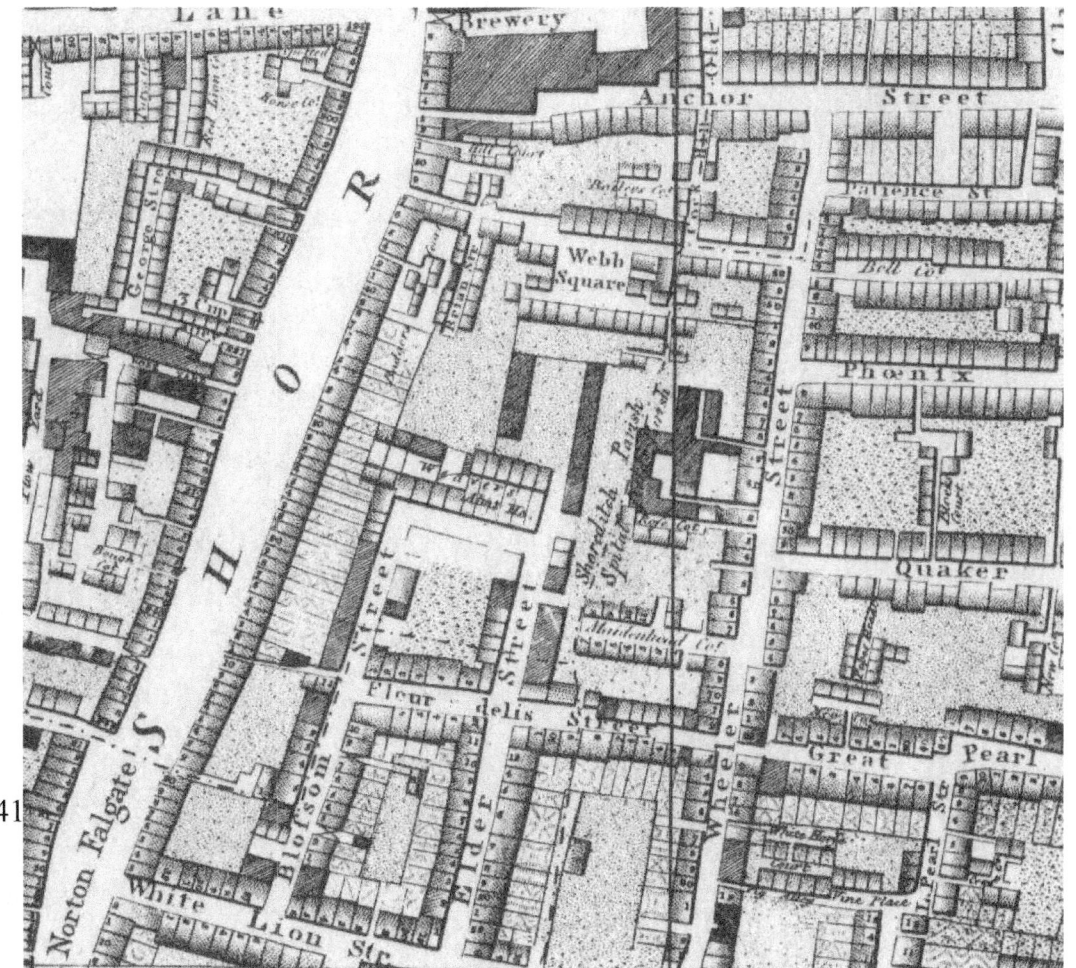

London politics and for a while held the post of Sheriff of London, being knighted

while in that post in 1818 – again demonstrating a City of London interest in gas lighting. He actually lived in Stratford Place, Notting Hill and later on the Portman Estate in Mayfair. He also had a country estate at Aston House in Rutland where he was High Sheriff of Oxfordshire. In future years he was to support many new initiatives and inventions.

It may be of interest that James Soames, later the Greenwich soap maker, took out a patent for making artificial light in 1829. He gave his address as 65 Wheler Street. His wife was Eliza Desanges and they had married in Christ Church, Spitalfields. Francis Desanges' Wheler Street factory must have been, in effect adjacent to Soames soap factory.

HUDDART'S PATENT ROPEWORKS

The gas making apparatus installed at Huddart's ropeworks is another example of an innovative new industry investing in new technology. This works was in the heart of the East End of London close to the vital port and ship building facilities. In this example in the Birmingham archive there is a full set of drawings of the gas lighting scheme and its integration with the power plant at the factory.

When the Elder Brethren of Trinity House came to witness the demonstration of gas lighting mounted by Hatchard and Champion in Pimlico in 1789, described above, one of the witnesses was Joseph Cotton His son, William, was to become the managing partner in a Limehouse rope works. This works may have been the site of one of the earliest gas lighting plants in London. Cotton's partner was Joseph Huddart who had patented a new method of making rope and the Limehouse factory was set up to make rope by his methods. Clearly it was to be a technologically advanced works and Boulton and Watt were asked to install the power raising equipment.

It seems likely that Huddart had known and investigated gas for lighting for some time. It has been suggested that Trinity House spent £500 on 'spirit of coals' as a lighthouse illuminant in the 1780s but that it was seen as too unreliable. Huddart later carried out experiments for Trinity House, which are recorded in their minutes, but reported badly on the brilliancy of the light produced, and also that coal for such plant would be difficult to use in isolated lighthouses and in addition Trinity House staff would need special training.

Huddart and Cotton had already purchased a steam engine for the ropeworks from Boulton and Watt, and it was to them that they also went to for gas making plant sometime between 1806 and 1811.

Plans for the plant at the Limehouse Ropeworks were drawn up by Boulton and Watt's gas design team. The drawings, as fresh as if they were prepared yesterday, can be found in the Birmingham City archives. They even still have pencilled-in alterations, which look like the result of working discussions. Boulton and Watt's team sited the gas-making plant alongside the steam engine and boilers, which they had already supplied and perhaps, therefore, they saw the ensemble as one installation of gas and steam together. All of the equipment was in a single building alongside the main works.

In the first set of drawings, dated 1809, two retorts and a 'gasometer pit' are situated next to the boilers with the engine at right angles beyond them. A wall was built between each part of the installation. Between the retorts and the '*gasometer*' is a '*condenser*' with pipes going to a '*tar pit*' and a '*drain for waste water*' sited below the retort and alongside the '*ash hole*' for the boilers. There is also a '*rat trap*'.

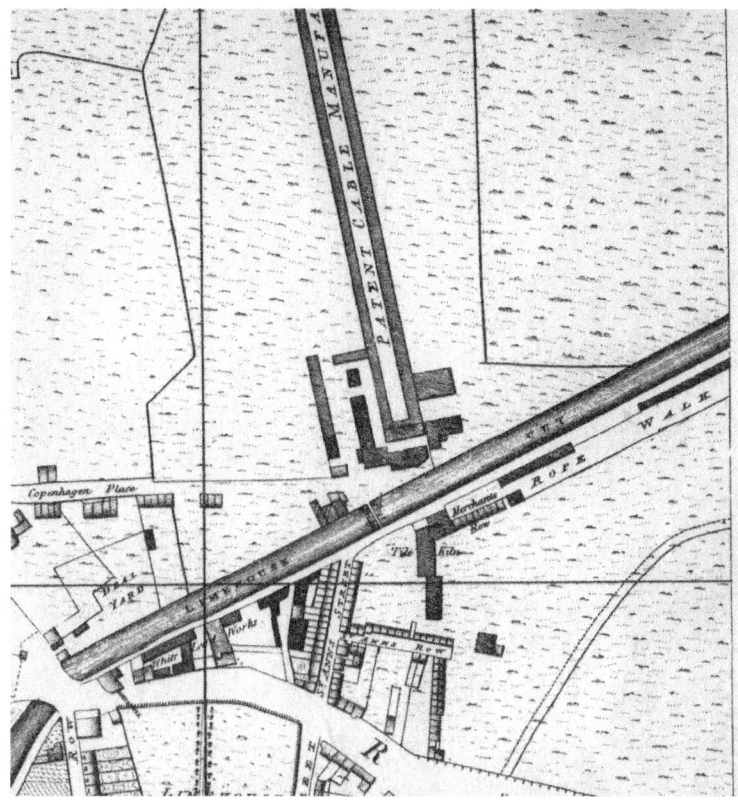

The gas making plant was probably installed after 1809; a note of 21st June 1811 gives instructions: '*Huddart & Co. Desire their Gazometer, Retorts, etc. to be sent as soon as possible*'.

Detailed instructions and plans are included for the lighting installations in the ropewalk and factory. For the rope walk itself - '*a pipe to join 2 cistern pipes and reserve 1 3/4 wrote iron pipe, upright. 160 feet 1 3/4 inch pipe 2 [angles]. 6 burners to fit 1 3/4 pipe*'. The run of pipe work is shown going from the '*gasometer*', down the length of the ropewalk, with a branch to a three storey building and '*cable warehouses*' and another to the '*cordage warehouses*' and '*turners shop*'. The position of burners is marked throughout.

The workings of this early gas lighting plant are not recorded. Huddart's rope works later became a lead works, and the site has since been redeveloped. In the late 1980s members of the Greater London Industrial Archaeology Society told me how they were able to walk the site and identify the sites of the rope walk, factory and service buildings.

It perhaps should be said that this site is not in what many people today would recognise as Limehouse. The 'works' where the gas making plant was situated was just north of today's Commercial Road alongside the Limehouse Cut. The rope walk itself stretched north into an area which was then roughly known as Bow Common and which covered a number of local authority areas. Today it would probably be thought of as part of Bow or Stepney.

LIPTRAP

This early gas making plant was probably in a large distillery it the heart of the industrial East End. It was in Whitechapel and near to Aldgate and Spitalfields to the west, Mile End to the east and not too far from the river and the port.

Whitechapel, in east London, must have had one of the highest concentrations of early gas works and they will continue to turn up in these pages for some time yet. The only evidence for the plant at Liptrap is in the Boulton and Watt archive in Birmingham. There, scribbled on a piece of paper, which, from other evidence, dates from around 1811, are the words '*Liptrap, Whitechapel*'. The words seem to be associated with a sketch of a gas making plant, which was pointed out to me by Tim Smith. Liptrap were certainly customers of Boulton and Watt who had supplied them with an engine in

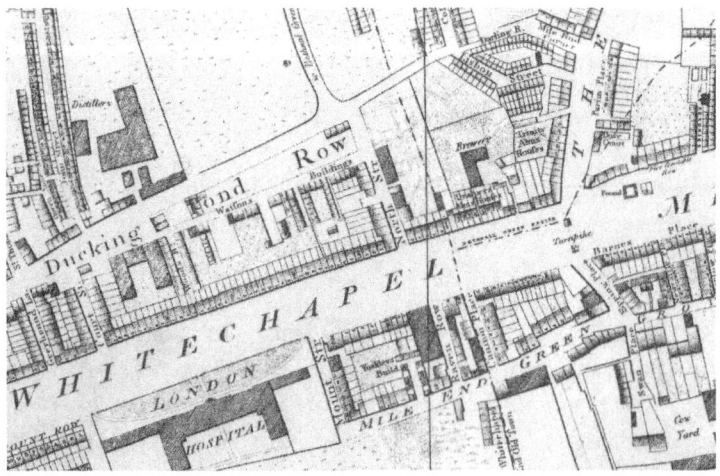

1786. *Dickinson* in *James Watt & the Steam Engine* gives some detail of their unusual gearing arrangement. Several of Boulton and Watt's customers diversified into gas making equipment when it was available, and so why not Liptrap?

Who were they? Davey E. Liptrap appears in the Mile

End Old Town Rate Books but the site location is not clear in that source. In 1800, in the dense urban area of Whitechapel a number of authorities were able to levy rates. While Mile End Old Town collected money to support the, no doubt very numerous, poor, money to pay for sewage disposal went to the Spitalfields Sewer Commissioners. It was in the Sewage Commission rate books for 1818 that I found two entries for adjacent sites on 'Tickle Belly Common' - they were 'Liptrap. Prop, 8 Bucks Row' and 'Liptrap & Thomas Smith, whole premises'.

Bucks Row is not hard to track down. It was a triangular open space at the back of Whitechapel Station, on which an old school stands. At one time I worked in an office whose window actually overlooked it along with a line of derelict brick coal drops. This is all gone now; modern flats have been built with a boring flat park. Unrecognisable as the same place, somewhere full of interest and variety has been eliminated. On the 1813 edition of the *Horwood plan* it is quite clearly shown and called 'Ducking Pond Row' – another place name which implies a rural past for Whitechapel, something that, I am sure, was just a very distant memory even in 1800.

Who was Thomas Smith? Munby says, in Industry and Planning in Stepney from evidence he found in a Parliamentary report, "The firm of T. & G. Smith of Whitechapel ... was one of twelve distillers in England in 1832, and the second largest of these'. The current Survey of London gives a detailed history of the distillery. On the Horwood Plan there is indeed a large distillery site on the north side of the street, which today is under a Sainsbury store (what else?). A tiny scrap of paper has taken us to the second largest distillery in England.

Did they have an on-site gasworks? There may be no way of being certain - but it does seem very likely.

What I do know is that if we add in all the distilleries around East London, that area was producing a very, very large percentage of the total alcohol produced in England.

STEIN, SMITH & DITCHLEY

Another rope works and one which may, or may not have had a gas lighting plant. Once again this works would have been set in the heart of the East End's shipbuilding and port area.

The Boulton and Watt archive contains drawings for a gas making plant commissioned by Stein, Smith and Ditchley of Whitechapel. It is not clear if this plant was ever installed.

Stein, Smith and Ditchley seem to have been rope makers - perhaps the proprietors of one of the numerous rope walks in east London. A reference to them in a 1784 directory also mentions a Walter Sims as the proprietor. Sims' rope walk was at Sun Tavern Fields so perhaps this early factory gas making plant was in fact the precursor of the Ratcliffe Gas Company's works which was later to open there.

There were a large number of rope works in east London at this period. Rope was of vital importance to the huge London shipbuilding and ship repair industry and it is interesting that two of them should have been the first to consider gas lighting in their works.

ACKERMAN'S PRINT SHOP

This small gas making plant has been described by most gas industry historians writing about this period. It has attracted attention as one works undertaken by Samuel Clegg, before he went to work for the Gas Light and Coke and Imperial Gas Companies in London – the first such works by Clegg in London, although he had set up several elsewhere. It was set up by an enthusiast who had the ideal conditions for

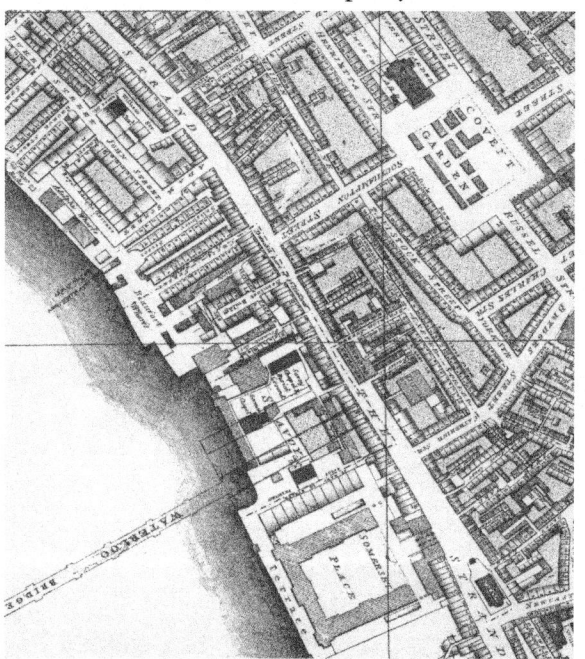

demonstrating gas lighting at his shop and art gallery in a busy commercial area on the edge of the fashionable West End. Sadly he does not seem to have used it for very long.

Rudolph Ackerman had come to London from Germany as a coach maker and opened The Repository of Fine Arts at 96 The Strand, expanding later to a school at 101 Strand. It was on the south side of the road on the corner of 'Beaufort Buildings', 101 is a few doors further up and next-door-but-one to the corner of Fountain Court. Today this area lies to the west of Waterloo Bridge and the Savoy Hotel.

Ackerman also published the *Repository of Arts* magazine. In 1813 it featured an illustration of his library lit by gas.

Clegg came from Manchester to build the plant and Ackerman reported that the plant cost £1,940 to install and consisted of 24 small retorts. The actual cost of running it was £151 a year but £111 was recovered from selling by-products. He estimated that the gas light cost £40 a year but that amount of lighting would have cost him £250 had candles and oil been used instead.

This was apparently the first works in which a dry lime process was used to clean the gas, following complaints about the discharge of wet lime effluent into the Thames.

Ackerman said that the light was like '*bright summer sunshine compared to a murky November day*' without the former suffocation from the fumes from charcoal and candles and without danger of spillage of candle wax on valuable books and prints. After that, in order to help minimise damage to prints, Ackerman's workers heated their plates by gas rather than on a charcoal fire.

Despite his pleasure at his new gas installation, Everard says that Ackerman asked the Gas Light and Coke Company for a connection to their mains in 1815. Brian Sturt has speculated that this was a cheaper option

ROYAL MINT

A small gas works built for a Government owned factory in the East End of London. Although the factory – The Royal Mint – had been equipped with machinery by Boulton and Watt, they do not seem to have provided the gas making apparatus.

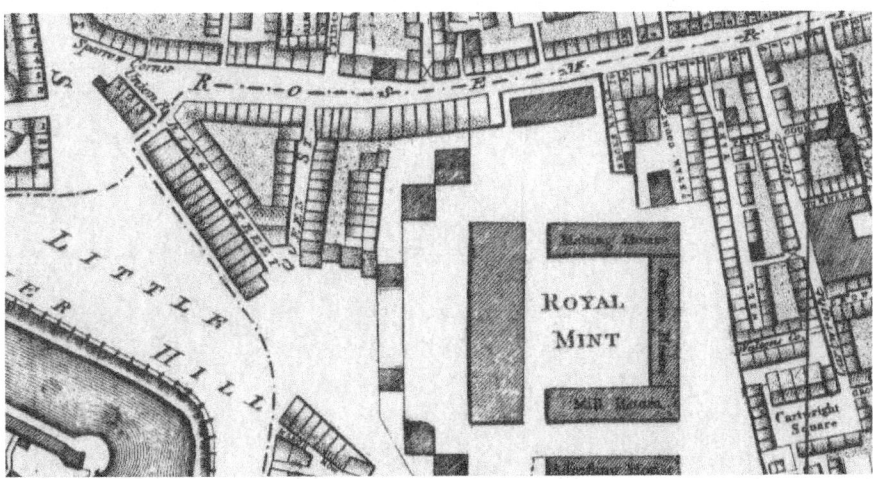

There is some confusion over the construction of the gas making plant built to supply the new Royal Mint constructed on Tower Hill – the grand buildings of 1809 are still there, now flats, the Mint having moved in 1967. Arthur Elton said that it was built by Frederick Accum, who illustrated it in his '*Description of the Process*'. Everard found records, which indicated that Samuel Clegg had told the Gas Light and Coke Company in 1816 that he had been asked to build and manage the works, and there is every indication that this is what in fact happened. However, Boulton and Watt had been on site in the Mint for some time installing machinery and one of their staff, James Lawson, was retained there as described in Dickenson's *James Watt and the Steam Engine*. Lawson was to be one of the members of Congreve's Commission of Enquiry into the early gas industry. It seems

47

very strange therefore that Boulton and Watt were not asked to install the gas works, unless of course, they recommended Clegg as a sub-contractor.

Once the works were built, George Holworthy Palmer, one of Clegg's assistants at Westminster, was installed as superintendent. I have given some details of Palmer's work at the Mint in an article in Journal of the History of Engineering and Technology (Vol. 89 No.1-2). Palmer is a saga in himself and there is no space to go into his background here, nevertheless it is remarkable that during his stay at the Mint there is no record that the works either fell down or blew up! He was till there in 1822 when he went to work for the Imperial Gas Company and their minute books record their annoyance at his attempts to 'borrow' equipment from them to help out at The Mint.

Some accounts remain of the Mint gas works which show that Palmer earned £63.14s.6d. a year and that they were able to sell coke, tar, liquid ammonia and burnt iron. In 1828 it was discovered that the works was costing twice as much to run as an ordinary commercial works outside. Palmer was sacked - which was nothing new for him - and another, unnamed, manager employed. By the 1850s gas was being supplied by the Ratcliffe Gas Co.

GENERAL POST OFFICE

Another gas works in a Government workplace - but this time using Taylor and Martineau's new oil gas system. This one is in the centre of the City of London, adjacent to The Bank.

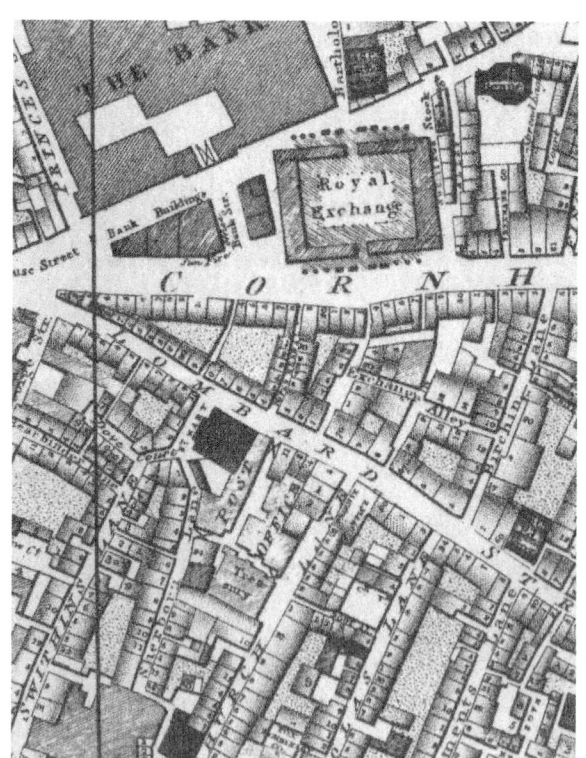

This was an oil gas installation undertaken by Taylor and Martineau. The original site of the Post Office was at the south-western end of Lombard Street where Post Office Court still runs between Lombard and King William Streets and where, indeed, a Post Office can still be found on the corner of the court at 10 Lombard Street. It was rebuilt at St.Martin le Grande before 1829.

The architect to the Post Office in this period was Joseph Kaye, who had previously acted as a consultant and surveyor to the Gas Light and Coke Co., but had clearly since joined the oil gas camp and gave evidence to the Enquiry into Oil Gas as Surveyor to the GPO. Kaye was also Surveyor to the Foundling Hospital and also eventually to Greenwich Hospital Estates, being responsible for much of the current Greenwich town centre.

The decision to install the gas works would have been taken at a time when the second Marquess of Salisbury was Postmaster General. Kaye himself had been a pupil in the Cockerell architect's practice - Christopher Cockerell was involved in the Gas Light and Coke Company. Kaye's main work with the Post Office was however, involved the new buildings at St. Martin le Grand where a coal gas plant was used.

WHITBREAD & COMPANY

An oil gas plant in yet another factory complex in the industrial area to the north of the City.

As mentioned above, the early gas making plant at the Golden Lane Brewery has often been confused with the nearby Whitbread plant. It is quite clear that there was an oil gas plant at the Whitbread Chiswell Street Brewery. However there is apparently no reference to it in the Whitbread archives – although 'thank you' to their archivist for trying to find it.

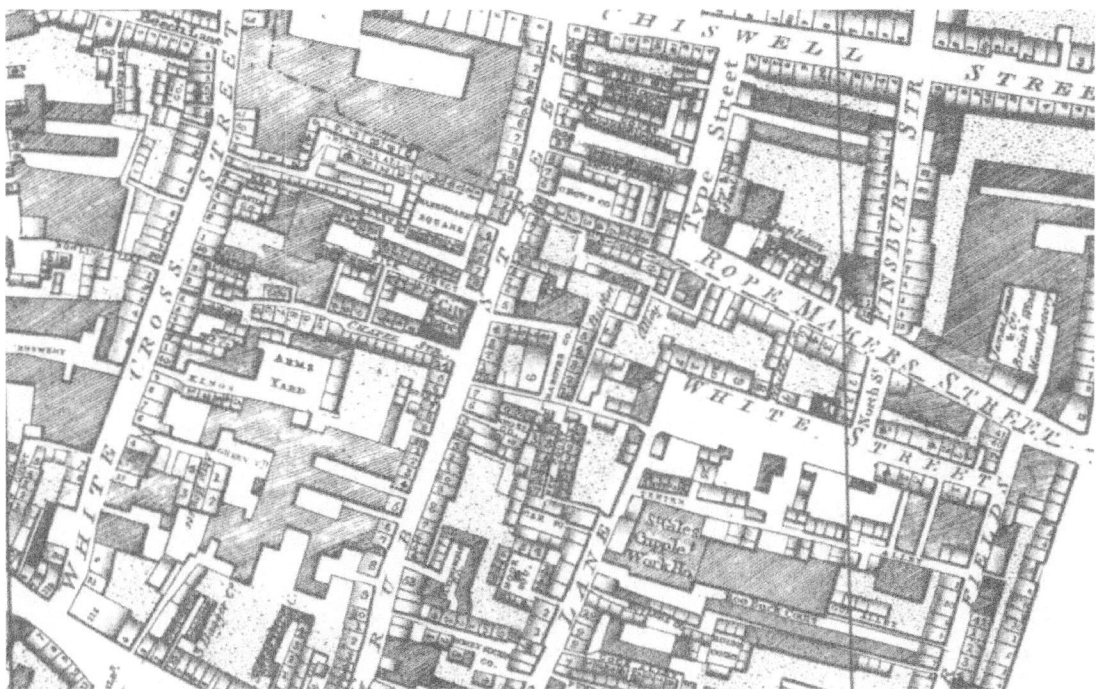

The evidence in the Oil Gas Enquiry is quite clear. First, a Samuel Lay, who worked for the Gas Light and Coke Co described a visit to the brewery in search of a gas escape. Another witnesses, one of the Martineau family, described the efficiency of the works.

There is another dimension to this story. As an oil gas plant it would undoubtedly have been set up by John Taylor and John Martineau whose original White Cross Lane works was very close to the Whitbread Brewery. Since 1812 John and Joseph Martineau had been partners in the Whitbread Brewery and since 1815 had been the managing partners while the Whitbread family pursued their careers in politics. Although there was more than one John Martineau alive at this time, nevertheless, there were close family links.

The Oil Gas Enquiry had been set up to decide whether an oil gas plant should be allowed in Westminster although in effect it became a sort of trial between the relative merits of gas made from oil as against coal. In such circumstances it is interesting to note that the Chairman of Enquiry was one Samuel Whitbread. This was Samuel Charles Whitbread, who was Member of Parliament for Middlesex from 1820 and who had joined the Brewery in 1819. It should also be noted that John Martineau eventually died in the great Porter Ton Room at Chiswell Street in 1834. Having 'suffered an apoplexy' he had fallen into the porter vat.

The Brewery itself remained in use by Whitbread's until the present day, although latterly offices. Very recently however Whitbread's have 'come out' of brewing and Chiswell Street has been sold.

WELLCLOSE SQUARE
THE EAST LONDON THEATRE

A small gas works set up to light a large east London theatre - it seems that at the same time it was involved in the public supply of gas. I have kept the title 'Wellclose Square' which was used by Stewart, although that is not really where this works was.

Both Stewart and Everard noted that an early gas works existed in Wellclose Square, E1. Everard said that it had been taken over by the Chartered Gas Light and Coke Co. in 1820 and then closed down. Like many things in the early London gas industry this turns out to be very much more interesting than that and it involves a gas works which was neither in Wellclose Square nor closed down in 1820.
Wellclose Square is to the north of The Highway and its original buildings have now been replaced. To the west of it runs Ensign Street, formerly Well Street, where in 1785 the Royalty, or East London, Theatre was built. Today a disused home for sailors stands on the site. It was opened by a John Palmer *'of the most versatile and eminent talents,*

but destitute of prudence'. Palmer died in 1798 but he may have been involved with some of the dramatic illusionists who demonstrated gas in theatres before 1800. In *'The Lyceum and Henry Irving'* Austin Brereton described how Palmer's brother, Robert, took part in a display of an *'Aeropyric Branch'* at the Lyceum in 1789 which it was claimed was actually a demonstration of gas lighting. This story is outlined in a collection of contemporary press cuttings in Tower Hamlet library

To cut a long story very short: a disturbance on the first night led to a relation of his, a Mr. W Palmer, being imprisoned as a 'rogue, vagabond and sturdy beggar'. John Palmer went out of business and the building was used by a number of different theatre companies over the next forty years of its existence.

At some point, a gas-making plant was installed to provide lighting for the theatre. Nothing is known of who built or commissioned it and it does not appear in the list of works built by Boulton and Watt. However a Mr. Van Voorst who lived in Wellclose Square and wanted to know about gas making equipment wrote a letter to Boulton and Watt, which is now in the Birmingham Reference library. This is the same Van Voorst who was a prominent and vocal shareholder in the infant Chartered Company.

In 1820, the theatre and its gas works were sold to the Chartered Company. It was then known as the

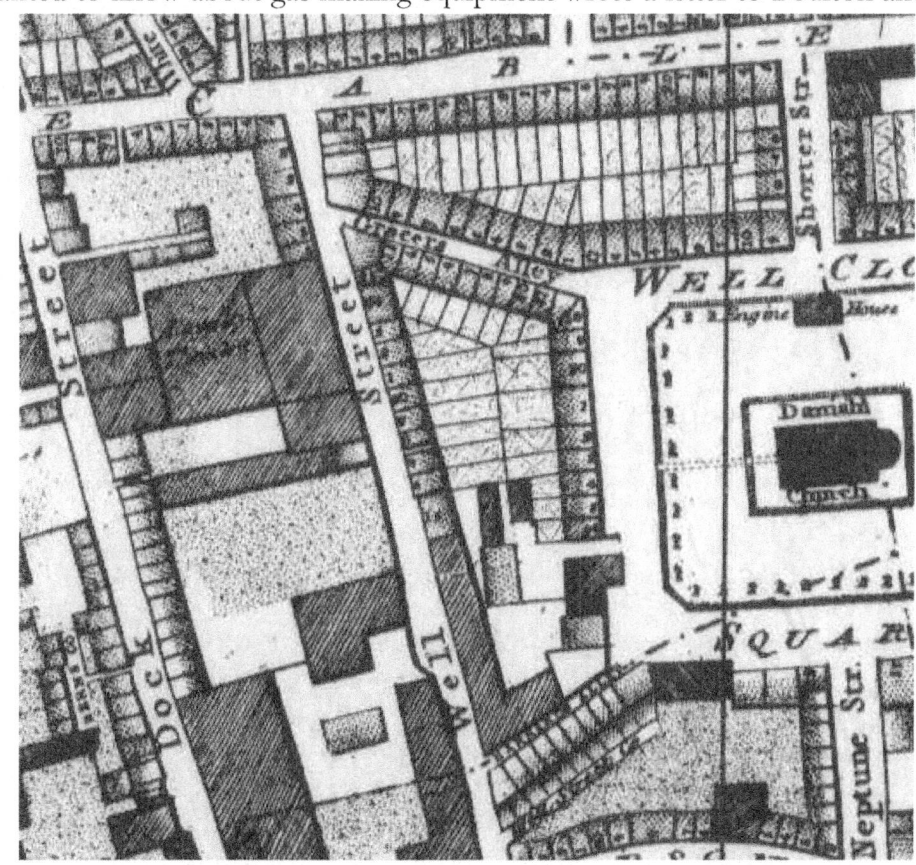

East London Gas Works, and was making and selling gas to *'a prosperous manufacturing district'* for a profit of £1,000 a year. There was a *'gasometer'* as well as *'main and service pipes'*. The 'works' was to the north of the theatre building and adjacent to the stage.

51

Something strange was going on, because a Mr. Vickers seems to have owned the theatre both before and after it was sold by auction in 1820. His son was appointed by the Imperial Gas Company to a post at 'Wellclose Square' in 1824. None of this makes an awful lot of sense but we assume that there is a rational explanation somewhere.

What is known is the final fate of this little gas making plant? One night in April 1826, a Mr. Evans was making gas for *'the use of the house on Tuesday night'*. Evans is a name well known in the early history of the Chartered Company and it may be that he was moonlighting from their works at Brick Lane. Evans looked out from his stoke hole and noticed that some of the scenery above the adjacent stage was on fire. He raised the alarm. So fierce was the fire that the firemen could only stand '*at either end of the theatre and throw the water on the flames as well as they could*' and there was much worry that it would spread to two adjacent sugar refineries. They were saved but the theatre was burnt to the ground with the loss of everything except the grand pianoforte '*snatched from the Green Room*' by '*an unknown sailor*'. The losses included a costume for Richard III '*worth at least £50*'. How had the fire started? It appears that the performance that night, of '*Kendrick the Accursed*', had required the eruption of Mount Etna on stage. For this '*about half a pound of powder*' was used. It also seemed that the gaslights on the side of the stage had not been properly turned off.

By 1834 the works and the theatre had closed. In 1835 it was opened as the Destitute Sailors' Asylum, although its present use is unclear. The East London Gas Company was to have a renaissance in due course, as we will see.

In 2019 Pieter van der Merwe gave a talk to Greenwich Industrial History Society on this event, but from the point of view of a theatre historian, providing a contrast to its context within the early London gas industry.

COVENT GARDEN THEATRE

Theatres were some of the first public buildings to take on gas lighting, both for the auditorium and for special stage effects. This famous theatre is in the centre of the 'entertainment' district slightly to the east of the West End.

Captain John Forbes gave some evidence to the Oil Gas Enquiry about this gas making installation. It had been installed by Taylor and Martineau and, therefore, used oil. The theatre was of course the predecessor of the present Royal Opera House. It had been built in 1809, but in 1820 the management had passed to Henry Harris. The Theatre had been supplied with coal gas by the Chartered Company, but, following a dispute about non-payment of bills an oil gas plant was built. There is a competitive aspect to this involving both good lighting and safety.

The theatre had had several fires and, in 1828, perhaps because of the incident at the East London Theatre, they were told by the Lord Chamberlain that such in-house installations were unsafe.

In 'New Flame' Hugh Barty King quotes the theatre's statement about this: "When the brilliancy of gas attracted public admiration the proprietors of the Theatre anxious to adopt any improvement which would give brilliancy to the scenery .... and to prevent the accidents which the best street illumination is liable to   ... at great expense, constructed gasometers, finding however that with the utmost care and skill in the introduction of gas in the audience part of the Theatre produced an offensive odour and the Public suffering inconvenience and disappointment in their amusements by the mischievous agency of some malignant and interested persons .. the Proprietors have determined to remove the gas.

Once the work had been done and the theatre reopened in December 1828 a certificate was produced by John Evans of the Chartered Company and Thomas Edge, the gas equipment manufacturer, to say that any apparatus which had been used for gas manufacture on site had been destroyed. The management completely stopped using gas and went back to oil and candles.   Was this perhaps the same Mr Evans who had caused the accident at the East London Theatre?

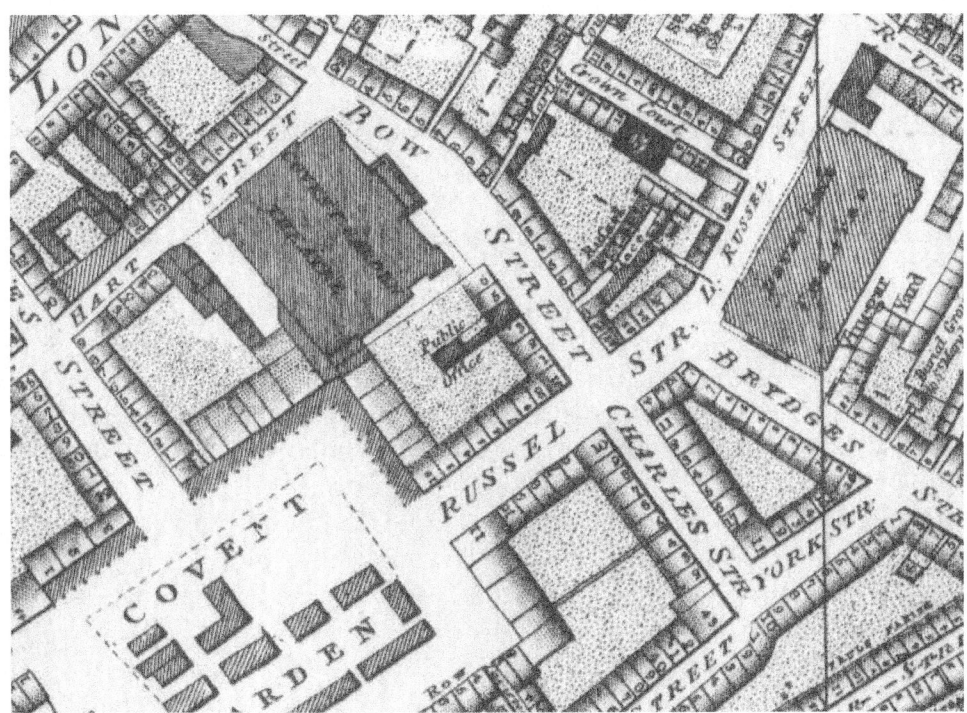

THE ROYAL COBURG THEATRE

This was another theatre which used one of Taylor and Martineau's Oil Gas plants. It was set up, safely, under the stage in what is now the Old Vic Theatre in the Waterloo Road.

The Coburg Theatre was built soon after the original Waterloo Bridge in 1811 and opened in 1817. In the 1820s, a manager of the theatre was a son of the radical, William Godwin, and the theatre staged a performance of 'Dr. Frankenstein,' by Mary Shelley, Godwin's daughter with Mary Wollstonecraft. In 1825, Ira Waldridge, a black American actor made a notable stage debut at the theatre. The theatre has had a number of names and in the 1872 map extract shown it is the Victoria Palace Theatre.

Henry Hornblower, the Theatre's Treasurer, gave evidence to the Oil Gas Enquiry on the effectiveness of the operation.

And -

THE WESTMINSTER GAS SUPPLY CO.

Westminster too had a small and obscure gas making plant

It is not really clear if this small works was purely for demonstration purposes or set up to supply gas, as the name of the company implies. If so then it is clearly 'the first gas works in the world although there no evidence of any customers at all. It was sited on the industrial riverside adjacent to Westminster, both the Abbey and the Palace of Westminster, to supply a perceived demand in that area.

So, it appears that Winsor had an experimental gas making plant on Millbank. I found out about it in a footnote to an article about the Marquis of Chabannes by Andrew Saint in *Newcomen Society Transactions*. Chabannes was involved with the infant briquette industry around 1800 – and the article illuminated many corners of his busy life.

In the *Newcomen Society Transactions* it is described how the Marquis set up a manufactory for briquettes on Millbank around 1799 and – tracing it through the rate books – they note that by 1808 the site was '*in the hands of another vagabond entrepreneur of talent and ebullience, Frederick Albert Winsor*'. So was this the site of Winsor's demonstration gas making plant? They also note his company name – '*The Westminster Gas Supply Company*'. Is this in fact the first public supply gas company? If so, it puts the great Gas Light and Coke Co firmly into second place.

It has been commented to me verbally that` given the level of incompetence at the early Gas Light and Coke Company's Westminster works, it is unlikely that this earlier plant would have been run efficiently.

One question remains. Exactly which site on Millbank does this note refer to? I am very aware that the Gas Light and Coke Co. had a wharf in that area from about 1814. They seem to have acquired it from a Mr. Sergeant, a coal merchant who was to deal extensively with many of the London gas companies. Was this in fact Winsor's old site?

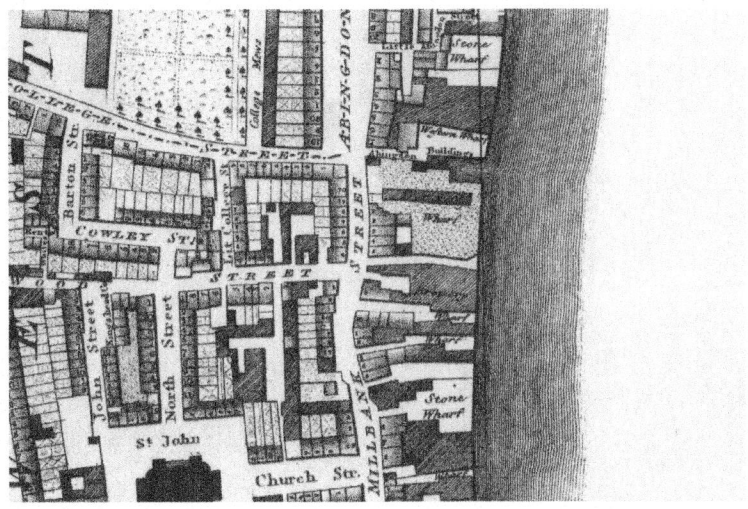

NATIONAL HEAT AND LIGHT COMPANY

As time went on the provisional committee of what was still called the National Heat and Light Company began to take charge of affairs and put forward their own ideas.

So who made up the membership of the National Heat and Light Company? The list is substantially that given a few pages back as Winsor's backers. Any analysis will be only partial and flawed through lack of information. There are some among the list of names who have been very resistant to research – for example James Hargreaves, the future Deputy Governor. His background has been investigated by a number of historians, but much of his life still remains a mystery. There are others of whom I, at least, know nothing about or very little. All of them, even those we know something about, may have had hidden interests and attributes which have not been discovered.

From the little we know:

There are four obvious members of the aristocracy and four with clear links to the Royal family – including, for example one of George III's doctors.
There is one professional soldier, and one professional sailor – although three others have links to the Navy.
There are at least four Members of Parliament and four with links to the East India Company, including its sometime Chair.
Professionally: there are three medical doctors, two lawyers, eight 'merchants' and five bankers – indicating a clear bias towards the business sector.
Two more may have had interests in the fishing industry.
There is one member of the Royal Society and three whose interest may be described as 'enthusiasts' – one with a clear interest in horticulture.
Perhaps most interesting is the one member who does not appear to be wealthy but who spent a lifetime promoting the cause of putting public services underground.

Within this list of men shows some links to others, through families, or for another example a relationship to an architect used by others to work on their grand houses

So – here are some details. Do these biographies help us to find out, or guess, why these individuals were involved?

James Ludovic Grant. Grant was the leading figure in the supporters group. He headed the Committee of Backers and went on to become the first Governor of the Gas Light and Coke Company. A member of a Scottish noble family he had close connections to the Murrays, Dukes of Athol. His father, Francis Grant, was a career soldier and MP and his mother was a Lady of the Bedchamber to George III's daughters, as described in *Recollections* by Amelia Murray. Grant was a career sailor, who joined the Royal Navy at the age of 13, became a midshipman and accompanied the future William IV on HMS Prince George. He became a Lieutenant in the Royal Navy but resigned after continuing a voyage to the West Indies on HMS Flora after the captain's death. From 1788 he was with the East India Company and in 1794 married Anne Bazett whom he had met on St. Helena where her father was superintendent. He was Captain of the East Indiaman, *Brunswick* which was captured by the French off Pointe de Galle in Sri Lanka in July 1805 and wrecked. He resigned as Governor of the Chartered in December 1813 following disputes and challenges – and his wife, Anne, died only three weeks later. He lived at Windmill Hill, sold because of losses in the gas company. It is now called Farnborough Hill and was later the home of Empress Eugenie. It is now a school. Grant went to Madras for the East India Company and died at sea on his way to St. Helena in 1827.

James Hargreaves. Hargreaves was the new Gas Company's first Deputy Governor. Everard described him as '*A doctor with an interest in mechanical matters from Ruthin in North Wales'*. Everard's source for this information has ever been identified. The late David Loverseed, who worked on early gas industry genealogies, was unable to identify a medical James Hargreaves - except for a '*surgeon and man midwife'*. Hargreaves family leased a house in Ruthin, 'Woodlands', in 1795. David Loverseed found three generations of James Hargreaves there and by elimination thought that the generation was the relevant when the family included both a James and an Augustus. Augustus Hargreaves was involved in the Chartered Company but failed to take his seat at the Court. In 1818 James Hargreaves was in Liverpool where he founded a gas company and then another in Macclesfield where he recruited George Holworthy Palmer from London onto the staff. Augustus was made trustee to James in 1825; maybe because of James' bankruptcy. James and Augustus were described as 'Merchants of Manchester' but also gave an address in Size Lane, City of London. In 1830 a Manchester based Augustus Hargreaves was a fustian manufacturer.

John Murray. 4th Duke of Athol. The Dukes of Athol are based at Blair Athol, Aberdeenshire where this Duke and/or his immediate forebears had a bad reputation for Highland Clearances and were freemasons at the highest possible level. John Murray succeeded to the Dukedom in 1803. He had some scientific pretensions, being a Member of the Society of Arts and Fellow of the Royal Society as the result of his book "*Observations on Larch*".

He had written this book as part of an attempt to find a rot-resistant wood for naval shipbuilding, something for which gas tar was also considered. This interest could explain his interest in gas lighting. Athol had a family connection with J.L.Grant, the first Governor of the Gas Light and Coke Co., and both of them were very close to the Royal family. His London address was 30 Great George Street, and in 1801 he built Castle Mona on the Isle of Man where the family have rights as hereditary governors of the Island.

Viscount Anson. Thomas Anson, né Adams, 1767-1818. A great-nephew of the famous Admiral George Anson, he was created Viscount in 1806 and became a Whig Member of Parliament. He undertook 'improvements' at the ancestral home of Shugborough, including the provision of a model farm together with specially designed and heated greenhouses, described, by William Pitt, as '*a kind of Academy for the study of Horticulture.* Perhaps, in this context, Winsor's pamphlet about the use of gas in hot houses should be taken into account. Anson married the daughter of the agriculturist, Thomas Coke, and was also a keen huntsman.

Christopher Baynes Christopher Baynes was born in 1755 and died in 1837. His father was William Baynes and his mother Mary Roberts. The family seat was at Kilburn, Nr. Thirsk where an '*ancient looking building, called the Old Hall, was formerly the property and residence of the Baynes family*'. Christopher's career followed that of many wealthy men in the 18th Century - in 1773 he had been sent on the Grand Tour, in 1777 he was appointed a Lieutenant in the First West Yorkshire Militia, and became a Cornet in the Horse Guards. A year later he married Nanny Gregory and had three children, William, Mary & Walter. In 1791 Baynes was appointed a Commissioner of the Peace for Middlesex. He went on to become Deputy Lieutenant for Middlesex and Hertfordshire as well as Major Commandant of the Uxbridge Gentlemen and Yeomanry Cavalry. He was created a Baronet in 1801. He was also Chairman of the London Docks Company and lived in Harefield, Middlesex.

Charles Cockerell. Cockerell was one of a family of whom several were architects. Charles himself was a banker who had made a fortune through the East India Company. In England he was a Member of Parliament with a country house, Sezincote, near Broadway. This house – the gardens of which are still open to public view – has been described as '*an extraordinary blend of English and Indian architecture in a country house.*' It was designed by his brother, Samuel Pepys Cockerell. The Prince Regent visited it in 1807 and the design is thought to have had some influence on the Pavilion at Brighton. Cockerell resigned from the Gas Light and Coke Company Court of

Governors in September 1812 on pressure of business, but a bank called Cockerell Paxton continued to be used by the Company.

John Turton. He was one of George III's doctors who also lectured at 53 Dorset Street on scientific subjects with 'commanding ability'. Turton was physician to many famous people of the day – including Garrick, Oliver Goldsmith and Horace Walpole. In 1784 he bought Brasted Place in Kent – and the house is said to still contain some mementoes of his patronage by the Royal Family. He died in 1810 and so missed seeing the gas company in which he had invested come to fruition.

Isaac Oliphant. According to Winsor's *Notice Historique* Oliphant was a medical doctor – in fact he was a Member of Royal College of Surgeons who lived in Chelsea.

Matthew Bloxham. In 1806 Winsor said that Bloxham had been his banker for twenty years – and he was also banker to the early Gas Light and Coke Co. Bloxham's banking partners were Wilkinson & Taylor based at 27 Gracechurch Street and Birchin Lane. He had originally been a stationer and a partner of the Foudrinier Brothers, who introduced papermaking machinery into England. He came from Worcester and was married to William Baker's daughter. He went on to become MP for Maidstone and may have died in Spain in 1838.

William Devaynes. Another banker (Devaynes, Daws & Noble of Pall Mall (later 'Attwood Spooner') who were also appointed as the Chartered Company's bankers. Devaynes was Chairman of the East India Co., a Government Contractor, involved in the African Company and MP for Barnstable. As such he was among the seriously rich and powerful. He is said to have been a promoter of vaccination. His father was John Devaynes, an apothecary who served the Royal family. William lived in Dover Street and at Cheltenham. Between 1789 and 1797 he was the owner of Highbury House near Islington.

Arthur Noble According to Winsor's *Notice Historique*, Noble was a banker based at Cock Street in the City – and presumably a partner of William Devaynes, above. He is described as of 'Johnson's Fens' in Ireland and of Hertford Street. It is very possible that he was relation – or even a descendent – of the American 'folk hero' Arthur Noble, who went to Massachusetts from Ulster and died in a battle with the French in Nova Scotia in the 1740s.

Edmund Cobb Hurry. Another banker (1762-1808), Hurry came from a family of ship-owners and Yarmouth merchants. The Hurrys were involved with the whalers of the Southern Oceans. Fishing interests supplied oil for street lighting and it was recognised at a very early stage that gas lighting would be a threat to this industry, hence it would make sense for someone who had made money out of fish oils to invest in gas. Hurry was chairman of the Portsmouth Railway and died in Clifton, Bristol.

Joseph Garland. A London businessman but there is also a suspicion that he might have been based in Newfoundland. A Joseph Garland of Trinity, Newfoundland was born in 1750 and the son of a *'substantial yeoman of East Chaldon, Dorset'*. Two directors of the Imperial Gas Co were a Marmeduke Hart and a George Richard Robinson – both of whom appear in a Canadian genealogy as Garland's sons-in-law. Garland was also a director of the Imperial Gas Co., from which post he was later disqualified. Everard gives no reason for this, except to describe him as 'honourable'. George Richard Robinson resigned at the same time. Both Everard and Matthews, writing about the Imperial Gas Company in this period, tend to ascribe every activity of the directors as attempted fraud! Garland may well have been disqualified because he lived abroad. The family, based in Trinity, is known to have had considerable connections with Poole in Dorset and the Atlantic fishing industry.

William Paxton. Paxton was an industrialist, described by Winsor as 'a banker' – the bank of Paxton, Cockerell and Train appears in the Gas Light and Coke Co. Minutes. He had gone to sea as a boy, made a fortune in India and returned to buy Middleton Hall, near Carmarthen in 1787, and then improved it – with gardens inspired by his time in India. The house was built by Samuel Pepys Cockerell. Paxton's mines near Middleton Hall supplied coal to early gas companies and a chalybeate well at Middleton Hall was analysed for him by Frederick Christian Accum. He stood as a Whig in the 1802 election, but despite lavish spending he was outdistanced by 139 votes. With the money he had promised to build a much needed bridge over the Towy but instead he built Paxton's Tower – a 'folly' dedicated to Nelson after the Battle of Trafalgar, visible throughout the area. At Middleton there was a specially constructed heated fruit growing area with an intriguing double wall which has been the subject of an archaeological investigation. Middleton Hall is now the National Botanic Garden of Wales.

John William Henry White. A Magistrate who sold the lease on Providence Court to the Gas Light and Coke Co. for the Westminster Gas Works. His address is given in the company records as Parliament Place, Westminster.

Joseph Cooper. 'A Merchant' who worked with Accum to find the Norton Folgate gasworks' site. He is reported as having made a chance visit to the new gasworks and reported on slackness there. His address is given as Bishopsgate Street and Clapham.

George Cooper Ridge. A Merchant. Lived at Morden Park, Lower Mitcham and was an army Captain

Thomas Saunders. Solicitor and member of the City of London ruling Court of Common Council.

John Ambrose Tickell. A Merchant, possibly the owner of a West Bromwich ironworks, holding a patent for waterproof cement. There are however other candidates, despite that this is an unusual name: A clergyman with this name was based in Castle Acre & Colston, Norfolk while covering for the notorious Vicar of Stiffkey. Another John Ambrose Tickell was based in Lambeth and patented home security devices.

Baron Wolffe. Jacob Wolffe naturalised in 1762. He was a Baron of the Holy Roman Empire and ex-British Consul for trade in Russia. In later years lived in Woodbine Cottage, Tunbridge Wells.

William Holmes. From an Irish brewing family, he was MP for a variety of English seats and was Tory party whip. Said to have had a '*life of intrigue*'.

William Belcher Parfitt. Lived in Eversley '*in the County of Southampton*' where he was a brewer.

James White Barlow. He was a merchant with offices at 8 Tokenhouse Yard, Lothbury, City of London. It seems reasonable to assume that he was one of the Barlow family of gasworks constructors. Perhaps he was the James Barlow whose death notice appears in *Journal of Gas Lighting* for January 1858. Whether or not this was so, James Barlow was nevertheless clearly interested in the practical side of gas manufacture, since he volunteered ideas for equipment and set up an experimental plant in 1811 at Westminster for the Gas Light and Coke Company. In the Charter document Barlow's name is given without the middle name 'White' and his address is given as 'Bowes near Chipping Ongar'. Bowes House and Bowes Road are locations there in this period.

John Williams A stationer with a business selling ledgers, etc. to offices in the City. He does not appear to have been a particularly rich man and he must also have fairly young in 1809. For the next thirty years he was to agitate and write promoting the use of subways for underground services. He eventually died, ignored by the new Metropolitan Board of Works, while subways on his pattern were built by them.

PROGRESS

In the February or March of 1808 the committee of backers issued a pamphlet – *Considerations on the Intended Light And Heat Company*. Elton makes the point that this was an opportunity for the committee 'to return to sanity' and to disown some of Winsor's claims – since they needed to rescue the new company from any misconceived ideas about gas lighting. The new pamphlet pointed out that the '*invention*' of coal gas was not Winsor's – a point, which they made no doubt aware that is would become crucial. Winsor's publications were, they said '*ill adapted to promote his cause. and have thrown an air of ridicule and improbability over the whole scheme*'.

The leaflet also describes a demonstration of coal gas manufacture, which Winsor had made in front of an examining committee of subscribers. There was also an interesting additional observer – Dr. Jenner, the promoter of vaccination. Presumably he was recruited as a known a reputable scientist – or perhaps Winsor's' *Cowpox and gas lights*' has a relevance which has escaped me. The Committee announced that they intended to apply for a Charter of Incorporation.

In May 1808 James Grant reported on progress. He said that there were more obstructions than the Committee had first realised – for example local Paving Committees were not co-operative in allowing the opening of pavements for pipe work. They had been told by the Attorney General that they could not get a Royal Charter directly from the King but would need to get an enabling Act of Parliament which could not go ahead until the next Parliamentary session. They had lobbied the Chancellor of the Exchequer for support – at that time Spencer Percival who was apparently not convinced of the need for the company. He was soon to be Prime Minister and it was under his administration that the gas industry began.

BOULTON AND WATT INTERVENE

As the National Heat and Light Company's Committee struggled to get a legal status, so their problems began to escalate. The Boulton and Watt Partnership in Birmingham had been selling coal gas-making apparatus for some years – but it had never been patented and they had been watching events in London. To maintain their position they needed to establish that the idea of using coal gas for lighting belonged and originated with their Partnership. To be quite sure they would have to show that such an idea pre-dated anything developed elsewhere in Europe. They set out to show that the first attempts at gas lighting had originally been developed by Boulton and Watt's employee, William Murdoch. The process of consolidating the National Company's position continued through a series of interactions inside and outside of the Parliamentary process – but increasingly challenged by Boulton and Watt. This is covered in almost day-to-day detail by Leslie Tomory in his *'Progressive Enlightenment'*.

Initially Boulton and Watt lobbied and fostered links with Royal Society grandees. Then in 1808 a paper, ostensibly by Murdoch, was published in the *Transactions of the Royal Society* Volume 138. This was *'An account of the application of the gas from coal to economical purposes'*. The Partnership continued to push Murdoch's claims despite his total personal absence from the proceedings.

Meanwhile the committee of Winsor's London supporters continued to prepare their case for an enabling Act of Parliament. Winsor's flow of publications ceased – presumably the Committee had persuaded him to keep quiet. Tomory notes that *'there was a definite shift ... away from Winsor .... toward the business interests'*.

In early 1809 a Bill was submitted to Parliament for the new gas company which was not only to make and sell gas, all the associated apparatus and by-products, but which also included the all-important right to open the pavements to lay pipes. Lobbying continued with letters and pamphlets. In the background was a discussion about public and private ownership of businesses which were in the public interest, along with fears of monopolies and ultimately the form in which the ownership and management of such bodies should take.

In May 1809 the whole question of the gas company bill was considered by a Parliamentary Committee – for which, as *Griffiths*, says in *The Third Man*, Boulton and Watt *'pulled out all the stops'*.

THE PARLIAMENTARY ENQUIRY

A Parliamentary Enquiry was set up in 1809 to examine the case put forward by the National Committee. It is when all the arguments come out but then, at almost the same time, change. It was set up to examine the viability of coal gas manufacture and the rights of those who could claim to have first discovered it. This essentially was a challenge from provincial manufacturers about the equipment they made and sold, against the Londoners' idea of a central 'gas factory' which supplied the public. The enquiry explored not just the uses to which coal gas itself could be put but also the uses of the other products of the distillation of coal.

The Enquiry was chaired by Sir James Hall, chemist and geologist. However as proceedings began the evidence given was not what might have been expected. Witnesses for the proposed gas company appeared who gave detailed evidence, not just on light, but also on the use of coke, tar and ammoniacal liquor. The London activists needed to move the argument away from Murdoch's position as first 'inventor' if they were to prove their case.

This strategy of the London "*Winsorians*" was revealed twenty years later in 1828 by Joseph Hedley, one of the family of ready-made gasworks' suppliers. In his *Letter to the Rt. Hon the Lord Mayor on the Supply of Gas to the City of London,* he described how the Londoners' evidence to the Enquiry depended on the "*celebrated Mr. Accum,*" their consultant. Their object was to show to the Committee the "*immense value of the by-products*"... "*The Company were anxious to claim this as a discovery of their own*" and so "*represented these products therefore as being more valuable than the gas itself*". Such a claim would not interfere with Murdoch's priority of invention but would let the Enquiry disregard his petition and allow the Bill to proceed.

Lawyers for Boulton and Watt were well aware of this tactic and lobbied hard. In the case papers now in the archive at Birmingham, are bills for entertaining witnesses to steaks, oranges and brandy, and lists of Members of Parliament to be lobbied. There are also day-to-day notes on evidence given at the Enquiry, with the lawyer's comments. Accum's unfortunate statement to the Enquiry that "*with the tar I have made no experiments*" was particularly noted by underlining in the lawyer's briefing document to James Watt Junior.

By comparing sets of notes the preparation of evidence can be seen. When James Watt Jnr gave evidence to the Enquiry on 13th May 1809 he was asked what Murdoch had done with the tar and ammonia produced by the gas making process, and replied that '*the pitch has been sold to boat builders in the neighbourhood*' and also that '*Mr. Murdock has made experiments on the ammoniacal liquor, which I have seen, to ascertain the quantity of carbonate of ammonia contained in it*'. Watt Jnr. seems to have written to William Henry and asked for details on this and on 29th May Henry wrote to him from Manchester, apparently in answer, and mentioned '*experiments with condensed liquid from coal made long ago with a view to procuring carbonate of ammonia*' and gave some details of experiments he had undertaken, ending with '*the purification of this salt I suspect would be a matter of some difficulty. We are all anxious to know the event of your opposition to Winsor's importunate and uninformed claim*'.

Minutes of the 1809 Parliamentary Enquiry describe a wide range of prospective uses for the residual products of coal gas manufacture. A selection of witnesses was called, some of who were already using these or similar products, others had been asked to test specimens from "*Winsor's stove.*" It is irrelevant whether or not the new gas company actually intended to develop these uses, or whether they were put forward only to impress the Enquiry.

The Bill was lost. It appears a weak link in the Londoners' case had been Frederick Accum who under questioning had been made to "*appear a fool... another greedy foreigner,*" together with Winsor's "*outlandish claims.*" Brougham, Boulton and Watt's lawyer, *had no difficulty in exposing Accum's ignorance of gas, despite his high scientific reputation*'. In Parliament opposition centred on '*the general principle of granting chartered monopolies to any great body of men, to the preclusion of all competition'*. Rawlinson, in *Regulation of the Gas Industry* points out that '*chartered monopolies'* were under attack and that Parliament '*had recently authorised three new companies to break the monopolies in the London water supply'*.

The National Committee continued with their work and the plans for the new gas company were changed by reducing the capital to be raised to £200,000 and excluding Winsor. The Bill was re-submitted a year later and by then Wilberforce, who had opposed and spoken against the original bill, had changed his mind following a campaign of lobbying and it passed through Parliament with no trouble. In the Act the new 'Gas Light and Coke Company' was given powers, restricted to the Metropolitan area and explicitly denied a monopoly in that district – hence the many other London gas companies, as will be described in due course.

Through Boulton and Watt's lobbying powers the Gas Light and Coke Company was prevented from making gas fittings – hence the cluster of fittings manufacturers which were to grow up around some of the earliest gasworks. Sugg, for instance, remained in Marsham Street long after the Westminster Gas Works had closed. Other clauses in the legislation protected the rights of oil suppliers and defined some of the conduct of relationships between the gas company and local authorities.

Everything was now in place for the opening of the first gasworks – something which it was to turn out was not nearly as easy as it appeared.

At around the same time Winsor was moving out of central London to somewhere more upmarket.

WINSOR IN HIS NEW HOME

Meanwhile Winsor seems to have moved to Woolwich. It might be interesting to look at Woolwich itself – a disregarded down-market town down river and in 1811 still firmly in Kent. Can we change our minds about it and see it as a key place in British technological development – and in the early 19th century a centre for academic scientific research? This has to be important to the nascent gas industry

WOOLWICH

In the late 18th century, a few miles outside London, was an institution of learning which may well have had an interest in coal gas for lighting (or more likely for its use in explosives). This was the military research complex in Woolwich, which included the Royal Military Academy.

Woolwich has had very little, if any, attention as an academic centre, but in the Royal Military Academy it had one of the few institutions in Britain where research staff were employed on technical subjects. A number of Fellows of the Royal Society lived and worked there. Some of these Woolwich-based scientists had a special interest in gases: for example, William Cruickshank, Professor of Chemistry at the Royal Military Academy, who published relevant papers before 1810. Later, another Chemistry Lecturer, John MacCulloch, wrote on wood distillates, a subject of particular relevance to a study of coal gas residuals.

There was also the Royal Arsenal, a huge and largely secret complex for arms manufacture – heavily focussed on research, which, later in the 19th century, had its own research-based chemical department. Everything about it was on a massive scale – and we know tantalisingly little about most of it. The Royal Arsenal itself did not install its own on-site gasworks until 1857, when it was described in Journal of Gas Lighting. Nevertheless the establishment had several close links with the early gas industry. One prominent person involved was the younger William Congreve who was Comptroller of the Royal Laboratory which was based in Woolwich. He was the Government's Inspector-General of gas light companies in the 1820s and responsible for an influential Select Committee on Gas Lighting in 1823. Congreve also played a part in the industry as an inventor, a company backer and a promoter – more about those later.

We do not know why the interest in coal gas manufacture by some of the Woolwich establishment was not translated into an early gas-making plant there. It was suggested by Arsenal historian, O.F.G. Hogg, that there was a deliberate decision not to site a gasworks there because of the perceived danger of explosion, although clearly the Arsenal authorities do not seem to have been frightened by the numerous other explosive substances on site.

We should also note the 16th Century Woolwich Royal Dockyard, also heavily research-based, together with the huge, Government promoted, rope walk. It was here that Clegg's associate, Mr.Lukin, experimented with the use of coal gas for seasoning wood – and blew up several buildings in the process.

All of these institutions are described in detail in the 2012 volume of the Survey of Woolwich.

It may also be of relevance that the promoter of coal gas manufacture in London, Frederick Albert Winsor, lived in Shrewsbury House, on Shooters Hill on the borders of Woolwich. He was probably there from around 1811, when his residence is recorded in the Woolwich Rate Books.

SHREWSBURY HOUSE

In the years between the first success of the Gas Light and Coke Company and his departure to France, Winsor seems to have lived in some comfort in a mansion on the slopes of Shooters Hill on the outskirts of Woolwich, Shrewsbury House – a

predecessor to the present Community Centre. There are a number of stories about gas-making equipment there.

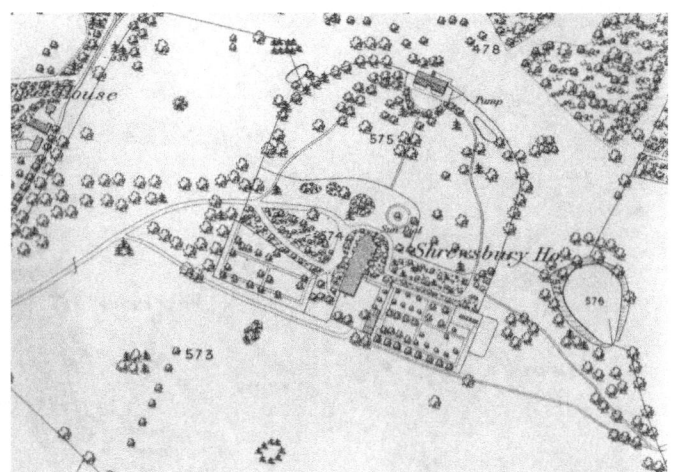

In 1883 discussion was under way about celebrations of the centenary of the 'first attempt' to make coal gas for lighting. Samuel Smiles, a Blackheath resident, lectured on the subject at the Royal Aquarium, Westminster. Around the same time a Mr. Thomas Bormann Winser of Shooters Hill Road in Blackheath wrote to *The Standard* about some old gas pipes found in a house being demolished on Shooters Hill. He linked this with handbills which advertised in 1807 demonstrations of gas lighting in London.

Mr. Winser probably knew the stories that the first ever "*gasometer*" had been sited in the grounds of Shrewsbury House on Shooters Hill. He neglected to tell the press that the "*old house*" under demolition was not Winsor's home – but some other unspecified building.

Modern Shrewsbury House is a community centre built in the 1920s, replacing the older house occupied in 1811 by Winsor. Before he moved there it had been a royal residence. In 1795, Princess Caroline of Brunswick had come to England to marry the Prince of Wales, the future George IV. When the marriage failed she went to live in Blackheath and their daughter, Princess Charlotte, heir to the throne, lived, as a child, at Shrewsbury House.

Frederick Albert Winsor's career in the London gas industry came to an end in 1813 when he seemed unable to give any sensible answers about gas-making to the Gas Light and Coke Company's Committee on Chemistry, subcommittee on gas manufacture. In 1813 he went to Paris where he died and is buried in the Pere Lachaise cemetery. His son, also Frederick Albert, remained in England. He became a barrister and had a lifetime's involvement with that first gas company – which grew to be the famous Gas Light and Coke Co. He died at his London address, in Lincoln's Inn Fields and is buried at Kensal Green. Strangely, the *Dictionary of National Biography* describes him as 'of Shooters Hill'.

THE 'CHARTERED'
THE GAS LIGHT AND COKE COMPANY

The next section describes the four gasworks set up by the Gas Light and Coke Company (commonly known as 'The Chartered') once their Charter was obtained. The first, Cannon Row, was very short lived and together with those works which were to provide the first public gas supply and continue over the next sixty years, is shown below.

CANNON ROW

A small, unsuccessful and short-lived attempt to build a public supply gasworks. Constructed by a group of enthusiasts it had the advantage of a riverside site in Westminster, close to the area where the first customers were to be found.

With their legal framework in place, the new 'Gas Light and Coke Company' next took the big step of setting up their first gasworks. A wharf and house were rented at Cannon Row, slightly to the north of Westminster Bridge, in 1812. One of the directors, Mr Barlow, was asked to provide apparatus. Barlow does not seem to have any obvious connection to the Barlow family of iron mongers from Sheffield who were to build and set up many small gasworks. It is however very possible that he was one of them – and if so had recourse to some of their expertise.

The site was managed by James Hargreaves, the company's Deputy Governor, while plans were made to light the areas immediately adjacent to this site. It is very probable that gas from Cannon Row provided the first public gas supply, to Westminster Bridge in September 1813.

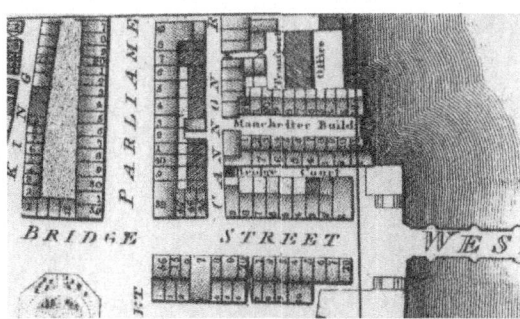

At first everything proceeded very badly, as various self-professed experts were shown to be both ignorant and incompetent. The Company was obliged to recruit an expert in coal gas manufacture and this was Samuel Clegg who arrived from Manchester 1812 with a group of other workers. Clegg said at once that the works at Cannon Row would not do – so, in due course, it was closed and the site sold in 1814. Everard remarks that the lease went to a Government body – The Transport Board – and on the *Horwood Plan* a riverside site at Cannon Row is marked *'Transport Office'*. It can therefore be assumed that the site was adjacent to this. The area is now covered with Government Offices and Cannon Row itself is not accessible to the public.

GREAT PETER STREET

This was the first fully functioning public supply gasworks. It was designed and initially managed by Samuel Clegg. He had trained under Boulton and Watt and had a strong scientific background. It was built in the centre of Westminster to be near customers – and showing a strong presence near the seat of Government. It was however in the middle of crowded streets and with no water transport access – although the river was not far away. It was to become a showpiece works and continued to supply gas for about sixty years. The site remained as the Head Office of the Company until nationalisation in the late 1940s – and its remains are still important enough to be the subject of a great deal discussion in Parliament and elsewhere.

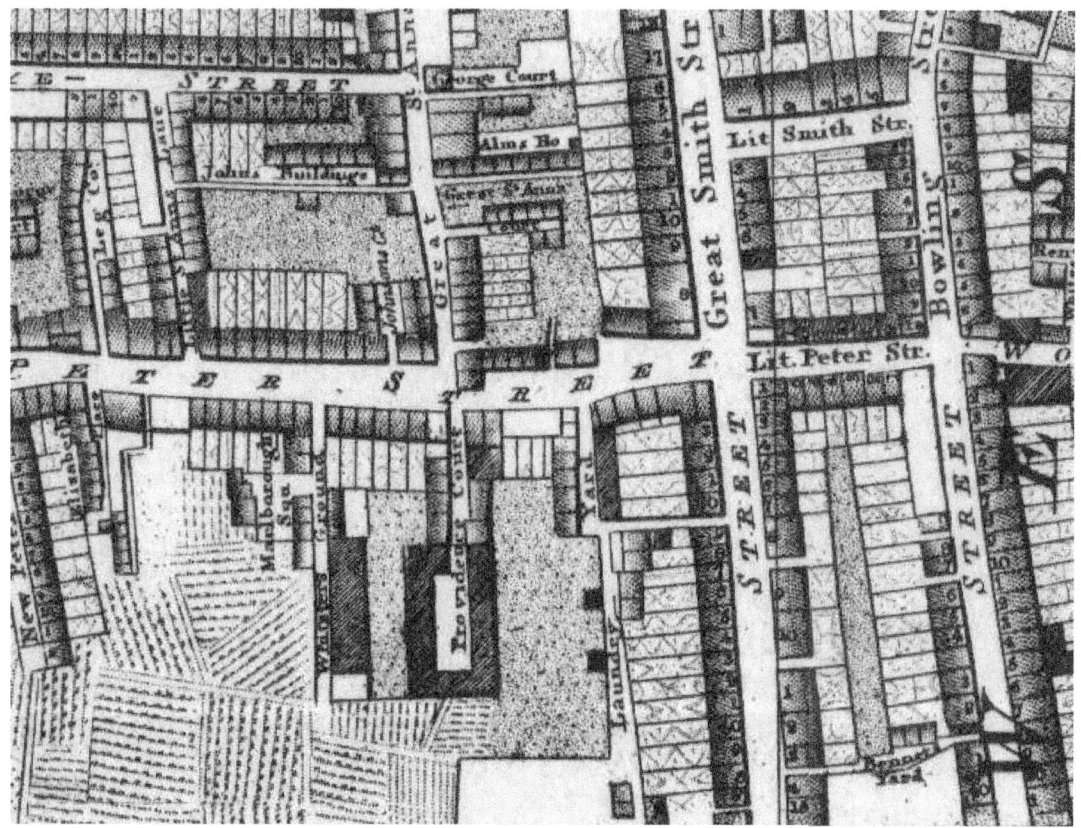

The Gas Light and Coke Company were to build three works in the first few years of operations but initially they opened a new works in Great Peter Street, Westminster.

On the Great Peter Street façade of the Seacole Building, 2 Marsham Street (almost opposite the end of St Ann's Street) is a green City of Westminster plaque. This states that you are at the site of the Gas Light and Coke Company (GLCC) gasworks, which provided the first public supply of gas in the world, in September 1813. The building is used as Government Offices and named for 19th Century nurse, Mary Seacole, although ironically, 'sea coal' is what was processed here in the gasworks. Initially in 1813 pipes were to be laid to the Parliament buildings. The first paying contract, in November, was with the Church of St. John (now the concert venue St John's Smith Square) which lay between the works and Parliament. The use of gas rapidly expanded over the next few years so and by September 1815 the mains had extended as far as Covent Garden.

Hansard of 1st March 1975 records a House of Lords discussion about the demolition of its replacement, Department of the Environment's Marsham Street, SW1, building. Viscount Ullswater told the House that this was the site of 'the first public gasworks'. From the gas historian's point of view the site is anything but obscure. It was the 'first operational public gasworks', set up by Winsor, Grant, Hargreaves and Barlow, and made to work by Samuel Clegg. For nearly sixty years the works functioned on the doorstep of Parliament – and even today, 130 years after its closure it is still making news.

The first contracts for lighting parts of Westminster had been agreed with some difficulty. Everard records that Grant was *'assiduous in pursuing contracts'* but without any *'expansion of the works'*. The first gas lights went into operation sometime between August and October 1813 – this was for public street lighting, but some private lights were installed shortly afterwards. It became increasingly clear that the Company needed a *'practical engineer'* – since little sense could be gained from either Winsor or Accum. The Board, which they called 'The Court', therefore recruited Samuel Clegg, from Manchester. He had been trained by Boulton and Watt as a consultant, and had already designed and opened a gas-making plant at Stoneyhurst College. He recommended the construction of new plant on a larger site and a site just off Great Peter Street was acquired.

Before 1811 the site, Providence Court, had been the site of a cudbear works. 'Cudbear' was a lichen- and ammonia-based dye developed in Scotland by the industrial chemist, Charles Mackintosh, but illicitly passed by one of his workers to a Mr. Grant. It may be co-incidental that the first Chairman of the Gas Light and Coke Co. was also a Mr. Grant. The lease was however owned by a different director, John White, and it was through him that the site was acquired.

In due course Cannon Row was closed and Providence Court became the first functioning gasworks of the first functioning gas company. Soon, it began to expand, initially to neighbouring Laundry Court. There was however, a problem with the site, which was to cause endless difficulties as time went on. Unlike Cannon Row, or indeed unlike Winsor's Millbank site, it had no water access. Deliveries of coal and removal of chemical waste products were to become a problem. Coal was delivered to a wharf at Westminster and taken to the works by road.

71

The first accident with gas, an explosion in a gas storage area, was recorded in October 1813. With it began the long history of public concern about inner city gasworks. As a result the Government made its first attempts at regulation of the new industry.

In October 1813, a small group of shareholders began to press for changes in the Company. From this group emerged Thomas Livesey, who was to become Deputy Governor of the Company for the next twenty-five years and was the first of a gas-making dynasty of Liveseys.

Gradually, with some difficulties, the technology was sorted out and things began to improve. This is not the place to go into detail about all the different technologies that were developed at Westminster as well as at the Gas Light and Coke Company's two other works. It was one of the earliest gasworks and unforeseen problems were inevitable. Samuel Clegg had brought with him a group of experienced workers - *'Clegg's young men'* - and many of them were very young – who went out to start gasworks of their own around the country.

This inner city site was never really big enough and expansion began almost before things had started. By 1814 there was a problem with increasing amounts of noxious effluent. It was even considered floating grea*t* lakes of the stuff in the area now covered by the Tate Gallery! There were continual and increasing complaints about pollution of the river and sewers. The works grew and grew and by the end of 1822, as the largest gasworks in London it fed coal gas into 57 miles of mains, serving 10,660 private burners, 2,248 street lamps and 3,894 burners in public buildings and theatres.

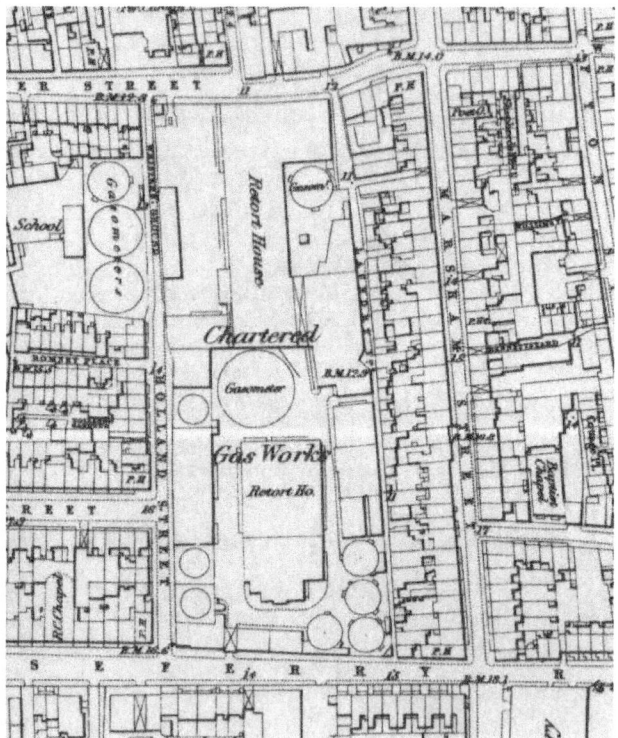

Because the Westminster Works was so central and so famous, visitors were allowed to look around, providing they had a ticket of admission. One of these was a Frenchwoman, Flora Tristam, who looked round the works in the early 1840s. She was appalled at what she saw there – *'a veritable hell'*. The place smelt *'foul exhalations of gas and the stench of coal and tar pursued me'*... it was dirty – *'pools of stagnant water and piles of rubbish'*... and *'appalling'* ... *'nothing*

could be more terrible and majestic than the sight of so many mouths all pouring flames'. Even worse were the conditions for the workmen *'Dear God! Have these men no mother, sister, wife or daughter waiting at the door as they emerge from that hell?'*

In 1848 the plant at Westminster was very largely rebuilt by Frederick Evans, their then engineer, and a wharf at Millbank was specially designed for coal deliveries to Westminster. When plans for the Victoria Embankment jeopardised the future of this wharf plans were put forward for a dock system in Pimlico but this was not built. Instead an extension to the works for gas storage was built at a site later known as Vincent Street. By the early 1870s the Westminster works was thought to have a 'discreditable appearance' – which, given its site so near the Houses of Parliament and Westminster Abbey is not surprising! The works was then reduced to supplying only the peak load and in 1875 it was closed for gas-making. In 1883 the site was cleared and two large gasholders were built on it.

By the 1940s the offices in Horseferry Road could be described as 'a charming survival of the early 19th century. The main entrance flanked on either side by decorative gas lamps. Behind it was concealed a jumble of added offices'.

The two gasholders built in Marsham Street appear on contemporary maps. Put out of use for gas, they were adapted in the Second World War for use as bomb shelter 'citadels' and a new steel frame building was also added in 1941. The citadels were designed to survive a 500 lb bomb and had 12-foot-thick concrete roofs. In 1943 one became the reserve to the Cabinet War Rooms. They were replaced by Marsham Towers which was completed in 1971 and housed the Department of the Environment. Anyone who walked down Peter Street could see that the holder sites appeared to match the large circular structures on which the 1960s office block rested. In 1958 E.G. Stewart explained how the tanks of the two holders had been converted into *'heavily reinforced underground strongholds each equipped to house several thousand Government officials ...joined by tube railway to similar strongholds'.* He gave no source for this information which was repeated in several books on 'secret' or 'underground' London.

I have met several people who claim to have seen inside the rotundas, which are alleged to go down at least four storeys. However most of my informants cited the Official Secrets Act as a reason for not telling me more. However members of Subterrania Britannica researched the holders and the secret rotundas – and the bunkers built in them – plus a civil service sports club. A report of their visit it is on their web site https://www.subbrit.org.uk/sites/rotundas/ . The citadels were eventually demolished by explosives in 2003.

Meanwhile – as other works began to be planned – gas-making plants continued to be set up for demonstration and research.

CURTAIN ROAD

The second works of the Gas Light and Coke Company, was started by Accum, and finished, more practically, by Clegg. Situated to the immediate north of the City of London it was built to supply gas to the tiny 'Liberty' of Norton Folgate. Like Westminster it had no water access being a long way from the river or canal. In the very first years of the Gas Light and Coke Company, the Court of Governors worked very hard to get local authority lighting contracts. 'The Liberty' now appears to be no more than a short stretch of road.

When I researched Curtain Road I was able confidently to place it near a taxi depot on the eastern corner of Hearn and Worship Streets. I had previously been on a walk round the site, looked at the defunct railway viaduct out of Broad Street station and guessed where the gasworks was. There were even some suspiciously relevant looking bits of wall. Now the whole site is a large construction called The Stage – based loosely round a Shakespearean theatre on the site. To be fair to the archaeologists, for a change they did take in this very early gasworks on site and recorded what they found. There are reports on various Shoreditch-based websites.

One of the GLCC Governors had influence over 'one of the Norton Folgate Trustees', who acted like 'vestrymen'. The Trustees were interested in the constant issues of

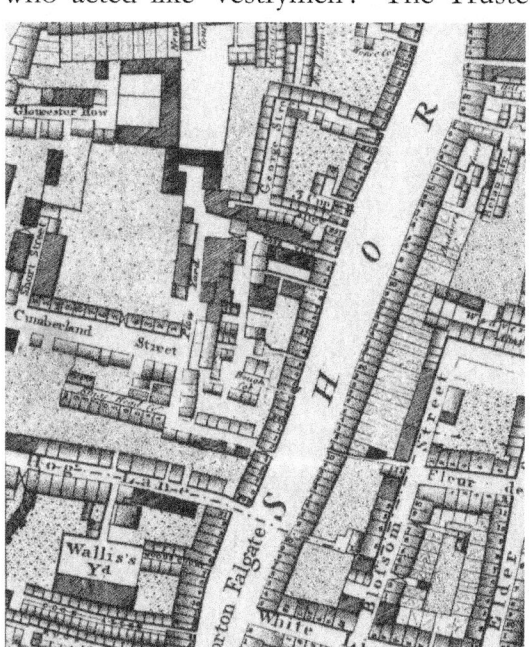

lower rates and cutting crime and so, by deciding to find a solution in improved street lighting using gas, this tiny area became the one of the first to have its own public supply gasworks as recorded in their minute books.

The site was leased from two coal merchants, James Weston and Thomas White, and the works was designed and begun by Accum, working with Joseph Cooper, one of the other directors. Accum, faced with his first practical chance of implementing his theories on gas lighting, made a mess of it and, as Everard records, Samuel Clegg finished the works.

Everard gives details of the problems caused by the single gasholder, the collapse of which caused a crisis and a resolution that future works must have two holders. Everard also tells the story of an early visit of directors to Curtain Road in 1813. He quotes a letter warning of springs underlying the works at Norton Folgate, springs which must lie on the line of the upper reaches of the Walbrook.

Despite the underground river Curtain Road was, like the site in Westminster, not on a navigable watercourse, which meant similar problems with coal delivery. Coal had to be carted across the City from the Westminster Wharf.

This is not the place to give a lot of detail on the works itself – what became known as 'Curtain Road' had an interesting history as one of the earliest gasworks in the world. As time went by it became less and less important, always on the brink of being closed. From 1865 the new North London Railway lines into Broad Street Station passed down the east side of the works and a complicated agreement was entered into with the railway whereby coal sidings would be built into the site and the railway would deliver *'coal and all other materials'* from Poplar Dock at 1/2d. per ton. Other arrangements concerned the use of Gas Light and Coke Co. gas for lighting in North London Railway stations and works and a promise that they would try and persuade LNWR to do so too.

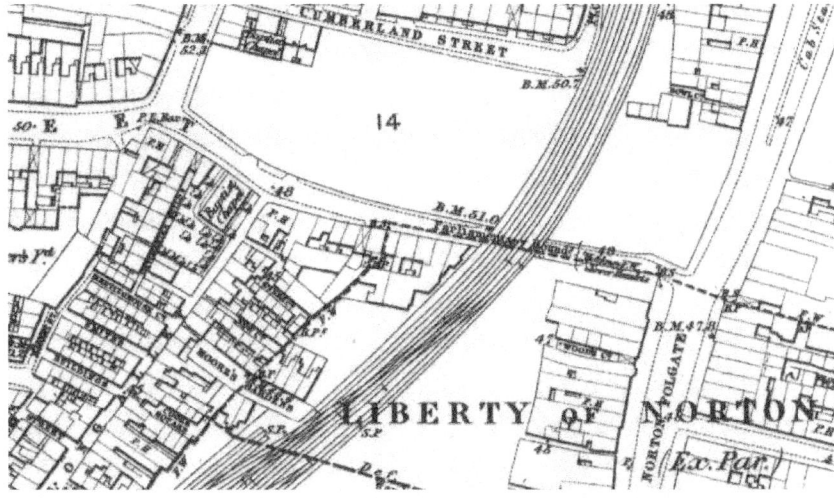

Within six years of the railway being built, the gas company had decided to close the works. A giant new works on a greenfield site in Barking, which became known as Beckton, allowed the Gas Light and Coke Company to close Curtain Road. A print of the works under demolition is sometimes reproduced with the claim that this was to enable the new Great Eastern Railway terminus to be built. However, the site shown in the print, is west of the existing North London Railway, whereas the Great Eastern lines are to the east. Plans in the London Metropolitan Archive make it clear that demolition was actually carried out to allow for a widening of the North London Railway into Broad Street Station. Until recently it was possible to stand in Hearn Street at the same angle from which the print was drawn large gasholder stood at the eastern end of the site, now partly covered by the railway. There is no apparent sign of this within the site itself.

In the late 1870s the site returned to its previous use as a coal yard and is shown as that on subsequent maps. Remains of a coal delivery system from the railway could still be seen on some of the walls in the 1980s. The future fate of the railway viaduct is not clear but will presumably be demolished eventually. Detailed investigation might still throw up clues to the past of this interesting old site.

75

BRICK LANE
THE GREAT GAS MANUFACTORY

The Brick Lane gasworks was in some ways the most successful of the three early works of the Gas Light and Coke Company. Brick Lane is now Central Street in what was once the parish of St. Luke's - to the east of Clerkenwell and Islington.

I was going up Goswell Road one day in the early 1990s when I saw that the office block which had stood in front of Samuel Clegg's Brick Lane Gas Works – and used as offices by the gas company - had been demolished. The gasworks had been *'The Great Gas Manufactory'* and justly famous. Now, for a few months, the buildings of the old works were there to be seen from Goswell Road. This alone of the earliest generation of gasworks is still in use by the industry, as a depot for Transco. I had always hoped to get on site at Clerkenwell and describe it from the inside, but there is little chance of that while it is still in use.

A developer will one day make a tidy profit on the site which cost the Chartered Company £3,000 to buy in 1814. It was called 'Brick Lane' because that was the name then of what is now Central Street – and nothing to with the more famous street in Aldgate

Brick Lane closed as a site for coal gas manufacture in 1871 when the giant out-of-town works at Beckton was opened but it stayed in use with showrooms and workshops. Some holders remained there until 1898. British Gas, and later Transco, vans could be still seen around in 2020s. This site in Clerkenwell has been in use by the gas industry for longer than any other. It will be regrettable if it were to pass from them without any commemoration.

The works opened in the world of Georgian Clerkenwell – very different from today. Before gas manufacture began on site, it is shown on the Horwood Plan (1813) as a 'cooperage' which it appears they had purchased from the Golden Lane Brewery Co. The street plan of Peartree Street, with its little kink, was much the same then. Between the site boundary and Seward Street was a burial ground and north of Seward Street was a ropewalk. All around were dye works and chemical manufactories of all kinds.

Clerkenwell is one of those areas that turned Britain into the '*workshop of the world*'. An enormous list could be drawn up of industries which started there — Hancock and rubber, a different Hancock and cables, Bessemer, Moreland, endless breweries and distilleries, print works, all sorts of workshop trades, and much, much more. Many moved out to larger premises and their London origins were forgotten. These trades were lit with gas from Brick Lane — and sometimes it supplied waste products for raw materials to the nascent chemical industry in the area. Without the gasworks would industry in the area have flourished so much? What role did the gasworks have in the development of surrounding trades?

Once again the builders of Brick Lane Gas Works made no provision for coal deliveries. After this, gasworks were usually built on navigable water or beside the railway. Here everything came in by road — imagine the coal carts coming in and the coke carts coming out. Sulphuric acid and lime came in, and the noxious waste known as 'Blue Billy' went out to be dumped — as well as tar and ammoniacal liquor for the chemical trade — all carted through the streets of Clerkenwell.

Visiting the site today it seems small and narrow — the gasworks originally occupied about a third of what is there now. Yet, people came from all over the world to marvel at it. Those big dark holders overlooking narrow Peartree Street were stared at by young enthusiasts. 'Clegg's young men' have already been mentioned. No doubt they were as excited by the new technology they found in the gas industry as young men are today by computers and electronics. Who knows what lies hidden there? This was one

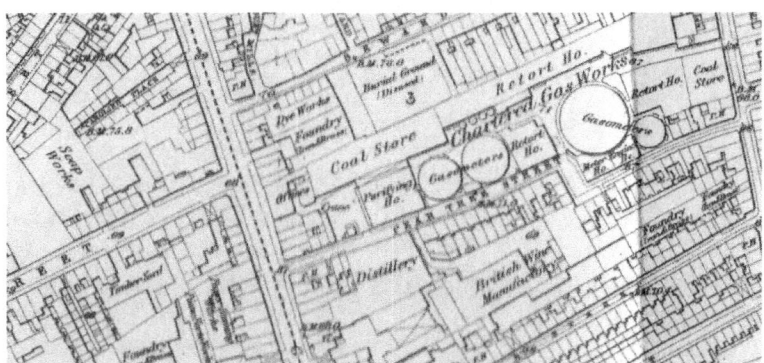

of the earliest gasworks ever, and it has been in the same ownership ever since. There is no other site like it. It could tell us so much. It may be that development can take place on the site without any return to the planning process — and if so then any chance of investigation is lost. Hopefully the gas industry will stay on site and preserve what remains for the future. However, that does not seem to be how things happen these days.

THOMAS LIVESEY
A BIOGRAPHICAL NOTE

Thomas Livesey was probably about forty when he moved into the London gas industry. Livesey is a common name in the north west of England but there is no reason to believe that this Thomas was other than a Londoner. He had done well in a wholesale hosiery business based in Wood Street in the City of London. Wood Street is near the Guildhall and surrounded by the halls of City Livery Companies including the Haberdashers – so perhaps, after all, he had connections with some dyeing and spinning Liveseys from Lancashire. He lived in Mare Street, Hackney – a much more prosperous area then than now. He was probably unmarried and was almost certainly childless.

The story of the setting up of the first gas company has been told a number of times. By the autumn of 1812 the company had a Royal Charter, an office, a Court of Governors and a muddle. In September of that year five men applied for a block of forty shares between them. One of these men was Thomas Livesey. His first action was to ask what the qualifications were for filling vacancies in the Court of Governors, his next was to visit the new gasworks which was being set up at Peter Street, Westminster. Thomas Livesey and his friends went to look at the new gasworks, which were still under construction in May 1813 – and in July they went to Curtain Road 'station' in the northern boundary of the City of London. They arrived there unannounced and did not like what they found. Thomas wrote a strong letter to the Governors ... *there appears a defect or imbecility somewhere...*

The group of angry shareholders, which included Thomas Livesey, began to grow and in October 1813 a meeting of 54 of them demanded that an Extraordinary General Meeting be held. Directors resigned, were reinstated, and a Committee of Investigation was set up. In November Thomas Livesey was elected to the Court of Governors. He immediately began to take a leading role and within two years was elected Deputy Governor, remaining in that position until 1840.

Thomas Livesey had joined the management of the first ever Gas Company at a time when it was still, dimly, beginning to work out how to build gasworks, make gas, distribute the gas and sell it. The hosiery business seems to have allowed him enough spare time to take on what must have been an almost full time task – which is not to say that he did not find ways of making money out of gas, as time went by. Once in the gasworks, first he took charge of the internal organisation, setting up a series of sub-committees to deal with the tasks to be undertaken – works, finance, lighting and experiment. He went on to look at the necessary activities and to regularise them.

Contracts with suppliers were generally tightened. The main purchase of any gas company was coal – and before 1813 the Chartered Company had bought it as it was needed — sometimes on a daily basis. The company had already been warned that direct buying of large stocks of coal from London sources would lead to price fixing by the tightly organised group of coal factors operating in the port. Livesey took a decision on coal purchases himself, against the wishes of the rest of the Court, and began to deal directly with a Newcastle coal factor — which meant increased transport costs but ensured a future supply and some control of its price. Later, together with another director, he went to Newcastle on a fact-finding mission. As a result coal buying was reorganised.

Another vital area for the new gas company to sort out was to whom and how the gas was to be sold. The early gas companies sold mainly to institutions rather than individuals and every contract needed negotiation. Initially most gas was sold for street lighting and therefore it was important to develop contacts within the local authorities that had to decide what lighting method was to be used. Even before Livesey became a Director of the Chartered Company it was noted that *'Mr. Livesey has influence with one of the trustees'* of the Liberty of Norton Folgate - a small local authority on the outskirts of the City of London. A few months later Livesey, although still not a board member, was negotiating with Norton Folgate and they became one of the first local authority areas to sign up for gas lighting. Livesey was also in discussion with the adjacent parish of St. Leonard's, Shoreditch and in 1816 he met Soane, the architect, to discuss gas lighting at the Bank of England.

Equipment was needed for the works. For example, casks and barrels were needed for the storage and dispatch of waste products. Livesey unearthed supplies of second hand oil and treacle barrels as well as *'porter puncheons'*. He saw to the ordering of bricks from Messrs Rhodes — the Islington based property-owning family of whom Cecil Rhodes was a member.

Gas needed to be cleaned — 'purified' — and at this period lime was used almost exclusively for this purpose. Livesey arranged for lime to be bought from Rosher *and Co '3 cwt lime at 15/- a barge load'* — Roshers were the Northfleet lime burners after whom Rosherville is named. He also arranged for a 'a circular lime machine' to be bought 'from the Horsley Co.' — that is a special new piece of equipment designed by a member of the company staff and commissioned from Horsley Ironworks in Shropshire. Horsley, under Aaron Manby, were already beginning to specialise in gas industry equipment. Manby was to describe him as *'friend Livesey'*.

Piping for mains and indoor supplies, as we would recognise them, hardly existed and was certainly not manufactured on anything like the scale needed. The Gas Light and Coke Company set up a Committee, which recommended standard specifications for different applications. Gas companies would place orders with a manufacturer to make tubing as required. Something had to be done with the *'residuals'* — the by-products of gas manufacture. Tar and ammoniacal liquor were building up in vast quantities in the works. It had been hoped they could be used to manufacture new and profitable products but nothing had been done. Livesey began to make arrangements — for

79

instance, in 1814, he had several gallons of ammoniacal liquor sent to *'Messrs. Barchard, Hilton and Platt, dyers, Montague Close, Borough'* to see if they could use it in their work as a mordant.

New offices for the company were needed and Livesey found these away from the works in the City of London — by what must have been a co-incidence they were almost adjacent to the second ever gas company's works at Blackfriars.   Once there he set about employing an accountant who was asked to do a detailed analysis of company finance and to set up proper systems.

As time went on Livesey continued to work on an effective coal buying policy for the company. The three works had all been built without water access and wharves had to be identified and cartage organised. In 1827 Livesey went north again and obtained advice on freight costs. The company began to buy directly from the pits. They chartered collier ships and from 1830 began to own ships themselves. In 1839 he negotiated to purchase Pelton Main Pit. The company did not buy the colliery but secured an exclusive agreement with the new owners.

Livesey was also the person in the company who interacted with the rest of the gas industry. The other companies all knew Mr. Livesey, it was him with whom they liaised. In 1822 the City of London Gas Company had put a main through Cornhill in the City of London and it was Livesey from the Chartered Company with whom they negotiated. In almost every reference to the Chartered by other companies before 1840 Mr. Livesey is found and not just in London — he appears in company minute books throughout the country. A tribute to his energy.

What was he like? Sterling Everard who wrote the History of the Gas Light and Coke Company described him as 'a Victorian, direct, forceful, pugnacious and impatient. The sort of man who could be found building up the fortunes of his business in almost every industry in the England of the time.' This was Georgian England. The history of the gas industry of the period is a saga of fraud. Livesey was not above taking his chance like the rest. The deal with the Newcastle Coal factor, which he had negotiated behind the backs of the rest of the Court, quickly came to grief. A Committee of Enquiry into the matter found him innocent of complicity with the dishonest factor. Livesey left the company in 1840, apparently under a cloud about coal cartage contracts.

He seems to have made a lot of money. Livesey had originally lived at an address in The Triangle, Mare Street, Hackney. At this time this was still a pleasant area on the southern borders of Hackney on the main road as it came north from Bethnal Green. Some old houses still remained in the area, although industry was creeping up from the City and down from Hackney itself.   He later moved, just up the road, to 2 Clapton Place. This must, by any standards, have been a moderately small house for a rich man. It was part of a terrace, which later became shops in the central area of Hackney and directly opposite St. John's Church.

At his death in 1847 he left some property, houses, in Bethnal Green. He also left a remarkably good reputation for philanthropy *'by his death we have lost a kind benefactor and the uneducated a zealous advocate'*.

I think it is important to note his work in sorting out the administration of the Chartered Company. We hear a lot about technological developments but very little about getting wages paid and invoices out on time.

In noting Thomas Livesey we should also pick up on some of his family members. He took two nephews into the Chartered Offices in clerical jobs. One of them, William, was to become an expert in the legal and parliamentary procedures necessary for gas companies. The other, Thomas, in taking over the management of South Met, Gas Co. In the 1830s was able to show how it was possible to run a company competently and honestly and to ensure its long term financial future with astute decisions on areas of gas supply. His son was the amazing George Livesey who was to revolutionise the late 19th century gas industry and laid the basis for its future in the 20th century,

Within a few years other gas companies were founded. One of the earliest was set up to serve the City of London.

THE CITY OF LONDON GAS COMPANY

FETTER LANE

This was another demonstration works — perhaps originating from a display in a shop window — which seems to have begun an involvement in public supply. It was probably, despite the name, based in Fleet Street, on the western edge of the City of London, in a busy commercial district.

This possible gasworks like so many at this time, has a vague and insubstantial existence. It might have been in Fleet Street, or Fetter Lane, or it might not have existed at all.

Everard says that the works was set up by a William Knight of Duke Street, West Smithfield, who had previously displayed lights at an office in the Strand. He has proved very resistant to any research and does not appear in later lists of directors of the City of London Gas Company — of which this gas-making plant appears to be the forerunner. Hugh Barty-King in 'New Flame" quotes a Times report of April 1814 which describes illuminations in 'Knights Gas Light Office in Fleet Street' with a display in which gas lights are the leaves of a laurel bush. Stewart, in the supplement to his 'Historical Index of Gas Works' gives the address as 183 Fleet Street. From the numbering shown on Horwood this was a couple of doors down from the Fetter Lane junction, to the east and next door to St. Dunstan's church. Everard also says that it was closed in 1814 following a prosecution for nuisance.

This is all very vague and relies entirely on notes by Everard who had access to the Gas Light and Coke Company archives before they were split and scattered following nationalisation and, since he gives no references, they cannot be verified unless found by chance. It seems most likely that this was a small demonstration plant set up by an enthusiast — perhaps in order to persuade people to join with him to form the City of London Gas Co.

Knight's absence from the City Company's records can be explained by another note by Everard, which says that on an unspecified date, but probably in the mid-1820s, Knight's widow appealed to them for money.

The City of London Gas Company itself moved to a permanent site in Blackfriars soon after 1814.

Thomas Hadland	Cheesemonger.	34 Holborn Hill
Charles Hutchins	A cow keeper.	Water Street, near Arundel Street off the Strand
James Lynn	Shell fishmonger including brawn & herrings.	Fleet Street
William Pocknell	Fish and shellfish monger. Selling oysters with beer brewed on the premises to those leaving theatres late evening.	134 St.Martin's Lane
Samuel Fish	Snuff and tobacco factory. In 1798 considered getting a steam engine from Boulton and Watt, via John Rennie.	St. John Street, Clerkenwell
Timothy Stansfield	Tobacco Merchant. Owned a mill on the Isle of Dogs	Originally from Bristol Lower Thames Street. Field House, New Cross
Frederick Sparrow	Tea dealer, but described himself as a grocer.	Ludgate Hill and Oxford Street
Henry Sparrow	Tea Dealer.	95 High Holborn and 26 Aylesbury Street, Clerkenwell
Anthony Weatherhead	Grocer and tea dealer.	18 Coventry Street
James Smethurst	Lamp manufacturer & oil warehouseman.	New Bond Street
John Blackett	Deputy Chair of the Ratcliffe Co and subscriber to the South London Co. Possible shipyard owner or a ships' biscuit baker of Wapping.	Brixton Hill.
James Blackett	Woollen draper. Brighton Gas Co. subscriber Blackett family were colliery owners in the North East.	New Park Hill, Brixton West Smithfield
Richard Ford	Treasurer and City Magistrate Superintendent of Aliens who dealt with political matters on London for the Home Office.	
William Fortescue	Member of the Royal College of Surgeons.	St. John Street, Clerkenwell, 9 Smithfield Bars

William Kimpton	Surgeon.	Old Kent Road
Timothy Tyrrell	City Gas Company solicitor. Solicitor to other Gas Cos. & the East India Dock Co. Remembrancer of the City of London. Master of the Worshipful Company of Upholders	
Harbut Ward	Bricklayer.	Water Street, Bridewell Carshalton
Charles Cofield	Plasterer.	Burrows Buildings, Christ Church, Surrey
William Pitcher.	Carpenter and builder. Shipbuilder with large yards at Northfleet and the Isle of Dogs.	Dorset Street, Salisbury Square Northfleet Canal Dock, Blackwall
James Sidney		

BLACKFRIARS WORKS

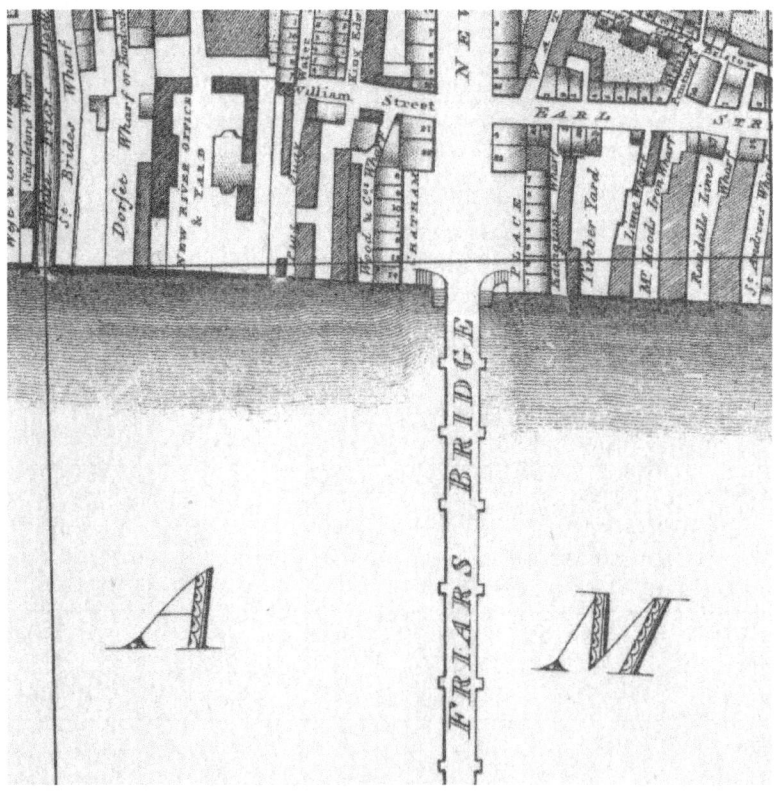

An important and successful gasworks built by a new and aspirant gas company on the banks of the River Thames on the western side of the City of London.

I was sitting at a meeting once, listening to a City of London planner explaining that they could not let any old, scruffy, boat moor along the Victoria Embankment because they had *'to preserve the original integrity of Bazalgette's design'*. I was forced to point out that

84

when Bazalgette built the embankment he had to accommodate a gasworks in his design and so included a tunnel underneath for coal transfer purposes — and scruffy colliers must have continued to deliver coal alongside.

This was The City of London Gas Company, whose holders can be seen in early photographs of the Embankment. Its Blackfriars works was slightly west of the mouth of the Fleet at Blackfriars on a site almost overburdened with historic interest. In the 17th century it was the site of a theatre, later Savery's workshop, later still headquarters and wharf of the New River Company.

It was, perhaps, the second gas company to be set up in London and was started by merchants and shopkeepers rather than grandees. However William Murdoch and James Ludovic Grant are reported in the *Monthly Magazine* for 1814 as establishing a gasworks in Water Lane along with 'Messrs. Knight'. In addition sources close to the Royal Society said that the works was set up by James Ludovic Grant and James Hargreaves, then Governor and Deputy Governor of the Chartered Gas Light and Coke Company. While Knight was certainly involved, there are no references to Grant, Hargreaves or Murdoch in the actual company records or in the list of supporters taken from the preamble to the Company's first enabling Act of Parliament and which describes those who were prepared to put their name to it.

Most of those listed appear to be City Traders — they are not financiers or 'businessmen' nor are most of them particularly prominent. Mostly they are men who would hope to use the gas made by the company on a daily basis. Among them are a number involved in tobacco and tea — and while this might just represent groups of people, who knew each other, it might also involve shipping connections with the West Indian and India trades. A number of them were based in the area around Smithfield and Fleet Street — that is in the western part of the City.

Twenty names are given in the supporters list, of whom only four appear to have business addresses in the City, three are in Clerkenwell, two in the West End, two in the Strand. They include seven shopkeepers — of whom four deal in tea and two in shellfish. There are two officials (or ex-officials) of the City Corporation, one of whom appears to be the current Remembrancer. There are two doctors and two tobacco merchants. There are others who may have wider interests but it is not always possible to identify every name with certainty. In addition, on the original indenture document of 1817 is found the name of William Caslon, type founder of Dorset Street — again almost adjacent to the gasworks site — who is thought to have built another gasworks himself elsewhere some years later.

The City Company's first works was at the bottom end of Fetter Lane but by 1815 was relocated to Dorset Street, or 'Water Lane', as it was then also known. In 1819, it was rebuilt again and it is from this date that the proper company records start. Everard wrote a detailed history of their first years, describing them as '*money making, grasping and litigious'*. By the 1820s, the company was in the hands of the New Cross based, Stansfield family.

An early engineer was John Perks, who designed the Blackfriars works. He was associated with Congreve who acted as a consultant to the company. Perks and Congreve were to go off with George Landmann, to tour Europe building gasworks. Everard describes how one of Perks' successors was thrown over a gasholder by an explosion and killed in 1822.

In 1815, the proprietors – Frederick Sparrow and William Knight were in court for polluting the atmosphere; this was seen as a test case and the City of London never let the company off the pollution hook again. As the years went by it became increasingly clear that the works would not be allowed to remain on this congested inner city site. Brian Sturt has commented that '*Blackfriars Gas Works seemed to be the whipping boy for local political ills – while it cannot have been the most ideal neighbour, it is unlikely it was quite as bad as made out*'. The political pressure of the 1860s was not to improve efficiency of this gasworks but to have it removed from the City.

Despite the reasonably successful future of the Blackfriars Works, its early years had not been so easy. In 1816 Sparrow and Knight had opposed a Parliamentary Bill put forward by the 'Chartered' Gas Light and Coke Company, saying that a statutory

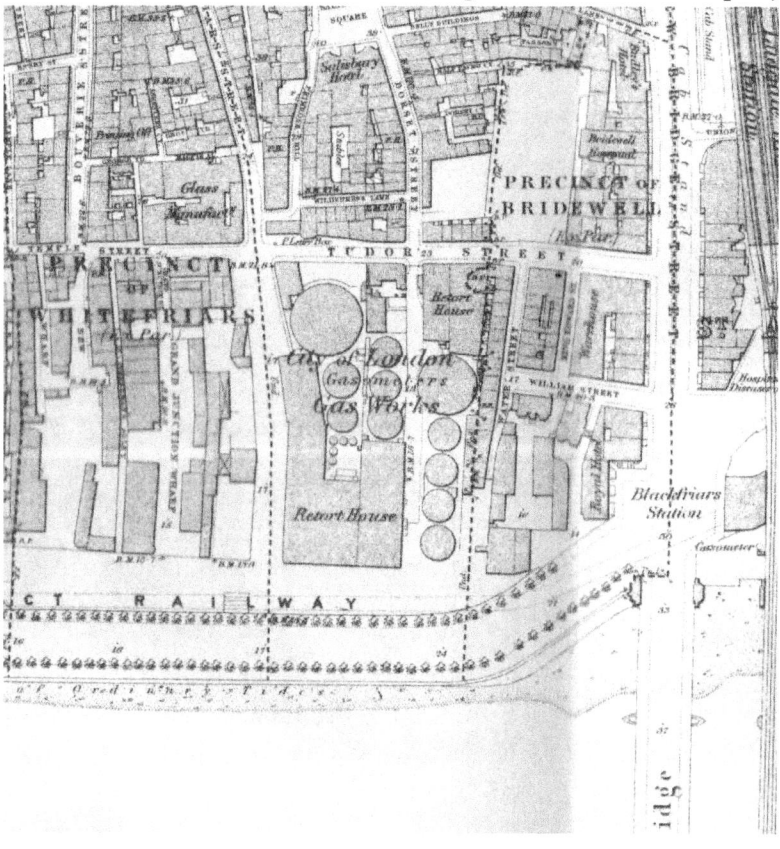

company had an unfair competitive advantage. Chartered had been in discussions about the Blackfriars Works for some years and in 1817 Sparrow and Knight offered to sell the works to the Chartered for £45,000 – an offer which, if accepted, the Chartered Court of Directors said would '*lead to mirth and derision*'. Thus, Knight and Sparrow felt that they had no alternative but to seek statutory powers themselves. Their Act was obtained without difficulty, following expensive alterations because of a prosecution for nuisance. In an agreement with the Chartered Company the new City Company agreed not to invade the Chartered's district nor steal its customers, and to exchange technical information.

The story of the City improvements is a long and complicated one and gas supply played a major role in it. City of London activists including Charles Pearson, the City Solicitor, aided and abetted by Angus Croll, promoted the Great Central Gas Company out at Bow Common to supply the City. That works is outside of the time frame of this book and so is not included. However it is worth noting that considerable remains still stand on the north side of Bow Common Lane albeit, as I write this in 2020, they are about to be removed for a housing scheme. The Bow Common works was soon to set new standards in bad practice and inefficiency, together with a number of actual scandals. Nevertheless it was opened by the Lord Mayor of London.

Political pressure to make gas companies more efficient led in the end to amalgamation of the City Company with the Chartered and subsequent closure of the Blackfriars works in 1873. Brian Sturt comments that '*Out of the many and complex issues that grew out of the construction of Beckton was that it enabled the closure of all the original Gas Light and Coke Co.'s works and also Blackfriars*'. As Beckton and its associated distribution system developed, other works were also closed. '*The Gas Light and Coke Company eventually came to regret that they did not purchase the City Company when they were able.*'

In the early 1880s, the City of London School was built on the site of the Blackfriars Gas Works. At the back of that building, in Tudor Street, part of a governor house survived into the mid-1980s, with art-nouveau motifs from the Gas Light and Coke Company. (Why did I never photograph it?) In the 1980s, the school was converted into the Morgan Bank. The Museum of London undertook a dig on the site. Some of us went down to see but it was clear that what the archaeologists were really into were the Roman remains some way beneath the interesting bits. A report was published into the dig, giving the briefest possible amount of space to the gasworks. Today, although the frontage of the school remains, the sheer walls of the bank make it difficult to imagine what used to be there. This is one of the key sites in the City of London and the siting of such an early gasworks on it demonstrates the importance of gas in the economy of the City.

Since my proof reader has expressed surprise that a school should have been built on a polluted site like an old gasworks I must explain that, until very recently, these things were thought of very differently. As the ensuing narrative will reveal, there are a number of schools in east London built on old gasworks sites, one as recently as the late 1960s.

87

ALDGATE GAS LIGHT AND COKE COMPANY

- OR IS IT THE WHITECHAPEL COMPANY?

One – or perhaps two - tiny works in an overcrowded inner city area. A gasworks here would find it difficult to be viable, – with little chance of expansion and water transport unavailable. There is little indication as to who was responsible for this scheme, or what happened to them.

The story of the gas companies and their works in the East End – Whitechapel, Wapping, Stepney, Limehouse, Poplar and Millwall – is a complicated and tangled one. From the evidence available to us we may never know how many works there were and where they were sited. In the early part of the 19th century Aldgate, Whitechapel, Spitalfields and Mile End were a ferment of innovative small works and inventors – engineering, chemicals, and sugar. Gas lighting was one of several exciting new technologies.

Stewart listed two Whitechapel Gas Works: the first in 'Castle Alley', and a second, in Goulston Square. He gives Everard's *History of the Gas Light and Coke Co.* as his source for both works. Everard gives no references and both he and Stewart seem to have

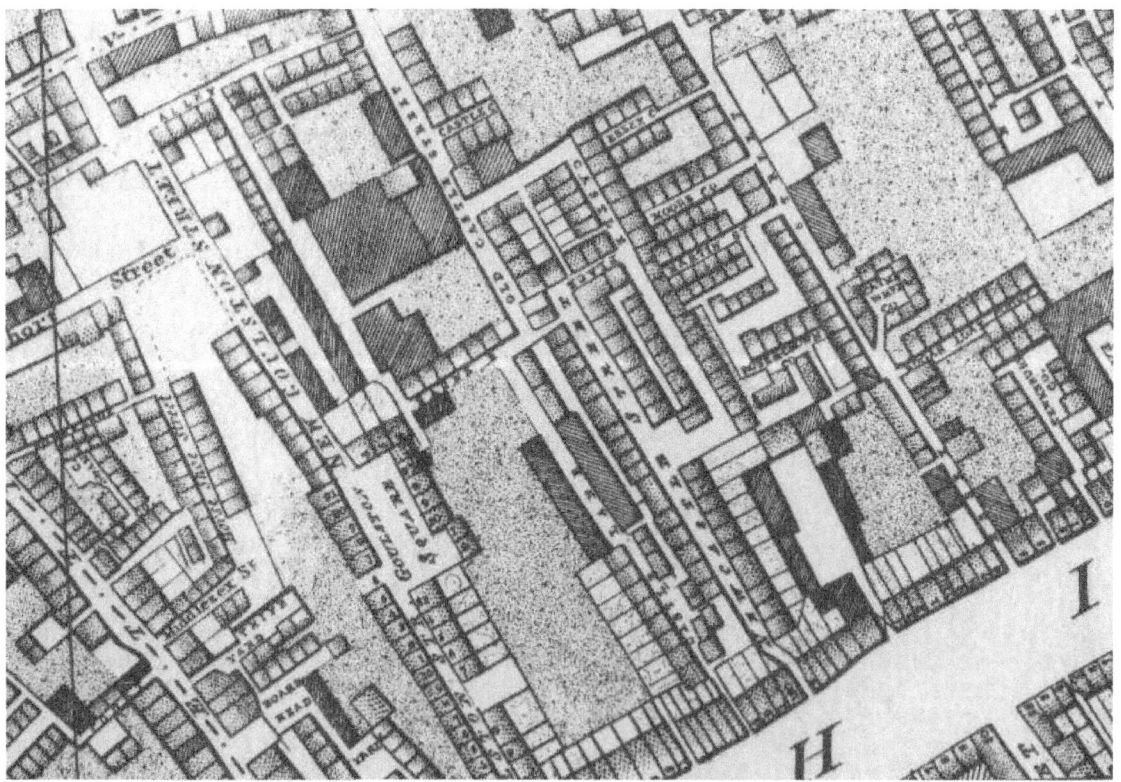

had access to information, which I have been unable to trace. The very early Aldgate Gas Company has left no records and its existence can only be traced by brief comments and inference. However, a lot of walking round the site has given me some doubts about what both Stewart and Everard had to say on this subject.

Goulston Square was, in effect, a widening half way up Goulston Street and buildings of the London Metropolitan University now cover its area. Behind this is the site of the 1851 Whitechapel Baths (a pediment saying '*Wash House*' is still to be seen in Old Castle Street, which runs parallel). Castle Alley is now under the buildings of the City Guildhall University but it ran from Whitechapel High Street, between Old Castle and Goulston Streets to the rear of the old baths. The Alley had an earlier name of '*Moses and Aaron Alley*' and it is still listed as such in the rate books of 1818. The St. Mary's rate books show a '*Gas Light Co*' in Whitechapel High Street next to the entrance to this alley way. The Sewer Commissioner's rate books however show a '*Gas Light Co*' which is round the corner in Goulston Square. (On the next site there was a '*Mr. Grant*' - why is there so often a Mr. Grant in the vicinity of early London gasworks?). No rate book gives two gasworks.

The sites are so close as to throw considerable doubt – in my mind at least – as to whether these were two completely separate works. In those days, factories took up a much smaller space than would seem reasonable to us and here in the inner city everything was huddled up to everything else – there was also at least one sugar refinery in Goulston Square in 1815. Nevertheless, the two rate book entries are for sites so close that they could easily refer to different ends of one quite small works. I very much doubt if either Everard or Stewart ever walked round Whitechapel to see how close together these sites really are.

We do not know who opened this (or these) works – the mysterious Mr. Grant perhaps? Stewart says that the Castle Alley works was built by 'J.Peto' – was he perhaps a connection of Henry Peto of Peto and Grissell? In 1815 ownership passed to the Aldgate Gas Light and Coke Co. and it is said that they then built the Goulston Square works – or was this in fact an extension and re-equipping of the existing works?

In 1816, the Aldgate Gas Company approached Aaron Manby, the Shropshire ironmaster, for gas making equipment. They wanted it '*on the same plan as the old gas company*'. What 'old gas company'? Did they mean previous equipment, which had been bought by the Aldgate Company or a different company altogether? He was also approached by the 'Whitechapel Company'. Were they the same as the 'Aldgate Company' or different? 'Whitechapel' tends to be a loose definition for a very large slice of east London. Is Stewart right that there were perhaps two works – one owned by the Whitechapel Company, and one by the Aldgate, and that one of these replaced the other? The rate books throw no light on this at all.

Stewart says that the equipment at Aldgate/Whitechapel included a '*Clegg collapsible tent gasholder*' – this must be the '*flexible*' gas holder which was sold to a George Mackintosh

89

in 1820 — described as '*two large canvas bags of about 15,000 cubic feet each — a blacksmiths forge placed near to one of them*'. This Mr. Mackintosh was the man who built a gasworks in Limehouse and who Stewart and Everard both assume to be the contractor who built the docks — but that contractor's name was not George — so who was he? Mackintosh's identity is discussed later under 'Limehouse'.

Everard says that the Aldgate Company was taken over by the Blackfriars-based City of London Gas Light and Coke Company in 1819. The reasons for the takeover seem, inevitably, to have been financial. In November 1818 Mr. Peto told the City of London Gas Company Board that he needed money quickly because Mr. Mackintosh was suing him for a large sum, that it would come to trial next Monday and that his '*character would be injured*'. Was the story of the Aldgate Gas Company the usual one of fraud and incompetence?

Stewart says that the City of London Company closed down the Aldgate works in 1823. The superintendent had been a Mr. Gronous, described, by Everard, as a '*half-pay naval purser*'. He was kept on and eventually became superintendent at Blackfriars - despite, as Everard again records, a spell in a debtor's prison in the 1820s. I am informed by a Greater London Industrial Archaeology Society (GLIAS) member, Richard Graham, that John Gronous was a purser appointed to HMS Mercurious on 25th April 1812 and his first warrant was '*27 later amended to 30 December 1813*'. He does not appear in any Navy Lists after July 1815. Richard Graham suggests he may have fallen victim to 'defence cuts' following the defeat of Napoleon. He continues to appear, without a ship, until June 1837.

Although Stewart calls these two sites 'Whitechapel', in other references, they are called 'Aldgate'. In reality the boundaries are so close that what is strictly Aldgate and strictly, Whitechapel is anyone's guess. Goulston Square and Castle Alley are more at the Aldgate end of the area than Whitechapel proper — but some distance from the City gate of that name. To understand these sites you need to walk round them, and to know the East End.

SOUTH LONDON AND THE PHOENIX

Gasworks were being on the south side of the river at the same time as those in east London. The earliest works in South London was on the riverside almost opposite another early works — that of the City of London Gas Company at Blackfriars. This south London gasworks was on Bankside, down River of Blackfriars Bridge, and its earliest days — like so many others — are clouded in mystery.

There are no records for the earliest years of the Bankside Works. It appears to have been built and managed by 'Monro and Evans'. William Evans came from Twyning near Tewskesbury. A Robert Monro seems to have been involved for many years, as was, later, a William Monro who from the early 1820s was employed as Works Engineer and, according to a deed in the Western Gas Collection, Robert was his son. A Robert Monro, connected with the gasworks lived in Nelson Square, Southwark. He is mentioned in her diary by Elizabeth Pearson, one of the family which owned the Greenwich and Deptford copperas works. He later moved to Wimbledon — and it might be speculated that they were brothers, or father and son.

In 1821 Monro and Evans became, or were taken over by, the South London Gas Co. Monro stayed with the company, but the chairman of the new company was Alderman Christopher Smith, a wine merchant with a London-based business with links in Oporto. He had already stood for Parliament and would eventually become Member for St. Albans — and Lord Mayor of London, according to the Drapers' Company records. In the mid-1820s he was also Mayor of Southwark. Later it seems that, after John Jones death, Evans and Monro were accused of deceiving his heirs as to the prosperity of the company, in a case that appears to have made legal history

In 1824 the South London was itself taken over by the Phoenix Gas Light and Coke Co. but Monro continued to manage the works. Smith too continued as Chairman.

In its company history '*A Century of Gas Lighting*', the South Metropolitan Gas Company described the original Phoenix Company, as having '*a philanthropic, if not a Whiggish, tinge*' and this is certainly true. The original Phoenix subscribers list, given below, includes many of the great and good of the era — Whigs, Quakers, Anti-Slavers — together with a strong element of local Southwark business men, many of whom would fit into several of these categories. The list contains some highly principled politicians. There are also a number who can be identified as family and connections of the prison reformer, Elizabeth Fry. Even Derek Matthews in '*Rogues, Speculators and Competing Monopolies'* was unable to find very much evidence of corruption — except in the dishonesty of a company secretary in the early 1830s.

PHOENIX GAS CO – THE ORIGINAL SUBSCRIBERS

Lord Holland **Henry Richard Vassall**: nephew of Charles James Fox.	He made Holland House a centre of political and artistic influence. A Whig, Lord Privy Seal and active in the abolition of slavery.	Had a development project in Camberwell, to be known as 'Holland Town'.
Rt. Hon Sir James Abercromby RA, MP, Judge.	Speaker in 1835. A "Reform" member who became Baron Dunfermline.	7 Carlton Gardens
John Key "Don Key" City Alderman. Lord Mayor 1831-2. MP for City of London.	Wholesale stationer and Master of the Stationers' Company.	Denmark Hill.
Matthew Wood City politician, eventually Lord Mayor	Pharmacist and chemist from Exeter. Supporter of Queen Caroline. Brewing and copper mining interests.	Responsible for the street lighting demonstration in Beech Street from the Golden Lane Gasworks.
Henry Hunt 'Orator' Hunt. By 1830, MP for Preston.		Hunt was a farmer from Wiltshire and, latterly, East Grinstead, who became involved in radical politics.
James Scarlett Tory MP Cockermouth then Norwich. First Baron Abinger. Attorney General 1827	'The most successful advocate in England' due to 'an abundance of clever artifice'	Lived Abinger in Surrey.
Mathias Attwood Banker of Gracechurch Street and Birmingham. MP for Whitehaven. Treasurer to the London & Greenwich Railway and other railways. Investor British Gas Co	The Attwoods promoted many industrial projects	Muswell Hill 27 Grosvenor Street. Lease owners, Shropshire and Streatham Park. Family from the Corngreaves Estate. Dudley. A family member was Thomas Attwood the radical MP.

David Barclay Quaker, Banker, Merchant Liberal MP Sunderland.		8 Belgrave Square Eastwick Park, Surrey
William Fry Banker. Joseph Fry's brother.		Involved with Mesmer and animal magnetism. Partly responsible for the downfall of the Gurney bank.
Joseph Fry Quaker banker. Husband of Elizabeth Fry.		Plashet House, Stratford
William Heygate City Sheriff 1812. Later Lord Mayor and MP. Treasurer of the Leicester and Swannington Railway Pares' Leicester Banking Co.		Originally from Leicester where his father was a banker. He lived at Roecliffe. Also Blackfriars and Holwood, Kent
James Heygate Father of William Heygate	Founder of the Leicester Bank of Heygate and Hodgson.	
Charles Barclay MP for Southwark. Connection of the Gurneys.	Bought the Anchor Brewery, Southwark, from Perkins.	43 Grosvenor Place. Inherited Bury Hill Surrey from his father. Horstead Place, Norfolk.
John Calvert Clark	Merchant. Peacock brew house and Purfleet lime burner	Lived Teddington Place, Teddington.
Charles Allen Young	A brewer who, in 1831, bought an ailing Wandsworth brewery and turned it into Young's Ram Brewery.	

93

Thomas Fowell Buxton. Married a Hanbury. Director of the Brick Lane Brewery. Whig MP Weymouth. Presented the London petition against slavery.	Involved with John Taylor in South American mines.	Philanthropist and a Baronet, Lived Hampstead. Also Cromer Hall, Norfolk - described as a 'respectable old mansion, the woods are particularly delightful'.
William Miller Christy Director of South Metropolitan Gas Co. He died in 1858.	A hat manufacturer who began in Gracechurch Street & a factory in Bermondsey. From a base in Droylesden near Manchester he made a fortune from a looped Turkish style towel.	
Abel Chapman Involved in Whitby shipping. Partner in the Gateshead Shipping Co	Ship owner. Director of Hudson's Bay Company and East India Company.	Low Stakesby near Whitby Woodford
William Frampton	Saddler	Bermondsey. Lived in Peckham.
Isaac Lyon Goldsmit University College, Royal Institution, Penny Magazine. Statistical Society	Bullion broker Bank of England. Associated with philosophy, radicals and social reform. Diffusion Society and close to Ricardo. Proprietor of the Imperial Continental Gas Co.	1827 lived Champion Hill but by 1846 in St. John's Lodge, Regents Park The Wick, Brighton.
Richard Heale	Colonial broker	Mincing Lane. Peckham Lodge, Peckham
John Petty Muspratt	Director of the East India Company.	Russell Square Dulwich.
Charles Pott	Vinegar maker in Southwark Bridge Road where the house was one of the earliest to be lit by gas.	Plaistow, Nr. Bromley, Kent. London address: The Foundling Hospital. Freelands Bromley.
Joshua Blackburn		Owned Brockwell Park, which he sold cheaply to the local authorities
Benjamin Currey	Member, House of Lords	Eltham Park;

		Old Palace Yard
Francis Cresswell (the younger) Married to Rachel, daughter of Joseph & Elizabeth Fry.	Judge.	
Emmanuel Goodhart	Sugar refiner of Horseferry, Limehouse later 4 Ratcliffe Highway.	Langley Park, Beckenham. Investor in Whitechapel Road scheme.
Charles Perkins	Possibly one of the brewing family.	1846 lived 1 Upper Harley Street.
Frederick Perkins	Perhaps one of the brewing family.	Lived Chipstead Place, Nr. Sevenoaks Manor House, Lee
Thomas Wilson. Might be the encloser of Hampstead Heath, who also owned much of Charlton or the clergyman friend of John Wilkes.	Treasurer of Highbury College and financed the building of several chapels in the Islington area.	
John Garratt Lord Mayor 1825,	A dealer	Bishop's House, Clyst Sackville, Near Exeter.
Arthur Holdsworth Commissioner of Woods and Forests.	Connection to the Newfoundland fisheries. His company was involved in West Indies and America. Left a collection of American Indian artefacts to a museum	Kingsbridge, Devon
George Bridges Lord Mayor 1820.		Aston Lodge, Tog Hill, near Bath
Jacob Foster Reynolds. Son of east London linen bleacher His son married daughter of Sir John Pelly, Hudson's Bay Company.		
John Adophus Young	Solicitor in the City and Great Ormond Street.	Hare Heath, Maidenhead, Berkshire
Charles Hampden Turner Brother in law to	A partner in the rope works and a director of the East India Company	Rooks Nest, Godstone Green, Surrey

95

Huddart.		
Rev. John Vane. Chaplain House of Commons.	Vicar at Wrington, Devon	
John Plummer		
Charles Bevan Within the Frys' circle of friends.		
Jonathan Chapman	In 1842 a John Chapman was owner and manager of the Harrow Gas Works	
Richard Fell. Surname of family of Southwark Quaker leather merchants..		Belmont House, Uxbridge.
John Fell the Younger.		
Haden Turner.		
Archibald Corbett	Salter	Marsh Street, Walthamstow
Horatio Ripley	Partner in Ripley Bros	
Thomas Perkins		
George Thackrah	Lawyer in Tooley Street. City connections	
Thomas Allan Shuter		Lived at Lee, claimed to be a farmer

BANKSIDE GAS WORKS

An extremely successful works in South London which remained on site for over a hundred years. It was on the riverfront and placed on the boundaries of two local authority areas. It had a recognisable management from the start and was – as the Phoenix Company – to have a group of proprietors including of some of the wealthiest liberal and philanthropic minds of the day.

It has been said that the Bankside gasworks was opened in 1814 but the evidence for this is unclear and it seems likely that historians in the past – who were usually company employees – might have had access to deed information, which has now disappeared.

Zeriah Colburn in *'The Gasworks of London'* said that the works was built on *'Rennie's site'*. This seems unlikely since Bankside Gas Works, although adjacent to Rennie's wharf near Blackfriars Bridge, is not actually on it. There are however some early reports that the gasworks itself may have moved from its first site early on in its existence — in which case it could indeed originally have been on Rennie's Wharf.

In *Johnson's Directory* of 1817 '*Morrow and Co.*' are listed as '*Gas and Coke Merchants*' at 64 Bankside- in 1870 the Phoenix Gas Works was 70 Bankside, which might imply some continuity of use.

This works seems to have run reliably for almost 120 years and — perhaps as a credit to Monroe's management — very little of note seems to have happened there. The company went about its business, supplied its customers with lighting gas — and, as a sideline, filled numerous balloons. There are a few sparse references from outside sources — for instance, in March 1822 Elizabeth Pearson, living in Greenwich, recorded that her brother, a friend of Munro, came home late because of an '*accident at the gasworks*'.

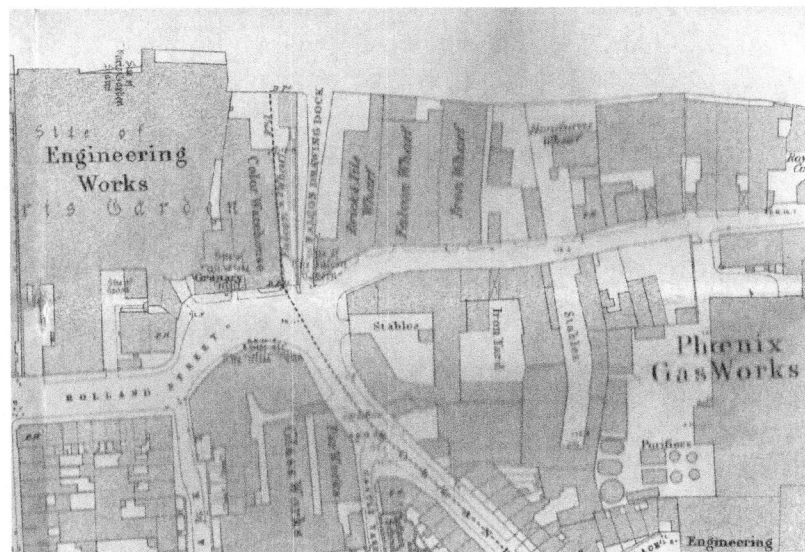

The 1873 Ordnance Survey map shows this works at its height — the chief works of a large and successful gas company. It stands on the south side of Bankside with a relatively restricted access to the river and is surrounded by the factories of industrial Southwark, which, no doubt, it helped to power and light.

The site today is entirely under the Bankside Power Station, now part of the Tate Modern Gallery. *Grace Goolden* in *Old Bankside* remembered its last years "*the illusion of a dark world lit only by the glare of burning coal gas from an open retort... the glitter of lurching pistons*" but she remembered more practical details too — that the retort house was opposite the gateway, that river water was used in the '*cleansing house*', that tar and ammoniacal liquor went into barges lying at the wharf, the generating station built over the river and provided power for the pumps and lifts throughout the works and that the meter house was the '*holy of holies*' where '*accuracy was worshipped*' and gas was measured in '*a meter decorated with Doric pilasters and pediment*'.

In 1888 Phoenix became part of the South Metropolitan Gas Co's. empire. The site of the Bankside works was eventually sold in 1938.

97

THE EAST LONDON GAS COMPANY

The 'East London Gas Company' is not easy to pin down. The name seems to be used in a number of contexts, and more than one small company, or even individuals, lay claim to the name. It will appear in the next few pages in a number of confusing settings. The first works which was claimed as the 'East London Gas Company' was that at the East London Theatre described above.

THE RATCLIFFE GAS LIGHT AND COKE CO

A second gas company in East London joined the Aldgate Gas Company at much the same time as the City and South London Companies were opening. It was a half a mile or so to the south of Aldgate and nearer to the river. Whether or not this works was the 'East London Gas Company' is far from clear. However, whatever its somewhat mysterious antecedents, a gasworks on the site about to be described was managed for most of its existence by the Ratcliffe Gas Co. There were to be others.

A list of the men who set up the Ratcliffe Gas Company is below. It is taken from the preamble to the Company's first enabling Act of Parliament and describes those who were prepared to put their name to it. They were mainly City and East End businessmen — but most of the names given are so common that accurate research is impossible. Articles detailing the history of the Ratcliffe Company were published before the Second World War in successive issues of The Commercial Gas Company's house journal Co-partnership Herald.

Thomas Davies	Distiller	Old Street
William Jones	Landlord of the City of London pub house in the City Road. 1839	
William Martin		Hornsey, Gent.
William Stone		Sun Tavern Field.
Robert How	Coach maker.	Queen Street
William Gardiner.		Ratcliffe Highway, Gent

SUN TAVERN FIELDS

A gasworks set up to serve the public by a group of local shopkeepers. It was in the heart of the industrial and port area of the East End of London – but, once again, with no water access.

Stewart said that the Ratcliffe Gas Company opened the Sun Tavern Fields gasworks site in 1817 – although he gives no source for this date. An account of the early days of the Ratcliffe Company published in *Co-partnership Herald* cites a lease document for the site – a document presumably now in the North Thames Gas collection at the London Metropolitan Archive, but not yet traced there. The Horwood Plan of 1812 shows Sun Tavern Fields as a large piece of open land stretching east from King David's Lane between what is now Cable Street and The Highway. The works was not sited on the Fields themselves, but to the north of them on the northern boundary road, Back Lane, now Cable Street. It was on a long narrow site fitting between ropewalks, which ran north-south down from the Commercial Road. Interestingly it sat just inside the angle of the boundaries of the Parish of St. George in the East with the parishes of Ratcliffe and Shadwell. On the Horwood Plan a large institutional building of some sort it shown with a frontage marked as 'Crown Court' – perhaps a site was acquired from the local vestry.

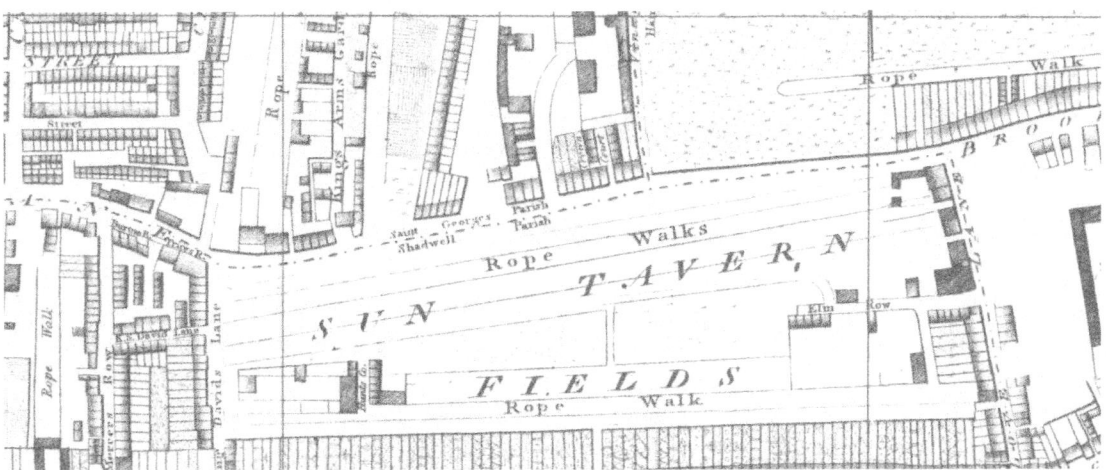

A possible earlier gas-making plant on this site, or nearby, has already been described. This was the apparatus supplied, probably in 1811, by Boulton and Watt to Stein, Smith and Ditchley, and managed by a Mr. Sims. Sims' rope walk was in Sun Tavern Fields. Rope was of great importance for the maritime industries locally and was a major manufacture - there are several walks in the tiny area of Wapping shown here. Rope making was a skilled trade and a worker could cover thirty to forty miles a day walking backwards with swathes of fibres round his torso which he twisted into rope as he went down the length of the 'walk'.

Although there were a number of rope walks on Sun Tavern Fields in this period, none of them appears to be on, or adjacent to, the site on which the gasworks was to be built. However, it is possible that this existing plant was taken over by the promoters of the Ratcliffe Gas Company and used by them.

The Ratcliffe Gas Company appears to have been set up by a group of local businessmen. According to articles in Co-partnership Herald the works opened for public supply in 1817.

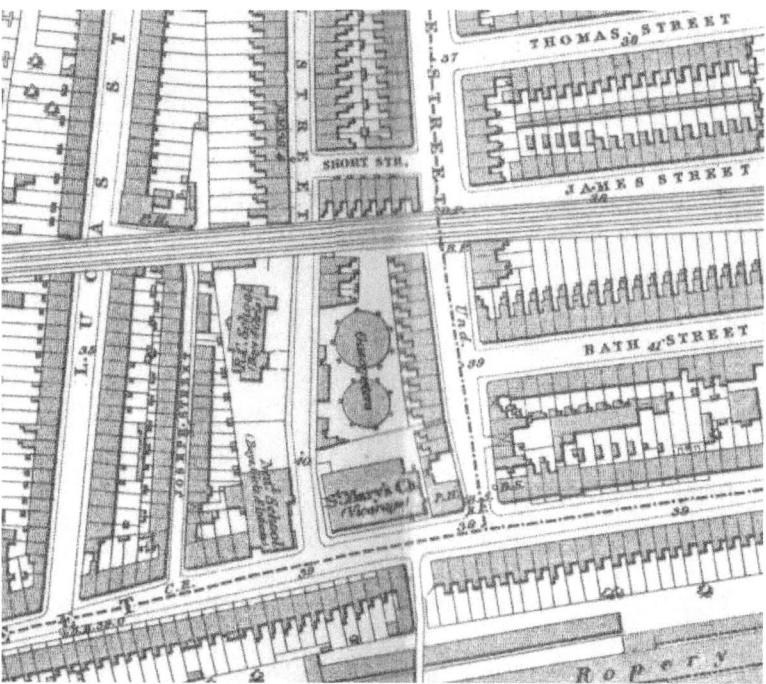

By 1828 they were running out of money and became involved with Robert Munro who had set up the Bankside Gas Works and the South London Gas Company. Following his advice they secured an Act of Parliament as the Ratcliffe Gas Company. They were soon, however, under great pressure of competition from other local gasworks, as we shall see. There was also a problem that the site of the works was landlocked and it became necessary to acquire land for a wharf. A site near the riverside was duly leased – more about this later.

In the 1830s a railway line, the London and Blackwall Railway was planned, to run between the Minories (to the west and nearer the City) and Brunswick Dock at Blackwall (a few miles east on the river). This was to be cable-hauled along a viaduct through East London. Cable haulage meant that the line had to be straight and could not deviate from its line, which was to run parallel, and slightly north of Cable Street. The Docklands Light Railway today uses the viaduct. It went straight through the Sun Tavern Fields Gas Works site and the railway company purchased the central section of the gasworks. The gas company was thus forced to move the majority of their manufacturing to another site and to use the remaining portion of the Sun Tavern Fields works solely for storage of gas in holders.

In 1875, the Ratcliffe Gas Company was taken over by one of its erstwhile rivals, the Commercial Gas Co. Sun Tavern Fields seems to have been closed as a gas holder station at some time towards the end of the 19th century although it is still shown as a 'gasworks' on the 1888 *Geographia Atlas of London*. It then lay with Johnson Street to the

West, the Blackwall Railway to the north, Hardinge Street to the south and St. Mary's Church, fronting Cable Street to the south. By the 1914 Ordnance Survey map a hall, convent, and some housing are shown on the site and these remain today.

STAR BREWERY SITE, WAPPING

The Ratcliffe Gas Company's inland site at Sun Tavern Fields has already been described. The company soon realised that they needed a wharf – like all companies with land-locked gasworks, they had a problem with coal supplies. They needed to be on the riverside.

Ratcliffe leased the site of the old Star Brewery in Wapping according to articles in Co-partnership Herald. The Brewery can be seen on contemporary maps – it stood with a street between it and the river and was a large industrial building, which once stood on the north side of the road at the junction of Wapping High Street, New Gravel Lane and 'Prusom's Island'. As such it would have had access to the river in the area near the pub, *The Prospect of Whitby* – now one of the most popular tourist venues in the East End.

We'll get back to Wapping Gas Works later, but, first, a complication...............

...... the American gentleman ....

MR. PINKESS AND THE DOMESTIC GAS COMPANY

I find it very hard to believe in a gasworks at 49 Ratcliffe Highway, although Mr. Pinkess (or Pinkus, or Pincus) certainly had some dealings with such a body. The reference to this address comes from the minutes of the City of London Gas Company when they were approached by Mr. Pincus about the *'new olificiant gas'*.

Ratcliffe Highway is today's 'The Highway' and number 49 is shown on Horwood. It would have been sited on the south side of the road, roughly opposite the end of Cannon Street – near St.George's Church. It is not that far from Wellclose Square and the East London Theatre, but on the other side of the road. More importantly Horwood shows just a small house or shop in row of similar buildings. I guess Mr. Pincus lived, or had some sort of office there. Who was Pincus and why should we be interested in his claims to be part of the East London Gas Co?

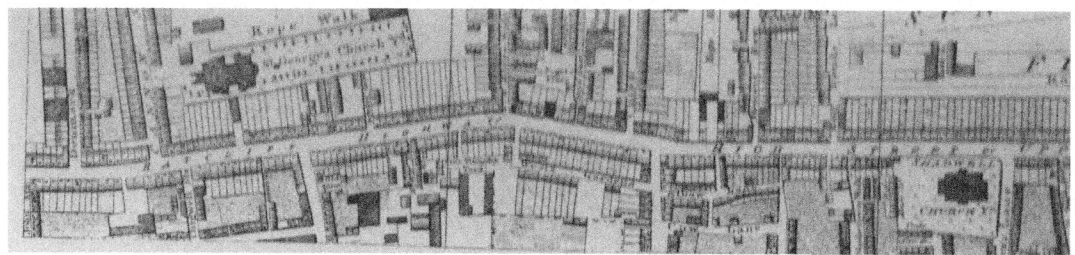

Henry Pinkus came from Philadelphia and in 1826 had done a deal with one Hercules Poynter (or Paynter). The nature of this deal and its relation to the East London Gas Company was to be crucial some ten years later. Pinkus and Poynter set up something called the Domestic Gas Company. This was a 'new method' of making gas (weren't they all!) in which rather than get your gas from a gasworks you made it at home yourself. The gas was made in your ordinary domestic grate and then safely stored in *'the cellar or some other convenient location'*. Pinkus and Poynter promoted this from an address in the Strand. Whether any of them were ever bought is not known – the suggestion being in *'Newton's London Journal'* that the smell kept the customers away.

In the next few years Pinkus acquired a string of patents which related to gas-making and similar subjects. It might be noted that at the same time a Henry Pinkus enrolled at University College for a course of natural philosophy, heat and chemistry.

In the 1830s Pinkus seems to have changed his interests from gas to locomotion. In 1834 he advertised a model of atmospheric propulsion, claiming to have been experimenting on this since 1825. He demonstrated this at an address in Wigmore

Street in the West End. The project was seen by a number of prominent engineers of the day and, following some changes, a demonstration railway may, or may not, have been built along the Kensington Canal.

The really strange thing about this is that the person who made atmospheric traction work a couple of years later – and who had undoubtedly seen what Pinkus was up to – was none other than Samuel Clegg himself, the father of gas lighting! Within a couple of years Pinkus was suing Clegg for infringement of his patent. As we will see this was not the first time that Pinkus had seen the inside of an English Court of Law.

WAPPING
THE EAST LONDON GAS COMPANY (AGAIN)

An important gas-making site built by the Ratcliffe Gas Co. On the riverside in the heart of the shipbuilding and port area – surrounded by the cosmopolitan and impoverished people of the East End of London.

While Hercules Poynter was (or was not) tied up with Henry Pinkus on the subject of do-it-yourself gasworks, he was also being persuaded by the people of east London to set up a gasworks on their behalf.

Local businesses in the area of the Ratcliffe Gas Company had decided that its prices were too high and that they could do better on their own. This was not an uncommon feeling by businessmen in the vicinity of early gas companies and several such protest movements developed – usually led by local publicans. The deputation then asked Poynter to set the works up. He did this at a site known as Prusom's Island which was, in fact, the site adjacent to the Ratcliffe Company's Star Brewery wharf. This works first supplied gas in September 1829. It seems very likely that the works was another Barlow construction since the first manager was none other than George Barlow, himself.

In 1831 a 'proper' gas company was set up to manage this site, calling themselves 'The East London Gas Light and Coke Co'. A price war soon developed with the Ratcliffe Company and accusations began to fly around the Wapping area. The East London Company began to complain that their profits were not as high as they had expected. Competition was very stiff in the area by then with a number of gas companies vying for consumers.

As has been described, the Ratcliffe Company was about to lose half the site of their works at Sun Tavern Fields to the Blackwall Railway, and Ratcliffe bought the, by then, ailing East London Company's Wapping Works – conveniently next to a site of their own. At that point Mr. Pinkus appeared claiming to hold 500 shares in the now defunct East London Company and claiming to be in partnership with Hercules

103

Poynter who had just, conveniently, declared himself bankrupt. Pinkus promptly sued for £18,000 damages and claimed fraud by the board of both Ratcliffe and East London Companies. Affidavits were filed by everyone who could conceivably have had an interest in the case at all – as can easily be seen from a quick look at the big bundle of case papers in the London Metropolitan Archive. Although the case was initially dismissed, Pinkus carried on arguing up to the House of Lords and for another eight years afterwards.

Shortly after, the Wapping Works was amalgamated with the Star Brewery site and continued in use as one works – n fact the main works of the Ratcliffe Company. In 1875 Ratcliffe was bought up by the Commercial Company and the Wapping Works continued to be managed by them until 1935 when, following a major fire, the works was closed.

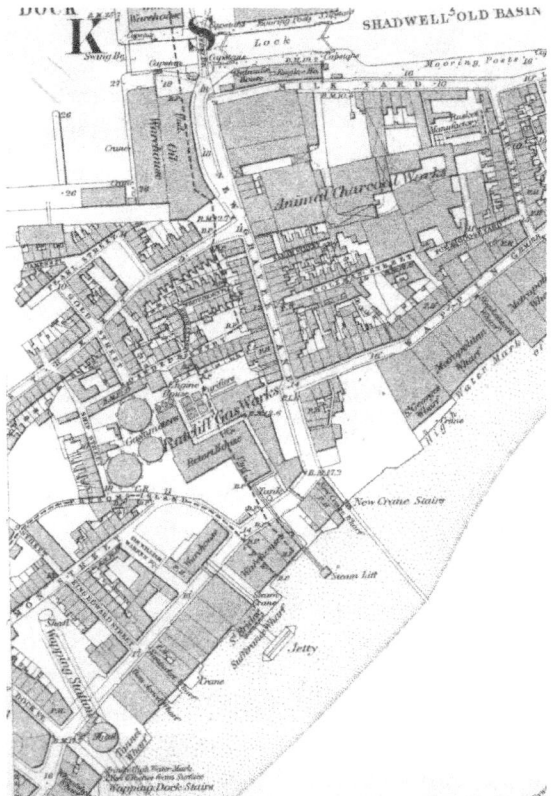

Although the Wapping Gas Works was an important one which served the people of East London for over a hundred years, the remains of it are very hard to find. It is not even easy to find it on maps – usually appearing as an unmarked industrial site with no sign of the gasholders which once stood there. Only in old photographs of the riverside can the holders be seen sticking up above the roofs of warehouses and surrounding buildings.

Wapping is no longer industrial and since the 1980s has rapidly gentrified. Those areas which were once warehouses are now upmarket housing. There is no sign of the riverside wharves where coal was unloaded to power London's industry. The site of the Wapping gasworks – always slightly inland – is now an infants' school. In the 1990s, as consciousness of the dangers of old gas making sites grew, the school was asked – did they know the past of their site? Yes, they replied, they had known for a long time and were always careful with playground activities. Most of the people who now live in the expensive flats all around the area will have no idea!

OIL GAS

And something new was stirring down in what is now east London – but in the 1820s was the Middlesex/Essex border – Bow, Poplar, and over the Lea to Stratford and West Ham … and a bit south of the River too, as we will see.

There were some curiosities in the great world of gas manufacture. We tend to think of town gas as having only been made from coal. This was really only because coal was cheap and easy to get in bulk. In the earliest days of the gas industry – when gas lighting was 'invented' by Lebon, wood was sometimes used as a raw material and after that a number of industrialists began to develop gas made from oil. Oil had been used for street lighting for many years and an infrastructure for obtaining it existed. Oil came from whales hunted in the Arctic and Antarctic seas but also from more mundane sources – tallow imported from Russia, for instance. It was thus seen as expedient to produce gas from oil and use a raw material which was readily available.

Much of the evidence for its use in east London is described in a Parliamentary Enquiry into Oil Gas. This is a most interesting document – or would be if it was not so hard to locate. I found half of it in the London Metropolitan Archive and the other half in the London Library. It is well worth reading.

Oil Gas is a subject, which, if properly written up, would take much more space than the whole of this book. In the early 1820s, a number of public supply gasworks used oil as a raw material.

The process was patented by John Taylor and/or his brother Philip in 1815. The Taylors were some of those Georgian engineers/entrepreneurs who set out to exploit, and change the world. There is a biography of John by Roger Burt where he is described as *'the foremost mining engineer in Europe'* but he sometimes described himself as *'manufacturing chemist of Stratford'*. – er – that is Stratford east London, or, technically, Essex, of course. I have never been able to track down the Taylors' Stratford chemical works and it emerges that the actual inventor of the oil gas process was his brother Philip, who lived, before 1824, in Bromley by Bow and was a chemist who had taken out a string of patents. He ended with a massive engineering practice in Marseille and a ship yard at Toulon. Why is it so hard to find out anything much about them? There were several other brothers, all in key positions. Members of the Taylor family – John and Philip in particular – turn up in many episodes of early 19th century industrial history.

Any oil could be used for gas production and it was thus useful for scrap from the soap and other oil-based industries, including the oils and fats replaced by coal as the raw material for street lighting. The oil was liquefied and trickled down a hot metal pipe. The resulting gas was cooled and collected. It then went through a red-hot iron pipe to a gasholder, as described in detail in *King's Treatise*. Oil gas lacked the sulphur compounds found in coal gas, it thus was not thought to need purification and it was promoted as both safer and cleaner.

John Taylor and his partner, John Martineau had an engineering works at Whitecross Street, just north of the City, moving to Winsor Ironworks in the City Road. They made a range of equipment, including steam engines, printing, and sugar-refining machinery – chapters could be written about all of these. 'Martineau' at the time was an important family name in sugar refining. Oil gas-making equipment was produced and supplied on a franchise basis.

It is clear by the mid-1820s that a war had developed between the oil gas and coal gas interests. The Parliamentary Enquiry into the London and Westminster Oil Gas Bill brought out a glittering array of contemporary scientific opinion and a propaganda campaign outside the courtroom.

Oil gas interests were intertwined with the massive sugar refining industry. The oil gas enquiry had been foreshadowed a few years previously by an insurance claim in respect of an explosion in the east London sugar works of Severn and King. This had involved equipment designed by a Daniel Wilson who worked for Aaron Manby. The equipment was designed and involved a technique, which was very similar to that used in preparing oil gas. Wilson and Manby were both better known for their gas-making equipment and later went to France where they were involved in the Paris gas industry. Some of their work will be described later. The same scientists gave evidence to both Oil Gas and the Severn and King enquiries.

Oil Gas was presented as cleaner as, and safer than, coal gas but the sub-text was about the economic interests of the suppliers of the raw material – coal or oil.

HAWES SOAP WORKS

So, our first look at oil gas is just about in South London – another industrial gasworks using Taylor and Martineau's system. It was sited to the immediate south of Blackfriars Bridge. Of interest is the later connection of the owner with the Gas Light and Coke Company. and – er – some 'interesting' marital connections

If you go down the Old Kent Road and look behind the shops on the corner of Trafalgar Avenue, you will find a big old house. In 1860, an old man died there looked after by his daughter, a Mrs. Donkin. Despite his 90 years the old man had been, until the previous week, the active Governor of the Court of Directors of the oldest gas company in the world, the Gas Light & Coke Company.

Although this old man is not in the *Dictionary of National Biography,* you will find his father and son there. His father was a doctor, who founded the Royal Humane Society, and his son was a politician. His name was Benjamin Hawes and he had founded what became the largest soap works in London. It was at Old Barge House, on the riverbank slightly to the west of Blackfriars Bridge. It was near to where the revolutionary Albion Mill had been burnt down just over thirty years previously.

That Benjamin Hawes was Governor of the Gas Light & Coke Company demonstrates a remarkable change of allegiances, because in the 1820s Hawes' soap works had been the site of a gasworks fuelled by oil. For a soap manufacturer to make gas from oil made a lot of sense because oils used to make soap could be used for gas, and an onsite gasworks could take oil rejected by the soap maker for reasons of quality. Sadly, most of the oil came from whales, but palm and coconut oils were also used. About 100 cubic feet of gas was made from one gallon of oil.

The gas-making apparatus had been supplied to Hawes by Taylor and Martineau. The plant, about ten feet from the main works, was run by one man *'chosen for his regularity and sobriety'.* There was a *'gasometer'* in the yard. The gas was not purified in any way, nor even washed. Smell, he said, did not matter; soap making was after all *'not the most savoury operation'.* The works is described in *Dodds' Days at the Factories.*

The gas was made for lighting the soap works, in particular the cellar, which was lit day and night. Gas was also supplied, at 45s. per 1,000 cubic feet, to neighbourhood shops and pubs, via a two inch main. In Old Barge House itself, gas was burnt in lights in the bedrooms, dressing rooms, nursery, hall and stairs.

The soap works was run by another brother, William. The Hawes were an influential family, the names of Benjamin and William permeating industrial enterprises of the 19th Century: breweries, dock companies, railways. Many of projects which they supported were those of I.K. Brunel who was a frequent visitor to Old Barge House both before and after his sister's marriage to Benjamin Jnr.

It is not clear when the oil gasworks closed and Benjamin Snr. became a leading light in the coal gas world. The family influence in gas was to continue, through the

107

engineering company into which Caroline Hawes had married – by the 1860s the Bryan Donkin Company Ltd. were to be leaders in the supply of gas distribution equipment.

Old Barge House has recently been cleaned up and turned into a complex of restaurants, art galleries and smart businesses – long forgotten are the soap works and the associated gas making plant.

So, after that brief incursion into inner South London let us go down to the banks of the River Lea, the boundary between Middlesex and Essex – Bow and Old Ford over into Stratford – an area where industrial innovation was as common as dodgy business practices.

BOW GAS WORKS

This was a public supply gasworks was set up near Philip Taylor's home at Bow. It was managed by Dr. Moses Ricardo, the brother of the economist David Ricardo, and had been built to supply lighting for the Whitechapel Road. It had an Act of Parliament, which allowed for gas lighting but, unusually, not the works. Many local industrialists were among its subscribers together with some scientific associates of the Taylors and John Martineau.

In due course another Parliamentary Bill was submitted, to light London and Westminster by oil gas. In the course of the enquiry into this Bill evidence was given which – at the very least – brought into some disrepute the management methods at Bow.

It emerged that, on May 5th 1825, Henry Holman, a brewer, had been returning from a visit to friends at Forest Gate. Coming into Stratford and still a mile and a half from Bow he began to smell something very offensive. As he continued down through Stratford and on to Bow Bridge it grew worse and worse. People were leaning out of their bedroom windows to try and find out was going on.

When he reached his home, which was only ten yards from the Bow Gas Works, he found his wife was ill from the smell. He went over to the gasworks and knocked and rang but could get no reply and had no choice but to go back indoors and try to sleep.

The next morning he went back to the works and examined the drain, which ran into the river Lea. There he found '*some glutinous matter of a dark colour*' which he took home in the hope that he could use it as evidence. He put it in his office, but the smell was so horrible that he ended up by burying it in despair. In addition, his water supply was so contaminated that he was unable to brew that day.

108

Throughout the night, Joseph Search the Bow watchman, had noticed the smell – 'It affected me; it made my head ache a good deal; it got inside of me, in the throat, and it affected me a great deal.' He described how 'After I had cried one o'clock ... I turned back into the town, and the first that I saw was Mr. Crawley'. Crawley was the works' superintendent but he did not go to see what the problem was, or even get up, he just 'asked me what this smell was, it was very affecting, and had woke Mrs. Crawley out of her sleep'. Next Mr. Baylis the journeyman at the linen drapers 'asked me what it was that smelt so shocking bad' and so he went on to Bow Bridge 'and the water was in a shocking state; it was entirely covered with nastiness; it appeared to me like oil, or something like that, swimming on the top.'

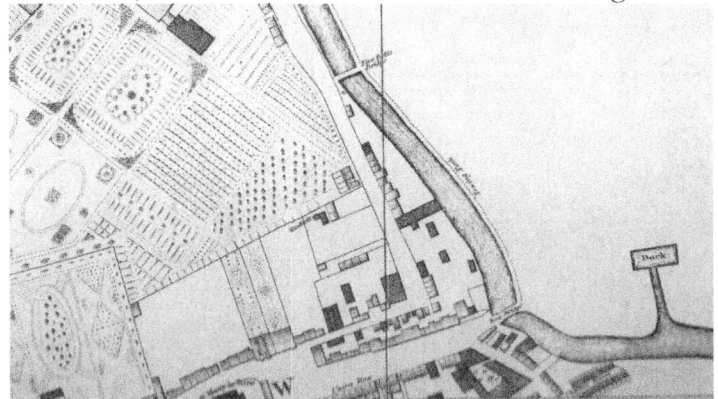

Of course, this evidence about the state of things at Bow Works was given by enemies of the less respectable elements of the Imperial Company. Stewart says that it became a coal gasworks and was taken over by the British Gas Light Co. in 1829, who sold it in 1852 to the Commercial Co., who closed it down. The new management does not seem to have changed things much. In 1831 they were ordered by Bow vestry to glaze their windows because of the *'quantities of deleterious matter being emitted'* and to *'remove refuse'* because of the cholera outbreak.

Where was this works and what happened to the site? A caption to an illustration in a *Co-partnership Herald* helpfully describes it as *'behind the houses in Bow Road'* – which might mean any one of a lot of buildings. The area has been radically changed with the construction of the Blackwall Tunnel Approach Road in the 1960s and the Bow roundabout and flyover. From evidence given at the Oil Gas Enquiry it appears to have been built over the River Lea and thus it existed in a sort of no-man's land between London and Essex and so is ignored by mapmakers from both sides. It is almost certainly not the row of gasholders shown in the 1880s alongside the Great Eastern Railway line east of the Lea since the address of the works was 1 Old Ford Road, putting it firmly on the Middlesex Bank. Since Old Ford Road ran north from Bow Bridge it must be assumed that the gasworks was the first building in the road on the riverbank. My guess is that it is today either under the motorway or on a piece of spare land now isolated in the middle of the traffic which was the site of a late Victorian chemical works and is now a the location of a branch of a well-known brand of cheap fried meat sold in buns.

Who were the people who set up the Bow Oil Gas Works? A list is taken from the preamble of the Whitechapel Road (Lighting With Gas) Act, 1821 is in an appendix.

109

This was an Act as to improve the streets. It does not set up a gasworks but gives permission to light by gas. It is in essence a Bill to support the Taylor and Martineau Bow Oil Gas Works.

There is a very definite input of investors from the Hudson Bay Company – who, no doubt, probably wanted an investment in something, which would use fish oil and oil from the other marine wild life in which they had an interest in killing.

Martineau No forename is given in the schedule - John is the Engineer. David the sugar refiner.		
Abraham Lancaster		
Archibald Barclay Secretary to the Hudson Bay Company.		Lived (1846) 12 Burton Street
Archibald Borde (Clerk)		
Archibald Campbell	Soldier Had been Governor of Jamaica	The Grove, Harrow-on-the-Hill
Charles Welstead		60 Berners Street 1846 Valentines, Ilford
Emmanuel Goodhart	Sugar refiner	Limehouse 4 Ratcliffe Highway. Beckenham
Frederick Hodgson In 1825 he is said to be Chairman of the Oil Gas Company.	Hodgson and Co., Brewers of Bow. They invented India Pale Ale. 1846 MP Barnstable. Deputy Lieutenant. Tower Hamlets	3 Carlton Gardens 1846
George Buck		14 Assembly Row, Mile End
George Dacre Had been the Oil Gas Company's Secretary.	West Ham Vestry Clerk, ousted by the parish in 1845. Became an activist in water politics, criticising arrangements in West Ham.	
George Hardess	Merchant, Wapping.	Rosherville, Kent

A family web site tells of a George Hardess, a refugee from a German aristocratic family, who changed his name. A Rosherville resident was a member of the younger generation and apprenticed to a Gravesend printer.		
George Minshaw Glasscot	Brass founder	Great Garden Street, Whitechapel
Henry Brookman		
James Boote Master of the Butcher's Company.		Also subscribed to the Mile End Act.
James Brand		Lived Tulse Hill.
James Gale	Ship owner and rope maker	Love Lane, Shadwell.
John Brooks	Printer	421 Oxford Street, 1812-38
John Giles		
John Henry Pelly Governor Hudson Bay Company.		
John Hillson Giles		
John Stanyer		
John Taylor His role, with his brothers, is central. With John Martineau he set up a company which made equipment for making gas for lighting from oil. Another brother, Richard, was the Editor of *Philosophical Magazine*	Mining engineer with a wide range of industrial and scientific interests	
Jos Norbury	Coppersmith	202 Whitechapel Road.
Joseph Foster Partner in the Walthamstow Copper Mill. This could be the Quaker involved with William Allen and Joseph Lancaster in the Borough Road Schools but not connected with Foster Bros. of South Met. Gas Company.	Joseph Foster and Co., Calico Printers, Bromley by Bow, 1796. Scarlet dyeing for East India Co. Sold out to Hugh Mackintosh in 1823	Upper Clapton
Joseph Giles	Carpenter	Bow.
Joseph Sumpner Joyner		

Leonard Currie	Malt distillery at Bromley by Bow	
Mary Tennant had considerable land holdings in the area. Mother in law of William Curtis		Bow
Moses Ricardo Brother of economist, David Ricardo. Member Royal College of Surgeons 1820.	First Manager of the Bow Oil Gas Works	Living in Bow. Later Brighton
Nicholas Charrington, Jnr Also subscribed to the Mile End Act. The Mile End brewer's son.		
Nicholas Charrington Also subscribed to the Mile End Act.	Mile End brewer	
Philip Taylor John Taylor's brother	Trained as a pharmacist developer of numerous chemical processes	Bromley-by-Bow and chemical works at Stratford.
Richard Carpenter Also subscribed to the Mile End Act.	Probably an Aldgate based publisher	
Robert Emans Crawley Committee of Management of the Bow Works. had to take over management in an emergency.	A grocer	Bow
Robert Surridge		
Robert Wilson	Surveyed the Strand for Taylor and Martineau. Otherwise had no occupation and helped out in his sons' office	Dartmouth Street, Westminster
S.M. Townsend	Collector, grocer	
Samuel Jones Vachell Born 1766 and married a Mary Millward, perhaps of the Bromley Steam Mill		Bromley- by-Bow and West Ham
Sir Elias Harvey MP, Admiralty. A hero of Trafalgar who later resigned following accusations by Thomas Cochrane.		Rolls Park, Claygate, with considerable Essex connections. Later lived in Chigwell
Thomas Chalk	Quaker	

112

Thomas Drane	Merchant	11 Leadenhall Street.
Thomas Hillson Giles		
Thomas Kinghorn		
Thomas Langley Hudson Bay Company director after whom Langley, British Colombia is named.	Wax and tallow merchant	8 Irelands Row, Mile End Cock Crow Hill, Southborough near Kingston.
William Blackbone		
William Meggy MP for Great Yarmouth.	A printer	

THE OIL GAS DISPUTE

Scientists sometimes worked with the early gas industry, and the building of experimental gas-making apparatus in London was monitored by William Brande, and others. Increasingly the early gas companies employed scientists as consultants and this sometimes meant that they were required to give evidence in court for one side or another in disputes. In the 1820s a series of enquiries, all in some way connected with the manufacture of gas from oil, rather than coal, brought gas manufacture into the realms of scientific dispute.

It was realised that there was a great deal of money to be made out of gas lighting – and money to be lost by those who had invested in existing oil lighting technology. Increasingly companies were prepared to risk a great deal to get the legal rights to provide lighting. It made sense to use the new lighting technology with the old raw materials.

In 1805 William Henry, the Manchester chemist who had acted as consultant to Boulton and Watt on gas for lighting, had published a paper in the Journal of Natural Philosophy, which cited the existence of "*light carburetted hydrogen*" for which he "*relied on the sole authority of Mr. Dalton*". The involvement of John Dalton must be noted here. Although he is well known for his work on the atomic theory, Dalton was, of course, based in Manchester and had undertaken theoretical work on gases. He knew William Henry well and they had worked together and seem to have supported each other's research findings. Dalton is also said to have known and taught Samuel Clegg and, if so, much of the technology as well as the theory of gas manufacture must have been influenced by him.

William Henry's 1805 paper had also drawn a parallel between the '*light carburetted hydrogen*' and the "*fire damp of coal mines.*" He followed this in 1808 with a paper in the Philosophical Transactions of the Royal Society, which attempted to explain his analytical methods and apparatus and their application to gas made from coal. In 1820

113

William Brande, by then Professor of Chemistry at the Royal Institution, challenged his findings.

Brande's apparatus for research into gas at Apothecaries' Hall and at the Royal Institution has already been noted. His paper, also to the Royal Society, in their Philosophical Transactions of 1820 was, in effect, an evaluation of the "cost benefit" of various coals compared with other substances for making gas. Brande was in a senior position, but he was young and probably concerned to consolidate his position. In his paper he seemed to be supporting the virtues of coal gas but, by 1819, *"for reasons that are not clear"* he had changed his views and was putting forward the cause of oil gas, pointing out that a process for making gas from oil was now available. Articles supporting oil gas were not only written by Brande.

In doing this Brande met with opprobrium from other scientists. In 1821 the position put forward by Brande was opposed by a contributor to the scientific press, writing in the Quarterly Journal from Derby, George Lowe. He said of Brande's article that "t*he chief object of this paper was to prove that no other gaseous compound of carbon and hydrogen exists but the one usually called olifient gas"*. It was, he said, based on "*material error*s." Lowe was a young man, experimenting alone in the laboratory of his father's brewery – his career, as one of the foremost gas engineers in the 19th Century had not yet begun.

William Henry joined the debate and challenged Brande with a series of articles in the Memoirs of the Literary Society of Manchester, the Monthly Magazine and in Philosophical Magazine reviewing the progress of his research on coal and oil gases. He explained, in detail, that his "*hypothetical conclusion coincides even more nearly with the facts ... while the opposite explanation is at variance with this general law of chemical union*".

SEVERN AND KING

The Oil Gas Enquiry of 1826 had been preceded by a series of court hearings about insurance claims following an explosion in a sugar refinery. The latter had some elements in common with the Oil Gas Enquiry in that it involved many of the same personnel and was concerned with the potential for explosions.

An apparatus for heating sugar had been developed by Daniel Wilson and manufactured by Aaron Manby. Wilson has already been noted here in the account of the Aldgate Gas Company. He had gone to work for Manby at the Horsley Ironworks in Shropshire. At the same time he was developing a coal gas purification process and would eventually go to Paris where he founded the first effective Paris Gas Works – all of which is an illustration of how close the technologies and personnel were.

This trial, it has been said '*made visible the members of an invisible college whose subject was the chemistry and chemical technology of oils'*. It might be added that for many of them this

114

included a study of coal and coal gases as well as coal oils. They included both William Brande and Michael Faraday and several others.

OIL GAS ENQUIRY

The dispute moved to the gas industry public supply when the Taylors tried to promote an oil gasworks for Westminster. At the resulting Parliamentary Enquiry, many of these chemists, and some others, gave their views. The Oil Gas Enquiry looked at the polluting nature of coal gas, its comparative heat and efficiency, and compared it with that from fish (whale) oil. In both enquiries, theories on gases, evolved by Henry, informed the background of much of the discussion
.

Evidence to the Oil Gas Enquiry, on behalf of the oil gas interests, was given by chemists working at the Royal Institution: Faraday, Brande and Richard Phillips. Evidence for coal gas was given by a group of Scottish chemists:

Adam Anderson: member of the Royal Society of Edinburgh and lecturer at the Perth Academy. Invented a lime purifier for coal gas, which was used at Perth Gas Works.
Andrew Fyfe: the younger. Doctor and future Professor of Chemistry at Aberdeen. Wrote and researched extensively on coal gas issues. Wrote *Elementary Chemistry* (1827). Member Chemical Society.
John Leslie: Professor of Natural Philosophy at Edinburgh University. Had written on heat.

Evidence was given by London shopkeepers on the polluting and inefficient nature of coal gas, and scientists were asked to validate this. Background questions were "What is coal gas?" "What is oil gas?" Richard Phillips answered "*that I do not know excepting that it is made from oil and has the properties I have stated*". Philips was a Lecturer on chemistry to the London Institution and editor of the *Annals of Philosophy*. His involvement in the discussion on coal gas and its constituents was such that William Henry, the Manchester chemist who had acted as consultant to Boulton and Watt on gas for lighting, sent him a copy of his book on the subject. '*On the Gas from Coal*' – the copy in ex-Patent Office collection is inscribed '*To Richard Phillips from the Author*'. Gas company minute books contain many references to "*Mr. Phillips*" acting as a consultant on chemical matters.

George Lowe answering the same question said that the chemical composition of coal or oil gas was then unknown "*it is carbon and hydrogen in some sort of combination*".

Towards the end of the Enquiry, evidence on behalf of the coal gas interests was given by John Dalton, whose work Brande had admitted not reading. He opposed the evidence of Faraday, Brande and Phillips, praised Lowe, and referred to his own work on *"carburetted hydrogen gas in the definite proportions."* He said *"coal gas when purified consists of the gas which I call carburetted hydrogen … super olifient gas"* and *"oil gas is much the same but in different parts"*.

The employment of scientists on different sides of a debate was to continue. William Henry himself had worked as a consultant to Boulton and Watt and, as has been noted, his partisanship against Winsor was only too clear. Lowe went on to a pursue a distinguished career with the Chartered Company, who had recruited him on the basis of his paper in response to Brande. Many of the other chemists involved in these enquiries went on to act as consultants in a wide range of applications to the early London gas industry. In later disputes on methods of purification, some were asked to act as referees for a particular protagonist.

In his evidence to the Oil Gas Enquiry, George Lowe, had made the most telling point in demonstrating that work on coal gas purification was beginning to overcome the difficulties of smell. Continuing to make gas cleaner and to produce an effluent which was also clean was to be the next big challenge for the industry in which chemists were to be involved. More on that, below, in due course.

The London and Westminster Oil Gas Company failed to get their Bill through Parliament and the hopes of establishing a viable oil gas industry collapsed with it. It was said that – *'despite the well advertised failings of the Bow Oil Gas Works'* – the telling evidence had been Lowe's which said, in effect, that the coal gas industry was beginning to overcome its initial problems. That John Dalton backed him so wholeheartedly shows how the role of chemists in the gas industry was endorsed both by the industry itself and in government circles.

LONDON PORTABLE GAS CO.

The early 1820s were a time of great innovation in the provision of gas for lighting. One of these new ideas was that of 'portable gas'. We are familiar today with gas canisters, used for many reasons — for instance, domestically to provide cooking fuel and light for campers. The idea of gas provided in containers like this, dates to the earliest days of the gas industry — to the London Portable Gas Company, and its twin, the Provincial Portable Gas Company.

Portable Gas was the idea of a Scottish engineer called David Gordon — he was the father of a more famous engineer, Alexander Gordon. Between 1819 and 1825 David Gordon took out eight patents. Two of these were concerned with a 'portable gas lamp'.

Samuel Clegg is also said to have used gas, which had been compressed into copper cylinders as early as 1811 while still in his pioneering gas making plant at Stoneyhurst College. The main antecedents of 'portable gas' seem to come through the application of compressed air. The invention is interesting in that most of those involved in its early application were also involved in the development of road and rail locomotion — several such will emerge in the next few pages.

One of these was, of course, William Murdoch, who has often been cited as the 'inventor' of gas lighting but who was always more involved in the application of steam power. Early in his career he had designed a steam road vehicle which, although it never got beyond the stage of a working model, was the precursor of both road and rail steam locomotives. *Fletcher*, in *Steam on Common Roads* relates how William Murdoch designed applications for compressed air as a motive force for machinery.

David Gordon is said to have worked with Murdoch at Boulton and Watt's Soho Foundry in 1819 on this use of compressed air to propel road vehicles. Perhaps also he had heard stories of Cornish miners who walked around with 'portable' lights made from bladders filled with gas by William Murdoch — stories which Philip Taylor, the real 'inventor' of oil gas claimed to have heard from the miners themselves.

By 1821 David Gordon had attempted to set up a company to promote road locomotives propelled by a high pressure engine, or a gas vacuum engine, or a pneumatic engine supplied by his portable gas. When this failed he turned his attention to steam locomotion and produced a number of designs, which would seem to us to be eccentric, and which explored paths which were ultimately unsuccessful.

117

Other engineers with involvement in the gas industry were also to explore the relationship of gases to locomotion – the best example is, of course, Samuel Clegg who was involved in work on the atmospheric railway, as was Henry Pinkus, who was also closely involved with gas in east London. As we will see, David Gordon's success was in the application of his compressed gas to lighting.

The London Portable Gas Company had been set up in 1819 and exploited a patent taken out by David Gordon jointly with Edward Heard. Heard has already been discussed in relation to the gas lighting display in Larder's Piccadilly shop. He had been an early assistant to Frederick Albert Winsor and had since pursued his own career in gas lighting. One of the key points about the Portable Gas Company is that the gas itself was not made from coal but from oil and in this connection the involvement of John Taylor, better known as a mining engineer is crucial.

The London Portable Gas Works was probably opened in 1819 and an attempt to set up a statutory company made in 1824 with the following subscribers:

David Gordon	Engineer and founder
John Taylor	Engineer
Joseph Watson	Probably a City Corporation Officer
Matthew Wood	City Politician – involved with Golden Lane Brewery & the Phoenix Gas Company
John Garrick	
Henry Alex Dyson	
George Methen	
David Maclean	
Henry South	
N.P.Woodbine	

Almost everything that is known about the Company and its operation comes from an article in the *Gentleman's Magazine* for 1819 – and this is quoted in detail by Stewart, but without a reference. It says that the gas was compressed into copper cylinders and sold at about £3.2s.6d. for 1,000 cubic feet of gas. This included collection, delivery and the loan of lamps. Delivery was by cart within a radius of seven miles of the works.

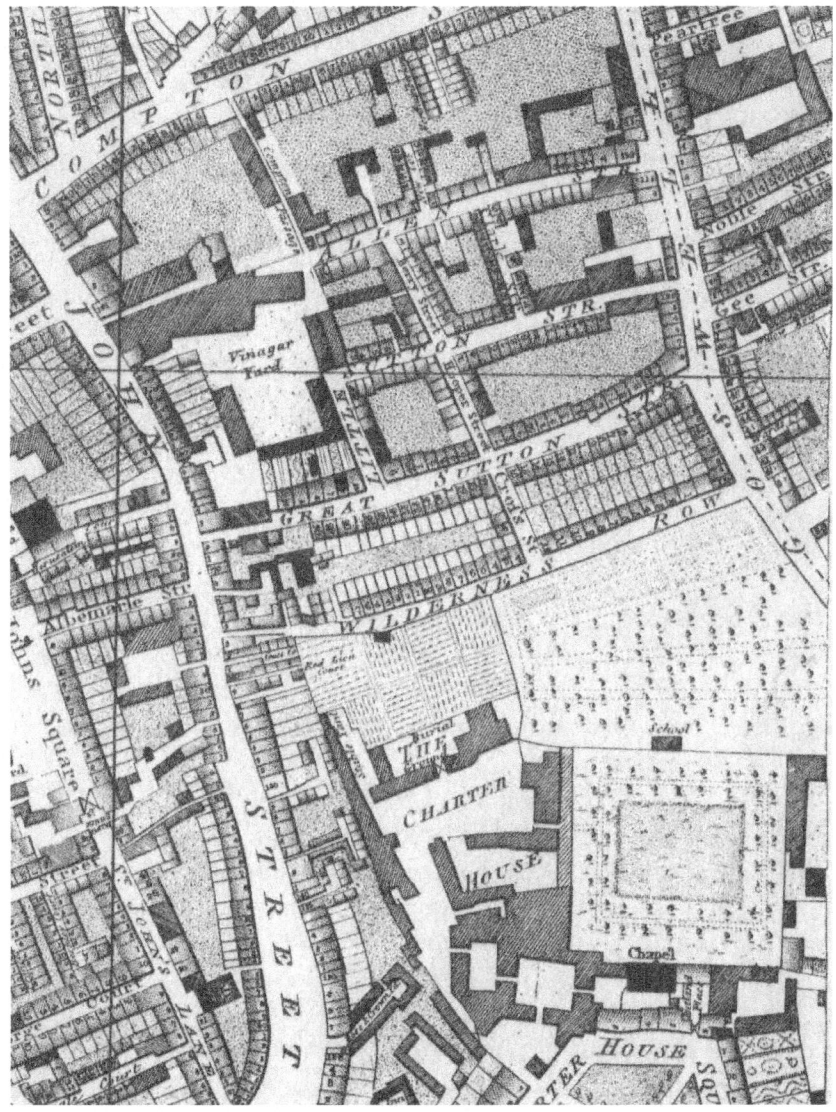

The actual works and its location does present a problem however. The address given is 38 Great Sutton Street — just off the Goswell Road and a short distance from the Chartered Company's Brick Lane Works. Great Sutton Street is small and narrow. The *Horwood Plan* shows number 38 as a single dwelling with a garden. Remaining houses in Great Sutton Street (no. 38 is now a modern brick office block) show that they were single fronted, two storey dwellings with a front door off the street. How did they fit a gas making plant into it? It might be thought that the works was a small one and would have taken up very little space — but we do have some idea of the size of the London Portable Gas Company's sister works, that of the Provincial Portable Gas Company.

The London Portable Company was accompanied by others outside London set up by the Provincial Portable Gas Co. — for instance in Edinburgh and Bristol. Another was

119

built to provide Portable Gas in Manchester and a gasworks was built in 1825 by the Portable Gas Company at Gaythorn, Salford. In the early 1830s this was sold to a Mr. Fernley who turned it into a conventional gasworks. It was then bought by Manchester Police Commissioners in 1837 and went on to become a major gasworks supplying the Manchester area. A picture exists of this works in 1857, after considerable improvements had been made. It shows a large and conventional gasworks, which would not have fitted into the site at Great Sutton Street.

Did the London Portable Gas Company have another, larger works somewhere else? The company remained in production in London until 1834. Where was the gas made if not at Great Sutton Street? There is nowhere, which can be considered suitable, but in looking for a suitable nearby industrial premises some intriguing relationships emerge.

Firstly, and very obviously, there is the role of John Taylor. His brother Philip Taylor's involvement included, among many other things, in an oil gasworks at Bow, described above. However Taylor and Martineau's engineering works, where machinery for making oil gas was manufactured, was also in Clerkenwell — at Whitecross Street in a works they had acquired from the print machinery manufacturer, Koenig. It has been claimed that, at this works, under John Martineau, Perkins developed a pump for use with portable gas. Taylor and Martineau were later to move their engineering production to the Winsor Iron Works in the City Road. It was at these two sites that their steam engines were made.

The other relationship is more complicated and even more intriguing. After the Portable Company had moved out of the Gaythorn works in Manchester it was used by the Mackintosh Company to supply them with 'naphtha' for the manufacture of rubberised materials.

'Mackintosh' was the generic name for the company, which had originated with Charles Mackintosh, the Scottish chemist, who had patented a method of making such materials. However, Mackintosh had not been the only researcher in this field and a patented process for rubber emulsified with coal tar naphtha had been developed in London by Thomas Hancock, whose work with rubber will be discussed in more detail in the chapter on coal tar naphtha. As the Portable Company made oil gas, it could not have provided the 'coal tar naphtha' which Mackintosh needed. There appears to have been a relationship between H.H.Birley, the owners of Chorlton Mill, and both Hancock and Mackintosh. For instance the mill records show that Birley had bought a gas holder himself in 1825 while the Portable Gas Company still owned the works.

Mackintosh himself was well known to John and Philip Taylor, and Mackintosh said that he had visited Philip Taylor at Bromley-by-Bow during the period in which he was working on oil gas.

Intriguingly the London rubber works, at which Hancock had developed his process, was only a hundred yards or so further up Goswell Road from Great Sutton Street. The site was later used by Gordon's Gin Distillery and is now a data centre. In the 1830s it was adjacent to the Brick Lane gasworks.

Some years later Thomas Hancock's brother, Charles, was to open a Gutta Percha works a few hundred yards away in Wharf Road. There was an even more famous Hancock brother, Walter, who, unlike David Gordon, produced a successful steam road vehicle. In the small and competitive circles of the inventors of steam road vehicles it is inconceivable that David Gordon and Walter Hancock did not know each other – indeed David Gordon's son, Alexander, wrote in *Elemental Locomotion* what was very largely a commentary on such vehicles and their inventors.

To return to gas lighting. There is some indication that the Portable Gas Company contacted several of the existing London Gas Companies with a request, although details of what was asked are not given in gas company minute books. For instance in 1827 a Mr. Palmer contacted the Imperial Company and was told that they '*declined the arrangement*'. As late as 1834 the Company was in touch with the newly set up South Metropolitan Gas Company. What did the Portable Company want? Was it perhaps a means of making gas at sites closer to their customers?

The Portable Gas Company continued into the 1830s – it has several successors in the continuing existence of firms such as Calor Gas. David Gordon died in 1836 but his son, Alexander, wrote a great deal about his aspirations to make an effective steam vehicle. Alexander was also to spend time in America and Canada, and built several lighthouses around the world.

The gas produced by the Portable Gas Company was the subject of scrutiny by some of the scientific community. In 1821 William Henry noted that the gas '*forcibly compressed in Gordon's portable gas lamp*' deposits '*a volatile essential oil* ' and noted that this part of the subject is well worthy of further investigation. The challenge was to be taken up by no less than Michael Faraday himself. Faraday's elder brother, Robert Faraday, actually worked for the Portable Gas Company and Michael was asked by David Gordon to analyse the liquid – it is of course inconceivable that Faraday had not read Henry's article on the subject. Faraday succeeded however in isolating a new compound which he called bicarburet of hydrogen – later known as benzene.

BACK TO MORE CONVENTIONAL GAS WORKS

And the Barlow family.

POPLAR GAS COMPANY

The Poplar Gas Company is an early example of something which was to become very common in the gas industry – a purpose-built works provided by a contractor – often described then as an 'ironmonger' or, more accurately, an 'iron founder'. The entrepreneur set the site up, provided some sort of management and then passed it on to another body – in some cases this would be a local authority and several works like this were built at the request of local people. A number of companies developed which provided this sort of service and some others will be described in regard to works at Greenwich and Woolwich. Members of the Barlow family seem to have been some of the earliest to undertake this sort of activity.

The Poplar Gas Company was set up by members of the Barlow family. The first proprietors were

John Barlow	The Sheffield iron founder.
George Barlow:	His brother.
William Wheatcroft	Had previously worked for the City Co. In 1839 name of a brass founder in Clerkenwell.

.

POPLAR GAS WORKS

This was a speculative gasworks built in order to be passed on to a management body. Sited in the heart of the East End and very near the new West India Dock complex and port activity. It may be an interesting question as to how far the continued development of the port area in this period influenced and was influenced by the number of gasworks built nearby.

This site was in Docklands – it is now covered by road widening in Ming Street, Poplar (once called 'King Street' and, before that, 'Back Lane').

The gasworks site can clearly be seen on *Crutchley's New Plan of London* (1829). It was known as Poplar Gas Works and was built by members of the Barlow family on behalf of a Mr.Wheatcroft. He had previously been employed as a foreman with the City of

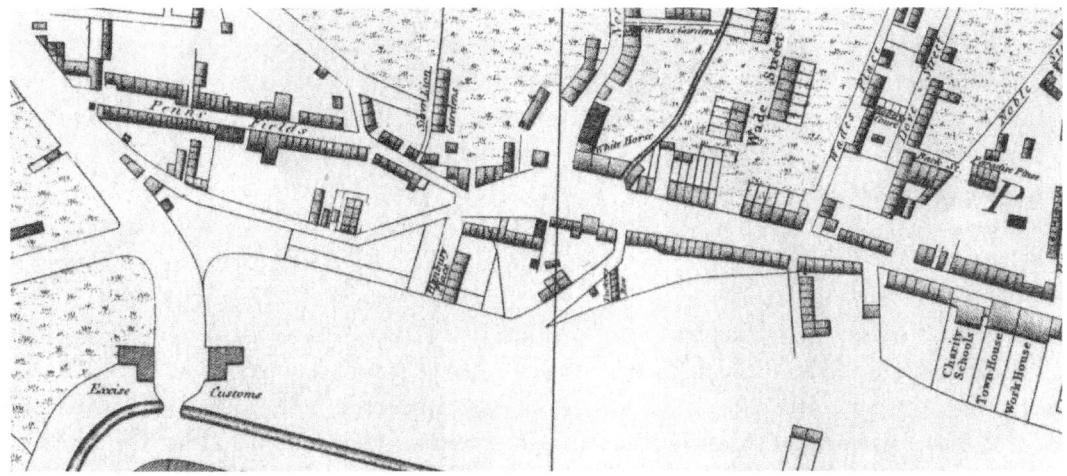

London Gas Co. and was probably one of many contemporaries who thought that they were onto something good with a gasworks. In 1824, 17 people living in Robin Hood Lane signed a petition, now in Tower Hamlets Local History Library, urging Poplar Vestry to buy gas for street lighting and the Barlows were all ready with a gasworks for them.

The Poplar works cost £16,000 to build and was adjacent to the West India Dock wall. The Dock Company, frightened of fire, insisted on certain standards of gasholder design. Barlow seems to have '*failed*' before 1827 and the works was run by a committee of unnamed proprietors under the direction of – '*William Smith, Clerk*'.

They were under pressure of competition from both the Commercial and British Gas Companies and in 1846 lost the parish lighting contract. The works closed in 1852. Stewart says that between 1840 and 1849 it was run (like so much else) by F.J.Evans, of the Gas Light & Coke Co. and sold to the Commercial Company in 1849. Poplar was typical of many small gasworks, which mushroomed in the early 1820s, suffered a bankruptcy and were gone within a few years.

The area has undergone numerous changes since the works was built and closed. In the 1980s it became part of the London Dockland Development Corporation's area and was cleared as part of a road widening scheme. It is still possible to find Ming Street but the old gasworks site is now near the junction of two major, and busy, roads.

THE BARLOW FAMILY

Sadly an article about the Barlow family, written by those who knew them, is missing from the only known set of the periodical 'Gas Engineering'. The Barlows are ubiquitous from the earliest days of the industry and were key influences on it.   The

123

influence of James White Barlow, of Tokenhouse Yard, in the earliest days of the industry has already been noted under the Gas Light and Coke Co. Another Barlow with an early interest in gas and its chemistry was an R.Barlow of Cockspur Street who sponsored *'A System of Chemistry'* in 1803 and who in 1814 wrote a booklet on gas-making by-products.

These two may, or may not, have had a connection with a John Barlow who was an iron founder in Sheffield. He came to London and opened the Wenlock Iron Works, City Road Basin as a manufacturing base. Family history web sites tell us he married a Ruth Greaves in Sheffield and had eleven children – eight sons were to work with their father. The third of these sons, Thomas Greaves Barlow, was to become editor of *Journal of Gas Lighting,* the most successful gas industry periodical in the 19th century, and still today as *Gas Journal.* He went on to become the second president of the British Association of Gas Managers in 1868. He had been preceded by an uncle, George Barlow, who had founded a short-lived *Gas Gazette.*

Members of the Barlow family seem to have realised very early on that there was money to be made in the fitting out of gasworks and that one way to encourage this was to found a gas company themselves, build the works, and then to pass it on, as a readymade enterprise to another body set up for the purpose of management. *Braunholtz* in his history of the Institution of Gas Engineers quotes an undated, but very early, document, in which *'Mr. Barlow'* proposes to set up a gas company in South London using his *'new carbonising stove'.* The Poplar Gas Company was another such scheme – and there were to be more. At the same time, the family sold equipment to existing gas companies like the Chartered and Phoenix. They would also tender for complete gasworks when required.

John Barlow appears to have designed some early gas cooking apparatus. In *Mechanics Magazine* of the 1830s, there is a long and acrimonious correspondence about this. A demonstration *'all gas'* house had been set up at 19 Colebrook Row in Islington and there were accusations that Joshua Beale, of Whitechapel and later of Greenwich, had sent spies to steal the ideas.

Thomas Greaves Barlow was to become enormously influential in gas politics in due course – but the influence of his father, uncles, and brothers was also enormous – and, as yet, under-researched.

OTHER GAS WORKS OF MANY SORTS

WOOLWICH
AN EARLY GAS WORKS

A public supply gasworks built by two speculators who hoped to sell it on to a management body – but failed to find anyone interested. Woolwich was a heavily industrialised town in Kent - but at the same time very near to London and contributing greatly to the riverside industrial sector.

In the early days of the gas industry entrepreneurs began to look round for towns in need of a gasworks. Woolwich was a flourishing centre with some big industrial sites, clearly in need of a good source of lighting. It is no surprise, therefore, to find a speculative gasworks built there.

In 1817, or thereabouts, a Mr. Livesey and a Mr. Hardy built a gasworks in Woolwich. If the name Livesey is familiar, it is because he was George Livesey's great-uncle, Thomas. Thomas Livesey was a hosier based in the City of London. A great deal has been written about the invention of the technology of gas manufacture but it is rarely mentioned that it was Thomas Livesey who took over the management of the Gas Light and Coke Company and made it work effectively – and at the same time set the pattern for how a gasworks was to be run. Busy as he was with this role, he clearly had time for other things, and like many others, an eye for a profit. A short biography of him is given below.

The other partner in the Woolwich gasworks was a Mr. Hardy, a coal merchant. Hardy and another gasworks entrepreneur, Joseph Hedley, operated a gas equipment and ironmongers business out of an office in King's Arms Yard off Cheapside in the City of London. Thomas Livesey also used this address sometimes, although his hosiery business was round the corner in Wood Street.

The Woolwich waterfront in the 1860s was very different from today and is described in detail in the 2012 Woolwich volume of the *Survey of London*. The industrial riverside lay between the Dockyard and the Arsenal, and Livesey and Hardy's gasworks would have been near the centre of it. They built their gasworks in Woolwich on a site known as 'Roff's Compound' or 'Edgar's Coal Wharf', which was on the riverside in the area of today's Bell Watergate and next to the Waterfront Leisure Centre. Roff was a well-

125

known wharfinger in Woolwich for many years and his wharf was still marked on a map in 1853.

Whatever the plans for the works were, it seems that it was not successful and after only six or seven years Livesey and his friends tried to dispose of it. In 1824 they attempted to sell the works and the South London Gas Company recorded their approach to them. When this failed they waited a couple of years and then tried to sell it to South London's successor, the Bankside based Phoenix Company — which by then also had a works in Greenwich. Phoenix minutes record that they were approached by the Woolwich company in February 1825, and then in November 1827 and again in December 1828, when they offered it to them for £6,500. Phoenix turned it down.

One of the reasons why Livesey and Hardy were so keen to dispose of the Woolwich Gas Works was that, as Thomas Livesey was Deputy Governor of the Westminster-based Chartered Gas Light and Coke Co., he was not supposed to have an interest in another gas company. In fact the Chartered took a very dim view of his extra-curricular activities and in May 1827 their records tell us he had to make a sworn statement to the effect that he had disposed of his interest in the Woolwich Gas Company. This, as it turns out, was not true.

It seems that Livesey had transferred the legal ownership to a corporate body of which a Mr. Ainger was a trustee. Ainger was yet another coal and iron merchant — this time based on Bankside. Livesey must have known him well, since Ainger had been selling coal to the Chartered Company from its inception.

The years went by. The works was offered around to other gas companies, but apparently no-one else wanted it.

In 1823 another group tried to set up another gas company in Woolwich and went so far as to obtain an Act of Parliament for it. This once again involved Samuel Hardy, this time working with Joseph Hedley. Others involved were Frederick Hardy, a Francis William Vant and a Joseph Wickendon.

In 1832 in Woolwich, yet another gas company was set up, the Woolwich Equitable and Ten years later another company was set up to rival it – The Woolwich Consumers Protective Gas Company. There was to be talk of 'serious defalcations' at the Woolwich Equitable and the rows between the two rivals fill many pages of the *Kentish Mercury*. The Woolwich Equitable tried to buy up the old works in order to replace it and they began to negotiate with Mr. Livesey and Mr. Ainger. This should have been no problem since they had been trying to get rid of it for at least the previous ten years. A valuation was commissioned from Mr. John Barlow (builder of the Greenwich Railway Gas Works at Deptford), and, in the interests of honesty and fair play, a second valuer was brought in. This was a Mr. Robert Brown of Royal Hill, Greenwich. I assume that this is the Robert Brown, Architect of Royal Place, in 1839 not the Mr.

Robert Brown, Plumber, of Blackheath Hill who was also extant in 1839 (or perhaps they were the same person).

Brown's valuation report was very long and very damning – the works was 'very dilapidated' to say the least. In negotiations Ainger and Livesey began frantically to talk the equipment up – they explained that the wooden tanks were after all, only fifteen years old and the pipe work would last at least a hundred years. Brown apparently did not agree with them. Ainger then accused the Woolwich Equitable Board of trying to cheat him, as recorded in the minutes of the Woolwich Equitable Company.

The new gas company decided that it was desperate to *'buy up the competition'* and continued negotiations regardless. Livesey began to talk about problems with an Act of Parliament and the Board of the Equitable brought their solicitor along to see him. A settlement was reached in July 1832 at a meeting between both sides and their lawyers. In the following January a list was produced of Messrs. Livesey and Ainger's various misdeeds and Woolwich Equitable Directors were perhaps most annoyed that £245 of the purchase money was to find its way into Mr. Livesey's pocket.

The old Woolwich works was taken over, run for a while, and closed down. While negotiations had been going on with Livesey and Ainger, other arrangements were taking place for a new works to be built especially for the new gas company. It is nice to know that the contract to build the new works went to Mr. Barlow, who had lost the contract to survey the old works.

The sketch map above is taken from an article on Woolwich Gas History in South Met's *Co-partnership Journal*. It shows the two later gas works but is also itself a historic document. The Free Ferry, as shown, then ran from a site near the current (but soon to be demolished) leisure centre known previously as Bell Watergate. The power station is long gone.

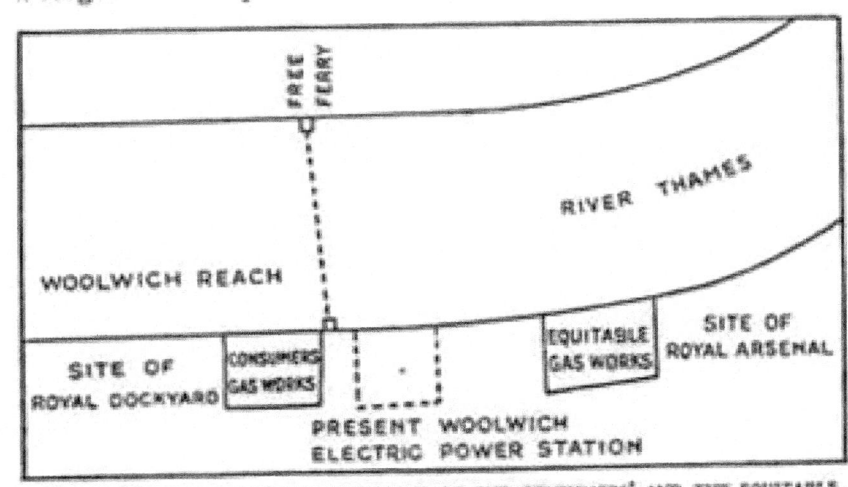

PLAN SHOWING THE RELATIVE POSITIONS OF THE CONSUMERS' AND THE EQUITABLE GAS COMPANIES' WORKS.

A PRIVATE WORKS
CASLON
DUTTON STREET

A small private gasworks, apparently built to supply lighting to a new housing development.

In 1823 The Imperial Gas Company bought a gasworks in 'Dutton Street' from a William Caslon. There are several subsequent references to the equipment at this site in the Minute Books of the Imperial Company.

Dutton Street is not easy to track down, since both the road and the road name seem to have vanished with the construction of tenement blocks on the site in the late 19th Century. It was a turning off what is now Lucas Street at the Kings Cross end of Grays Inn Road. Lucas Street was previously Cromer Street and a long thin strip of land to the north of it had been acquired by a Joseph Lucas and developed for housing from about 1800, some details of which are in *Survey of London* Vol. XXI. In April 1817 the estate's management committee opened discussions with a Mr. William Caslon about gas lighting for the area, according to the minutes of the local Paving Commission.

Both Everard and Stewart say that this was '*the type founder*' and, as the William Caslon who subscribed to the City of London Gas Company, is described as such, it is likely that it is the same person. 'Caslon' as the name of a type founder and the type style he designed is, of course, famous. This William Caslon had, however, died in 1766 and, whoever it was that had an interest in gas manufacture, was of a generation likely to be one of his grandchildren.

By the 1820s there were two Caslon type-founding businesses. The original Caslon foundry in Chiswell Street had been managed by the wife of the first William Caslon's son, and then by her daughter-in-law. From 1809 onwards this business was in hands of her son, Henry Caslon. The present company has no information or knowledge at all about either a gasworks or Dutton Street.

A third William Caslon had sold his shares in the original business and bought a different type foundry, which had belonged to a Joseph Jackson, and from 1807 this business was run by his son, yet another William. It must be assumed that the Dutton Street gasworks was set up by one of these, either father or son. This Caslon type foundry was in Dorset Street, Salisbury Square, immediately adjacent to the works of the City Gas Co. and so it is likely to be the same man who invested in the City Company.

In 1800 the Cromer-Lucas estate had considerable pretensions. There were gates into the estate and an elected residents committee, sworn in as Commissioners of Paving, who employed staff, a scavenger, watchmen and so on, and who negotiated with

Caslon and tried to impose some sort of standards on the gasworks and the lights it provided.

The gasworks was actually on the estate, among the houses and soon things started to go wrong. By November 1821 there were complaints that the lights were not '*properly lit*' and in June 1822 a very strong complaint was made that the gasworks '*had of late become so great a nuisance that it was almost impossible to live in the neighbourhood*'. There were threats that the works would '*be indicted*'. Perhaps inevitably, it was soon closed. The Paving Commissioners received a letter from the Imperial Gas Company in May 1823 to say that they had purchased the works and the Commissioners replied that Mr. Caslon had not told them of an intention to sell. In June Caslon told them that the works would be '*gone in two months*' – which implies that a great deal of pressure was being applied, perhaps by local residents, to close the works down. It was indeed closed by the Imperial Company, and some of the equipment was transferred to their new Fulham works after 1829.

The site in Dutton Street must have been difficult to relet and the estate records show it vacant for many years, let for short periods to other industrial concerns. It was not until 1851 that it was permanently let, and then to a private school. A school is shown on the west side of Dutton Street on Bacon's Street Atlas of 1888.

By the late 1880s the Cromer-Lucas estate had descended into slum property and around 1900 a number of tenement blocks were built by the East End Improved Dwellings Company – and most of these still remain on site. At the eastern, narrower, end is a more recent block of flats. It is difficult today to work out the exact street pattern of two hundred years ago and the location of Caslon's Gas Works. In the early 1800s residents felt sufficiently insecure to provide gates and new street lighting.

MACKINTOSH'S LIMEHOUSE GAS WORKS

The only thing known about this works is that it was built in the east end of London.

E.G. Stewart listed a gasworks in Limehouse, which he attributed to Mackintosh the building contractor, who was currently working in the area. They probably meant a Charles Mackintosh. Neither Stewart nor I, have any idea where this site was – 'Limehouse' being an unclear definition, which can be used loosely to cover a section of the London riverside as well as, more straightforwardly, the parish of St. Ann. I would also suggest, however, that the works was not necessarily built by or for Mackintosh, the contractor.

129

The main evidence for the existence of this works comes from the various London gas company records. In 1819 the City of London Gas Company took over the Aldgate Gas Works. They reported that the then owner, Mr. Peto, was being sued by a Mr. Mackintosh and also that that a 'Mr. Mackintosh of Limehouse' had bought the equipment from the Aldgate works — and it can thus be assumed that this equipment was to be used in Mr. Mackintosh's own works. In 1824 the Imperial Gas Company recorded that they had agreed to buy 'Mr. Mackintosh's Limehouse works'.

There are, however, more details to be found about the works in the Oil Gas Enquiry Report, There, Mr. George Mackintosh with a works in Limehouse registered his wish to lodge a petition with the enquiry. Unfortunately he failed to turn up and so we will never know what he intended to say — but the first name of 'George' is given and is the only clue we have to the identity of Mr. Mackintosh.

Stewart assumed that Mackintosh was a member of the family of contractors who were busily engaged in east London in that period. This firm was currently involved with a number of gas companies on construction projects and, what is more, had significant land holdings in the area having bought land in the Bromley by Bow area from the Foster family in 1824. Ten years later Samuel Clegg Jnr. worked for them on the London and Greenwich Railway. The head of the firm in this period was Hugh Mackintosh, to be succeeded by David Mackintosh - no 'George' seems to be involved.

'George' was however a name in the family of which Charles Mackintosh was the then head — both his father and son were 'George'. Charles Mackintosh is the man after whom the raincoat is named and some information about his links with the London gas industry is given in the chapter on Portable Gas. He also wrote a 'Memoir' in 1824 about his family and their work. He was based in Glasgow but, in the 1820s, was clearly involved and interested in the London gas industry with a view to making tar — in fact, in 1800 he had seriously considered moving his whole business to the south of England. Charles Mackintosh probably also had an interest in a tar distillery in the Bow Common area — the Bromley by Bow Court Book seems to indicate that he may have been involved with one of the many tar distilleries there.

Also of note is Mr. Thomas Parker of Bow Common who, in 1821, visited Bristol to extol the virtues of oil gas. Mr. Parker's tar distillery was somewhere near the top end of Bow Common Lane — in the same area as that in which Mackintosh may have had an interest.

It seems a reasonable hypothesis therefore to consider that 'George Mackintosh' was one of Charles Mackintosh's relations and that they decided to upgrade a tar works into a gasworks, perhaps in conjunction with Mr. Parker in 1821. Then having bought equipment from the Aldgate Company found it did not pay and so disposed of it to the Imperial Company. In 1824 Charles Mackintosh visited the Gas Light and Coke Company to discuss buying gas tar from them.

130

Maps show numerous chemical and tar works along Bow Common Lane. It is not easy to disentangle the ownership of these since five local authorities, none of which list ratepayers in any particular order, covered the area. It could of course be argued that Bow Common is not Limehouse — but some sites at the south end are in the Limehouse Parish and many chemical works, along the Limehouse Cut, could be described as 'Limehouse' as much as anything else in that area.

All of this is guesswork and Stewart could as easily have been right in attributing this mysterious works to Hugh Mackintosh, the contractor.

WELLINGTON STREET

A probable public supply gasworks built by an unknown company but taken over and managed by the Phoenix. It is unlikely that gas was ever made on the site. It was just off a main road out of London south of the river in an area containing both industrial and residential property.

The 1872 Ordnance Survey the 'Phoenix Gas Works' is marked, just off the Blackfriars Road. It is a long narrow site, crammed full with twelve gasholders. The site seems to be that of Friars Primary School in Pocock Street, SE1. The Phoenix Gas Company's records show that the site, described as Wellington Street, was used as a holder station, until closed down in the 1870s and later sold. *Garton* in his *History of the South Metropolitan* serialised in *Gas World* in the 1950s, tells us that in 1823 it belonged to the Phoenix's predecessor, the South London Gas Company. It is has proved very difficult to find out anything more.

The South London Co. minutes begin in 1823, by which time the company had been working for several years from their works at Bankside. Was the Wellington Street site their second works or was it the first works of the Phoenix Company — or something entirely different? There are indications that the South London was negotiating with a Kennington and Camberwell Gas Company — both a bit too far away to have had a works in the Blackfriars Road. Who were they? Trying to find out has proved an exercise in frustration. I started with the rate books — lists of who owned what — for 1820, administered by the local parish. However Pocock (ex-Wellington) Street has changed its name several times since then and was, confusingly, on a parish boundary.

It took a lot of searching to find it. The works was listed first in the Christ Church Blackfriars Road rate books 1818, as 'Gas Light *and Coke Works*' — no help at all. Were there any deeds for the property, which might help to tell me who had been the first owner? The site is now a school, so there should be something in the public records. Staff at what was then the Greater London Record Office discovered a record that a parcel of deeds had been passed by the London Residuary Body to the London Borough of Southwark, but they could not be located.

131

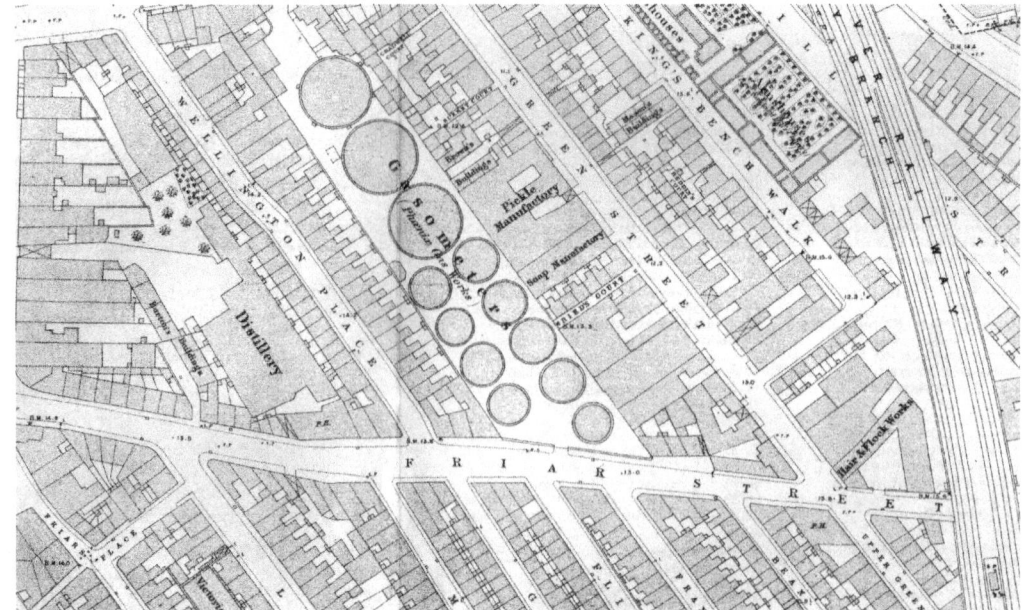

However GLRO had a list of the deeds and they showed that in 1818 the site had been leased – but who from? Did the original ground landlords still have records? Bridge House Estates and the Society of Friends owned adjoining sites – but not the site itself. So, despite a lot of help from archivists, I know no more than when I started.

I only have one small theory about the origins of the Wellington Street site. In the British Library is a piece of paper, an advertisement, about *'Mr. Barlow's proposals for establishing ... a company to light the County of Surrey from the end of Blackfriars Bridge to the Obelisk, Borough'*. Mr. Barlow is most probably the speculative builder of gasworks in the 1820s. Wellington Street would be a good site for a works to light Blackfriars and the Borough. If Barlow built the works, perhaps he then leased it to South London. For lack of other evidence I would like to suggest that he did.

Another theory has been put to me Brian Sturt. Gas companies had designated areas of supply agreed between they – basically to stop fights over whose mains went where. Brian points out that at this time the area of Pocock/Wellington Street was still in the designated area of the Gas Light and Coke Company but that these rights were bought out by the Phoenix Company in 1825. He asks *'although it is a long shot, was Wellington Street, originally a bright idea of the Gas Light and Coke Co.?'*

In 1823 Sir William Congreve reported to the House of Commons on the London gas industry, and gave some details about Wellington Street. No gas was being made there but three gasholders were in action taking in 73,565 cubic feet of gas. It appears that the intention was to make gas when retort houses were built and in the meantime the holders were supplied with gas from Bankside Works. It seems very unlikely that gas was actually ever made there but the site was used for storage until 1882 when the great, No.13, holder was built at the Old Kent Road.

132

BRITISH GAS LIGHT CO

It is a great pity that there is so little to say about what was probably one of the most important of these east London works. The British Gas Light Company (not to be confused with British Gas!) was a large, national and very successful gas company, which remained in business - although not in London - until nationalisation in 1949. It appears, however, that none of their earliest records have survived and very little is known about their early London operations.

Brian Sturt has commented that 'the British Gas Light Co was originally set up as, in effect, two concerns, one of which was to supply gas in London. After the London side of the business was sold off the provincial section was successful'. Several such concerns were established to supply provincial towns and their success rate was low — the British being an exception to the rule. British Gas Light survived until nationalisation in 1949 when the various works were hived off to the appropriate Gas Boards.

The British Gas Light Company — which closely mirrors the international Imperial Continental Gas Association — was set up by a group of rich industrialists among whom banker members of the Attwood family were prominent. The Company's Engineer was George Landmann, ex Royal Engineer and constructor of the Greenwich Railway. William Congreve was also involved.

The following list of subscribers to the British Company will demonstrate that these were people of a very different sort to the local traders and businessmen who had invested in the many other east London gas companies. These men were rich, often self-made and making an investment in both technology and politics.

Benjamin Attwood	A glass manufacturer.	Also a director of the
The Attwood family roots lay in the Corngreaves Estate, near Dudley, West Midlands, where their ironworks was used to promote other industries. A younger generation set up their own industrial empires elsewhere in the country — chemicals, iron and steel, glass, railways and so on. Thomas Attwood was a radical member of Parliament. Wolverley Attwood, became MP for Greenwich.	He was very rich and gave widely to charity.	Imperial Continental Gas Association.

Mathias Attwood MP for Whitehaven. Lived Muswell Hill also Leasownes, Shropshire	Banker of Gracechurch Street and Birmingham who had made his fortune from a monopoly in Swedish iron.	Muswell Hill Leasownes, Shropshire Streatham Park, 1846,
Thomas Starling Benson Benson family were active in the West Country and South Wales, contributing to the economy and politics of the area.	A Timber Merchant. Imperial Continental Gas Association and the South London Dock Company. Founder member to the Imperial Continental Gas Association and the South London Dock Company.	Russell Square. 2 Paper Buildings, Temple. The Manor House, Teddington. Sanderstead Court, Purley.
Thomas Hamlet	A goldsmith and jeweller based at 1 Princes Street, Leicester Square.	Cavendish Square Denham Court, near Uxbridge.
John Key 'Don Key' – City of London Alderman, Lord Mayor 1831-2. Master of the Stationers Co. MP for the City of London.	Involved with 'Golden Lane Brewery. Wholesale stationer.	Denmark Hill.
George Landmann Royal Engineer, trained at Woolwich who continued with a distinguished career in Canada and the Peninsula War as Lieutenant Colonel.	Engineer to the Greenwich Railway Co. A close personal friend of Congreve.	.
James Lett	Director of British Steam Navigation	Woodford
Samuel Eustace Magan		Austin Friars
Alexander Milne	A surveyor who worked with Nash on West End improvements. Commissioner for Woods and Forests, and for Improving London.	Court Yard, Eltham, adjacent to Eltham Palace but gave his address at 1 Whitehall.
Edward Stewart	Merchant.	Broad Street
William Thompson	Lead merchant	All Hallows Wharf and

MP for Westmorland and a City of London Alderman.		Upper Thames Street 2 Whitehall Place. Pennydarryn House, Merthyr Tydfil. Underley Hall, Westmoreland.
George Byrom Whittaker In 1824 Sheriff of London and Middlesex. An MP	Bookseller of Ave Maria Lane. Railway director	20 Upper Phillimore Place.
John Wilkin	A lawyer and a member of the Queen's Bench.	Spring Gardens
Jacob George Wrench	A seed merchant of King William Street.	Grove Hill, Camberwell
Thomas Harrison		

The Company set up a number of provincial works, initially in areas where whale oil, for oil gas, would be readily available. These 'provincial' works were in slightly different commercial structure to the London works and most survived into the 1940s. According to their Centenary book the Company was set up to serve the nation and to do it efficiently.

SCHOOLHOUSE LANE
THE BRITISH GAS LIGHT CO. WORKS

A public supply gasworks set up by a major gas company in the heart of the east end of London and the area of the port. Given the international business links of the founders, the closeness of the port area and the growing number of other gasworks in the area – it is very likely that there was an underlying aspiration to involve the works in the growing trading activities of the area.

The British Company were said to have initially taken over and run the elusive Mackintosh Limehouse works and then to have built a large works of their own. The description of 'Stepney' comes from Stewart, although the address is not in an area, which is easily described as that – since the site is actually in the hinterland between Wapping, Ratcliffe, Shadwell and Limehouse. It was not particularly far from either the East London Company/Ratcliffe Wapping works or from Sun Tavern Fields. It was actually in the Ratcliffe parish area for local government purposes.

Stewart gave the address as '*Schoolhouse Lane, Wharf near River Thames at Cock Hill*'. I have found no mention of this works on any map of that area. Schoolhouse Lane ran, and runs, between Cable Street and The Highway at their eastern ends. It is parallel with

Glasshouse Street where a glass works must have been in existence at the same time as the gasworks. On The Highway at the end of Schoolhouse Lane, stands a large London School Board School, now The Shadwell Centre. Between it and the River stand the Ziggurat flats on the site of Free Trade Wharf — which again would have been in active use as Saltpetre Warehouses in the 1820s. Alongside it today is the park on an area, which in the 1820s was crowded with tiny wharves.

On the Horwood Plan School House Lane is home to a Quaker Meeting House, a foundry and the Coopers' Almshouses. Walking round the area it seems even smaller and more cramped. School House Lane itself is a narrow alleyway, which you can walk in half a minute. The gasworks appears to have been on the west side of the road the British Company having leased the site and adjacent wharf from the Bowles family who had no need of it. It is described on their family history website.

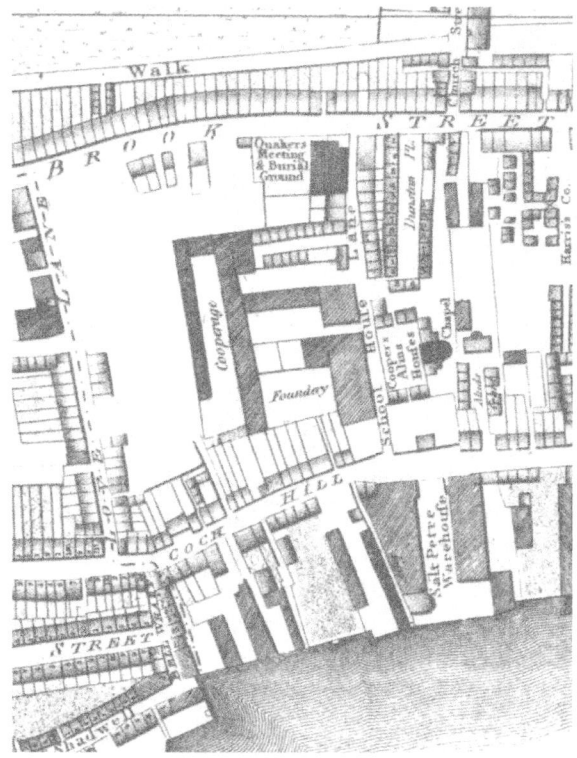

The British Company decided to leave London in 1855. The works was sold to the Commercial Company which immediately closed it. The site eventually passed to the London School Board and the wharf was subsumed into the area of Free Trade Wharf where it is now completely covered by the Ziggurat flats.

The site of the works was in Schoolhouse Lane. On the other side of the Lane, between it and Glasshouse Fields, stood glassmakers, which had been there since the 17th century. The glass makers, eventually T. &W.Ide, were owned by Hetley and specialising in art glass, and remained on site until at least 2005. They were then taken over by the Liverpool firm of Pearson's Glass Ltd following the collapse of T.&W. Ide with whom Hetley was associated. Glass now seems to have left Glasshouse Fields. The road is now the usual succession of overbearing identikit flats with no apparent reference to its four hundred year association with glass manufacture.

Roads in the area have changed enormously. The Ziggurat flats, which now stand on what was once Cock Hill and Free Trade Wharf, are alongside the ancient line of Ratcliffe Highway — now 'The Highway' which has become a six-lane road, which disappears into the mouth of the tunnel, which now runs under the Regent's Canal Dock (itself renamed as Limehouse Basin).

THE IMPERIAL GAS LIGHT AND COKE COMPANY

The Imperial Gas Light and Coke Company got its enabling Act of Parliament in 1821 after a number of false starts. It allowed them to serve the whole of north London. They were to be even larger and even grander than the Chartered Gas Light and Coke Company. Everard, who wrote a chapter on them, commented that *'everything was to be done on a large scale'*. Despite the famous names and the money they raised the company was riven with financial and other scandals.

The three works, designed by Clegg, were sited alongside canals so that coal deliveries would be simplified. The initial plan was for three works strategically placed around the metropolis.

This book does not include the Imperial Company's Fulham Works — since it is clearly not in east London. At Fulham however, the company has left the oldest gasholder in existence, the site of Sandford Manor and a fine set of 19th Century workers' cottages in Imperial Square.

THE PROMOTERS OF THE IMPERIAL GAS COMPANY

Everard and Derek Matthews, in their accounts of the Imperial Company, make great play of the financial mismanagement and irregularities in its early years. It is also true that some of the leading players — in particular the Clarks — have eluded very much research into their exact identities, although, as with many others, those with common names are often very difficult to pin down.

What has emerged from those proprietors is that there are three strands of mutual interest:

One — those members who seem to come from the London area and often have a connection with clock and instrument making and, perhaps, the Worshipful Company of Clockmakers. The influence of City Livery Companies in new initiatives like gas making should never be underestimated.

Two — the possible input of investors from the American and Canadian seaboards — and some irregularities noted by Everard and Matthews, which could be explained by absentee shareholders. People who made money out of whale oil and fishing may have a felt a need to put their profits into a new technology which might be heralding the future demise of their business — that of supplying fish oil for street lighting.

Three – investors coming from leading interests in North East England – Newcastle and Sunderland. Members of the Surtees family were major figures in financial and civic circles in Newcastle on Tyne and it is wholly understandable that they should invest in a new industry destined to become a major coal user.

Provisionally – Four – I am tempted to make a fourth category for those known to be involved in financial scandals – there seem to be a disproportionate number of them!

Who were the men who set up the Imperial Gas Company? The following list is taken from the preamble to the Company's first enabling Act of Parliament and describes those who were prepared to put their name to it. Sources are standard street directories of the period or information from Everard and/or Matthews.

Rowland Edward Williams The Company's first Chairman: Both Everard and Matthews interpreted his "Shaking signature" as that of "a senile old gentleman" and took it as a sign that he was put into post as a malleable, dummy candidate. Nevertheless very little is known about him. He died in 1826 soon after the Company began business.		
Francis Edwards Laid out and built the Imperial's St.Pancras Works, and the Millwall Products works.	An artist and architect who won prizes and exhibited at the Royal Academy. As an architect he had been described as a "*public house and brewery man*". a pupil of Sir John Soane.	
Joseph Clark His career in the Company was outlined by Everard, who said that Clarke '*made himself indispensable*' along with his brother, Henry, the Company Clerk. In 1825 the Company borrowed £10,000 from Joseph Clarke to pay a dividend following accusations re Henry Clarke's financial management. The Clarke brothers were involved, along with William Congreve, in the Arigna Iron Company scandal. Subsequently	He and his brothers were said to be '*scavengers and contracting dustmen*'. Subscriber to Imperial Continental Gas Association and United General Gas Company.	Lived at Kilburn Priory

shareholders voted Henry Clarke out of office. In 1829, after another embezzlement scandal, Joseph Clarke was asked to resign, which he did. He was then taken to court by the gas company, but had gone to Ireland. He was eventually jailed over the Arigna affair.		
George Clarke Maybe another relative of Joseph.		
James Henry Deacon In 1824 accused the rest of the Board of misappropriation of funds. He was later disqualified on a technicality.	Stock and Exchange broker, based at 9 Finch Lane, Cornhill. A Director of British Steam Navigation.	
Joseph Hawker	Possible member of the College of Heralds.	Lived Alfred Place, Bedford Square.
William Healing	Possibly a solicitor.	20 Lawrence Lane
Richard Oakley	Perhaps a stockbroker.	Bartholomew Lane, City
Timothy Francis Power	Wine merchant	Cornhill
Daniel Adams Master of the Barber-Surgeons' Co. 1793.		Lived in Islington
William Campbell	Merchant	Great St. Helens
Thomas Dodd	Perhaps one of a family of instrument makers – violin bows.	Premises in Soho
Thomas Dyer	Broker	Mincing Lane
William Styan Treasurer of the Merchant Tailors' Co., 1828.	A tea dealer	
James Beck	Watch and clock maker, Sweetings Alley, Cornhill & Mare Street, Hackney.	Wrote at least one book on gas lighting.
Evan Roberts The City Corporation Guildhall Museum has the Evan Roberts Collection of Watches – although they do not know the identity of	Slate merchant	Mayfield Street, near Dalston. 29 Mill Lane, Tooley Street.

139

the donor. The original Chairman of the South Metropolitan Gas Company, resigning after an apparent financial scandal – Matthews says "*in the habit of issuing cheques and pocketing the money*".		
Isaac Rogers A prominent watchmaker – His watches are collectors' items. Member of the Clockmakers' Company Everard says he 'ran off to Paris' as the result of financial scandals in the Imperial Co.	Member of the Levant Co	Business in Little Bell Alley.
Charles Francis	Roman cement maker. Limeburner, cement & marble merchant. City of London Corp. broker. Subscriber to the United General Gas Co.	Works Earl Street, Blackfriars & Phoenix Wharf, Nine Elms
James Birch Connected through marriage with the Northleet based Rosher, lime burners – and through them with the cement industry.	Ship's chandler, tar and colour manufacturer. London agent for Dundonald's British Tar Co. and St. Patrick's Marine Insurance. Partner of Cleverly, Northfleet shipbuilders,	Lived Crete Hall, Northfleet in 1854 – a riverside house built in a chalk pit and surrounded by shipbuilders, cement works and lime burners.
Aubone Altham Surtees The Surtees family were leading citizens of Newcastle upon Tyne with numerous business connections – banking, shipbuilding, and mining. Aubone Altham's sister Bessie had eloped with Jack Scott, a future Lord Chancellor (Lord Eldon).	Appointment in the Navy Pay Office.	Both Everard and Matthews outline numerous accusations of corruption made about Surtees and the Imperial Gas Co.
Matthew Surtees:	The Imperial Co's	

Brother of Aubone Surtees	coal agent. Lived in Kenton Street.	
James Griffith	Merchant of 23 Great Knightrider Street, Doctors Commons.	May also have been a landowner in County Durham, with links to the coal industry.
James Hartley	Possibly a Solicitor, of New Bridge Street, Blackfriars. Or perhaps the innovative Sunderland glass manufacturer.	
George Richard Robinson MP for Poole and, later, Tower Hamlets. was Chairman of Lloyds and was an East India Co. Proprietor. Family history sources give a George Richard Robinson as the grandson of Joseph Garland - an early subscriber to the National Heat & Light. Later disqualified as a director of Imperial.	Lived at 27 Chester Terrace	The Garland family had links with Poole in Dorset and, Newfoundland.
Marmeduke Hart Hart was the son in law of Joseph Garland of Trinity Newfoundland.		
Samuel Guppy	Merchant – maybe Bristol connections	
George Edward Watts	Gold and silver dealer Hatton Garden	
Henry Cadwallader Adams Married Emma Curtis, daughter of William Curtis (banker and MP for the City of London).		Anstey Hall near Coventry
James Alexander de Reimer Voted out of office in 1827 following misappropriation of funds. It has been supposed that this is a name of Huguenot origin.		
David Dickson Reportedly bought Henry Clark's bond of indemnity for £2,700 in gold.		

Peter Anderson		
James Dunstan		
James Cole		
John Cole		In 1816 a shareholder in the Bristol Gas Light Company.
Henry Johnson Hope		
Richard Gaunt		
Benjamin Hill		
Rickman Moore	63 Bishopsgate Within. Stationer and a paper hanger.	
Joseph Packwood	Possible career sailor. Royal Navy Lieutenant 1796 and Commander in 1806. Retired 1811	
James Parton		
Charles Roberts Perhaps a relation of Evan Roberts		
Catherine Van Dam		
George James Watson		
William Meggy MP for Yarmouth.		

PANCRAS WORKS

The prominent, and listed, gasholders which everyone used to see as their train pulled out of Kings Cross and/or St.Pancras have now in part been turned into housing as a 'feature' of some sort. They were, as E.G.Stewart said, '*A fine example of gas making practice*', and they were part of what was known as 'Pancras Gasworks'. Until 1869 it was the largest works in London with every facility available to the modern gasworks of the mid 19th Century.

The works was opened by Sir William Congreve himself on 16th June 1823. This was to be followed by dinner at the nearby Albion Tavern, although since the Albion had some last minute problems that day they actually went to the Freemason's Tavern instead. Before the dinner however was the ceremony with '*the acclamation of the multitude of spectators attracted by the fineness of the weather … the trowel and apparatus employed for the occasion were presented to Congreve.*'

The architect for the works, present at the ceremony, was Francis Edwards, the company architect. It was typical of the pretensions of the Imperial Gas Light and Coke Company that they should employ an architect of some merit for their gasworks.

The works was probably designed by Samuel Clegg. The Works Minutes exist but it is not easy to distinguish between orders for St.Pancras and those for what was then called Shoreditch Works - later known as Haggerston Works. They do however show George Holworthy Palmer taking a multiplicity of direct instructions from the Committee.

Once open and in business from 1824 'Pancras Station' became the headquarters works of the company. The first superintendent being John Vivian – who was also in overall charge of the company's other works. He was followed by John Kirkham, appointed in 1830 and who remained at the works for many years. It was said however that the works *reached their greatest perfection* in the 1860s and 1870s under John Methven and his successor, John Clark.

The area surrounding the works became less and less salubrious as time went on – to which Mr.Kirkham's pigsty must have added some effluvia. Dust shoots, chemical works and, in time, railways and their goods depots, came to the area.

By 1860 the works had six retort houses and covered eleven acres and it was claimed by the Imperial to be the largest and the best gasworks in the country – if not the world!

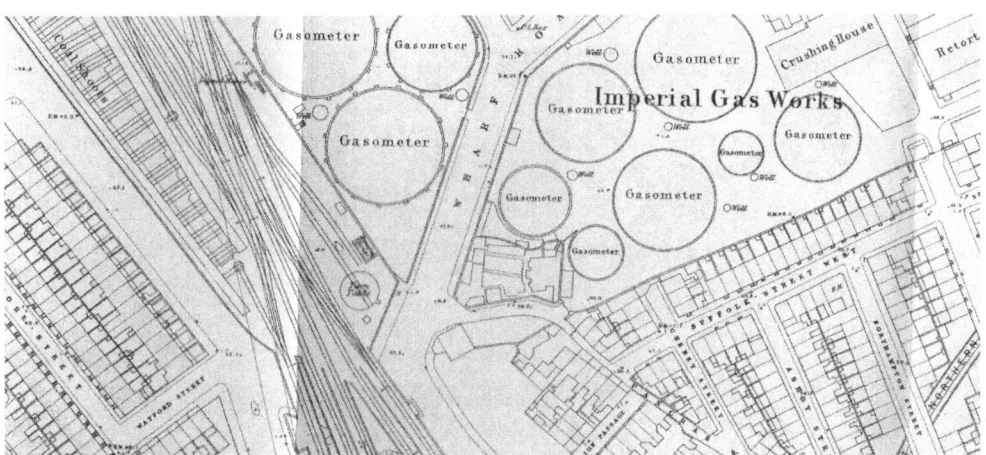

The original site was that portion south of Goods Way (once known as Wharf Road when it ran only as far as what is now Camley Street) and north of Battle Bridge Road (once Suffolk Street). To the east of the works the railway was built and beyond that ran York Way. Here there was an entrance into the works along a road known as Congreve Street. A gasholder still stood on this site in the 1990s and some outline of the shape of the works could still be seen. There was an entrance off Battlebridge Road with gateposts and remains of a gatehouse and other buildings.

Before the construction of Goods Way from what is now Camlet Street, the northern boundary was formed by the canal. A basin was built off the canal into the works and a large unloading pier was built across it. Careful investigation revealed some remains of this inlet which can be seen in the canal walls and in the local road layout.

In 1846 part of the area of Congreve Street was compulsorily purchased by the Great Northern Railway Company, deeming a detour into the basin to be necessary, and in due course a connection from the railway was made for rail-borne coal deliveries. However, as each new rail extension into the area was planned, so the Canal Company made an improved offer to the Gas Company to persuade them to retain coal cartage with them.

The dramatic holders, which make the site so distinctive in fact, date from fairly late on in the site's history. They were ordered in 1860 and built gradually over the next seven years. Tanks were constructed by Aird with structural ironwork by Westward and Wright. They were telescoped in 1880. Their closeness and the 'triplet' effect is merely a device to save space on a very limited site – something, which was discussed at length at the time. The Imperial Company's records give a great deal of detail about the construction of the holders – including the difficulties in finding riveters prepared to work at the height required to finish them. One of the holders has not been in use since bomb damage in World War II and the visible framework is purely decorative. As part of their restoration by Dorothea Engineering they were carefully recorded in detail.

As early as 1862 the gas holders at St. Pancras had drawn comments from locals. The Company recorded complaints in particular from a Mr. John Butler of 13 Spanns Buildings Agar Town, saying that *'he would like to know to whom he is to look for compensation for the injury done to his house by the erection of those frightful things opposite'*. He was followed by a Sam Sawyer, grocer and Chandler of 10 Spanns Buildings, who said *'his business has been injured by the erection of the new gasholder*. Not everyone it seems was an admirer. Spanns Buildings however would soon be under the railway lines.

In due course, the biggest and most modern gasworks in the world became old and cramped. Under demolition it was thought that there was *'no room to swing a cat anywhere, and the wonder is that so much gas was produced'*. The old equipment, so modern in its day, continued to be used. To quote E.G. Stewart again: *'Until the end it remained a fine example of gas making practice as developed by that company .... in 1904 the only modern equipment was the coal unloading cranes"*. Wet lime purification of gas continued here for longer than anywhere else – perhaps again because of the shortage of space – though Brian Sturt comments: *'the methods of purification at Pancras were rather unorthodox – the description quoted should be treated with some caution. Why this survived, just possibly, is that replacement would have been prohibitively expensive"*.

144

The works was closed for gas-making in 1904 and finally in 1907. The separate extension with the 'triplet' holders remained in use but controlled from Staines. Visiting the site in the 1980s we saw those famous holders close up – they were dramatic but the site was very quiet and bleak in an otherwise busy area.

THE IMPERIAL'S SHOREDITCH WORKS HAGGERSTON

At the same time as the St. Pancras works were built, Imperial constructed another works. This makes for some difficulty. In theory we should have the best possible description of the building and setting up of these two works because the works' minutes, with day-to-day instructions to the engineers, still exist. However, because the two works were built together it is often difficult to disentangle to which works a particular set of instructions refers.

The 'Shoreditch' works were in Whiston Street (once Gloucester Street) to the north of Shoreditch, on the area now known as Haggerston Park. This leads to some confusion since it was known originally as the 'Shoreditch Works' – yet it is not particularly near what would be described as Shoreditch today. Another nearby 'Haggerston Works' belonged to an entirely different gas company to be described later.

The site was taken on a 60-year lease from Rhodes, the north London builders and brickmakers. There was a chapel on the site, which had to be demolished, and a large pond at the southern end. The works was built, as we have seen, at the same time as St. Pancras but with the attentions of George Holworthy Palmer who was 'superintendent'.

The Works' Minutes show Palmer being given daily orders on how work was to proceed. Palmer was never the most amenable of employees and as early as September 1822 he *'accosted the Clerk at Shoreditch... and considered that much of the company's money would be wasted, or words to that effect'*. For these comments he was admonished as *'being disrespectful to the Committee.'* He continued however with the daily work of building a new gasworks *'making an inventory of all drawings for the committee'* ... and was directed to *'put the new purifying engine together ... and fix the same ready for work in the spot alongside Scott's pond'*.

Disaster was not far away and in February 1823 the two gasholders fell because *'Strutton's tackle had failed'*. The Committee of Works had been suspicious for some time about the nature of the materials used and they were not impressed. Six months later, in October, Palmer was warned to be *'very circumspect in his conduct towards other officers'* and the Board refused to fund a staff dinner, which he had proposed. The shed erected for the purifying apparatus needed to be moved nearer to the pond and in December Palmer was sacked, the committee being *'deeply impressed by his negligence of insufficiency'*.

145

With Palmer's departure, the works seems to have settled down into unremarkable gas-making for the next 130 years. In February 1824, a stretch of canal was opened to the *'acclamation of the proprietors'* as 'Haggerston Basin' from the Regent's Canal, into the works. This basin formed the western boundary of the works and, although filled in long ago, can be traced in Haggerston Park today along with its junction with the main canal. This canal junction became increasingly important since no railway ever ran near enough to the works to effect a rail junction for coal deliveries.

The site was a very limited one and, although near the canal, had no frontage on it. Very soon space was needed for storage and, as early as July 1824, negotiations were underway for a site further to the west near the Rosemary Branch pub (which still stands near the canal). In 1853 a site was bought on the Regents Canal nearer to Bethnal Green and it is this site, where two gasholders – once four – stood until very recently, the last one about to be demolished by a developer at the time of writing this. Once again, the site contained a large pond, and an inlet with a lime wharf alongside was included.

In 1911 an article in *Co-partners Magazine* described what they felt was one of the most 'interesting' features of the works – the Hunt automatic railway. It is not clear when this dated from since it is not apparent on maps and plans, nor is it clear who 'Hunt' was. It was said however that it provided a *'great fascination for the onlooker'* and that those who saw it were *'charmed by its simplicity of action'*. It ran, loaded with coal *'apparently (and*

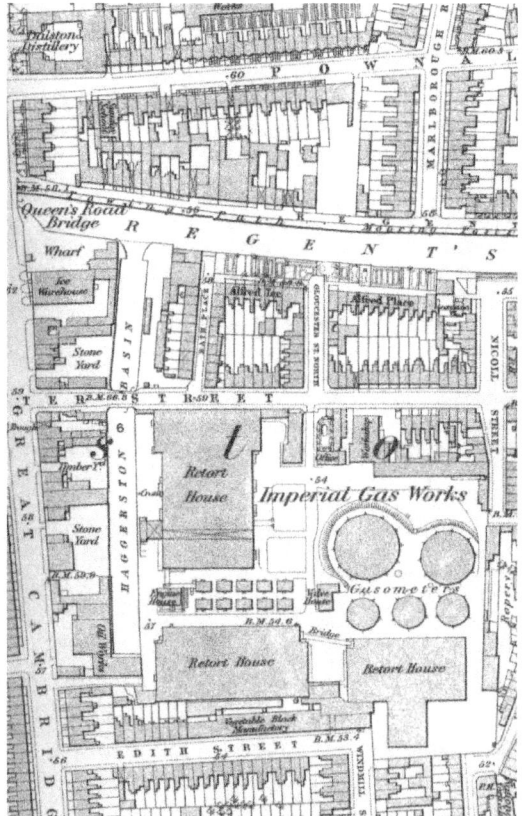

actually) of its own volition' to the *'desired spot'* and then *'closes its own doors and returns to the place from whence it started'*. In a special article, Co-partners Magazine went to some lengths to explain how this was achieved.

The Shoreditch works continued in use until 1954. Its longevity was attributed to its good position for coke sales – despite its smallness, its old-fashioned equipment and lack of a rail connection. The coke presumably went to local industry and the impoverished population of the surrounding Hackney streets.

The site is now Haggerston Park, opened in 1956, where an investigative walk will find outlines of the canal, holders, etc. to be traced in the flowerbeds. The fine stretch of the great brick wall of the works still exists along Whiston and Queensbridge Roads – providing an intimidating screen.

146

THE INDEPENDENT GAS CO.

SHOREDITCH INDEPENDENT GAS CO.

The Imperial Company's works on the Haggerston/Shoreditch borders tends to be called 'Shoreditch' and the Shoreditch Independent Company's works nearby tends to be called 'Haggerston'. They are remarkably close to each other.

The Shoreditch Independent Gas Company was started in the mid-1820s – the minute books date from June 1824 at which time they were trying to find a site. They began to make gas about a year later. It was opened by two employees of the Gas Light and Coke Company – Edward Hinde and Joseph Hartley – to objections from the Imperial *'alarmed at this arrival on their doorstep'* to quote Everard.

Initially they intended to deal with the local authority in St.Marylebone (a saga which took place outside the area of east London) but instead settled for Shoreditch and a site in Haggerston – buying the land from Rhodes, the building and brick making contractors.

Those proprietors who can be traced were local businessmen – the first meeting was chaired by James Andrew Welch, a surgeon from Dalston. Shareholders also included Charles Snewin, a publican, and George Bailey White, a grocer from Shoreditch. *Derek Matthews* in *'Rogues, Speculators and Competing Monopolies'* says that because of the *'mood of the time'* the shares were oversubscribed and that *'at a share auction at Galloway's Coffee House the police had to be called.'*

HAGGERSTON WORKS

A gasworks built by the Shoreditch Independent Gas Co. in the suburban area north of the City.

The works was, like Imperial's Shoreditch site, off the Great Cambridge Road but to the west of it on what is now Laburnum Street. It had a frontage actually on the Regent's Canal – lying between Haggerston and Kingsland Road bridges. The North London Railway was eventually to form its western boundary. An inlet for coal deliveries was built off the canal while the works was being constructed.

147

For the first couple of years, the works proceeded without too much incident, although they were soon sued by the Regent's Canal Company for disposing effluent into the canal. Matthews has described what happened after the company's shares had crashed in 1826 and a resulting enquiry in which the company was reconstituted.

THE INDEPENDENT GAS CO.

First the Subscribers to the Company. The Chairman was *a rather racy MP*, and almost all the rest can be found in local street directories of the period, and seem to be traders and businessmen in the area of Shoreditch and the City fringes.

Michael Prendergast MP.	Barrister Involved with Indian issues. He also fought a number of duels.	32 Castle Street, Holborn
Joseph Gratton	Corn dealer.	Shoreditch
Robert James Hendrie	Calico glazer.	Fleur de Lis Street, Norton Folgate
James Vernell	Silk manufacturer.	18 Steward Street, Spitalfields
Richard Tillyer Blunt	Solicitor	10 Union Court, Old Broad Street
John Townend	Grocer and tea dealer.	9 Shoreditch.
Matthew Warton	Surveyor.	Spital Square
Thomas Robinson		There are 13 businessmen with this name in the 1839 edition of Pigot's London Directory!
Thomas Beale	Surgeon.	Commercial Road
William Williams		There are 31 businesses in the 1839 edition of Pigot's London Directory with this name, so it is unclear which it might be.
William Rhodes	Brick, tile and chimney pot manufacture The Rhodes family were	Hackney Road. 'Chalk wharf' Regent's Canal.

	brick makers and major landowners in the area	
Charles Earith	Silk dyers	82 Goswell Street
Thomas Eaton	Surgeon	44 Shoreditch
Robert Penny	Barrister	Stone Buildings
John Jeffkins	Wine and spirit merchants	Crosby Square
James Kendle Browne	Corn factor.	Mark Lane
William Henry Burgess	Merchant	Mincing Lane
Ebenezer Fernie	Stone merchant. Later managing director of the British Commercial Life Insurance.	Cornhill .
William Lefevre	Carpenter	Plough Yard, Shoreditch (next to the Chartered's Curtain Road works) George Street, Mansion House.
Charles Montague Williams	Banker	St. Marylebone & Birchin Lane
Edmund Homersham	Head Cashier at the Bank of England	
John Blackwell		

The minute books stop and restart in 1827 with the name of 'Independent Gas Light and Coke Co'. The earliest records under this name are enlivened by the news that the Works Manager had given away tactical information about their current court case to the other side *'while insensible with drink'* – which they found to be an understandable reason. Complaints from the Regent's Canal Company on the contaminated waste water continued.

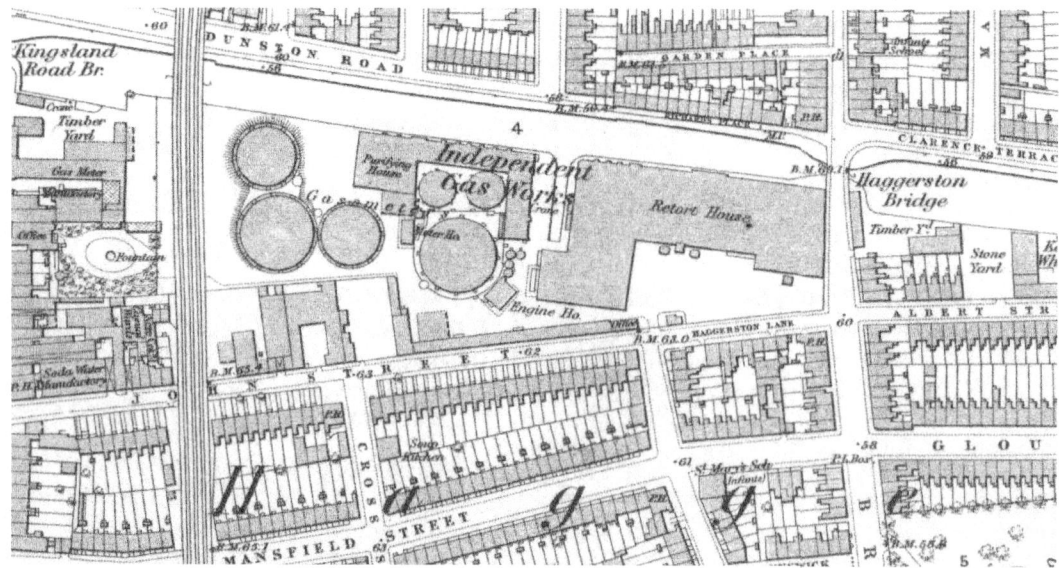

It took some time to sort out the problems with the previous management and Edward Hinde had to be removed from the company property in the midst of aggravated litigation. Derek Matthews describes how 'Hinde ... *had 120 of the company's directors and shareholders imprisoned ... and eventually had to be evicted bodily.'*

Despite setbacks the Independent Gas Company and its Haggerston Works continued until eventually taken over in 1876 by the Gas Light and Coke Company. They were always in competition with the Imperial Company and perhaps it was the need for constant cost cutting that gives the whole operation a slightly down at heel and shifty air.

Around 1900 the Gas Light and Coke Company closed the works for gas making and it became a factory for stove and meter manufacture. The whole site was eventually closed in the 1950s. There exists a very dramatic photograph of the large gasholder under demolition in 1911 – the great guide columns are falling and all around outside the wall are the tiny houses of Victorian London.

Housing was built in Laburnum Street in the 1990s but a few remains can still be seen if they are sought. The inlet from the Canal became part of a boating club for local children, inspired by the daughter of the Thames enthusiast A.P.Herbert, and around it has grown up an activities centre – perhaps not such a bad use after all

150

SOUTH OF THE RIVER

GREENWICH

A story of municipal dissent which outlines the process by which a gasworks might be set up by an entrepreneur. Greenwich was then a town in Kent – less industrial than the riverside areas which surrounded it, but nevertheless part of the port and its hinterland.

The advent of gas lighting threw a number of familiar themes into sharp focus. People in the 1820s were worried about the same things as we are. Public safety on the streets was important and improved street lighting was seen as a necessity. Another issue was 'keeping down the rates' – that street lighting had to be cheap. Local authorities were based on the parish and the vestry – but even so, their debates have a very modern ring. They discussed the same issues about private and public contractors, and about the responsibility for how public money is spent.

In Greenwich, as elsewhere, it did not take long for the vestry to realise that there was a new technology – although maybe they did not quite understand it. Before a parish could build a gasworks it would need Parliamentary permission to raise money and had to get an enabling private Act of Parliament. Happily there were those who were keen to guide them on their way. The story is told in an anonymous leaflet: *'Non I Ricordo – or the metallic influence of the gas upon the dark of the lampposts'* – and repeated in an almost identical official report.

In June 1822 Mr. Hedley of Coleman Street, iron merchant and gas light contractor, got an introduction to meet Mr. Bicknell, the Greenwich Town Clerk. He and his solicitor, Mr Tilson, went to meet Bicknell and Mr. Hargrave, Chairman of the churchwardens. He told them that new lights could be in place by late September and then asked for permission to dig up the streets. He also offered to get the necessary Act of Parliament which was steered through Parliament by Mr. Wells, MP for Maidstone and received Royal Assent in May 1823.

Then one of the Greenwich churchwardens, Richard Smith, began to complain that the parish was allowing *'strangers'* to form a gas company and that they would *'reap the profits'*. It should be set up by local people themselves and his committee reported that a *'good and proper light'* could be provided which would cost the parish absolutely nothing if it was done by a private company made up of local people.

In July 1823 Mr Hedley was asked to attend a vestry meeting with his tender documents. When he got there he discovered that a Mr. Gosling was there and had been called in first to meet the vestry. Hedley sat for two hours outside the meeting and

151

was then told that his tender was 'inadmissible' and that there was no record of his previous discussions. Mr Gosling had got the job with a contract for fourteen years.

Inevitably, as the pavements were dug up, complaints from the public began to roll in. And Hedley was plotting revenge. He made public the costs – his charges compared to Gosling's.

Gosling went to Parliament to set up a Ravensbourne Gas Light and Coke Co and many Greenwich residents petitioned against it. He refused to say who his shareholders were although it was said 'everyone' knew who they were. It was then admitted that the Greenwich vestry had broken its standing orders with Gosling's contract and Mr. Bicknell resigned as Vestry Clerk. A resolution was passed that this work was 'illegally and shamefully expended and misapplied' – although this is crossed out in the Vestry minute book.

It then emerged Greenwich had not levied a rate and a large majority of the vestry had voted not to do so, backed by the Royal Hospital. As a result a Writ of Mandamus was issued by the Court of Kings Bench – in effect an injunction forcing a local authority to fulfil its lawful obligations regardless of what it thought about it. Thus under duress, the vestry resolved 'to make a sufficient rate .... for lighting'. A vote of censure was passed on the parish officers for signing an 'improvident and harmful contract' with Gosling, not to mention the "gross neglect ' and 'expenses £10 for dinner at the Ship Tavern and £25 for a (another) dinner '.

THE NORWAY STREET WORKS

A plan in the National Gas Collection shows an 'old gasworks' site on the eastern side of Norway Street – on the current site of council flats – and the conclusion is that this was Gosling's works. In May 1824 it was been reported to the Vestry that Phoenix Gas Co. was about to buy it.

Phoenix – as we have seen – was the biggest and most successful Gas Company in South and Kentish London in the early 1820s and they were looking to expand. Gosling said he would sell to Phoenix 'at cost' plus a percentage of future gas sales. An assessment of the works was to be carried out by David Mackintosh's contracting firm. By the end of December an agreement had been reached including important details such as fixing Gosling's son's salary, as well as the Parliamentary expenses, and investigations on his title to the land. All of this was handled by the able Mr.Tilson and Greenwich's ex-vestry clerk, Bicknell and added to the bill on the rates.

Greenwich Vestry began to negotiate with the Phoenix Company for a supply of gas light. Phoenix said they intended to provide street lights in Greenwich by using Gosling's works in Norway Street, which finally closed in 1828 when the new Phoenix works was ready. Phoenix hung on to part of the site for many years and a gasholder built there by Gosling probably remained in use. It was advertised as a '*valuable property near the river, with brick buildings and a lofty chimney, suitable for an iron foundry or any trade needing large premises*'. By 1841 it was let to William Joyce the steam engine and ship builder.

WEST GREENWICH GAS WORKS – THE PHOENIX WORKS

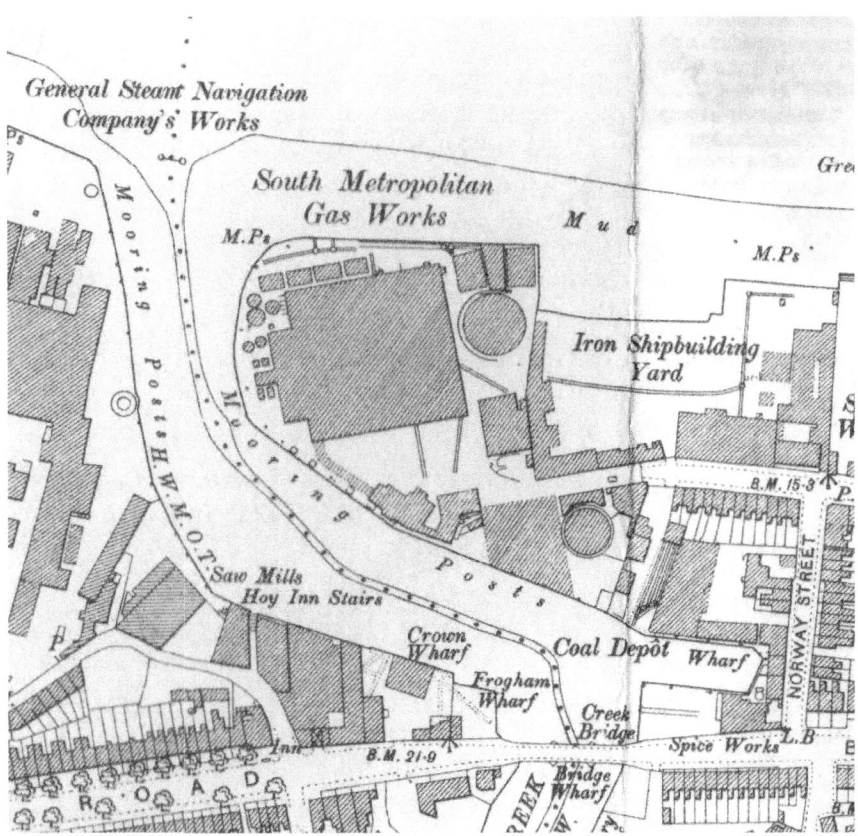

Meanwhile Phoenix had been building a Greenwich Gas Works of their own. This was at the end of Thames Street and occupied the site where Deptford Creek enters the Thames. They bought it from Mr. Horrocks, MP for Preston and cotton magnate. but first they needed to stabilise the land at the creek entrance and this was undertaken by David Mackintosh. The new Phoenix works was at the end of Thames Street on the site now occupied by the Millennium Quays flats and Waitrose. For which site they should really thank David Mackintosh since it was broken down marsh and reed bed before he stabilised it for Phoenix.

The trouble is that something <u>was</u> falling down, although sadly the Phoenix minute books are not entirely clear about which works it was. The Phoenix engineer reported that '*The Retort House at Greenwich is settling again*'. It had originally been estimated to cost

153

£4,400 and to carry the brickwork down 22 ft because of the nature of the subsoil. *'The (gasholder) tank has given way for the third time'* – and *'we have had to employ 150 men to renew the timber, and water has seeped through to Mr. Hartley's premises'.* *'The foundations were dangerous ... The sand had not been puddled first in the contract'.*

Phoenix Gas Light and Coke Company flourished and continued to supply Greenwich with gas for lighting from their works built on the east bank of Deptford Creek. In the 1870s Phoenix was taken over by the South Metropolitan Company, and in the 1880s their giant East Greenwich works demoted the old Phoenix Works to be renamed 'West Greenwich'.

West Greenwich Gas Works made charcoal throughout the Great War and was then closed. In the 1980s it was an aggregate works and, trespassing as usual, I was delighted to find aggregate stored in what was clearly an old gasholder tank. All now gone, along with the wharves, boat repairers, barge operators and so much more on the Greenwich riverside. Now just flats – same flats they have everywhere.

GREENWICH AND DEPTFORD GAS CO.

A scheme which never came to fruition. It is however one that can be seen to have a connection to the later and successful Greenwich and Deptford Company. No date, probably 1830s.

Those involved were:

Sir William Beatty Governor of Greenwich Hospital. FRS.	Beatty was Nelson's doctor who ministered to him at his death at Trafalgar	
George Barrett	Possibly the watercolour painter. The son of a more famous, Irish, father	Circus Street, Greenwich
Adam Gordon	Deptford shipbuilder	

Plus: Thomas Broadbent, J.W. Paris, Richard Edwards, Samuel Gordon, George Scott.

In the 1820s gas lighting in Greenwich was supplied by the Phoenix Gas Light and Coke Company from their gasworks in Thames Street. In 1829 the gas from the South Metropolitan's Old Kent Road works began to be supplied to some of the area to the west. Deptford lay between the two and, as more and more towns had gasworks of their own, Deptford people began to want their own gas lighting supply from their own works. In due course they were to get it – but from a very unlikely source.

In October 1834 the Kentish Mercury announced a meeting 'for the purpose of considering the expediency of immediately forming a GAS LIGHT ESTABLISHMENT'. It was agreed that Deptford 'presents peculiar local facilities for the advantageous formation' of such a body and it was proposed to call it the 'Deptford and Greenwich Gas Light Company'.

In due course the *Kentish Mercury* carried a notice of the formation of the company. After such a good start it is shame to have to relate that nothing else seems to be heard about this body.

The Mercury also reported that a Deptford Gas Works had received an Act of Parliament, although this cannot be found in the official records. A celebratory dinner was held in a pub on Deptford Broadway. This was a *'sumptuous entertainment'* for a *'numerous and highly respectable'* company. They toasted everyone and everything from *'The Old Oak Tree'* to *'The Army and Navy'* and everyone else – but I do not think they ever built a gasworks.

GREENWICH RAILWAY GAS WORKS

Meanwhile, as the 1830s progressed, excitement and innovation was in the air in Greenwich. A steam railway – the first suburban railway in the world - was to come to Greenwich. As plans advanced for the scheme, so the Greenwich pamphleteers and satirists were, as usual, out in force. Not only was this railway to be the first in London but it also would incorporate a number of novel features. Along with the boulevard and the inclined plane at Deptford there were plans for an integrated scheme of gas lighting.

The engineer to the London and Greenwich Railway Company was Colonel George Landmann. He had had a distinguished career in the Royal Engineers but had sold his commission in 1824. In the intervening ten years he had worked as Engineer to the Imperial Continental Gas Association – travelling round Europe to construct gasworks in Continental towns. In turning his hand to railway construction it is only natural that he should also think about how gas could be used as part of his railway scheme.

A separate company – The Greenwich Railway Gas Company was set up in 1836 with the same board membership as the railway itself. It was proposed to light the line with gas lamps –"*lights at a distance of 21 yards on each side of the railway and also a number of lights for the stopping places each end of the road making in all about 700 lights*" and to supply gas lighting to stations and to cottages built in the arches under the railways. In a

155

revolutionary step it was also proposed to supply the cottages with gas cooking apparatus. It seems very likely that another part of the plan was to make coke on site for use by the locomotives. The gasworks itself was to occupy the site upriver of the railway on the Deptford side of Deptford Creek – a site which is very easy to see from the train today and which now houses a local ecology centre, having been apparently derelict for many many years.

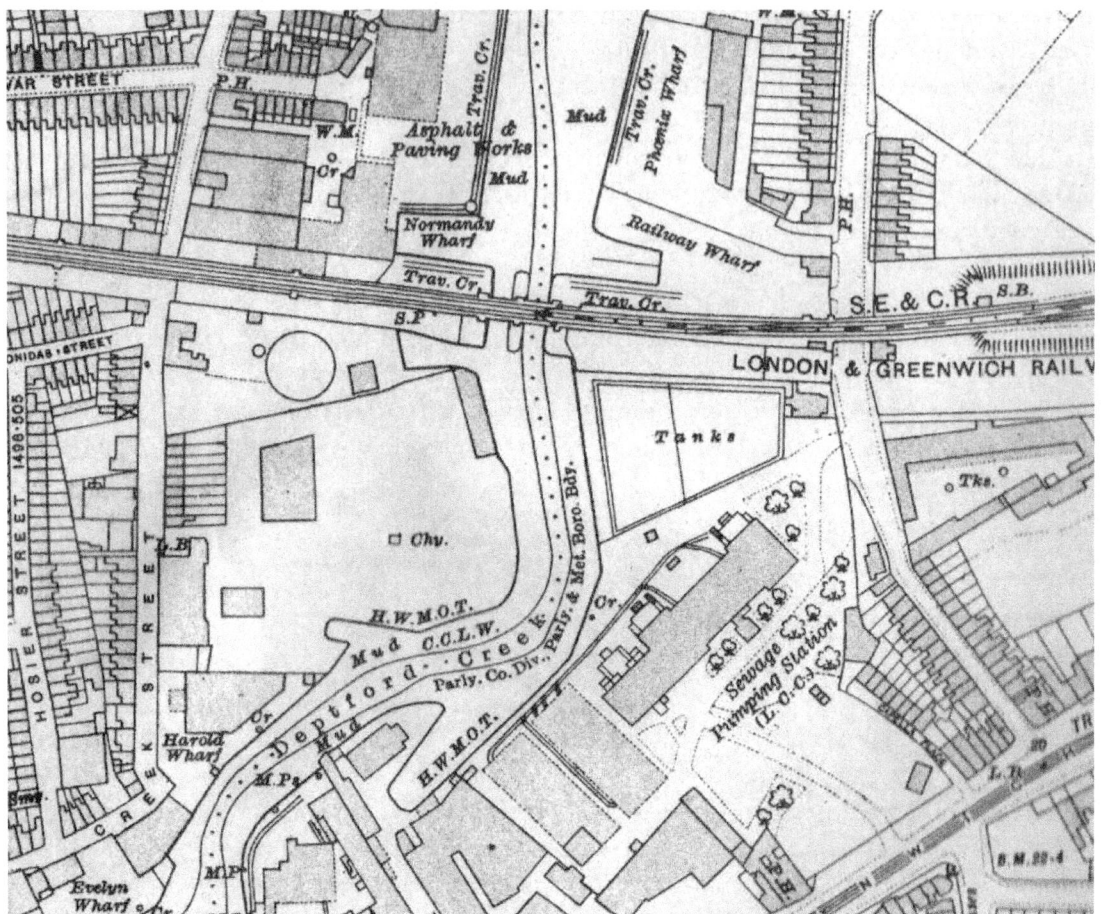

As plans for the railway began to emerge, the Phoenix Gas Company became concerned about the potential of the railway for damage to the gas mains and Mr. Tilson, now acting as the company's solicitor, took steps to ensure that a clause was inserted in the railway's Parliamentary Bill, requiring compensation for any damage. When the railway opened in 1836 Phoenix supplied the coke for their locomotives. What Phoenix did not know was that Colonel Landmann had been in discussion with the rival South Metropolitan Company, based in the Old Kent Road, on the question of a supply of gas for the stations and for the line. When Phoenix found this out in 1836 they were not amused and pointed out that they had not been allowed to tender for these lights. But, we should ask, why did the railway company not use its own gas for lighting, and its own coke for fuel?

The Greenwich Railway Gas Company does not seem to have been a success – and it is very unclear if it actually ever did supply gas to the railway line. Brian Sturt comments *'according to evidence given by Thomas Vince Barnard one of the reasons why the railway gasworks was not fully operational was a delay in delivering castings by the Barlows'*.

Did the Barlows continue to operate the works after the formation of the Deptford, Rotherhithe and Bermondsey Gas Company? There have been descriptions of lights which people saw in 1837 and 1838 but we now know that the gas for them was supplied by South Met., from the Old Kent Road works and not the railway's own gas-making plant.

By 1838 the railway company had given up trying to make gas, the new works was abandoned and the site was sold. The gasworks was taken over and finished by the new Deptford, Rotherhithe and Bermondsey Gas Light and Coke Co. This had a board consisting of:

Charles Barlee	Coke merchant	Deptford – a churchwarden at St. Nicholas Deptford, his name is inscribed on bells of 1842
Webster Flockton:	Tar distiller	Spa Road, Bermondsey
John Wells:	M.P., local shipbuilder. Deptford also with Wigram and Green at Bow Creek	Bickley Hall, Bromley Later Redleaf, Penshurst
John Twells:	Related to Philip Twells, City of London MP. Birmingham engineering family. Worked with Richard Foster.	
John Barlow:	Built and operated the works	

DEPTFORD ROTHERHITHE & BERMONDSEY GAS LIGHT & COKE CO

This represents the Company formed to take over the London & Greenwich Railway Gas Works Co.

The proprietors of the proposed company were as listed above for the ex-railway gasworks.

From 1838 onwards the Deptford Rotherhithe and Bermondsey Gas Company supplied gas to the people of the area in competition with the other local gas companies. Not too successfully however since, in 1840, Phoenix secured the contract to light the parish of St. Paul's, Deptford – the parish in which the works was located and an area that the new company could well hope to have secured. The reaction of both the older gas companies to the newcomer was to lower their prices and eventually in 1841 a limited agreement on competition was made between them.

By the early 1850s there was yet another gas company in South London – the Surrey Consumers based in Rotherhithe which posed yet more competition. They made several attempts to buy up the now ailing Deptford works but by that time the Deptford Gas Works had a neighbour in the shape of Frank Clarke Hills (about whom more later). He had a chemical works on Deptford Creek, next door to the gasworks and he seems to have found them useful for his own purposes.

It eventually transpired that the Deptford Works had been underwritten by Frank Hills to the tune of £10,000 loaned to them in order to extend the works. He had then claimed that he had used the works as a testing ground for his various gas purification schemes. The gasworks claimed that there was a footpath through the site over which he had rights. This version of Frank Hills' rights was contested by some of the ex-directors of the Deptford, Bermondsey and Rotherhithe Gas Co.

The Deptford Works was eventually sold to the Surrey Consumers Co. In due course that was taken over by South Met. and the works was closed down in 1856, but probably continued to be used as a holder station only. It appears on the Ordnance Survey for the 1860s with three holders, the little dock and some buildings. By 1914 only the largest holder in the centre of the site remained – and it then remained empty and unused until the 1990s. It is now the home of the Creekside Ecology/Discovery Centre – but the regenerators and their tower blocks are moving steadily down the Creek.

SOUTH METROPOLITAN
GAS LIGHT AND COKE CO.

The South Metropolitan. was to become almost the most important and famous gas company of them all.

1842 is the date of the Company's Incorporation but the building and operation of the Old Kent Road works dates from 1829 and gas making appears to have begun in 1833. The origins of the South Metropolitan are obscure. The Company seems to have been set up around 1829 by some of the following – taken from the South Met. Deed of Incorporation

Evan Meredith Roberts	Slate merchant	Imperial Company Shareholder	Dalston
Lewis Roberts Family history sources suggest that he was Evan's father.			West Hackney
William Clare	Bed making Tea agent		Charles Street, 46 Lime Street 8 Clerkenwell Close
James Davison Habe	Bookseller		Old Street
William Baker	Middlesex County Coroner		3 Crosby Square. Church Row, Limehouse
George Holgate Foster Family from Lincolnshire	Originally family drysalters, then merchants trading with Brazil and Portugal. In 1852 formed a bank.		Crutched Friars
James Foster			Walthamstow
William Lyall	Potato salesman		St.Mark's Place, City Covent Garden Cotton's Wharf, Tooley Street

South Met. had been set up as a 'cannel' gas company – that is making gas from expensive 'cannel' coal (a type of oil shale) to make a richer sort of gas. There are no records for the first five years of the Company and by the time the minute books start in 1834 there had been some sort of dispute. By that time the effective board consisted of the two Fosters, William Lyall, plus Frederick Blakesley (a tea dealer who lived on Brixton Hill) and William Bailey. The Fosters, and their bank, appear to be backing the Company financially, as they would continue to do, and their ethical and religious background was to become crucial in the later 19th Century.

In 1834 it appeared that two meetings of the proprietors were held; the second of these under the Chairmanship of Thomas Farncombe. He explained that the two Roberts had been discovered in *'fraudulent behaviour'* because a deficit of £11,000 and some false Bills of Exchange had been uncovered.

A new Deed of Incorporation was set up and the following people are listed as the first proprietors of this new entity. Once again they are largely City and local businessmen – but within those who can be found in directories there are some addresses which centre round particular locations, for instance Brixton Hill and St.John's Wood as residences. Within the list can be found those who took responsibility for the company over the next fifty years.

Thomas Parkin, Jun	Shipbroker		Threadneedle Street
Frederick Blakesley The company's managing director until 1840 – Matthews says *"more or less incompetently"*.			Bishopsgate Street Brixton Hill
Thomas Farncomb Master of the Tallow Chandler's Company. Magistrate of Surrey and Sussex. Lord Mayor in 1851, presided at the Great Exhibition.	Merchant, ship-owner, banker wharfinger – largest owner on the River	Described in opposition leaflets as 'an old Tory Queen.'	12 Holyard House, Kennington Common. Rose Hill, Surrey
L S. Baxendale	Lloyd and Baxendale		21 Lincoln's Inn Fields. 7 Great Winchester St.
Robert Edward Johnson			10 Hamilton Terrace, St. Johns Wood
George Elliott	Chemist and	Chaired anti-	Fenchurch Street.

There are many men with this name – this is a 'best guess'.	druggist	corruption group in Imperial Gas Co. 1830 & bought their failing Millwall residuals works	
Thomas B. Simpson Vice Chair company, Chairman 1859-1879 retired aged 92		Also involved in the Ratcliffe Co.	6 Albany.
Thomas Allen	Wrote a history of Lambeth.		
William Maugham			51 Guildford Pl. Kennington Lane.
George Park	Cow keeper		Union Street, Borough Road.
Samuel Bowring	Bowring Bros – - Liverpool ship owners - originally Newfoundland 'cod fishery'.	Founded early gas company in Newfoundland.	.
George Swayne	Wine and spirit merchant		19 Abchurch Lane. 2 Circus Rd, St.John's Wood.
John Barclay			Brixton Hill
Frances Roughton	Merchant		Brabant Court, Clapham
Thomas Baxter	Russia Broker Baltic Coffee House		
Joseph Lidwell Heathron Managing Director 1830. Son Chairman 1879	Ship owner	Said to have sailed his own ships.	Abchurch Lane Change Alley
Alexander Bell	Corn factor		Winchester Wharf, Clink St Bankside
W.E.D.Cuming	Coach maker		St. John's Wood
Charles Henry Stedman	Solicitor		Broad St, City
Samuel Arbouin	Wine & spirit broker		Mark Lane
Horton Ledger		Also Greenwich & Deptford Gas	Deptford Bridge

		Co.	
William Miller Christy	Hat maker and looped towel inventor.	Also Phoenix Gas Co.	
Henry Gaitskill			19 York Place
Richard Addams			22 York Place, Portland Square
Charles Price:	Oil distillery turpentine/linseed Banker Price Marryat & Co	Commercial Docks Negotiated for cheaper gas from Deptford & Rotherhithe Gas Co.	Millwall Blackfriars King William Street
Joseph Ivimey	Solicitor		89 Chancery Lane. 1 Ampthill Sq.
Benjamin Edgington Buried in Nunhead Cemetery	1835 marquee business and Britain's largest tent maker.		Charing Cross. Died The Elms, Tooting
Jonathan Fussell	Currier and leather seller	Related to Evan Roberts' wife.	Old Street, 20 Sidmouth St. Stoney Lane Little Elm, Bruton

Also – with no known further details:

Charles Farley	**John Fearnside**	**Elizabeth Foster**	**John Ware**
Donald Brown	**Charles Wood**	**John Stewart**	**Robert Illey**
P Stubbing	**John Sainsbury**	**J. L. Burrows**	**J. B. Langton**
John Dagleish	**George Mitchell**	**W. Bennett Jnr**	**Charles Jacob**
R. D. Jacob	**John Brown**	**Thomas Back**	**T Richardson**
H. Wane	**Richard Salisbury**	**James Foster**	**Thomas Black**
Sam Adams	**Thomas Jobling**	**Charles Newbury**	**William Dagleish**
Richard Price	**John Holgate**	**Stephen Sleasby**	**Jos Wilkinson**

James Carter	Benjamin Williams	William Bailey	Zachary Layton John Barratt
James Blake	Samuel Hunt	Mary Ann Christy	Samuel Travers
Charles W. Maxwell	Edward Sutor	A. Richmond	Benjamin Blake
Adam Catto	M. A. Arnold	George Greenwood	George Woodcock
Hugh Wade Macauley	Mr Southwell	John Whiffen Hooper	Richard Millhouse

To these must be added someone not in this list – but shortly to become the largest shareholder and one of the most important influences on the future of the company:

Richard Foster. One of the Foster family of bankers, Richard was born in Finsbury and later entered the family bank. He eventually moved to Chiselhurst – and throughout his life supported South Met. Gas Co. morally as well as financially.

He became very involved in the need for reform in the Church of England and personally financed a programme of church building in deprived areas – several churches funded by him are still very much still in business. He was influenced by a healer called Robert Brett. He was involved in many financial ventures both in England and overseas – and at the same time with a range of philanthropic organisations.

His backing for 'new' methods of workplace relations paved the way for South Met's innovative 1890s Co-partnership scheme – but that is yet another story.

OLD KENT ROAD WORKS

A gasworks – or the remains of one– still stands in the Old Kent Road. Almost everything that can be pulled down has been pulled down– and the statue of Sir George Livesey was been moved across the road to what was the Livesey Museum for Children, whose building is in transition to community use. No. 13 gas holder remains because it is listed but what its future use is seems to be unknown also – the rumours of an alligator park now having been dismissed. This is not, however, the site on which the works which opened in 1833, since successive land sales have moved it considerably to the east, although the portion by the canal remained operational for many years.

The Surrey Canal once crossed Old Kent Road slightly east of Verney Street but remains of it are increasingly hard to find. Hidden among the light industry is a terrace of pretty Georgian cottages – Canal Grove – and in 1830 they stood alone by the canal, by the main road, opposite the Kent Pond.

The Old Kent Gas works was built alongside the canal, and the cottages rented by the company as workers' housing. Maps show the area adjacent to the gasworks described as 'Peckham New Town'. The gasworks straggled out along the canal and a triangle was filled with little streets. Successive editions of the Co-partnership Journal in the 1900s included reminiscences and descriptions of the area and of a very different world in the early days of the gasworks. Backing onto the works was Caroline Street (now Sandgate Street) where a mission stood, frequented by gas workers.

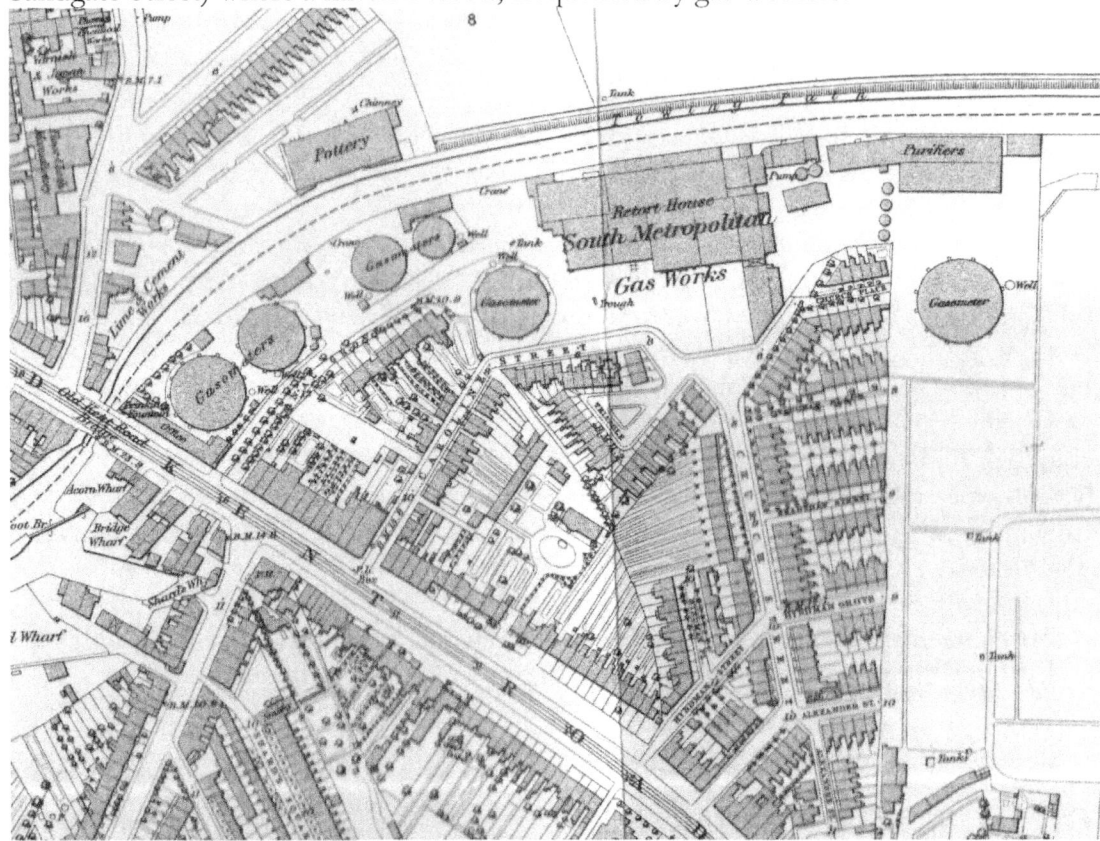

Church Road completed the triangle with Old Kent Road. It ran to Christ Church, built in 1838, immediately opposite the gasworks at the end of Caroline Street. Christ Church had been built to serve the district under the parish of Camberwell. Officiating there was a beadle with *'gold braid'*. The pinnacles of the tower were to eventually transferred to the clock tower in the gasworks. After the church was moved, Church Road became Ruby Street. To the south east of these streets was a large piece of vacant land into which the gasworks would move.

By 1834 the South Met. Works had already been built. The designer and engineer to the company was George Holworthy Palmer. Volumes could be written about Palmer, who had already had a very varied and lively career in a number of gas companies much of which has been mentioned in these pages. See my article on Palmer in *Journal of the History of Engineering and Technology*

There are no records of the start of Palmer's career with South Met. but at other companies he had tendered to build them a works, claiming a revolutionary design. Things would soon go wrong often because of Palmer's disputes with his employers. However, in 1834 the new works at South Met.were going well, and starting to make gas. The Board constantly reminded Palmer to *'think of economy'*.

The works grew and some important customers were supplied. Astey's Theatre for one took South Met. Gas. But the Board's relations with Palmer were so bad that by May 1836 he was no longer communicating with the Managing Directory, Blakesley and he had also *'made some allegations'*. The Board called on him explain. Palmer refused and was dismissed but remained in his company house.

The situation was resolved with some suddenness on the 8th of October when a major explosion shook the works. An enquiry showed that the explosion had been caused because of the lack of ventilation in Palmer's octagonal purifying house which a workman had entered with a naked light.

There was to be a happy ending to this saga – although one which takes us well beyond the remit of this work. South Met. took into employment a Thomas Livesey, nephew of the Deputy Governor of the Gas Light and Coke Company and with some years of experience of gas company management behind him. Thomas was to revolutionise South Met. – and was succeeded by his unorthodox and charismatic son, George. South Met by the 1890s was to *'take the lead'* in both London and the rest of the country.

THE WASTE PRODUCTS
OF
COAL GAS MANUFACTURE

The manufacture of 'town gas' was, essentially, a chemical process. Coal was put into retorts, distilled and a number of different substances were collected as a result. One of these – the best known and most obviously useful – was the 'gas' which could be burnt to provide lighting.

This activity of providing light became so important, that the other products of the distillation process were either forgotten or seen only as 'waste', 'residual' or 'by-products'. How did the early London gas industry deal with these other substances and relate to local industries as their customers?

'WASTE' PRODUCTS

The 'waste' materials which were the by-products of coal gas manufacture have rarely been considered as a commodity in the industrial world and only occasionally been noted as part of the coal-based fuel structure although *A.E.Musson,* in *Growth of British Industry* suggested that *'linkages with the chemical industry were gradually developed'.*

Some historians of the chemical industry have looked at some of these 'waste' products from outside of the context of the gas industry. They have noticed specialist manufacturers who made 'tar' rather than 'gas' – using the same process but for a different end result. Studies of this sort of work appear in accounts of chemical discoveries, biographical material on industrialists like Charles Mackintosh, or in studies of technologies like ship building and repair which used the end product. The gas industry, as such, is rarely mentioned.

The writers of generalist gas industry histories also frequently ignore "waste" products. Thus, there is often an assumption that gas industry by-products were normally disposed of, unused. Hence *Musson & Robinson* in *Science & technology in the Industrial Revolution,* describe them as *"an embarrassing problem, often being dumped in rivers'.* This disposal method is assumed to have gone on until the 1870s when, suddenly, coal tar was found to have a use in the manufacture of dyestuffs.

Regional histories of the gas industry sometimes give more detail about what happened. A history of the Scottish industry concludes that *'restrictions on dumping produced a strong incentive to find markets for by-product'* implying that there was no interest from producers or potential customers until pressure was applied from outside environmental interests.

166

By-products are mentioned in two histories of the London gas industry. Sterling Everard, an industry insider writing in the 1940s, showed that the early gas industry had customers for tar and ammonia products. However, Derek Matthews, in his 1986 Thesis on *the London Gas Industry* said *'in the early decades of the industry the London gas companies literally could not give their tar and ammoniacal liquor away'* while at the same time noting that some went to *'local chemical firms like F.C.Hills of Deptford'*. Matthews moved on to include a discussion on some of the problems of disposal of chemicals which resulted from the 'purification' of coal gas – in particular the *'blue billy'* which resulted from the *'wet lime process'*.

WHAT THIS IS ABOUT

The story starts in London at the turn of the 19th century; there was a buzz about – fuelled by strong drink, bright ideas and loose capital. Cynical Cockneys remained under-impressed and many waited their chance. It is not very likely that such a society would have allowed anything to be dumped in the river if there was any chance that something – preferably a profit – could be made out of it.

I do not think these gas industry *'wastes'* were really ever seen as rubbish at all – but as economic assets to be exploited. At first the early gas companies tried to exploit them themselves and, failing that, began to sell them to surrounding industry. Over the next twenty years sales proceeded to the local chemical industry. Some manufacturing chemists developed large businesses and capital to invest elsewhere while seeming to have proceeded without the benefit of much knowledge, and with standards of truth and honesty which seem remarkably low.

As the chemical industry grew it spread around the London hinterland. It was one of the industries which filled in the spaces left after everyone else had had their pick – on Bow Common, on the Stratford Marshes, on the Bermondsey Levels – and, ultimately, Hackney Wick. It settled itself down near the shipbuilders and the engineering workshops, which bought its products. Around it lived its workforce – the poor people of East London – who smelt its smells, breathed in the fumes, and died young. Management, mainly, moved to Blackheath and other such areas from whence it tried not to complain about the fogs and the smell – there were works at Erith that you could smell five miles away!

The last chemical works on Bow Common – the direct successor of one which will feature in this text – closed only in 1984. The greatest gasworks of them all – at East Greenwich – was the site of the Millennium Exhibition and as such is derided as a polluter. Alongside East Greenwich gasworks the most successful chemist of all had his works. and some of his money built the ships that fought the Kaiser.

COKE
THE FIRST BY PRODUCT.

Coke is the best known of gas industry waste products and in terms of early sales is the simplest to deal with. That is not to say that it is uninteresting – but that there is not much more to say than that the early company promoters said that it could be sold, and that it was sold – much as they predicted.

This chapter will look briefly at the background to coke manufacture and promotion in London and at the ideas which Frederick Albert Winsor and the early Gas Light and Coke Company had for it. A following chapter will briefly look at some of the subsequent uses by industry.

I am also painfully aware that, for many younger people, 'coke' will not be understood as the word for a fuel. Trying to find an instant definition of it I have flicked through five pages of Google before I find a reference which is not to a brown fizzy drink, nor to a drug. When I get there the first definition is "*a solid, grey substance that is burned as a fuel, left after coal is heated and the gas and tar removed*", so says a standard dictionary. I am not so sure about the 'grey' – perhaps an ashy sort of black. The definition is fine but what is remarkable is the way that a substance once so common has retreated out of the consciousness of most people. To the early gas industry it was incredibly important.

THE BACKGROUND

By 1800 coke had already been purposely made from carbonised coal for at least a hundred years. Abraham Darby's use of coke to smelt iron in 1709 is, perhaps, the example which comes to most minds most readily.

Development of manufacturing coke had however begun considerably before 1709 and some of the earliest recorded experiments had taken place, in Greenwich and Deptford. In 1656 John Evelyn described experiments he had seen in 'charking' sea coal near the Greenwich Ferry. This was in works set up by Sir John Winter, at that time apparently imprisoned in the Tower of London, but evidentially allowed out on some sort of day release.

This may be connected with the 1659 patent of Thomas Peyton of Deptford for a method of making 'Coke'. This patent is connected to the coal trade from Newcastle to London but may also be connected to the copperas industry. At least two copperas works opened alongside Deptford Creek during the 17th century – started by members of a loose grouping of Royalist entrepreneurs. This group included associates of both Peyton and Winter most of who would have been well known to Evelyn.

Coke, therefore, had been known, and used, for at least a hundred and fifty years before 1800 and was, probably, very familiar. The approach of the early gas industry to coke was different to that taken to the other by-products. Coke had a market, which was known, and sales proceeded.

Doubtless the promoters of the Chartered Company had done some homework on the subject first. In 1800 Bishop Watson, Professor of Chemistry at Cambridge, published a book *'Chemical Essays'* in which, among other things, he described coke, and its industrial applications. Frederick Albert Winsor acknowledged Watson's influence on him by sending him a copy of his coke pamphlet inscribed '*with greatest respects from the author'*. This is probably a very rare occasion on which it is possible to show some influence from academic world on the early gas industry.

COKE AND THE GAS COMPANIES

In 1809 the gas company promoters took care to draw to the public and to politicians' attention the use of coke in the workplace. One way of doing this had been to bring evidence to the 1809 Parliamentary Enquiry.

Some time at the beginning of the Enquiry was taken up with evidence given about the use of coke – this was a comparison between the coke from 'Mr. Winsor and from others – in a Lambeth furnace. Naturally 'Mr. Winsor's' was found to produce much better results.

There is however very little to be said about coke sales by the early gas companies beyond what can be deduced from ordinary common knowledge. Coke was sold, and continued to be sold from the start of the industry until coal was no longer used to make gas. Analysis of early sales is difficult because the gas companies left very few records about them. Company minute books and ledgers refer to coke sales but not on a day to day basis. They recorded the unusual – large or difficult sales – but not the ordinary. Even total sales figures over more than a very short period are rarely available.

Two elements of coke sales will be explored here. One is a comment on the original intentions of the gas companies towards coke. The other is a brief look at some of the known customers for gas company coke.

ORIGINAL INTENTIONS
GAS LIGHT AND COKE COMPANIES

The intentions of the early gas industry towards coke can be seen from the names adopted by the early gas companies. The proper name of the first gas company was the "Gas Light and Coke Company'. The first directory listing of another of the original gas companies was 'Morrow, Evans and Co. Gas and Coke Merchants' (someone had clearly misheard or mistranscribed Morrow for Munro here). In both cases there is equal emphasis on the words 'gas' and 'coke'. Their intention was to be known to be sellers of it. This raises, of course, the point as to whether coke is actually a by-product at all. In some cases might 'gas' be the 'by-product of coke manufacture?

The legal name of most gas companies included 'and Coke' and this continued to be the case with companies formed as late as the 1850s. Names are taken from their enabling Acts of Parliament.

In east London the 'Gas Light and Coke Companies' were:

The City of London Gas Light and Coke Co. (1816)
The Imperial Gas Light and Coke Co (1821)
The South London Gas Light and Coke Co. (1821)
The Ratcliffe Gas Light and Coke Co (1823)
The Phoenix Gas Light and Coke Co. (1824)
The Independent Gas Light and Coke (1829)
The South Metropolitan Gas Light and Coke Co (1842)
The Commercial Gas Light and Coke Co. (1847)

We can assume that these companies intended to make and sell coke as a major product. Those companies that described themselves merely as 'Gas Light' were:

The Poplar Gas Light Co. (1821)
The Woolwich Gas Light Co (1823)
The British Gas Light Co (1829)

Do these variations of company name show anything about the nature of the London gas industry? All of these companies must have made coke. Clearly some companies, not included here, made gas from oil and thus would not have produced coke – in east London this would have covered the Bow Oil Gas Works. The 'Gas Light and Coke' companies are mostly the earlier and larger companies while the 'Gas Light' companies are later, smaller and include some oddities, like the British which had a nation-wide remit, and were mainly based outside London. They also include the Poplar Company, one of the earliest of the "Barlow" works. The cut off point for this book is 1850 but it is worth noting that a number of works opened in the early 1850s were 'consumer' companies set up with 'consumers' – usually local authorities as shareholders. Their titles frequently omitted 'coke' – since they were set up to provide street lighting.

Gas Companies may have chosen their names for a number of reasons – some for reasons only known to them. Whatever they called themselves, all the coal gas companies had coke to dispose of and they all did this in the same way: they sold it. For the earliest companies the name 'gas light and coke' seems to serve as an advertisement of their intention to sell coke on the same basis as they sold gas. Thus the two terms are expressed equally in the company title. The gradual change to plain 'gas' seems to reflect a diminution of the need to advertise coke for sale through the company name and the growing importance of gas as a universal street lighting medium.

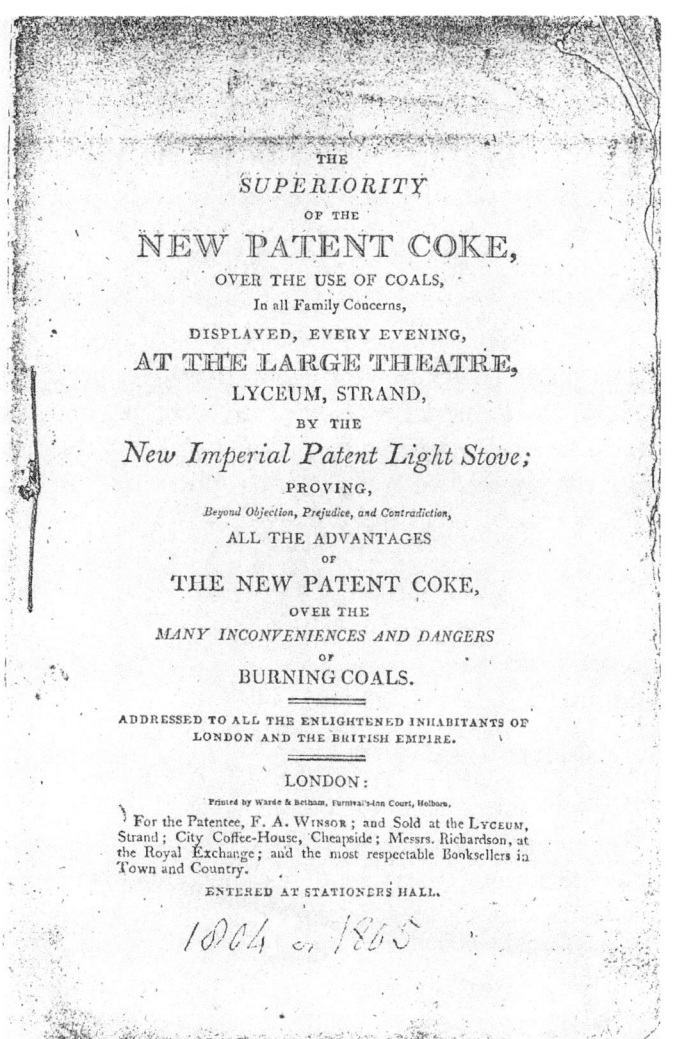

THE PATENT COKE COMPANY

To the first promoters of the Chartered Company it seemed that the manufacture and sale of coke was as important as the production of gas for lighting. Frederick Albert Winsor wrote several pamphlets promoting the company. His first, in 1804, was called:

'The Superiority Of The New Patent Coke Over The Use Of Coals, In All Family Concerns, Displayed Every Evening, At The Large Theatre, Lyceum, Strand ...' Addressed To All The Enlightened Inhabitants Of London And The British Empire'.

The second, which also appeared in 1804, was:

'New Patriotic Company, Imperial & National Patent Company, For Establishing Sundry Manufactories To Make & Extract For Home Consumption & Exportation,

171

Coke, Charcoal, Ammonia, Acids, Oil, Tar, Chemical Salts, &c. From All The Combustibles In Nature; & For Applying The Inflammable Air Obtained From The Raw Fuel To The Purposes Of Heating, Boiling, Smelting, Lighting, Illuminating'.

This second leaflet appears to say that the most important activity of the proposed company would be to make coke and chemicals. The manufacture of 'inflammable air' appears as the third activity by a very long way. It appears as if Winsor's first intention was to start a coke company – to which 'gas' was added as an afterthought.

There is more evidence for Winsor's original intentions. In 1818, seven years after the Chartered Company had begun manufacture of gas, 'coke' was included as an entry in Abraham Rees' *Encyclopaedia*. Rees highlights a patent held by *'Mr. Winsor ... for the manufacture of a superior kind of coke'*. That Rees picked on Winsor as a major element in coke manufacture suggests that Winsor's publicity methods had been successful and that he was seen as the purveyor of something new and that was – coke.

Of course many of Winsor's claims about coke were made before the launch of the Chartered Company were just 'puffs', aimed at attracting finance. The public might be more ready to invest in coke – which was already in use and profitable – than in gas lighting which was still unknown.

The Chartered Company's were to emphasis their production of 'coke' at the 1809 Parliamentary Enquiry and this can be shown to partly be tactical. Their defence strategy was described in a brief drawn up by Boulton and Watt's lawyers and now in the Birmingham archive. This speculates that Chartered were to mount *'the defence of a corporate coke company'*. It has already been suggested above that Winsor's supporters saw the promotion of by-products as a way of avoiding a confrontation with Boulton and Watt on any arguments about the priority of the invention of gas for lighting.

For one reason or another, before the Enquiry James Watt Jnr. sent a note to Winsor at the 'Patent Coke Office Pall Mall' – the pencilled address is in his handwriting. This is the same Pall Mall address as that at which Winsor was giving lectures and demonstrations on gas lighting.

Winsor was not the only person to produce something called 'patent coke'. He himself mentioned *'that celebrated haacter (sic) Doctor Clarke who set up a patent coke company in 1804.'* He also described a *'phantasmagory celebrity'*, a Mr. Philipstall 'who subscribed to a patent coke company'. Patent coke seems to have been a feature of the period. It was a way of identifying the product although what these patents were and who held them is more a matter for conjecture probably neither Mr Philipstall or indeed Dr. Clarke whose names are not clear in the patent lists for that date.

Winsor himself took out four patents. The earliest in May 1804 begins with an oven for *'inflammable air'* and leaves *'coke and charcoal to the end'*. In the next, February 1807, *'coal and charcoal'* have moved from the end of the citation but are not the prime subject

172

which is still the *'oven or furnace'*. There were two more – in March 1808 and February 1809 – these both put *'a superior fuel of coke'* as the main reason for the patent and *'inflammable air'* is now at the end. Clearly something had changed his mind.

Strangely, his leaflet about *'patent coke'* dates from 1804 when *'coke and charcoal'* were the last things to be mentioned.

Coke sales were to be either to industry or for use in the home but Winsor wrote his leaflet about patent coke to interest the potential domestic market and set his descriptions of use in the home. Coke used in a domestic setting would not necessarily be suitable for industrial use – although knowledge about types of coke was limited in 1804. Winsor avoided discussion on this point by saying that his coke could, with extra firing, be used by industry. Coke was well known to industry and perhaps needed less advertisement but nevertheless it was clearly hoped to appeal to potential customers both in the home and the workplace.

The Chartered Company, and probably several of its immediate successors, was set up with the manufacture of coke very much in mind. The *'Gas Light and Coke Company'* could just as well have been called the *'Coke and Gas Light Company'* and there would have been no difference to its activities.

When the new company began business, coke sales were relatively easy to set up, in contrast to some other proposed activities. There has been a great deal of emphasis on gas, its early manufacture and sale. It may have been the coke sales that got the first companies up and running.

PROPOSALS FOR USING COKE

There were good reasons why the gas company promoters thought that coke sales would be profitable – it already well known, particularly in industry. Both Winsor and the Chartered Company promoters gave publicity to it by listing a number of suggestions of how to use it – all of them based on current practice.

Frederick Accum described some of these practices at the 1809 Parliamentary Enquiry. He opened the proposed gas company's evidence and began at once with a submission on the use of coke and its virtues as a fuel. This coke, however, was special because it had been produced by *'Mr. Winsor's method'*. Accum said that this way of making coke was *'greatly and generally superior'*. He was not, however, he said *'permitted to disclose the process'* although he told the Enquiry that he had used *'Winsor's coke'* to smelt 'lead ore, copper and iron'.

Accum went on to give a report of a demonstration which had been specially set up for the Enquiry. This coke had been tested in a blast furnace at *'Mr. Joseph's foundry in*

Lambeth'. At a guess this is John Joseph who had a foundry on Narrow Wall on the Lambeth riverside. Mr. Joseph had previously made his own coke in a stove *'open at the mouth only'*. Winsor's coke-making process had brought the charge time down by ten minutes, and gave more heat. The resulting iron manufactured at Lambeth *'would run through the eye of a needle'*. David Walker, *'Mr. Joseph's foundry man'*, gave evidence to the Enquiry. He found that *'Mr. Winsor's coke ... gave more heat than my master's coke'* and said that he would definitely pay more for it *'if I had the business in my own hands'*.

The Chartered Company's promoters had a number of other suggestions about the use of coke. It might, for instance, be ground up as an ingredient in gunpowder. It would then substitute for charcoal bought from France – an obvious advantage since Britain and France were then at war. No more is heard of this idea but since any experiments conducted on such a sensitive matter would, no doubt, have been secret, the silence is not surprising. The potential of use for gas by-products in explosives may explain some of William Congreve's interest in the early industry. The *'cylinders'* in which charcoal was made for gunpowder in a process partly developed by Congreve are forerunners of the gas-making retorts, as Brenda Buchanan explained in her *Gunpowder, Explosives and the State*.

ACTUAL COKE SALES

From the start, gas companies sold coke; or rather, as Joseph Hedley explained, they sold what was left after they had taken about a third of the output for their own use as fuel.

Gas Companies employed special staff for coke sales. In the gasworks coke staff were autonomous and important. In a South Met. List of staff for 1836 the *'coke clerk'* has a different heading to staff in the *'indoor office'*. In the Co-partnership Journal in 1904, John Surman reminisced of the time when the senior coke clerk had his own office, not out of doors, but below the manager's office where it shared space with the store room and storekeeper. They were then easily available to the public. He was in effect a departmental head with two junior clerks under him. At South Met. in the 1850s, this was the same staffing complement as the Works Manager according to Layton in his *History of South Met.* The Chartered Company had staff like this from the start, as did every subsequent gas company.

The gas companies sold coke *'over the counter'* for cash. There are still many who remember the collection of coke by children for use at home in the 20th century. It is very likely that these sales of small amounts of coke began very early and that, from the start, anyone who wanted one bag or so only had to call at the coke office door. Sales at this level are very difficult to check on at any time – and at a distance of two hundred years, almost impossible.

174

Only one early ledger survives for the Chartered Company, and none for any of the other early London Companies. Unfortunately no records appear to have survived of day-to-day sales, if they were ever kept. Such sales provided a source of ready cash that could come in very useful in times of trouble. For example, in 1854, the Sydenham Gas Company's minutes record how they used coke income to pay the wages after their Company Secretary disappeared together with the names and addresses of their customers.

In the early years of the Chartered, coke sold steadily. Occasionally income was reported to the directors and was recorded in the minute books. These intermittent notes allow a snapshot of their sales. In April 1817 they took £187 12s.3d. for coke compared with £469. 16s. 6d. for gas. By January 1820 coke sales have risen to £305. 13s. 7d. but this time there is no corresponding gas sales figure.

Board Minutes usually recorded only the major sales and enquiries. For example when the Board of Ordnance – a very important potential customer – asked for coke in 1815 it was reported to the Board. These occasional references in the minute books give the only information as to who used Winsor's patent coke.

Some examples of the thousands who must have bought coke from the gas companies

Name of Customer	Gas Co.	Purchased	Address	Trade
Thomas Farmer	GLCC	Coke Sal ammoniac Sulphate of ammonia Carbonate of ammonia	St.Agnes Place, Kennington Later West Ham & Silvertown	Vitriol works using pyrites
William Coles Child	Phoenix	Coke	Lambeth East Greenwich	Coal merchant
William Gladdish	GLCC	Coke, breeze	Cliffe Cottage Shore, Northfleet	Lime merchant

CARTERS

Deliveries of coke to those customers, who did not collect it themselves, seem to have been undertaken by independent carters who dealt directly with customers. In 1817 the Chartered Company advertised for tenders *'per caldron for coke'*. A caldron, as a measure, rather depending on local custom and practice. These carters trimmed the coke 'for *threepence a caldron if required by the customer'* as well as delivering it.

Carters were not necessarily specialist hauliers but combined this activity with another. Their main profession seems usually, and inevitably, to have been that of coal merchant. The Chartered's three works were all landlocked with no water access — - it was not until later that the company acquired wharfage facilities. Carters serving their works would have had to use horse and cart, but as other companies built riverside or canal side works so cartage would have been done by barge. Coke was only one of many cargoes undertaken by barge owners, who often combined river haulage with lime burning, brick making and other activities. Perhaps more unusual was F.J.Bouchet who combined carting with ownership of a brass foundry in the Old Kent Road recorded by Chartered.

BARTERS

When gas companies minuted coke sales they naturally concentrated on those that needed a special decision by the board. Most of these were large industrial users. After 1820 these decisions include a number of barter deals, often involving coke, and another commodity which a gas company would normally buy in from an outside supplier. The Chartered Company records show the most frequent use of this practice as, although less often, do those of the Phoenix Company.

For example, the Chartered Company recorded swapping coke for oil of vitriol with Farmer, the Kennington chemical manufacturer in 1834.

Such barter deals were set up with suppliers who needed gas industry by-products. Gas companies used lime in their purification process — they got it from lime burners who used coke. The use of this type of transaction, throws even more doubt on the accuracy of any cash prices which are recorded.

It also illuminates the role played by the gas companies in the industries which surrounded them.

176

COAL TAR

COAL TAR BEFORE THE GAS INDUSTRY

Perhaps the substance, which most readily comes to mind when talking about gas industry by-products, is coal tar. The next few chapters will look at production of tar by the early industry and at what indications there are for the profitable use of it. It is not proposed to look at the more sophisticated chemical products made after the mid-century but at the simpler mixtures which preceded them.

TAR - COAL TAR -WHAT IS IT?

Up until the 1820s – and often afterwards – 'tar' meant a distillate of wood – sometimes called 'Stockholm' or 'Archangel' tar, showings its places of origin in Scandinavia and the Baltic States. Of course, words and what they mean can change a lot.

So – what was 'tar'? While that may appear obvious to us, in the early 19th century it was much less clear what the word meant. 'Tar' was the name of a black sticky substance derived from wood and which was widely used, particularly as a preservative in ships, and thus important to naval and commercial shipbuilding and repair. When coal gas was first made, a solid substance was recovered as part of the manufacturing process when the new gas was 'washed'. This was like 'tar' and seemed suitable for use in the same way and so it began to have the same name. But what we now commonly call 'tar' – coal tar – was then called 'mineral' tar.

This 'coal' or 'mineral' tar became available at the end of the 19th century when ideas about such substances were changing. Initially it was produced by specialist experimenters and companies but the new gas companies meant that it was suddenly available in large quantities. As its availability increased so did the research into its use. This led on to new ideas about what exactly 'tar' was. Two strands of research – for practical use and for ideas – ran in parallel and fed off each other.

Tar distillers – working with both wood and coal tars – used a wide variety of words to describe the tar fractions which they were dealing with. There is a great deal of confusion because the words they used have also changed in meaning over the last two centuries. Before discussing the gas companies, the tar distillers and their work, it might be useful to look at some of these words and what was actually being made.

When scientists identify new substances they coin names for them. One generation's batch of names is superseded by the next's. Such names often change their meanings in the process. A good example of this is 'creosote' – a word used in the 2000's for a coal-tar derivative commonly used as a preservative paint, and is available in every DIY store. George Lunge recorded that the Berlin chemist, Reichenbach, coined the word 'Kreosote' in 1830, to describe a product of wood tar and it was not used to describe a coal tar distillate until after 1836.

Frederick Christian Accum, whose role as an advisor to the Chartered Company has been mentioned above, described tar manufacture in two books published before 1820. – 'Practical Treatise' and 'Description of the Process'. As the Chartered's consultant on chemistry what he says can be taken as a good guide for the thinking of the company at that time. 'Tar', he said in the Treatise was made as part of the process of gas manufacture, during which it was 'deposited in a vessel to receive it'.

He went on to describe in 'Description of the Process' some of things which could he made from the deposited tar. It should be condensed to get 'essential oil or oil of tar'. Through evaporation 'coal oil' could be obtained – he described this as a 'yellowish inferior kind of naphtha'. Otherwise, he said, it could be boiled for 'pitch' which by the 'evaporation by heat gives asphaltum. What did it all mean?

Georg Lunge writing in 'Coal Tar', a century after Accum, discussed this problem of the names by which substances were known. As an illustration, he provided the various definitions of 'pitch'. 'This denoted many substances which have nothing to do with coal tar.. such as natural bitumen'. He went on to describe 'asphalt' as 'the residue in the retort once the light oil is distilled off' but adds that 'to tar distillers it is ordinary pitch' mixed with other things... and that in the past it meant 'bitumen'.

All of these words for tar distillates have meanings that were changing throughout the period of the early gas industry. Obviously, this leads to some difficulty in understanding the activities of those who used them.

PITCH

'Pitch' is perhaps the simplest. It was understood to refer to the residue left after distillation of the first 'coal oil'. It is the substance, which the British Tar Company sold, and which, as we shall see, the Chartered Company tried to sell to the Navy.

NAPHTHA

Many complications arise in the definition of 'naphtha', a word in common use in the 19th century. In a modern (Chambers) dictionary it is defined as a 'vague name for the inflammable liquid distillates from coal-tar'. Earlier use was more precise – Thorpe's 19th

178

century "*Chemical Encyclopaedia*" defines it as '*the volatiles observed in substances*'. H.Scherer, in his *Newcomen Transactions* article of 1952 says that the '*naphtha*' from tar was identified in 1779 by a Giovanni Fabricini although '*until 1823 it was called coal-oil, volatile-oil or spirits of tar*'.

Gasworks engineers used the word '*naphtha*' for some coal oils and in the 1820s labourers in the works referred to it as '*fat*', as described in *The Chemist* by 'a *Young Chemist*'. Meanwhile academic chemists like W.T.Brande' insisted that '*naphtha*' only applied to the products of distillation of natural bitumen'. Thus '*naphtha*' meant one thing to scientists and another to those working in the field. By the 21st century the precise meaning, already obsolescent in 1820, has been lost.

WHAT IS COAL TAR?

When newly-made gas emerges from the retort it is full of impurities and needs to be cleaned. Normally the gas is channelled from the retort, through a condensation process and then into wash water. One result, said Parkes in *Elementary Treatise* is the production of a '*tenacious bituminous fluid called tar*'. Coal tar was known before the gas industry began to produce it. It had been well-promoted and there is no reason to believe that it did not sell well within its market.

It is perhaps useful to look at a definition of tar in *A New General English Dictionary* of 1758:

"TAR. A gross liquor issuing or extracted from various trees, exceeding useful upon many occasions, especially for the smearing of cordage and planks belonging to ships"..... i.e. a wood-based product from the Baltic.

Some industrialists knew that a similar substance could be made from coal in theory but they had not found it easy to manufacture. They did not want to make gas, but to produce tar for a market they knew existed. Supplies from the Baltic were under increasing pressure during the Napoleonic wars and it was important to find a supply of tar from a source that was not under threat. Coal, or 'mineral', tar seemed to be the answer.

One industrialist who had tried to make coal tar was John Champion from Bristol, whose father's experiments with gas manufacture in Pimlico have been described above. He had registered a patent for tar manufacture in 1799. James Watt's friend John Roebuck, the Birmingham vitriol manufacturer, had also tried. Other experiments had been sponsored by landed estate owners – the Clerks of Penicuik and the Fitzwilliams at Elsecar.

179

In letters preserved in the National Library of Scotland Archibald Cochrane, Ninth Earl of Dundonald, was happy to point out that they had all failed but he had, to some extent, succeeded in coal tar manufacture.

AN OPERATIONAL TAR WORKS

Dundonald, was not alone. In 1791 the Society of Arts awarded a prize for an account of a tar-making plant at the Dudley Wood Ironworks. It was described in *Transactions of the Society of Arts* by the winner, a William Pitt, "*On Converting the Smoke*". Members of the Attwood family probably leased the ironworks at Dudley Wood and they certainly held it from 1800.

The next generation of Attwoods became very wealthy through a wide range of manufactures, which included chemicals, and investment in the London gas industry, while others, most notably, Thomas, went into politics. The Dudley Wood foundry itself was later managed by Philip Taylor, the inventor of oil gas and brother of John Taylor, the mining engineer.

The actual idea for the tar recovery plant at Dudley, which William Pitt described, came from the Earl of Dundonald.

At Dudley Wood *'smoke from steam engines'* was converted into tar. The process was itself a way of using waste products. Pitt described how *'the iron masters give the tar works raw coal gratis and in return get the coke'*, while the *'proprietors get the smoke for their labour and interest of capital'*. Tar was recovered from the condensed *'smoke'* through an elaborate process, described in detail in the published report.

THE NINTH EARL OF DUNDONALD

The Dudley Wood tar works was one of several opened as part of the pioneering work on the extraction and use of tar from coals which Dundonald had initiated.

The Earl's 'real' name was Archibald Cochrane – and it is worth noting that Cochrane was to become an important name in the Black Country where the Earl's brother was another emergent industrialist. Another famous Cochrane – Thomas the naval hero, discredited MP, revolutionary and future Admiral of Chile, Peru and Great Britain – was the 9th Earl's eldest son and he too was to have an involvement in the early use of coal tar. In general it could be said, about the Cochranes, that originality was a family trait. There are numerous biographies of Thomas (eventually the 10th Earl). He is the model for many a naval adventurer in novels and films. What are rarely included are his contributions to contemporary technologies or indeed the original and important work of his father and some other family members. There is however a large archive in the National Library of Scotland and some accounts of their scientific work – most notably in Clow's *'Chemical Revolution'*.

Archibald, the 9th Earl, had, in addition to eccentricity, *'scientific capabilities'*. He had inherited the earldom of Dundonald and the estate at Culross in 1778. Culross is an ancient industrial and mining town on the north side of the Forth between Glasgow and Edinburgh where coal was mined from the 17th century. Culross village is a showplace owned by the National Trust for Scotland who, when I visited in the 1990s, showed little or no sign of recognition of either Dundonald's pioneering tar works in the village or of his naval hero son. Indeed even the former "HMS Cochrane' naval base, just down the road, is now known merely as Rosyth Dockyard.

The ownership of an earldom might appear to be a way to get wealth and status. This was not so in the case of Dundonald who set about trying to rebuild the family fortunes by means of new manufactures. As an ex-naval officer, he knew that there was a demand for tar in shipbuilding, and that it was important to find a supply. Tar and pitch were, he said in letters to the Admiralty, *'essential to a maritime power'*. In 1781 he patented a tar-making process and the next year opened a tar works in Culross itself.

Although it was later said that *'from a naval nation Lord Dundonald deserves a statue of gold'* his tar sales to the Navy were not successful. From the 1780s Dundonald promoted the use of coal tar to be put on ships' bottoms to prevent the ravages of Teredo worm and his publicity leaflets –*'An account of Coal Tar'* include glowing references from ships' owners. Discussions were undertaken with the Dutch Navy but in Britain he had little success. Ship repairers were notably ungrateful for his work to prevent damage to ships – which threatened to put them out of business.

Another of his tar works was sited at Muirkirk where it was managed by his cousin, John Loudon Macadam. Macadam was the developer of a road building process but although *'macadamised'* roads are known for their use of tar, this is in fact a later development and Macadam himself did not suggest it Five Dundonald tar works were opened in the English Midlands – one at Dudley Wood, and another, better known, at Calcutts in Shropshire. Despite his involvement in a wide range of other chemical projects with industrialists in Shropshire, Newcastle and elsewhere, Dundonald's fortunes remained obstinately at low ebb.

THE BRITISH TAR COMPANY

Because of Dundonald's financial problems, the tar-making operations were taken into a manufacturing and sales organisation, British Tar Company. This organisation appears to have sold considerable quantities of tar although (despite the punning name) it seems to have been sold to industry rather than to the Navy. As time went by *'Dundonald revealed himself more and more as a potentially disastrous partner'* and management of

181

the company passed to other family members who made *'considerable fortunes'*. Dundonald *'led the life of a perpetual fugitive.... suffering from a profound, if largely justified, persecution complex'*.

In the British Tar Company's works, coal was burnt in the bottom of "*stoves*". Smoke from the coal went up into "*proper horizontal tunnels*" and then into a "*capacious and close tunnel 100 yards or more in length*" which was "*covered on the top with a shallow pond of water*". The reason for this pond was to condense the gases: "*the chill of the water condensed the smoke*" and the tar then "*falls on the floor of the tunnel*".

Tar was marketed by the company in grades that were each defined by a crown and number. Their instruction booklet: *Directions for Using Coal tar'* published in 1789 said that the products ranged from rough tar, straight from the kiln, sent out only "*if ordered*", to distillates for high quality work.

Dundonald could easily have added gas lighting to his repertoire of manufactures. He simply seems not to have been interested in developing it. He certainly knew about coal gas – it was included in the index to his unwritten book *'Contents of a Proposed Publication'* on the uses of tar. There is also some eyewitness evidence that he sometimes used gas for lighting in his house at Culross as described by Thomson in *Proceedings of the Philosophical Society of Glasgow* in 1843. He had no known connection with the gas industry itself, although he lived well into the era of gas lighting. He would also have had a good case for a challenge to the Chartered Company on priority of invention. Weston, Boulton and Watt's lawyer, whose brief, now in the Birmingham archive, says that the lawyers thought that the British Tar Company would issue such a challenge unless certain unspecified, clauses in the Chartered's Bill were dropped.

Dundonald had an unerring eye for not making his fortune. He was left with very little to show for his years of work. In the 1820s, when the gas industry was already very prosperous, he was reduced to writing to the Admiralty to ask for financial help and support. His long letters, heavily underlined in alternate red and green ink, stress his contribution to the Navy and the nation and that of his naval hero, albeit discredited, eldest son.

THE BRITISH TAR COMPANY
THE LONDON CONNECTION

In Northfleet, Kent, one of the roads running down downhill to the river is Burch Road. On either side of it the land falls sharply away to the old chalk workings with which the area is surrounded.

182

Despite the slightly different spelling a Mr. Birch was a key figure in tar sales before 1810. Burch Road once led to Crete Hall, built by Benjamin Burch. That Mr. Burch of Northfleet and Mr. Birch of Limehouse are one and the same can be confirmed by other comments about the marriage of his daughter to Jeremiah Rosher in Beck's *History of Rotherhithe*. Rosher was a lime burner after whom the surrounding area, Rosherville, is named, as we learn from Benson's *History of Gravesend*

In 1810 they are listed 'Birch, *Rhode and Cleveley of Walbrook and Limehouse'*. Cleveley also had a Northfleet connection having built warships there. At the Walbrook address they were also known as the *'British Colour Company'* and – of course – the British Tar Company.

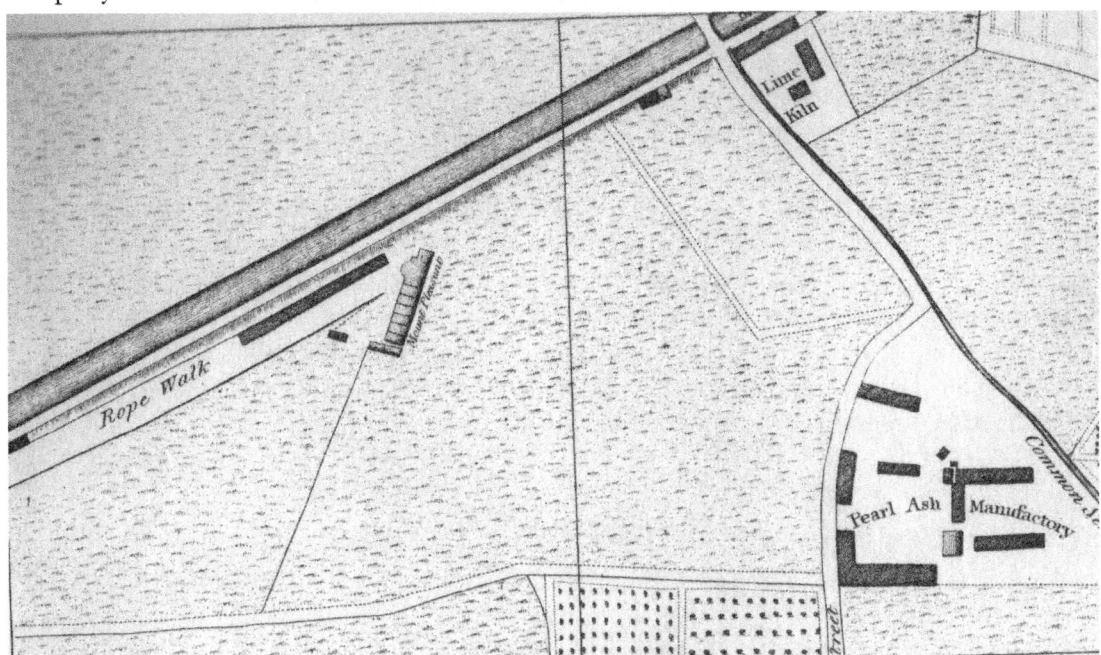

Birch ran a ship chandlery business, licensed to sell, and probably make, tar on behalf of Dundonald's company. Birch's tar works had been opened in 1787 on the Limehouse Cut – slightly south east of the point at which it crosses North Street on Bow Common and show by a lime kiln on the Harwood Plan.. In the 1790s, Dundonald set up a chemical works there in association with a group of Newcastle financiers – close to, if not on the same site as, the Birch tar works. At that date it was an ideal place for such a works, on a newly-built canal with excellent road links into the heart of the London shipbuilding area. In the location of their sites and in their families and partners, members of the Birch firm were well-placed to take advantage of Thamesside shipbuilding and its associated industries.

Wigram, one of the biggest shipbuilders on the River in 1809, bought tar from Birch and there is no reason to believe they were the only ones to do so. Birch claimed that his works was the only tar works in England that also made oil, colour and varnishes.

183

His tar sold in *'large quantities'* as witnesses to the 1809 Parliamentary Enquiry affirmed. Much of it would have gone to London shipbuilders. Tar was well-known in London before the gas industry came

WHAT DID TAR DISTILLERS SELL?

One of the clearest definitions of what tar distillers sold is the earliest. In 1789 the British Tar Company produced a sales booklet which described the different tar fractions sold. This is *Description of the Directions for Using Coal Tar & Varnish*, published suitably in Broseley, in 1789. It described: *'Tar No 1... Raw tar from the kiln. No.2. Freed by the kiln from added water.'* This was followed by three more *'marks'* This easily understood definition of types of tar by a simple gradation is very rare — usually there is an ever-changing mass of names, most with several meanings.

Winsor and his original supporters advertised their intentions for by-products before the Chartered Gas Company began business. When they describe tar it is far from clear whether they were advertising the raw or processed tar. They generally failed to mention the need for processing at all. They tried to explain what gasworks tar was — or rather what it was like, or what they thought it was like. Winsor explained in *'Considerations'* that coal tar *'resembles common tar'* and was *'applicable to the same uses as tar from Sweden'* — that is tar made from wood.

RAW TAR FROM THE KILN

The British Tar Company sold, *'if ordered'*, tar which was completely unprocessed. Tar of this sort was known to be a preservative if it was painted on wood — Lunge says that Phillipe Lebon, the subsequently murdered French scientist and tar manufacturer, had recommended it as such in 1799. In England some discussion, and promotion, appeared in the national specialist press.

A Benjamin Cook, of Birmingham, wrote to the *Journal of Natural Philosophy* in October 1808 to describe his experiments on the use of coal tar. Cook appears to have been a toy maker or a brass founder with an interest in gas manufacture — in December of the same year he also published an account of his gas making apparatus. He thought raw coal tar would make *'an excellent coating for all out-of-doors work such as gates, fencing and paling'*. Other letters and articles on this theme followed. In 1809 an article in the *Edinburgh Review* pointed out that tar was *'useful as a coating to prevent damage by wind and rain to timber'*.

Ten years later such use of raw tar for outdoor work was again put forward as a good idea when *Mechanics Magazine* published a number of letters extolling its use by farmers in December 1827. Christopher Davy described the uses of coal tar as — *'a most valuable*

184

product'. He said it could be used to paint on gates and doors; and for farmers used on hurdles and as a roofing material. Another letter came from *'Amateur Mechanic'* who had used tar to paint his roof tiles and as a result they no longer blew off or let in water.

Why were such letters written? They can only have been promotional 'puffs' – were Christopher Davy and 'Amateur Mechanic' trying to sell something? As the century progressed such uses of coal tar must have become increasingly better-known and such letters were no longer needed. These letters provide a pointer to the sort of ways in which coal tar, would have been used in the days of the early gas industry.

TAR PAINT AND VARNISH

Before 1800 varnish was made from various mixes of oils, many secret, and used by the *'carriage trade'*. Coal tar varnishes were rather rougher than that. In the early days of the gas industry a number of mixes for painting on wood were known as *'varnish'* or *'tar varnish'* or *'naphtha varnish'*. In the early days of the gas industry the British Tar Company's grades of tar sold before 1800 had included a *'pitch varnish'* and *'an oil used for varnish'*. In the 1820s Frederick Albert Winsor, Jnr. described *'essential oils in different qualities, applicable, instead of turps, in painting from the finest to the coarsest'* and *'asphaltum for ... japanning and varnish of the highest gloss'*. There were, no doubt, many recipes.

Initially coal tar varnish seems to have been considered as a substitute for other, more expensive, ingredients. In 1809, Benjamin Cook had said that it could substitute for *'the tar spirit brought from Russia and of vast importance to manufacturers'*. He described the first distillation of the tar as *'a substitute for turpentine'* because it *'takes as beautiful a polish'*. In addition, he said, the pitch left after the second distillation *'forms an ingredient for black varnish'*. Cook had produced a *'waiter... japanned with varnish made from the residuum and the volatile oil'* and said that he hoped to put items like this into production.

The subject of varnish had been investigated before the early gas industry made tar for varnish more widely available. Dundonald used tar to make 'varnish' in 1789 and Sir John Black, who examined Dundonald's work, described how *'volatile oil'* was distilled from boiled tar for it.

In 1808 Cook gave details about how varnish was made. He produced three specimens of spirit, each the product of a re-distillation and explained how these distillates could be used instead of the more familiar oil of turpentine. It made a varnish, he said, in which *'there appears to be no manner of difference'*.

One *'manner of difference'* however, may have been the smell and the 1809 Parliamentary Enquiry panel questioned Accum about this. Of course, he denied any bad smell, but the question is an indication of the image which coal tar varnishes always seem to have had as a cheap, and perhaps nasty, substitute for more expensive traditional oils like linseed and turpentine.

This was a bad start. Coal tar took a long time to lose an image of something rather nasty, the use of which often needed to be concealed. The next chapters will look at how the Chartered Gas Company and its competitors went about marketing the tar which, they had been assured, would bring them in a vast profit.

THE CHARTERED GAS COMPANY
AND
TAR SALES TO THE NAVY

The Chartered, the first gas company, had been set up with a remit to manufacture tar and sell it profitably. They had before them the example of Lord Dundonald and the British Tar Company. It was known that the Royal Navy (and commercial shipowners) wanted a means to protect ships from rot.

They were fortunate enough to find someone who knew about both shipbuilding and tar to make and sell it for them. It may have seemed that tar was going to be as easy as coke to sell – all that had to be done was to prove its worth.

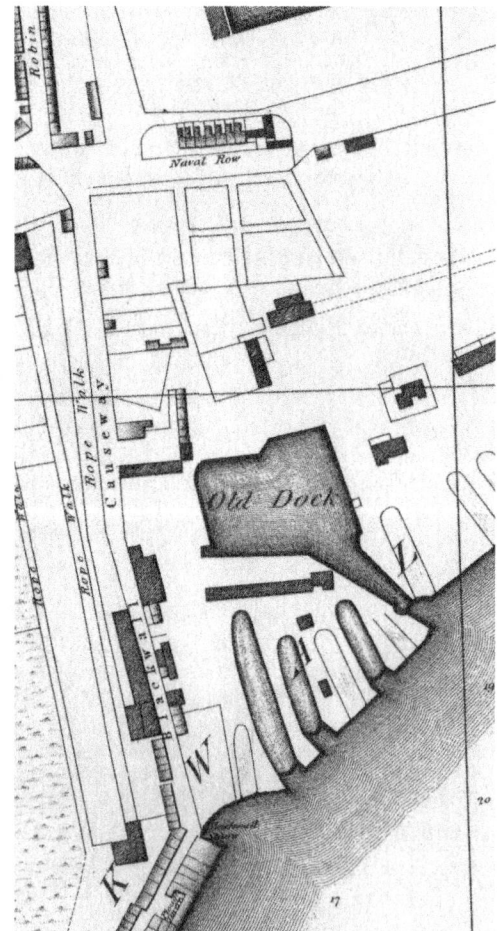

In August 1816 a Thomas Dalton wrote to the Chartered Co. *'about tar'*. He was foreman caulker at Wells, Wigram and Green's shipbuilding business at Blackwall Yard and as Banbury says in *'Shipbuilders of the Thames and Medway'* it was the *'oldest private business in Britain'* – and a working shipyard until 1988. The yard had gone through a number of changes over the years. The site had been laid out in 1587 and it had later, in 1614, been Perry's Yard'. In 1784 it was described as *'the most capacious private dockyard in the Kingdom and probably the world'*. Later George Green bought the yard, and a statue of one of his descendants still stands in the East India Dock Road. Robert Wigram and William Wells became partners in the yard around 1810. Wigram and Wells went on to become investors in the early gas industry. Dalton had been at the yard for 31 years in 1816 and must have witnessed the building of a dry dock still preserved on site today.

Dalton wrote to the Chartered Company from Strong's Buildings, in the recently completed East India Dock Road. He lived in Naval Row, next to the East India Dock itself and on the road to Wigram's shipyard. The area was still semi-rural and he had a large garden plot attached to his house. Like other Poplar residents of the time he kept a pig (which the Poplar Health Committee in 1833 recorded to be a 'clean' pig).

Leaving his domestic arrangements aside, Dalton was an expert on the use of coal tar in shipbuilding and gave evidence to the 1809 Parliamentary Enquiry about it. He told how Wigram had bought coal tar from Birch. It had been used in the shipyard, intermittently, for many years. In his employment in the shipyard Dalton had worked with this and other tars. He was a caulker — a profession once commemorated by the *'Jolly Caulkers'* pub in Rotherhithe now sadly a grocery store. Caulkers made sure that ships were watertight and Dalton described, to the Enquiry, how paper dipped into tar was used for the purpose.

The exact relationship between Dalton and the Chartered Company is not clear. He seems, initially, to have been employed to sell tar for them on some sort of agency basis. To start with he wrote, on their behalf, to the Navy Board — the civilian body in charge of naval purchasing. The Board agreed to let him undertake 'experiments' — in fact demonstrations — at Deptford Dockyard.

The two inner London Royal Dockyards at Deptford and Woolwich had begun to concentrate on repair work during the preceding century. Deptford, because of its proximity to the Navy Board offices in Seething Lane was used for experimental or new work and it was there that officers would make an assessment and then decide whether to place an order for the Chartered's coal tar.

...AND THE NAVY

In 1809 lobbyists working on behalf of the Chartered had pointed out that 15,000 tons of tar was bought from abroad every year for naval use. There was considerable interest in ways of preventing rot of various kinds in shipbuilding. Within the Chartered Gas Company itself some subscribers had a specialist interest in the subject- the interest of the Duke of Athol has already been noted.

The discussion on rot-proofing was not new and the Navy must have known a great deal about coal tar and its potential. Dundonald had tried to sell his tar to the Navy thirty years earlier and claimed in *'Account of the Uses'* that tests on it had been undertaken at Sheerness Dockyard. He had tried to sell coal tar as a preservative against woodboring marine creatures such as crustaceans (e.g. *Limnoria lignorum or gribble)* and

187

the molluscs commonly called 'teredo worms' (*Teredo navalis* or naval shipworm), which were a great scourge to wooden ships. On the other hand Dalton also hoped to sell tar for use in caulking.

There were other contemporary developments in the applications for coal tar being made by Naval architects, although this information would not have been widely available outside naval circles and was probably unknown to either Dundonald or Dalton. From around 1810 designers of warships considered the use of a coating of coal tar on ships for sophisticated structural reasons: to turn them into a *'solid body'*.

It is to be assumed, therefore, that the use of coal tar was not completely unknown to the Navy when Dalton drew attention to the use of tar for caulking. He pointed out to them possible savings of *'8/6d. per barrel in dipping paper beside oil and fuel'*. He followed by suggesting that they might like to take 100 tons *'for use on ships' bottoms'*. He later suggested tar in rope making and offered to demonstrate by making up some rope using Chartered's tar.

Dalton's persistence gained some success. In September 1817 the Navy Board officers discussed with him the purchase of coal tar *'in barrels similar to those in which [wood] tar is imported from Russia and Sweden'*. It was, however, nearly a year before they placed an actual order for 10,000 tons of coal tar at Woolwich.

Tar had, at last, begun to sell to the market for which the Chartered Company and their backers intended it.

POPLAR TAR WORKS

It was at this time, in 1817, that the Chartered took the decision to open its own tar works. Dalton was to be in charge and he set about preparing estimates setting up the new works. Premises at Poplar *'for one year certain at a rent of £61'* were obtained from Wigram who also agreed to build a wall dividing the site up.

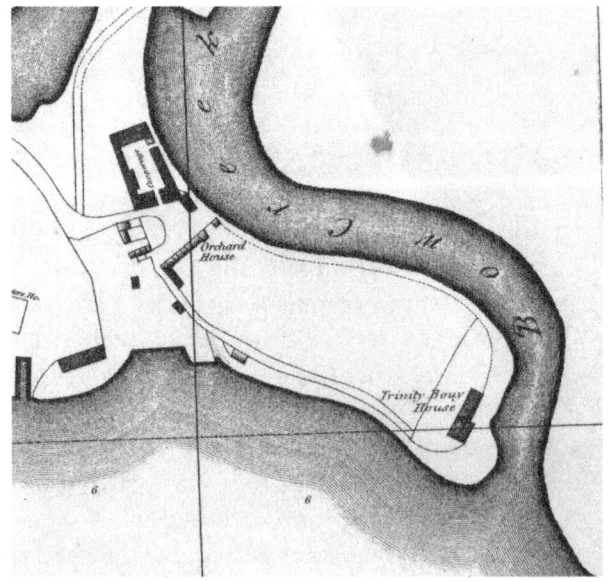

The place chosen was in Orchard Place, on one of the convolutions of the River Lea as it nears the Thames. It was on the southeast side of the northern spur of Orchard Place, and had a frontage on the Lea — in the

188

1990s it was part of the Pura Food complex and in 2020, inevitably, it is flats.

Thomas Dalton bought a *'crane and pans'* and other equipment and a special committee were appointed to oversee the works. They duly visited Poplar and reported to the main Court of Governors on the buildings and the products, which Dalton was considering for manufacture. So that future meetings could be held in the sort of accommodation to which they were accustomed *'a committee table, a Pembroke table, and 8 mahogany chairs'* were bought.

The works expanded and over the next ten years more equipment was bought: in 1820 a grinder for making colouring material and, four years later, a deal plank to make a tub for washing spirits.

Dalton worked hard to promote his products. He prepared information about the use of tar on ships, producing samples *'of felt dipped in first mineral tar and the other with Stockholm or Archangel tar'* with which to show the difference. He wrote to the Board of Ordnance asking them *'to try the black varnish on gun carriages'*. He contacted the King's Buoy Warden of Trinity House, whose wharf was next to Wigram and Wells's shipyard, asking them to try his tar on a buoy. The Chartered Court of Governors minuted its obligation to him for his *'perseverance'*.

TAR SALES - THE POTENTIAL

It must have seemed that there was an endless market for the new tar in the shipping industry on the banks of the Thames. The West India Dock was newly built and more docks were under construction and planned in Wapping and Shadwell. It was a time of experiment with new methods and new materials for shipbuilding. The powerful East India Company had a depot immediately adjacent to both Blackwall Yard and the new tar works. They had a potential worth as a customer second only to the Admiralty. In addition *'on both banks of the Thames, eastward to Blackwall and Woolwich there were thriving shipyards and dry-docks'*. All were potential customers.

What neither they, nor Dalton, could have foreseen was that Thames timber shipbuilding had reached a peak. Many yards were building their last warships and would soon close. When they reopened it was to build ships of iron.

ACTUAL SALES

Not all the Chartered's tar sales were local. For instance, Messrs. Bayley, pitch tar and rosin merchants of Ford Street, Stonehouse, Devon, bought *'70 barrels of prepared coal tar*

189

to be shipped via the 'London Captain Paul'. An agent was appointed at Ipswich for sale of tar and varnishes at 5% commission. Further afield, Von Dadeltzen and Co., on behalf of Peltzer of Hamburg, bought tar, as did a *'Mr. Tucker of Boston'*, Massachusetts, and the Company set up special arrangements for shipment to America. Tar went to New York in the ship, 'Marcus Drew'.

Sales were not always successful; 10 barrels of black varnish were returned from Havre de Grace *'for want of a market'*. As the gas industry grew the Chartered inevitably faced local competition outside London.

...... AND THE NAVY

The relationship with the Navy Board continued. By 1819 naval shipbuilders was using coal tar as *'the best prevention against dry rot ... and every ship is now completely saturated with it by means of a forcing pump'* which Andrew Lambert has described in *'The Last Sailing Battlefleet'*.

By 1824 thirteen battleships had been injected but then the scheme was changed and linseed oil was used instead. The reason given by the Navy was the unacceptable smell of coal tar. The Navy had commissioned considerable research from Humphrey Davy on protecting ships' bottoms against woodborers and rot. Frank James in *'Davy in the Dockyard'* describes this. Davy hardly considered coal tar, and other strategies were now being adopted. Coal tar, despite Dundonald's years of lobbying, was no longer thought suitable.

In 1827 an offer by the gas company to sell 60,000 gallons of *'mineral tar'* to the Navy Board was not accepted. By then the Chartered was not the only gas company in business. This meant that the Navy Board could now advertise for tenders for tar – the Chartered must face competition for its tar sales.

After repeated failures in getting orders for tar from the Navy, the Company Secretary took over from Dalton the job of replying to tenders. He succeeded in getting an order from the Navy Board Commissioners for *'mineral tar fit for making cordage'*. Rope making was a field which makers of gas tar could well expect to enter by providing a cheap substitute for Stockholm tar.

Within three months of their first sale for rope making it appears that the rope makers of Woolwich Dockyard did not like the smell of coal tar. G.Smith of the Navy Office wrote to say that *'the use of mineral tar in the manufacture of cordage is having a pernicious effect on the workmen'*. He *'desired the Superintendent at Poplar to remove what is left at the ropeyard at Woolwich'*. Peckston, writing in 1823 in *The Theory and Practice of Gas Lighting* confirms that gas tar was disliked for rope making *'because of the rawness and destructive nature of the ammoniacal liquor'*. The Gas Company quickly sent the Board *'37,000 galls of tar that we feel confident will not be injurious to the health of their workmen'*. The Navy Board cancelled the order but agreed to take the rest of the order under threat of legal action.

Once again tar had lost a market because of smell.

POPLAR TAR WORKS CLOSES

Although there are many references to tar sales in the Chartered's Minute Books, the Court decided that the tar works was not successful and that it should be disposed of. In 1823 the coal merchant, Davey (of Davey Sawyer, Bankside), had made '*a proposal about Poplar which we cannot entertain'* but the works remained in business for several more years. In 1827 more discussions were held on disposal of the works, this time to a Mr. Bromley. In 1828 bad debts of £41 13s. 8d from tar customers were written off.

Five years later the Company commissioned a report on the tar works from a Mr. Hopwood, described as '*the chemist'*. His remit was to report '*concerning the results of his experiments on oil of tar ... and his opinions of the Poplar Station'*. It was decided that there was '*not much advantage in his proposals'* — whatever they were. The Court of Governors thought that '*despite the volume of business the works failed to pay its way'* as Everard comments.

By 1833 Dalton, who had put so much energy into the works, must have been in his sixties. It may be that he no longer felt able to continue. Closure marked the end of the hopes of the flourishing tar derivatives business so confidently envisaged in 1809. As we will see, however, this was not the end of the story — the marketing role, which the gas companies had not been able to fulfil, was to be taken up by others.

MORE AND DIFFERENT CUSTOMERS FOR TAR

If the gas companies were not able to distil and sell tar themselves then there were those who would. Tar had to be disposed of somehow and some were willing to take the task on.

From the very start of their operations the London gas companies sold raw tar direct to customers. Records of day-to-day sales have not survived, but the companies occasionally recorded in their minute books reports of sales and enquiries — usually those transactions that were particularly significant. There must have been, in addition, innumerable sales for which no records remain or were never in fact kept.

191

Some companies recorded that regular reports were submitted from those in charge of such sales, but the reports were never appended to the minutes or reproduced with any consistency. This means that the surviving evidence is weighted towards the unusual in any account of such sales. Any attempt at evaluation of sales has to be biased by the evidence available.

Before looking at customers in general, here are two examples of tar buyers:

THOMAS KEMPSON

One, seemingly straightforward, early customer for raw tar was a Mr. Kempson. He appears in contemporary street directories as an iron merchant with a Bankside address. He was actually based in Hatfield Street – which today runs parallel to Blackfriars Road in SE1.

Now, as then, Hatfield Street ends in Upper Ground, near Old Bargehouse. In 1812 the Christ Church rate books show that this was the yard of Davey Sawyer, a coal merchant much involved with early gas industry. It was also the site of Hawes Soap Works – soon to be the site of an oil gasworks described above. The owner, Benjamin Hawes Snr., would eventually become Governor of the Chartered. A short distance up river Munro and Evans had opened the small gasworks which would grow to become the Bankside Works of the South London Gas Company. . It might be possible to speculate on the social interactions of these industrialists.

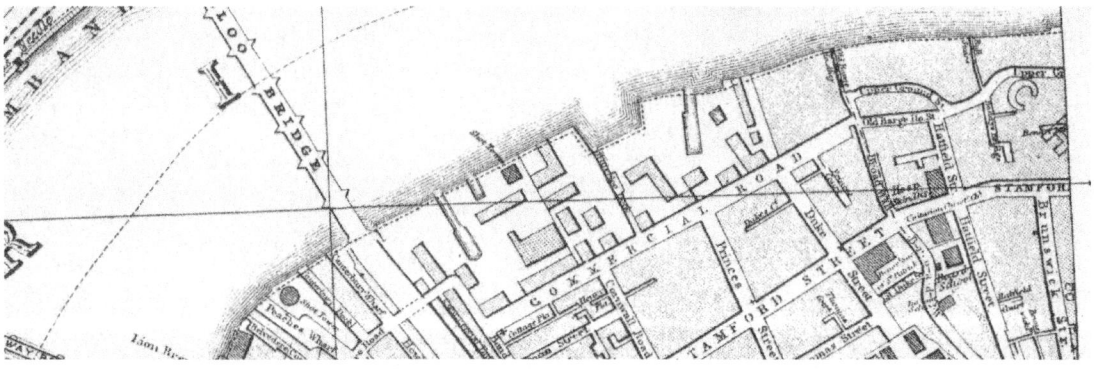

The Bromley St. Leonard Court Book shows that before 1814 Kempson had also had a tar works in Limehouse**Error! Bookmark not defined.**, in partnership with a Mr. Parke. Is this the same Mr. Parke who later made vitriol on Bow Common? In Limehouse were many shipbuilding yards and it was perhaps thought that this was a better place to process tar than Bankside. A large 'tar yard' is shown on the 1813 Horwood Plan just north of Narrow Street and there were many smaller ones.

Kempson and Parke would, before 1811, probably have made 'Stockholm tar' from wood and Kempson, perhaps, thought that coal tar would sell to the many existing and

192

new customers in this area. He was thus was an early customer of both Chartered and City Gas companies for coal tar. He probably had long term plans to distil tar from the seven-year contract he made with the Chartered.

Unfortunately Kempson's aspirations were not matched by reality. In 1820, after only a few years of his first purchase, he offered his Limehouse tar works for sale to the Chartered. He was, at the same time, being pursued for debt by the City Gas Company — another way in which he was a forerunner of many others to come. The Chairman and Deputy Chairman of the City Gas Company visited him in the East India Dock Road where he was said to be living. They did this to 'ascertain his sentiments — whether this means that they wanted his advice on tar use or (more likely) wanted the missing cash, is not clear. The City Company's solicitor advised them that their contract with him was not viable and no more was heard.

Although the implication in this story is that Mr. Kempson failed in his tar-making enterprise and disappeared when debts were called in — that is not necessarily what happened. Although he is no longer noted in the gas company records it is possible that he carried on buying tar from them, or from a different gas company, and that no records have survived.

On the other hand, we may speculate that perhaps he was the Mr. Kempson who was a partner in contemporary wholesale druggists, Kempson, Yates, Evans and Parkinson. They failed in 1823 and were reconstituted without Kempson.

Kempson is a good example of a business man who bought tar from the early London gas companies. He was in the coal/iron trade on the Southwark riverside and moved eastwards to diversify. He also got into debt. This is a pattern which, with variations, was to be repeated. His failures matched those of the Chartered Company itself.

WEBSTER FLOCKTON

In the case of Mr. Kempson, and many others, it is only possible to guess what their trade was and why they wanted to buy tar. There are, however, a number of recorded purchasers about whose intentions guesses are slightly better informed. One such was active later, in the 1830s : Mr. Flockton of Bermondsey.

By the 1830s, tar had found some markets and Flockton was one who seemed to know what they were and the best way of getting himself, and his tar distillates, into them.

Webster Flockton first bought tar from the Chartered in 1828. In 1836 he registered a patent for timber preservation, only a few months after the opening of the first railway station in London: Spa Road, on the London and Greenwich Railway. It may, or may not, be a coincidence that the station was next to Mr. Flockton's tar works.

193

It may seem natural that railways should need tar for the preservation of timber sleepers, as will be discussed later. The London and Greenwich used stone blocks for sleepers at first — an unused pile of which could still be seen at New Cross Station into the 1990s. The company changed to wooden sleepers, two years after opening in 1838. (see Ron Thomas' *History of the London and Greenwich Railway*).

The London and Greenwich Railway had, from the start, its own gasworks, intended to produce gas for station and line-side lighting. Mr. Flockton appears to have had an interest in this enterprise which, soon after opening, was taken over by the specially constituted Deptford, Bermondsey and Rotherhithe Gas Company, of which Mr. Flockton was a director.

In 1840 a meeting of the railway company shareholders questioned their Directors' interests in a number of companies supplying plant and materials to the various railway companies in the area, including London and Greenwich — perhaps Mr. Flockton was one of those they had in mind.

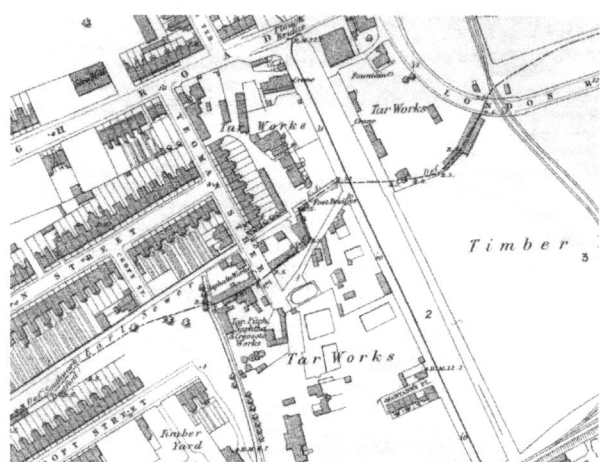

Flockton seems to have prospered. By 1839 there were branches of his tar and oil business in Bermondsey and Weybridge — both sites near the entrance into the Thames from the Grand Surrey and the Wey Navigation canals. The business was described as *'turpentine & tar distillers, and seed crushers'* — a common enough combination of activities for what was basically an oil distillery. Many such businesses, like the long established Charles Price oil distillery on Millwall, were to produce timber preservatives of various kinds. By the 1860s, in partnership with others, Flockton had moved to Plough Lane, Rotherhithe — nearer to the Surrey Canal and an area where several other tar distillers were sited.

TAR FOR SALE

Those who bought tar from the gas companies are mentioned intermittently in the minute books. They provide a record of the ideas and the efforts made to distil tar and to sell it. There were those who were prepared to buy it and sometimes income from by-products is recorded in the gas company minute books. During one week of 1817, for example, Chartered took £2 14s 3d. in tar sales.

194

Before 1820, as is clear, from sometimes increasingly desperate, minutes, that the Chartered had a surplus of tar and no very clear idea of where to dispose of it. Sometimes enquiries the

In 1823 Chartered advertised coal tar for sale. After that they, and other gas companies, negotiated contracts, which usually ran over a three-year period and sometimes included transport arrangements. By the late 1830s these contracts were with large specialist tar distillers although most of the gas companies also record a trickle of additional enquiries about tar. The system of awarding three-year contracts means that information in the minute books is very limited after 1840. Such contracts were never, in any case, given the same attention as other activities — like buying coal and making gas.

Several potential customers only appear once in the gas company records in respect of tar. These were sometimes established customers who dealt regularly with the gas companies for other products.

Richard Torr. The Chartered Company sold tar to this Deptford bone merchant in 1833 although he usually bought ammoniacal liquor.
Wilkinson. Normally bought ammoniacal liquor but bought tar in 1837.
Marmeduke George Featherstonehaugh. Bought tar from the City Gas Company in 1819 — he usually bought scrap retorts and sold coal.
Davey of Davey and Sawyer, Old Barge House. He usually sold coal to the gas companies but bought tar from Chartered in 1823.
Mr. Hardlen of London, Paris and Hamburg Asphalt Company and **Mr. Micklen** of Finch Street were both refused tar by Phoenix Gas Co. because Phoenix offered *'only one contract'*.
Mr. Parker was refused tar by Chartered in 1831 because the *'Company uses all the tar'* and by Phoenix because they *'could not consent to part with it for less than 3d. a gallon'* . It made difficulties for Mr. Parker who needed raw materials for his paint and varnish business in Deptford.

How much did the gas companies charge for their tar? Prices quoted have little consistency. The following list, taken from a selection of minutes, may serve to confuse things further, but demonstrate the difficulties of the available evidence.

1816 - 34/-d. a barrel
1818 – 2/2d. per gallon beer measure
1818 - 3d. per gallon beer measure

195

1818 - £5 per ton
1826 - 12/6d. a barrel
1831 - 2d. a gallon
1831 - 3d. per gallon
1833 - 1d. a gallon
1845 - 10d. delivered
1846 - 11/6d. a butt of 108 gallons
1848 - 10d. a gallon

LOCATIONS

Where did these purchasers of east London gas company tar come from?

Featherstonehaugh. He came from Sunderland and seems seems to have been a coal merchant. However there is a record of a lime burner in the Swanscombe area of Thamesside with that name.
Stephenson and Ritson. They came from Sunderland but have not been otherwise identified.
Mr. Bayley. He bought tar from Chartered in 1818, came from the Stonehouse area of Plymouth where he made tar, pitch and rosin.
Mr. Wills. He came from Tandridge, slightly to the east of Godstone and in the centre of an area of chalk and stone mines along the Kent/Surrey hills.
Pritchard. Chartered's earliest recorded customer had an oil warehouse in Smithfield but later moved to Battlebridge where he made asphaltum.
Crease. Another early customer for tar from Chartered. He was based in West Smithfield and then moved a short distance to Cowcross Street.
Mr. Davey was, as we have seen, at Old Barge House by Bankside
Mr. Kempson – in Hatfield Street.
Mr. Clarke was in Lower Chadwell Street on the Finsbury/Islington borders

By the late 1830s most sales were to buyers from further east.

Henry Hughes bought tar from Chartered in 1851. He had a tar distillery in Plough

Lane, Rotherhithe, like Mr. Flockton. There was still a Hughes Terrace in the area into the 1940s.

Henry Burt also opened a tar works in Rotherhithe Wharf, establishing the company which became Burt Boulton and Hayward.

Another concentration of tar distillers appears on Bow Common: Bush who bought tar in the 1830s and, later, Bethel and Battley. The only divergence from this eastward trend is a small cluster of tar works to the southwest in Nine Elms and Battersea.

There is nothing very unusual or surprising in this. Firms in many trades that had once clustered around the City boundaries began to move out in this period. There was a general and gradual drift east — both northeast and southeast and down river. As companies expanded they needed more space, and that meant that they usually needed to be near water for transport purposes.

There was also pressure on these smelly industries to move away from the inner city. Hunt's Bone Boilers were to claim famously that they were pressurised by by-laws in Lambeth to move across the Lea to Stratford. As late as the 1960s they were still there. My husband, as a public health student, was taken there on a site visit, and never quite recovered from the horror of what he saw.

Several paint and varnish makers were to claim in company histories that they felt pressure from 'regulations' to move, although it is often difficult to pin down exactly what they mean. It is usually clear that they wanted a larger site, and one well away from complainants. A good example, but a much later one, is William Davy who had a tar works at Hackney Wick. His move from there to Rainham Essex was partly forced by petitions against smell from residents in newly-built Cardigan Terrace alongside Victoria Park. At the same time extra space and a riverside location suited Davy very well.

Tar distillers and those who used gas industry tar did not only move east. Many went north of the City to Battlebridge and Belle Isle and out to Haggerston and Old Ford. By the 1880s they had moved again — to, for example, East Greenwich and Hackney Wick or, later, further down river to Rainham, Essex or Erith. Others went south to Merton and sites along the Wandle.

WHAT SORT OF BUSINESS BOUGHT THE TAR

Those who bought raw coal tar directly from the gas company intended to distil it for resale. Initially they are described in directories as *'oil merchants'* or, sometimes, *'varnish makers'* or *'seed crushers'*. By the 1830s they are nearly all described as *'tar distillers'*, with the odd exception of those like *'Mr. Lance for wharfaging at Greenwich'*.

197

While many of the early purchasers are obscure, later contracts were made with those who became famous for their tar products — in particular Burt Boulton and Hayward. Many, like them, used the tar to manufacture a range of products. It ought to be possible to find out what those products were, and, by discovering other manufacturers, to find out more about the effects of coal tar and its use in the wider London economy. Tar had moved slowly to start with but the fact that there were those willing to buy shows that it had found a market.

JOHN HENRY CASSELL AND GAS WORKS TAR

In the minute books of the London gas industry between 1820 and 1850 the name that stands out as the pre-eminent tar purchaser is Cassell. The volume of his purchases makes him a far from typical customer. Cassell's activities over thirty years provide a picture of how a tar distiller was able to use and presumably profit from what he bought from the local gas industry.

Cassell's business was to buy gasworks tar, to distil it and sell the product — an activity in which the gas companies themselves had failed. Despite some apparent problems Cassell, and at least one son, managed to survive in the business for many years.

THE START OF THE BUSINESS

There was, as we will see, more than one Mr. Cassell. They were based in Millwall where their name appears for several sites in the All Saints, Poplar, rate books from the 1830s. As with many sites in this area the relevant Survey of London volume is an important source of material — as well as providing a valuable commentary on local industries and much else.

In 1815, John Henry Cassell, probably the company originator, had a business in Poplar High Street where he made rainwater pipes and gutters. He then seems to have set up a tar distillery in Millwall and is first noted in the gas company minute books when he bought tar from the Imperial Gas Company in 1823. On that occasion he agreed to take all Imperial's surplus tar, supplying the casks in which it would be transferred onto barges. This implies that he had access to a wharf somewhere on the river — something not available at Poplar High Street — as well as enough capital to fund purchase of the tar. At around the same time he was concluding a very similar deal with the South London Gas Company and another with the Chartered. He also appeared to have a partner, a Mr. Morgan.

Cassell seems to have pioneered the use of gasworks' coal tar as an ingredient of

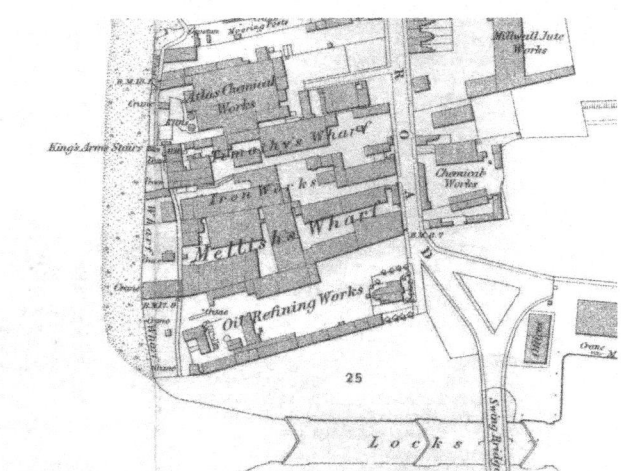

building materials — something that might give a clue to the identity of Mr. Morgan. *The Survey of London* tells us that in the 1820s a Mr. F.D. Morgan was in partnership with James Grellier on what was to become the site of the Millwall Atlas Chemical Works. On this site, very near to where Cassell was to set up his 'Lava Stone' works, Grellier and Morgan made Roman cement. Hopefully this is the right Mr.Morgan

THE CITY OF LONDON GAS COMPANY'S MILLWALL TAR WORKS

At some time in the 1820s Cassell began to operate the City of London Gas Company's failing tar works. This had been set up on Millwall in the early 1820s. The gas company had bought the site from William Pitcher, one of their original subscribers. He had a building business near the City's Blackfriars Gas Works and was also one of the Northfleet and Millwall shipbuilding family. Cowper in '*Description of Millwall* 'says he *lived on the road which ran from Blackwall to the Greenwich Ferry*' and had considerable land holdings in the area (see also Ken McGoverin's book on the *Northfleet Ship Yard*).

Chartered had already set up a tar works at Poplar. The decision of the City Gas Company to set up a tar works was made following a fire and losses through fraud.

Cassell signed a formal agreement for a lease on the works in 1830, working in partnership with a Mr. George Ward. Ward is a common name in wharfaging and chemical manufacture in this period — a younger George Ward was later to be involved in an East Greenwich tar works together with members of the vinegar-making Champion family.

The site of the City of London Gas Company's tar works has not been easy to identify but for reasons to be made clear later, it was probably the site which the Survey of London identifies as Lowe's Wharf. In 1828 Cassell expanded and took over the site of an old mast house further north on Millwall, and eleven years later extended this site again. This later became known as Patentia Wharf.

Cassell sometimes seemed to be in financial trouble. 'Cassell being taken to court for not paying tar bills' and 'Secretary went to Millwall for the purpose of getting a payment

199

from Messrs. Cassell' are two notes among several in this period. Despite this, however, his name appears most frequently in gas company records as a tar purchaser and presumably all this tar was eventually paid for.

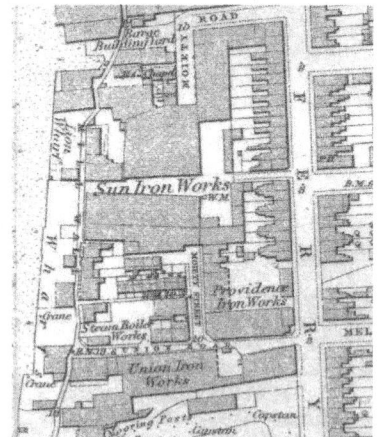

In 1843 the City of London Gas Company noticed that the Millwall premises, which Cassell still rented from them, were very dilapidated and there was no business going on there. Letters of administration were taken out against John Henry Cassell. The City of London Gas Co. then began to prepare to lease the site to a Mr. Blatchford. '*Blatchford*' is perhaps Mr. Blashfield who around this time actually leased the site on which F.D.Morgan had been operating his building materials business. Two younger Messrs Cassells then approached the City of London Gas Company. One of them, Edwin Edward Cassell, said that the partnership with his father had been dissolved. City then leased the Millwall site to him and he stayed there until the 1880s. It is this lease, noted by the Survey of London, which identifies the site as the old City of London Gas Company tar works.

CASSELL TAR DISTILLERS

What did the Cassells do with all the gasworks' tar which they bought? They were general tar distillers, selling tar products and fractions to whoever wanted them. A good example of their reputation was given in a patent case where the type of 'coal oil' was crucial and reported in Mechanics Magazine. The chemist, Richard Phillips, acted as a consultant in this case and was asked by the judge where he had obtained his samples of tar used for the demonstration in court. He replied 'from Cassell at Millwall' Similarly Thomas Hancock, who was to develop the emulsification of rubber using tar oils, went to Cassell to buy the selection of fractions needed for his experiments. These cases suggest that Cassell were well known as tar distillers and had a reputation for quality.

What they produced and sold to customers was a variety of specialist distillates, which were called by the names used by the British Tar Company, Accum and the early Chartered promoters. Elsewhere chemists were working on a more sophisticated codification and analysis of coal based oil fractions. Sadly, there is simply not enough information about Cassell and tar distillers like him to know how far they were involved with such chemists and how much they contributed to their work.

PATENT LAVA STONE

A possible connection of Cassell with F.D. Morgan and Roman cement has been mentioned above. John Henry Cassell 's site at northern Millwall was called the *'Patent Lava Stone Works* 'and advertised as such in his *Treatise on Roads & Streets*. He seems to have developed a type of bituminous material there. He carried out a number of contracts using this material, including the paving of Vauxhall Bridge Road, in front of the Horns Tavern in Kennington and the flooring of Giblett's slaughterhouses in Bayswater as noted in Survey of London. As a demonstration piece he paved the part of West Ferry Road behind his works. The material, which had all sorts of uses, seems in some ways to have provided an extension for his drainpipe business. He even used one of his mixtures for coffins in the crypt of the Brunswick Chapel, in Three Colt Lane, Limehouse. In 1837 he used it to cap the river wall in Greenwich for the Greenwich Commission of Sewers.

'Lava stone' is not obviously made with coal tar and Cassell 's publicity for it implies that it was made from natural bitumen. However, in view of the amount of coal tar he was buying, its true ingredients must be open to question. Cassell was one of several manufacturers of artificial stone at the time that had strong links with gasworks' tar and the subject will be discussed again later.

ROADS AND PAVING

Another use of coal tar is in 'asphalt' for roads and pavements. This subject will be discussed later but it should be noted that John Henry Cassell patented a *'Cement or combination of materials, applicable to the purposes for which cement, stone, brick of other similar substances may be used'*. This proposed the use of coal tar distillates for road surfaces and pavement – to quote the text of the patent itself.

Twenty years later, in 1853, he wrote a 'Treatise on Roads and Streets, where the advantages of a Patent Invention the Paving of Streets and the Making of Roads are fully explained'. This was primarily a sales document and in it John Henry describes his work and the uses for 'lava stone'. Sadly the price list is missing from the British Library copy.

LAMPS AND LIGHTING

Cassell also made lamps and provided the means of lighting them. He almost certainly had contracts for lighting because on one occasion he gave the fact that *'rental for lamps'* had not been paid as the reason for his own non-payment of City Gas Company bills.

The lighting may well have been oil-based street lighting — for which several systems were developed in this period.

It is also possible that Cassell had some sort of gas lighting plant himself. The evidence for this is confused and rests on an entry in the 1846 Poplar Rate book which records a gas factory on or near part of the site owned by Edwin Edward Cassell on Millwall. This 'factory' is identified by Survey of London, with some justification, as the Millwall Works of the Poplar Gas Company. However, the Poplar Company is not known to have had links with Cassell, and the rate books imply the site was his. E.V.Stewart located the Millwall Gas Works site much further south at Cahir Street. A large gasholder, shown on some maps but which probably belonged to a shipyard, may have confused Stewart. Whatever the truth about the Millwall Gas Works, if it can be gleaned from these tangled probabilities, it remains possible that Cassell had a small gas-making plant that could have been used to make gas for lighting.

THE CASSELLS CONTINUE

John Henry Cassell may have remained at his lava stone works into the 1860s and Edwin Edward Cassell operated his tar distillery until the 1880s. In addition, a Mr. Bruce Cassell had an ammonia salt making plant on Millwall and a Frederick Cassell opened a naphtha and paraffin works in the 1870s at Plough Road in Rotherhithe. All of this seems to add up to a busy, inventive and successful family. They appear to have been local to east London, as John Henry lived in the Commercial Road.

AND – THE PUBLISHER

There is one strange coincidence. John Cassell, the publisher, of Belle Sauvage Yard off Ludgate Hill, held 1860s' patents on obtaining fuel from coal, peat, etc. and the carburetion of gas. In 1862 he set up Cassell, Smith & Company, oil merchants and lamp manufacturers, who were involved with early petroleum. His Hydro-Carbon Oil Co. was based at Southall and Bow and he had a miniature oil refinery in his home. It seems remarkable that two people with the same name should have been in the same business — but Cassell, the publisher, is well-documented. His biographer, Nowell-Smith, Simon, noted no Millwall relations.

GAS WORKS' TAR
OTHER USES – OTHER BUYERS

Cassell was just one of several customers for gasworks' tar and they themselves sold their distillates to a number of outlets. Who and what these were can only be guessed at from the very scant surviving evidence. What was done with the tar by those who bought it is another matter for conjecture. The following paragraphs might provide some indicators.

CREASE, PRITCHARD AND JAPAN

Mr. Pritchard was the first customer for tar about whom the Chartered made a note. He wanted to know about using tar for *'refining oils and making japan'*. the directories list a remarkable number of Mr.Pritchards around the country who make 'japan'

A Mr. James Crease who was an established varnish maker with a business in Smithfield *'Inventor of Cheap Paint'* followed this enquiry with one of his own. He too was interested in tar for 'japan' and had published a booklet in 1808. *Hints for the Preservation of Woodwork'.*

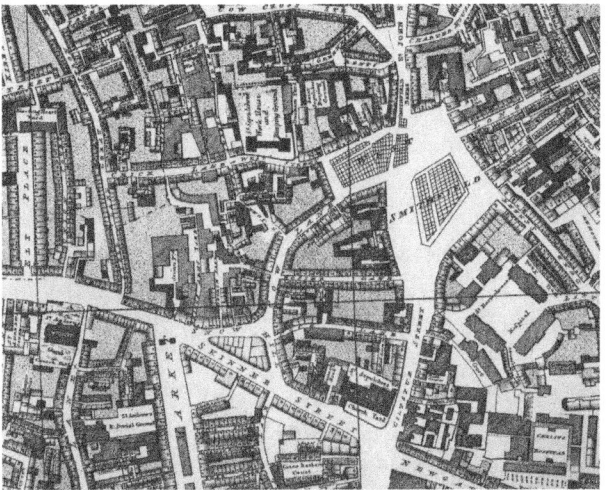

In giving evidence to the 1809 Enquiry Accum had said that *'the asphaltum could be mixed with the distilled spirit'* and used as *'an ingredient for making the black varnish used in japanning'*. 'Japan', in this context, is the name of a technology. 'Japanning' is a method of applying a decorative coating by a heat treatment to goods using a varnish mix, which could include, for instance, coal oils. In particular this was done in the manufacture of decorated tin ware in South Wales. The practice was, however, very widespread and the term appears to have been used to include goods, like leather, which could not have been subjected to high temperatures

In this period London directories list a wide range of manufacturers and sellers of 'japanned' goods. It was a popular form of decoration and no doubt manufacturers were hoping for a cheaper means of production. Gas company promoters naturally saw it as a technology that might provide an opportunity for the use of coal tar. At the

203

1809 Parliamentary Enquiry the Chartered Company's promoters put forward two 'japanners' to give evidence as witnesses. Neither has been traced through directories or relevant sources as active varnish makers in London at this time.

Coal tar used as paint seems to have applied to the cheaper and rougher end of the market. Japanning was a decorative, often expensive, process. There were many japanners working in London but the use of coal tar distillates for the process is not something they were likely to advertise — they were, in any case, likely to keep their mixtures secret from rivals. Because of this secrecy and despite these experiments on tar distillates it is probably impossible to know if tar was used commercially to any great extent by japanners in London, or indeed elsewhere.

RUBBER

Histories of the chemical industry – for example A. & N. Clow — have drawn attention to the Glasgow-based industrialist and chemist, Charles Mackintosh, and his use of tar distillates in the manufacture of rubberised materials. As is obvious from his name, Mackintosh has been credited with the invention of rubberised, and thus waterproof, clothing — but Charles Mackintosh was much more than that. The son of a successful Scottish dye manufacturer he was to become one of the foremost chemical manufacturers of the late 18th century. His influence stretched far beyond Scotland — he had many connections with industries in England and Europe and with bodies such as the Royal Ordnance.

Mackintosh made a contract with Glasgow Gas Works in 1819 to buy their waste tar and ammoniacal liquor which could be used by his father's company to make cudbear. He experimented with *'essential oil'*, for which he had no immediate use, and thought it might be useful as a solvent for caoutchouc (latex). In 1822 he patented a method of cementing two pieces of cloth together using rubber emulsified with coal tar spirits – or naphtha – producing a waterproof cloth. This led him to work with the Manchester-based Birley Brothers to manufacture items using this process, but problems with smell persisted.

Mackintosh was in London in 1824 and approached the Chartered for *'coal tar spirit'*. 'Crude' naphtha was still being sold to his company by the Chartered thirty years later. A Mackintosh coal tar refinery existed at one time between Mile End Road and Poplar Road. This location is not easy to identify, particularly within the confines of St. Leonard's, Bromley, Parish, but it could refer to a site in the same area as the Dundonald/Birch works mentioned in a previous chapter.

Nothing is as straightforward as it seems in this industry and it may be that London tar distillers had more to do with the development of rubber clothing than those in Glasgow. Thomas Hancock, who has been described by Sylvia Clark in '*Chorlton Mills & their Neighbours*", as, '*the foremost rubber technologist in the world*'.

204

Thomas Hancock, was one of a large family of talented brothers from Marlborough but with a coach-building works in Stoke Newington and the family is described in detail in 'The Hancocks of Marlborough' by Loadman and James. Thomas had been experimenting with rubber based on a patent of 1813 take out by a John Clark using turpentine as a solvent. Thomas went on to develop his 'masticator' which eliminated many of the problems. He described his experiments to find a suitable solvent and some of the problems he encountered. The 'masticator' enabled the rubber and solvent to be mixed in a particular way but this he did not patent. He then discovered that 'pitch and tar' were the best solvents he could find. He experimented with a number of distillates, which he obtained from Cassell in Poplar and decided that a wood tar distillate was

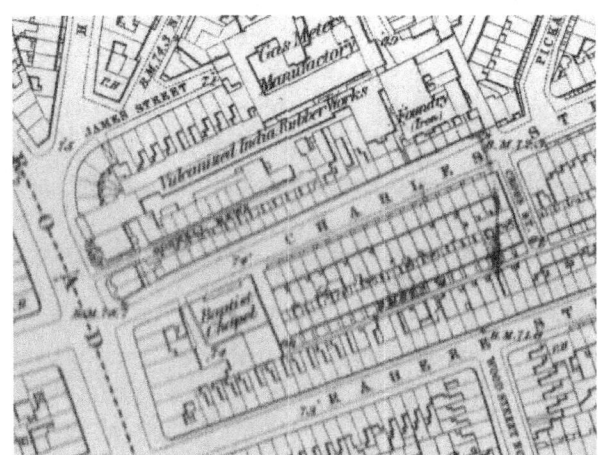

best. Thomas described all this in his 1857 booklet Personal Narrative of the Origin & Progress of the Caoutchouc or India Rubber Manufacture in England. He patented this process on 22nd March 1822 using coal tar naphtha as a solvent. Hancock did not claim however to have discovered the use this solvent for rubber but to have developed the way in which it was done via his 'masticator'.

Thomas Hancock had some contact with the early gas companies and bought spirits of tar from the Chartered Company in 1828. Company minutes show that they took good care to check that he was a suitable person for them to deal with first – a great contrast to their treatment of Macintosh who appears to have been met with some deference.

With his brother John, Thomas set up a factory in the Goswell Road to process items from rubber – they did well with specialist hoses. Another brother William, worked there on what is now known as 'perfect binding' of books. Their works were slightly north of the Brick Lane gasworks in what was then called Goswell Mews and later became the site of Gordon's Gin distillery. It is now a massive data centre.

In 1823 Thomas encountered Mackintosh's process and obtained a licence to use it but soon realised that his process gave better results. He wrote to Mackintosh and was at first ignored but by 1826 an agreement between them had been reached. Later Hancock said that Mackintosh was his partner. Indeed a statement made in court during a patent case it was clearly said 'Mr. Hancock and his partners are the firm of Charles Mackintosh'.

Eventually Mackintosh and Hancock worked very closely together, and a large manufacturing base in Manchester was set up. Sylvia Clark in her article on Chorlton Mills, shows that this factory had some connections with a gasworks in the immediate area. It may or may not be relevant that the Portable Gas Company may have been adjacent.

Eventually Hancock began to develop a number of manufactured goods from rubber using a range of different solvents according to need. He achieved the hardening of rubber, which he called 'vulcanisation' – on this there is also some suggestion of deathbed discussions with Mackintosh in his *Personal Narrative*. Over the next century what had begun as an experimental works in Goswell Road, grew and flourished and changed and, became part of other industrial empires but remained in some senses independent into the 1960s.

There were several other Hancock brothers whose careers are covered in '*The Hancocks of Marlborough:* John, who managed some of the works. Better known is Charles, an artist who was responsible for the processing of gutta percha and the subsequent breakthrough in cable-making. Another brother, Walter, developed the most successful steam road vehicle of the period and described it in *Narrative of 12 Years* – where he says that his vehicles ran on '*common gas coke*'.

Thus four of the six Hancock brothers had some connection with gas industry by-products and all made some ground-breaking contribution to industry and invention.

LIGHTING

Better lighting is what the invention of coal gas is best known for. However other new lighting methods were introduced which used the by-products of gas manufacture, like tar oils.

Up until the advent of gas for street lighting, most of the oil-based street lights used tallow – much of it imported from Russia. Tallow prices were controlled by the Worshipful Company of Tallow Chandlers – so we have to wonder if the Company members switched their allegiance to gas and/or gas tar oil methods of lighting. It is worth noting that, at South Met. at least, some of the earliest promoters were Tallow Chandlers' Company members.

Frederick Accum, writing in 1816, said distillates were used for lighting as a substitute for whale oil and gave as an example the illumination of Waterloo Bridge. Waterloo Bridge was then newly built, and it should be noted that the ironwork on it was coated with 'distilled tar'.

In 1820 Major Cochrane made an application to the City Gas Company for a supply of 'essential oil'. This was John, one of the sons of Archibald the Ninth Earl of Dundonald whose work on early gas light and coal tar has been discussed above. John was acting as agent for his brother, Thomas Cochrane, who had taken out a patent for purifying *'oil of tar for lighting and construction of lamps'* in 1818. Typically, for Thomas Cochrane, this had been done while inside the King's Bench Prison.

Thomas Cochrane, later the 10th Earl of Dundonald, was of course 'The Sea Wolf' and a great naval hero. It is a shame that his numerous biographies (I have five myself on my very modest bookshelf) give scant, if any, attention to his work on a number of technologies, lighting among them. One exception is a PhD by John Sugden.

The Cochrane brothers, working through Samuel Brooks, a Strand merchant, had an agreement to replace 800 traditional oil lamps with 400 new ones in St. Anne's Parish, Soho. There may have been another smaller scheme at St. John the Baptist in the Savoy.

London street lighting has not, as far as I know, been investigated on a parish-by-parish basis. Parishes that took on early gas lighting have sometimes been noted but there may well have been other oil-based street lighting schemes. My comment in a previous chapter about Cassell and a street lighting contract may be an example of this.

Sugden says that the Cochrane's' lamps were made by Mr. King of Cock Lane and probably copied by others as time went on. Directories of 1839 show both King and James Cochrane (another of Thomas' brothers) as *'meter manufacturers'*.

Oil lamps using *'mineral oil'* and *'naphtha'* were refined to a greater degree by others in east London. Joshua Taylor Beale for instance, worked from Whitechapel Church Lane from which address he took out two patents for lamp design. Beale was later to move to East Greenwich where he worked with Enderby Brothers, on using rubber with naphtha in specialist rope-making. I have written about Beale in this and other contexts elsewhere.

The use of tar oils for lighting persisted – local manufacturers went on to produce *'naphtha flares'* which became a feature of more casual outdoor lighting in markets and fairgrounds. 'Mineral' or 'dead' oil for the purpose of such lighting was described as an *'old established article of commercial enterprise'* in an 1860s work: *The Chemistry of Gas Lighting'*.

ROADS

It is often popularly supposed that John Loudon Macadam introduced a system of road making using coal tar incorporated in the road surface. As noted earlier, Macadam was a relation of Dundonald's and managed the Muirkirk Tar Works on his behalf. In London he is listed in 1817 as a coal tar manufacturer working under licence from the British Tar Company. Macadam's road surfaces were built up through layers of different sized stones and were <u>not</u> tar-based. Tarred roads were to come later and be undertaken by companies who used his name (in 'Tarmacadam') rather than his process– one such was J.H. Cassell's, whose *Treatise on Roads and Streets* is described in a previous chapter.

There is, of course, a clear distinction between road surfacing and street paving although both were under discussion in the 1830s and 1840s. Main roads were used by horse transport and many were in a bad state. In 1816 a Select Committee on Road Transport had discussed the problem. In this the state of Mile End Road were described in much detail: the mud, the ruts, and the difficulties were all given an airing.

The Carriage Pavement was a term used for those areas of town roads which horses and light wheeled transport would share with pedestrians. In 1839 an experiment was conducted in Oxford Street in which a number of different types of bitumen and asphalt were laid to see which was the most resilient. This is described in *The Mirror* of January 1839. The composition of some of these paving materials is very far from clear. One of them, *'Aberdeen Granite'*, seems obvious – Aberdeen is after all known as *'the Granite City'* so what was used in its name ought to be granite paving, although – as it does not seem to have lasted very long – perhaps not. Another sort of paving laid down was, *'Val de Travers'*, the name of a Swiss valley where natural bitumen is found – which makes that one seem clearer but the ingredients of *'Parisian Bitumen'* are not quite so easy to work out– and what were *'Claridge's Asphalt'* and *'Bastenne Gaugac Bitumen'*? The likelihood is that they were all coal tar mixtures which came from nowhere more exotic than the Isle of Dogs.

Down in Millwall and other parts of the Isle of Dogs, Mr. Cassell was not the only manufacturer with an interest in both tar and road surfaces. *'Parisian Bitumen'* for instance, was made at Atlas Wharf, Millwall by a Mr. Robinson of whom Survey of London says *'although using English coal tar rather than the superior natural asphalt... he claimed a particular foreign connection'*. Robinson paved the Woolwich Royal Artillery Parade Ground and part of the Strand. The Bastenne Asphalte and Bitumen Co. (proprietor Chas. Fred. Tilstone) was also based in Millwall.

Richard Tappin Claridge at his *'Seyssel Asphalte Company'* had patented *'Claridge's Patent Asphalte'* in 1835. The company had a list of distinguished patrons including the Brunels. It was, however, based at Stangate on the Lambeth riverfront rather than Switzerland, although it may have some connection with Seyssel Street, also on the Isle of Dogs. After the Oxford Street experiments *'an impression having gone abroad that the work started by this company failed ...... that part which had been of Claridge's Asphalte was in a state of superior order'* as an advertisement in Pigot's Street Directory claimed.

It is very difficult to say that the products of these companies were definitely coal tar based as there is no proof. It is just rather hard to believe otherwise!

Coal tar in various mixtures for road and pavement surfacing had had its supporters for some time. One of the most vociferous was Colonel Francis Maceroni who, since the early 1820s, had pointed out the usefulness of tar for road surfaces in his *Hints to*

Paviours. Maceroni was a flamboyant Italian from Manchester. He had a strong involvement in the promotion of steam carriages, which might explain his interest in flat tarred road surfaces.

Maceroni claimed in *Mechanics Magazine* in March 1838 that the first attempt at a tarred surface had been on the paths *'in Mr. Bell's garden in Blackheath'*. Attempts to identify *'Mr. Bell's garden'* have, thanks to Neil Rhind, led to a Mr. J.R. Bell who lived at Westgrove House in Westgrove Lane, at the southeast corner of Blackheath in the early 1800s. The garden has obviously been altered since 1816; and the chance of finding one of his tarred paths is remote! On the other hand, 'Bell' could be a misprint for 'Beale'. In which case a likely candidate is Joshua Taylor Beale, the naphtha lighting inventor already mentioned. Beale was to adapt steam carriages for Maceroni at his works in East Greenwich and, although he lived in Greenwich, not Blackheath, he was certainly in the area. He was in Conduit House in Trafalgar Road at the bottom of Vanburgh Hill where the site is currently flats converted in the shell of a large cinema. Ironically, his son moved to Blackheath where a portion of his cycle test track of the 1890s could until recently still be discerned in the garden layout.

Another experimental site for tarred surfaces is said to have been Margate Pier. Maceroni claimed that this was surfaced with coal tar at around the same time in the early 1820s. No definite information, beyond one letter in *Mechanics Magazine*, has been found to support this. Margate Pier, built in 1824, actually consisted of something called the 'Jervis Landing Place', which was an 100-ft. wooden jetty *'available only at low water.... it was not uncommon for unfortunate strollers to be cut off ... the result was a lucrative business for local seamen who carried the marooned visitors ashore and amusement for the spectators safe on dry land'*, according to S.H. Adamson, writing in *Seaside Piers*. However, the chance of investigating the archaeology of early tar there has been lost, because the present pier replaced Jervis Landing in 1851.

Maceroni had his critics, including J.C.Robertson, while pointing out in his *Improvement of the Carriage Pavement*, the practicality of coal tar as a binder for roads and pavements made the cryptic comment that Maceroni wanted to use *'Dogs meat soup from Whitechapel'*. Maceroni was an enthusiast for steam cars and his suggestions are clearly meant not only for foot pavements but for surfaces intended to take wheeled traffic. Steam car promoters are a sub-text to much activity on tar.

Maceroni and Beale played a minor role in the steam car movement compared to Walter Hancock, brother of Thomas the rubber expert. Hancock managed to run what was almost a public transport service using these vehicles. There were many others who tried to do so. One such was David Gordon, whom we have already met involved in the Portable Gas Company and who also patented a portable gas lamp. He built steam cars, and his son, Alexander wrote a book about them called *Elemental Locomotion*. Frank Hills who will feature very prominently later in this work built a steam car and worked with Beale on it. All of these can be found in Fletcher's *Steam on Common Roads*.

209

Many of these early steam carriages came to grief on muddy and uneven roads. Horses need a surface which their hooves can grip. Wheeled vehicles need smooth tarred road surfaces. Tar did not come into common use for road surfaces until horses were supplanted by motor vehicles with pneumatic tyres. Bicycles needed an even smoother surface, which, no doubt, was in the forefront of Beale, Jnr's mind when he designed his Facile machine. A great deal will be found on this in bicycle history web sites and you can even buy replicas. Thus, tarred road surfaces had to wait for powered vehicles to be perfected before they could be used. No doubt, the steam car makers thought, mistakenly, that the reverse was true.

CEMENT

Coal tar products were developed for use in many construction applications. There seems to have been a suspiciously close relationship between manufacturers who bought coal tar and those who claimed to make various fancy 'Roman' cements. For instance Turner, the Poplar tar distiller who had taken over the Chartered Gas Company's tar works, also described himself as a 'Roman cement maker'.

'Roman' cement could be any one of a number of artificial building materials developed at this time. Ingredients were often not clear and varied with the maker, and bore no relation to the pozzuolanic cement used in classical Roman times. The poet, Michael Baldwin, writing in 'The River and the Downs about cement in North Kent has commented 'I suspect that experts are less clear about what was really in James Parker's Roman Cement than they pretend to be'.

For example, Edgar Dobb of Southwark, had patented a cement the ingredients of which were 'clay, loam, mud, shale, road dirt, soil ochre, metallic oxides, ore, sandstone and earths', in which mixture A.K. Francis comments that 'the addition of a bit of coal tar would probably have gone completely unnoticed'.

In a similar vein, Francis quotes an advertisement from 1845 of 'P. & T.M'Anaspie bitumen cement works' (which preamble leads incidentally to the question about what exactly is meant by the word 'cement'?) M'Anaspie advertised their product as 'artificial hydraulic cement' and also claimed to make 'artificial stone and patent asphalte'.

Maceroni, more likely to be frank about coal tar, writing in Mechanics Magazine in October 1826, promoted its use in a mix with materials like pebbles and chalk 'to answer every purpose of building'. No doubt it was also cheap.

A list of eleven Roman cement manufacturers active in London in the early 1820s is detailed by Francis. Of these, Atkinson, Simpson and Sanders are also all listed as chemical manufacturers. Turner, as we have seen, was also a tar distiller; Morgan was involved with Cassell Francis and Mornay were gas company subscribers. Seen in this way, the manufacture of Roman cement becomes quite clearly a branch of the chemical industry.

Charles, 'Citizen' Earl Stanhope of Chevening was well known to the early gas industry and had even written a letter of support to the Chartered Company before the 1809 Enquiry – which is quoted in Winsor's *Considerations*. Stanhope had invented a type of cement that included tar, although exactly what sort of tar is a point on which he remained ambiguous. John Nash used Stanhope's tar on the roof of Buckingham Palace where it melted in warm weather, was the subject of some scandal and had to be replaced. General Pasley, who wrote a book on cement, said that the tar used on this occasion was wood tar although coal tar was used in similar installations. Contemporary comments point to the use of coal tar in similar circumstances and with an equal lack of success.

'Stucco' is another example of something whose constituent parts were far from clear. This popular material had a lime and stone based formula and, like 'mastic', it was widely used on the outside of those buildings that were in need of covering *'with great expedition'*. Mastic was made with linseed oil although some variants contained whiting, resin and glue. What really went on the walls of buildings, being built with an eye to speed and to keeping down costs, is anyone's guess. In most cases the main aim must have been to cover up quickly whatever it was that had gone up underneath!

'Asphalte' was used both for waterproofing and as a surface material. Advertising material hinted that it came from a Swiss source and was a type of natural bitumen Once again this is more than open to some doubt.

George Landmann, Engineer of the London and Greenwich Railway, mentioned above as a gas enthusiast, used *'asphalt as a waterproofing medium on the railway's brick arches'*. This came from the Seyssel Asphalt Company – and from evidence given above their most likely location was the Isle of Dogs.

Ron Thomas gives other examples of this in his history of the London and Greenwich railway. When the Croydon Railway joined London and Greenwich at London Bridge Station the platforms were covered with *'beautiful specimens of Bastenne bitumen'* – another Millwall product.

R.T. Claridge Esq., whose *'patent asphalte'* has been mentioned above, provides a good example of this confusion in the exact nature of ingredients. He patented a *'Mastic cement applicable to paving, and road making, covering buildings and various other purposes'*. In 1838 *Mechanics Magazine* reported on a case for patent infringement between Claridge and a Mr. Latrade which went to court. Latrade had actually intended to use *'mineral pitch'* in a paving scheme but had somehow found he was using *'Stockholm tar'*. There was much discussion in court on the two patents and unsurprisingly Claridge's specification was said to be unclear on the subject of the type of tar. Specimens of coal

211

tar from the City Gas Works were produced in evidence and passed round the jury so that they could see what they thought the difference was.

The likelihood is that there were as many mixes as there were manufacturers and that they mostly kept the contents of their mixtures to themselves.

COMPOSITION

Enderby, the Greenwich-based whalers and rope makers were interested in something called *'composition'* and discussed its manufacture in 1835 with the City of London Gas Company. Contact with the gas company suggests, of course, that it is tar that they were after for their 'composition'. A mysterious super-hard cement is said to have been found in the cellar of Enderby House in Greenwich and just might be something to do with it. The Enderby family built the house on the Greenwich riverside in the 1840s and it has since been used as offices by subsequent occupiers of the wharf and is now being converted into a pub.

'Composition' is a vague term that can mean any number of things. Its nature was discussed in *Mechanics Magazine* in 1838 when a report was given of a *'new Paving Composition in Paris'* which turned out to be *'pebbles in pitch'*. 'Compo' can mean anything from an unreliable mortar to a rubbery constituent of cricket balls. An 1826 recipe in Philosophical Magazine gave a mixture of oil of turpentine and coal tar as ingredients together with resin, size and ochre.

In the 1780s James Wyatt, the architect and builder, had invented something he called *'compo-cement'* for use as stucco. He was to use this in the *'self destructing'* Fonthill Abbey'. Observers noted in its ruined walls *'tarred packthread'*. At that date coal tar is unlikely to have been used, but Wyatt's successors very probably found it very useful indeed. It is not hard to imagine that coal tar was a real boon for those builders who wanted something sticky, quick and cheap.

BRIQUETTES

Attempts to make a fuel from scrap coal preceded the gas industry. In 1799 the Marquis of Chabbannes had begun a business on Millbank to combine small pieces of coal with other things and make the mixture into *'cakes'*. This is described by Andrew Saint in his Newcomen Transactions article of 1994. Interestingly Chabbanes wharf was later taken over by Frederick Albert Winsor who used it, in 1808, for one of the earliest gasworks to be built in London, as described above

It is not clear how successful the Marquis' enterprise was but, nearly a hundred years later, Georg Lunge described a number of patents for fuel briquettes using coal tar and other things — wood chips, sawdust, sand and similar ingredients of varying flammability.

In the 1830s and 1840s a number of makers of these artificial coal blocks sprang up in the Deptford and Greenwich areas. Colonel Francis of the Wylam Patent Fuel Co. owned what is described as a chemical works on Marsh Wall, on the Greenwich Peninsula. William Wylam took out a number of patents in 1845 for the manufacture of *'artificial fuel'* and for pressing machinery to be used for this. The Wylam Company used tar for their briquettes — in 1848 the Chartered Company refused to supply more tar to them because of defaults on payments.

Wylam were not the only manufacturers of briquettes in the area. A patent fuel wharf is listed for Scott and Eden in Broomstead place on the Deptford Riverside. Nearby, in 1867, a large wharf between the Royal Dockyard and General Steam Navigation was described as *'Patent Fuel Company's Wharf'*. William Buckwell who held a patent for *'compressed or solidified fuel'* owned another *'composition'* factory on Greenwich Marsh. Buckwell eventually went bankrupt and was arrested by the Italian police in the roof space of an Italian barn having absconded over the Alps — a riveting tale reported in *Kentish Mercury*.

WOOD PRESERVATION

One of the best known applications of coal tar is as a wood preservative. As railways, telegraphs and other outdoor users of wood proliferated so the need for preservation became more pressing. Several methods were tried which appear to use gas industry derivatives.

In 1814 a Royal Society Enquiry into the gas industry had been set up because of *'general alarm'* raised through an explosion in the *'searing house'* at Woolwich Dockyard. This had occurred two years earlier when a Mr. Lukin had experimented there with a new method of seasoning timber. Samuel Clegg giving evidence at the Select Committee into the Chartered in 1823 described Lukin as *'a partner of mine'*. This comment seems to suggest some sort of liaison with the early gas industry, in which Clegg was, of course, a leading figure.

What Mr. Lukin actually used is not particularly clear. John Maiben, a saddler of Perth, who wrote on the early gas industry claimed that he was using *'naphtha*. Clegg said that it was *'wood gas* and Lunge, writing a century later, said that it was *'creosote oils or similar substances in a state of vapour'*. *Mechanics Magazine* contented themselves by describing it as a *'secret process'*. Joseph Banks when commenting on it to the Royal Society Committee

213

said it was *'gas'*. Whatever, Lunge was probably right in his comment that it *'could not possibly answer'*.

A number of methods of wood preservation gradually became available that depended on the forcing of a preservative into the wood. Several works to undertake this sprang up in the Millwall area.

Sir Humphrey Davy's brother, John, researched a process using chloride of zinc. This was patented in 1838 by Sir William Burnett, the Inspector General of the Medical Department of the Navy, as a disinfectant — an action on his part which led to much outrage among the medical profession. In 1851 a works in Millwall was described as owned by the *'Proprietors of Sir W. Burnett's patent for manufacturing and disinfecting timber, corded cloth, wool, etc.'* The company did not leave Millwall until the 1970s by which time it functioned as a timber importer. Until recently they continued in business in Cuffley, in Hertfordshire.

JOHN HOWARD KYAN

The most famous wood preservation method was that of John Howard Kyan who patented a process using 'corrosive sublimate'. The term *'kyanising'* was widely used but it was its methods, rather than the use of sublimate, which were copied by others. Sublimate is a particularly unpleasant and dangerous substance: *'it has a sharp metallic taste and extremely poisonous ... it is used in medicine, especially in cases of syphilis and in surgery as an antiseptic in the form of a dilute solution'*. Its connection with syphilis had given it a particularly bad reputation.

Kyan told the Committee appointed to enquire into his patent in 1835 that he had taken 40 years to devise his patent, suggesting he must have begun in the 1790s. His antecedents are not clear — he may have been the J.H.Kyan who wrote to Boulton and Watt around 1800 as an Irish mill owner. He had a works in Pimlico where he lived at 'Gillingham Cottage' but later moved to 'Nailsea Cottage', Twickenham.

He said that he had devised his process through work at the Old Street Vinegar Works. This works, on what is now the north east corner of the Old Street roundabout, was owned in the 1830s by members of the Champion family. Other Champion family members were involved in Walker and Ward's Islington White Lead Works in which Fishwick was also a partner. Enderby — who also had connections with Kyan, had brought Fishwick's white lead process to London.

Kyan clearly had a reputation throughout the chemical community – the first name given to aniline on its discovery by the chemist, Runge, in 1834, was *'kyanol'* – a clear

compliment to Howard Kyan. Kyan took out a number of patents, all in the 1830s. Most were concerned with the preservation of a number of substances from decay but others covered the preparation of salts from gas industry by products and 'steam engines'.

In 1835 the Admiralty instigated an Enquiry into his process, having undertaken tests *'at Woolwich in the Foundry Pit and in pits at Margate Pier'.*

The process was tried in a number of other places. It was used in the building of a ship called the Samuel Enderby. It was the second Samuel who probably built the first Enderby House and a print of the ship, built in 1834, once hung in the building. A model of the ship is in the National Maritime Museum in Greenwich and her work in the South Seas whaling trade made her a particularly important testing ground for this new process.

Another place in which sublimate was tested was in the timber *'laid down in Mr. Pearson's father's house in Greenwich'* This was *'Ravensbourne House'* the old mansion, rebuilt around 1800, belonging to the owners of the Greenwich copperas works. In the 1830s Charles Pearson, the copperas works' owner, not only bought tar and ammonia from the Imperial Gas Co. but also acted as auditor to the Phoenix Gas Company.

Considering both Enderby and Pearson's interest in, and liaisons with, the early gas industry, both of these testing places must be particularly significant. The new railway companies took up Kyan's system. Perhaps the most famous relationship in this context is Kyan's work with I.K. Brunel on the Great Western Railway. A timber preservation works was set up on the Grand Junction Canal at Bulls Bridge depot where the wood to be preserved was immersed in tanks full of sublimate.

A similar 'kyanising' plant in Battersea caught fire with disastrous results in 1847 but, in this case, the tanks were said to be full of tar. Thus 'kyanising' eventually came to be used to describe a process that used tar distillates – in particular creosote – for wood preservation and the dangerous sublimate ceased to be used.

215

JOHN BETHEL

Perhaps the most successful process was that pioneered in the 1830s by John Bethell a barrister from Bristol. He was the brother of Richard Bethel who became Lord Chancellor. An interesting sidelight is that Richard Bethell acted in a judgement *'between Paynter and Pincus'* – part of a long and tangled case in the affairs of the Ratcliffe Gas Company.

John Bethell took out a patent in 1848 for *'preserving animal and vegetable substances from decay'*. Lunge described the apparatus which had first been designed in Paris: the dried timber was put on iron bogey frames, which were run into a strong wrought iron cylinder, and the air exhausted. The preservative was then forced in under what would have been a partial vacuum. Bethell issued licences and specified a number of preservatives including gas-tar.

He set up a tar distillery in Battersea in 1845 – probably the site of the fire mentioned above. He is said to have opened this works up as a creosote distillery because of an, unspecified, difficulty with tar supplies. Another tar works was opened by Bethel on Bow Common in 1844 and, in the early 1850s, a Chemical Works near Blackwall Point on a site leased from Morden College.

The Blackwall Point works seems to have made a general range of chemicals. Bethell is listed in directories of the 1840s as an *'oil of vitriol manufacturer'*, implying a much wider range of chemical manufactures than merely wood preservation. A range of workers' housing was built adjacent to the East Greenwich site.

When Bethell died in the 1870s his wife, Louisa, continued, to own the East Greenwich works. Mrs. Bethell lived in Bath and the company was managed from an address in King William Street, City of London. The works seems to have specialised in tarred wooden blocks for paving and in the 1880s it was taken over by the Improved Wood Pavement Company although the Bethel family still remained involved.

Bethel seems to have experimented with a number of other coal gas related chemical processes. In the 1850s he offered the Chartered Gas Company a purification process but this proved 'unsatisfactory'. Methods of wood preservation by tar remained his main interest. He said, in 1851, that he had got the idea of preservation by tar from examination of an Egyptian mummy. In preservation with coal tar pitch as used *'in the Mediterranean'*, ammonia should be distilled away, because that would cause rot.

HENRY BURT

At Bethell's Battersea works, Henry Burt experimented on what was soon to be called 'creosote'. He too was involved with a railway company: the Eastern Counties Railway. In order to fulfil orders he opened two tar works of his own: one on Bow Common and another on Millwall. In the 1850s Samuel Boulton and Thomas Heywood joined Burt and they acquired Bethel's tar distilling patents.

By the 1880s this partnership was described by Crory in *Industries of East London* as the largest distillers of gas tar in the world. In 1871 their Silvertown works, then open three years, covered eleven acres. This was achieved because they had gained the market in railway sleeper blocks and telegraph poles for much of Europe. In the 1980s the area of the works became the northern riverside of the Thames Barrier. It was called the 'most polluted site in Europe', in a 1994 report by Travers Morgan to the London Docklands Development Corporation.

The international success of Burt, Boulton and Heywood is a very long way from the early experiments carried out by Thomas Dalton for the Chartered Company and his attempts to sell gasworks tar for ship-building purposes. The intention has been to look at the relationship of the early gas industry with those who used its tar. After the 1840s many new ideas about coal tar began to bear fruit. Burt, Boulton and Heywood, and their works at the end of Prince Regent Lane were part of a world of successful tar distillers and far removed from the earlier experimenters.

BACK TO THOMAS DALTON
AND THE POPLAR TAR WORKS

To return to the Chartered Gas Company's Poplar Tar Works, closed as a failure and sold to Turner, Shakell and Hopkinson, but who were Turner, Shakell and Hopkinson and what happened to them?

The partnership at Orchard Place does not seem to have lasted very long because later directory entries only mention a Mr. Turner. In 1839 a William Hopkinson was an oil and colourman in The Barbican while Shackell and How were printing ink, varnish makers and oil merchants at Coppice Row, Clerkenwell. Did they find the use of coal tar for varnishes and oils unfruitful and leave the partnership and Mr. Turner in Orchard Place?

Turner had had plans to manufacture *'various articles'* from coal tar and had already been using it for ten years when he bought the Orchard Place works and he continued to buy tar from Chartered. Twenty years later, still there, he was in an *'advantageous position'* as the *'only varnish maker'* in that area. His Roman cement business has been mentioned above. The site was still a tar works in the 1880s and this continued use must indicate some measure of success.

Cassell had taken over the City Gas Company works in the 1820s and stayed in business there, in one form or another, until the early 1860s. Nearly thirty-five years of production from gas industry tar can hardly be called a failure.

These tar distillers were part of a movement in which the material was gradually exploited to make new materials. Several of these uses have been discussed above. The continued existence of these works raises the question as to whether the gas company tar works really failed. Failed tar works were bought by others who made them profitable and were able to help in the exploitation of coal tar by a wide range of industries.

AMMONIACAL LIQUOR

To return to 1800. A third by-product resulted from the processing of coal gas: ammoniacal liquor. The early gas companies had to find a profitable use for it. So, how did they go about it?

THE IDEA

It is less easy to describe the background to this third principal by-product. It might be said to have hardly existed before the gas industry began to produce it. '*Ammoniacal liquor*' is an ammonia-rich liquid that condensed on top of the tar after the gas was washed with water. Ammonia itself had been identified only in from the 1750s by Joseph Black, and further researched in the fifty years since. Some ammonia salts were known and commonly used but it should be noted that they were those commonly known by their older names: '*sal ammoniac*' and '*sal volatile*'. Knowledge about the use of '*ammonia and its compounds*' was thus confined to '*medical purposes and scientific investigations*'. Nevertheless the promoters of the Chartered Gas Company claimed that it had potential.

Winsor had advertised the uses of ammoniacal liquor by saying that it was '*one of the strongest lyes for tanning skin*'. 'Lye' was the alkaline solution used as part of the tanning process. Ammoniacal liquor also, Winsor said, in '*Account of the most ingenious… National Discovery….*' suitable for smoking '*hams, bacons, beef*' and '*very valuable in the fabrication of white lead, verdigris, copperas and alum*'. In his '*Considerations*' Winsor suggested the manufacture of '*chemical salts*', while at the 1809 Enquiry Accum talked at length about the various salts that could be made.

The Chartered's promoters while suggesting that the liquor had uses in dyeing and tanning also admitted that '*this has not yet been investigated*'. This point was not lost on Boulton and Watt's lawyers who had read the Chartered's advertising material with an eye to unsubstantiated claims. On their copy of the *Report of J.L. Grant* they highlighted extracts from a letter by Accum in which he said that ammoniacal liquor could be used for dyeing and calico printing – in particular they noted the words '*highly probable*'. Their barrister, the future Lord Chancellor, Henry Brougham, used these claims to some effect at the 1809 Enquiry.

What did the new company think they were going to do with this awkward and uninvestigated liquid? A point had to come when large quantities of it were being produced and the claims made by Winsor and Accum had to be turned into reality.

THE REALITY

One advertised application for ammoniacal liquor was for dyeing.

Ammonia itself was used to make cudbear, a lichen-based violet dye. In London 'Cudbear' was also called '*archly*'. There were two manufacturing works in Bethnal Green, that of Samuel Child, and that of Dent and Child. There was an even closer relationship with the industry in Westminster because the Great Peter Street Works of the Chartered Gas Company was to be built on the site of the Cudbear Company's works. A Mr. Grant had brought this enterprise from Scotland. The ammonia they used was often in the form of urine, but the production of cudbear meant that dyers were aware that ammonia products were useful in the manufacture of at least one dye.

The new gas company promoters suggested, in *Considerations* , that rather than be used as a dye, ammonia could be '*applied as a mordant for dyers*'. Hitherto sal ammoniac, had been used for this. A mordant (not defined in the 18th century dictionary) is the 'biting' solution used with some dyestuffs in order to 'fix' the colour.

A Mr. Bryan, described as a dyer from Spitalfields, had testified to the 1809 Enquiry on the usefulness of the liquor for dyers. His tests had been for the use of the liquor as a potential colouring agent rather than a mordant. He had produced '*a number of neat shades of drab - which will stand wearing*'. Asked about its use as a mordant, he said '*I'm sure… it may be used … as a substitute for potash*'.

EXPERIMENTATION

It was nearly a year after the Chartered began to make gas that they first investigated the potential of ammoniacal liquor. They then arranged for 'experiments' to be done. They had set up a Committee for Chemistry to decide which products '*are the most saleable and of the least bulk*'. Having got very little sense out of Accum, who demanded money before he would give any relevant information, they began to look for someone else who might know what do to.

At this stage a junior Frederick Albert Winsor appeared on the scene. Persuaded by Winsor, the Chartered directors agreed to ask his son to set up '*practical processes for... ammoniacal liquor*' and to make "*such articles as may best suit the interests of the company*". The lad was just fifteen in 1813. His career as a barrister, as director of a charity, and his long association with the Chartered, which did not end for another sixty years, could not have been foreseen. Within a few months the Court of Governors called a halt to his work on the project.

The laboratories, and the other Pall Mall buildings of Winsor's first headquarters, were to be demolished as part of John Nash's 'improvements'. An argument ensued when Winsor Jnr. asked for payment and no doubt he had done his best. This episode illustrates the Chartered Gas Company's commitment to fulfil their promotional promises to shareholders and the public.

Meanwhile some directors began to act on their own initiative. One of them was a Thomas Livesey who in 1812 had been one of a group who had organised a takeover of the Court of Governors. He stayed with the Company as Deputy Governor for the next thirty years and he intended to change things. Finding a use for ammoniacal liquor was a start. He arranged for a sample of the liquor to be sent, for experimental use as a mordant to *'Messrs. Barchard, Hilton and Platt, dyers, Montague Close, Borough'*. He also arranged to sell all the 'weak' ammoniacal liquor from Curtain Road at *'1d per gallon wine measure'* to *'Alcock and Co. of Haggerston'* together with *'strong liquor for experimenting'*.

John Van Voorst was a shareholder concerned to get some action and effect change in the company. He arranged for 'experiments' to be done by a Mr. Dunstan, an apothecary of Old Broad Street, who was to become a director of the Imperial Gas Co., where he was involved in the usual financial scandals. He was, however, probably more qualified than young Winsor to undertake chemical investigations. He concluded that ammoniacal liquor would be *'valuable to dyers'* and give a *'very considerable advantage in producing sulphur salts'*.

Word was also beginning to get around the manufacturing and scientific community that large amounts of ammonia-rich liquid was being produced. Individuals from outside the company also began to ask for samples on which to experiment – for instance, a Mr. Hoskins was sent liquor for 'his friends'. Sooner or later someone must come up with a good idea.

RAW AMMONIACAL LIQUOR

In due course the London gas companies sold raw ammoniacal liquor.

Liquor was produced in substantial quantities. An idea of the amounts can be seen from figures given by Samuel Clegg to William Congreve's 1823 Enquiry into the London Gas Industry. He said that the Great Peter Street, gasworks produced 102,102 gallons of liquor 1821. All this raw ammoniacal liquor had to be disposed of somehow.

Clegg's figures were taken up and publicised by Joseph Hedley in his 1826 *Letter to the Rt. Hon the Lord Mayor*. Hedley had a *'gas fitting and ironmongery'* business based in Cheapside and was the father of a family of gas engineers.

It is frequently said that the early gas companies found it hard to dispose of the ammoniacal liquor. Musson & Robinson described residuals as *'an embarrassing problem, often being dumped in rivers'*. Derek Matthews said that *'in the early decades of the industry the London gas companies literally could not give their ammoniacal liquor away'*. Rom the industry itself George Anderson in his 1871 paper on *'Manufacture of Sulphate of Ammonia'* given

221

to the British Association of Gas Managers remembered the disposal of ammoniacal liquor, which, he said, incurred *'great expense'* and had to be *'carted away in barges'*.

SELLING AMMONIACAL LIQUOR

Some raw liquor was definitely sold although often together with an agreement on bulk removal. At first the Chartered Company sold its liquor on an ad hoc basis but from 1818 the system was regularised. The superintendents of the three works at Westminster, Brick Lane and Curtain Road, were asked to prepare lists of all liquor purchasers together with the price being paid. In 1820, as a result of their findings from this survey, they set a standard price for liquor at 12s a butt. 'A butt' usually meant 108 gallons but sometimes this amount was qualified: as *'Imperial measure'*, *'beer measure'*, or *'wine measure'*.

Customers began to emerge and in 1823 Imperial agreed to sell the liquor from its Shoreditch Works at double the price of that from its other works. Strength and quality were bargaining points on both sides. The gas companies advertised for liquor purchasers. *'Secretary to put an advertisement in the Times for the tar and ammoniacal liquor'*, minuted the Imperial Company in 1825. Contracts were often made for a set number of years: usually three. In 1827 Independent agreed that *'MacMurdo would take the liquor weekly ..... without any complaint about quality until 22nd June.* Phoenix Gas Company noted, in 1833, that *'Pearson says it [the liquor] is very weak and not so good as that from other companies'*. Their reply was robust *'Let him try it at the other works'*.

In June 1831 'Wilkinson' was asked by the Ratcliffe Gas Co. to provide the name of someone who would act as a guarantor for his payment of bills. He provided *'Wilkinson late of Ludgate Hill'*. This was almost certainly H.Wilkinson who took over the gun-making company that later became known as Wilkinson Sword. George Elliott who was to take over the Millwall works of the Imperial Company, offered '1s 6d' for the City Gas Company's liquor *'for the next three years from midsummer'*. These financial arrangements would not have been necessary if payment was not being made.

One customer was Samuel Crane who had a turpentine manufactory by Stratford Bridge. It is tempting to speculate that he was a member of the family who made *'blue'* and *'celebrated Mexican jet'* at Kings Cross from the 1830s. In 1823, just before he began to buy liquor from the gas companies Crane's son took out a patent for *'improvements in the manufacture of inflammable gas'*. In 1826 Mr. Crane of Stratford was given a percentage discount on liquor by Ratcliffe Gas Co. And at around the same time he told the Independent Gas Company *'that he could afford no more than 8s a butt'*. It should be noted that Independent were then under threat of legal action from the Regents Canal Company for putting liquor directly into the Canal and clearly needed to get stocks off the premises. Soon after, Crane complained to them that the liquor *'was inferior to the usual strength'*. Still negotiating in the 1830s he told Independent that he could only afford 1s 3d and they agreed to accept this. Two years later he persuaded the City Gas Company to accept 10d, although for this they wanted him to agree to *'special guarantees'*.

There were, of course, problems. Inevitably the contractors did not take all the liquor in exactly the way that the gas companies wanted. In 1832 Imperial Company complained that Beneke's barge *'which was loaded with ammoniacal liquor on Thursday last …. within four hours of its arrival … still remains in the dock at this station and there is 22,000 gallons of liquor on hand'*. This particular episode continued for months with some suspicion on Imperial's part that both Mr.Beneke and his, usually missing, bargeman found the Imperial's wharf at Haggerston a convenient, and free, place to leave a barge which had no other work to do.

Who were these contractors?

Mr.Baldock - who unsuccessfully tendered for liquor from Chartered Company in 1837.
Mr. Barnett who was *'considering an offer'* from Chartered.
Mr. Mandeville, who received liquor from the Chartered in July 1829
Mr. Maples who offered to manufacture *'saleable products'* for Imperial in 1824
Mr. McPheron of Haggerston contracted to take all of Imperial's liquor in 1823.
James Hanbury, wanted to experiment with Chartered's liquor in 1824. Was he one of the Quaker banking and brewing family?.
Mr. Pruce, or Pryce, of Haggerston Chemical Works failed to fulfil his contract to take Imperial's liquor in 1824. Was he the friend of Benjamin Hawes who witnessed the oil gas experiments undertaken by Herepath and Rootsey at Bankside in 1826?
Smith & Cotton, contracted to take Chartered's liquor in 1823? Is Mr. Cotton the same man who had enquired from 'Kennelworth' about liquor a decade earlier?

WOMEN CHEMICAL MANUFACTURERS

Some contractors were women.

Mrs. Miles, who bought liquor from Imperial in 1843. She made sal ammoniac and complained bitterly when the price dropped – causing her to ask Imperial to reduce

their prices too.
Mrs. Hunt made sulphate of ammonia, on Bow Common and also bought liquor from Imperial in 1844. She too complained about their prices and gave considerable detail about her difficulties and the investment she had made in manufacturing equipment.
Charlotte Foot – also called Charlotte Elizabeth Condy – who from 1839 managed the chemical and dye manufacturing company of Foot, Brown and Co. based in Bolingbroke Gardens, Battersea. Also described as '*acetous acid manufacturers*'. She bought as much ammoniacal liquor '*as required*' from Imperial in the 1830s. It was at her works that experiments were undertaken in the 1850s to determine the validity of a number of purification patents that used ammonia salts.

To them we should also add Mrs. Eastwood who personally managed the largest barge haulier and brick maker on the Thames and whose business representatives in attendance at gas company offices and meetings were all women.

LIQUOR BUYERS - WHERE THEIR WORKS WERE

Customers for gas works liquor had works concentrated towards the east of London and all, except one was in the modern metropolitan area.

The exception was Firmin who bought ammonia salts and liquor from the 1820s. George (or Richard) Firmin was, like some others among this list, a friend of Philip Taylor. He was one of the principals in the chemical firm of the chemical firm of Firmin, Fenton, Haddock & Co., and one of the founders of the Colchester Gas works where he became manager and installed oil gas making machinery from Taylor and Martineau. By the late 1830s he had moved to an address in Great Alie Street near the Tower of London. The directory entries change to '*Mrs. George Firmin*' in this period and by the 1860s the company had moved to Borough Road. in Southwark. In 1853 George Firmin had a joint patent for lampblack with Henry Hughes of Rotherhithe. I was told by an unknown person in the audience at a lecture in 1992 at Essex University that he was involved in developing early photographic chemicals.

The most westerly identified, were Foot and Co, in Battersea, mentioned above.

SOUTHWARK - In the Borough was Macdonald's saltpetre works in today's Southwark Street then known as 'The Grove' Great Guildford Street. However he dealt with the gas companies from his City office at 62 Old Broad Street. He tendered for liquor from several gas companies and sold acids to them.

BERMONDSEY – The one Bermondsey based customer was MacMurdo. His name sometimes occurs in combination with Pitchford and together they were Stratford based. However, the same, or another Mr. MacMurdo operated chemical works in Abbey Street, Bermondsey, together with a Mr. Davey (another name that crops up in several other combinations). MacMurdo, along with Hills and some others, exhibited ammonia salts at the 1851 Great Exhibition.

BATTLEBRIDGE –this is the area to the immediate north east of today's Kings Cross. One customer listed is 'Wilkinson' described in 1823 as *'of Battlebridge'* - but there may be more than one Mr. Wilkinson. In 1839 a Thomas Wilkinson had a varnish and japan manufacturer in a Holloway Road, near Kings Cross, and this could be the same person. He is almost certainly a forerunner of Wilkinson, Heywood and Clark who were in 9 Caledonian Road before 1876 and later moved to West Drayton. However the connections of a Mr. Wilkinson with the future Wilkinson Sword company has been noted above and there are other candidates – in particular as the owner of a large chemical works on the Surrey canal.

HAGGERSTON – Pryce was in the Haggerston area as was Copeman.

MILLWALL – Millwall chemists include Richard Laming and Owen and Mertens. One important ammonia manufacturer was George Elliott who had bought Imperials' defunct Millwall products works.

STRATFORD – A number of chemists, like Crane, operated in Stratford. MacMurdo, also mentioned above, was in partnership with Pitchford at Tokenhouse Yard in Stratford where they are described as turpentine manufacturers. John Pitchford seems to have had interests also on Bow Common. He was another friend of John Taylor and a close personal associate of the Quaker banking families of Frys and Gurneys, themselves Essex-based. Elizabeth Fry, the prison reformer, lived in Plaistow and knew Pitchford. Pitchford was the son of a surgeon and a member of the Chemical Society. Pitchford Road in West Ham probably commemorates him.

Perhaps the most typical Stratford ammonia purchaser is Mr. Crow. Thomas Crow had an ammonia works and a laboratory near what is still known as Crows Road, in West Ham, on the edge of the Imperial Gas Works final site at Bromley by Bow. He dealt with several of the gas companies for a range of products. In 1836 Thomas Crow rented Westbury House in Barking, and was probably a Conservator of the River Lea – both implying considerable prosperity. In the 1850s a Mr. Edward Crow established a sulphate of ammonia works on the east side of Barking Creekmouth. It is very likely that this was a second generation of the same family moving to an expanded greenfield site.

THE GREAT IMPORTANCE OF BOW COMMON

The most important area for locations of ammonia purchasers is Bow Common – a large open area north of East India Dock Road and intersected by the Limehouse Cut and North Street. A number of firms in this area have already been noted above.

Chemical manufacture on Bow Common seems to have grown up following the opening of the Limehouse Cut in the 1770s. Dundonald's and Birch's activities there have been noted in other chapters. An early chemical manufacturer there was Brown who took over a potash works, perhaps Dundonald's in 1813. James and Thomas Brown are listed on Bow Common as *'ash makers'* in 1839. They bought ammonia from the gas companies through the 1820s and 1830s.

A later regular buyer was Bush who had a chemical works on Bow Common. He does not seem to have been the Hackney based aromatics manufacturer, a firm which became Bush, Boake and Allen. The Mr. Bush who bought liquor was on Bow Common from the 1830s until the 1880s.

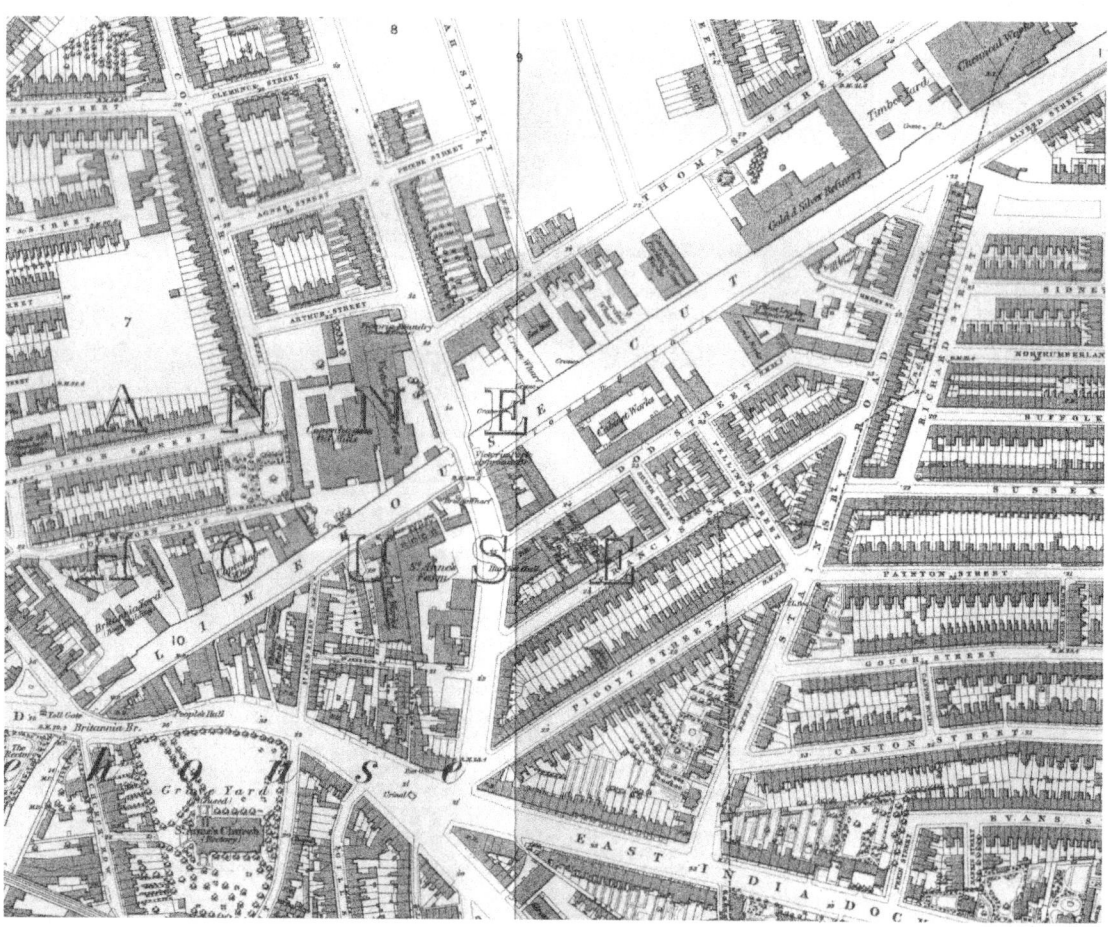

Pitchford and Torr also had works on Bow Common.

Cook bought liquor from the Chartered in 1827. In the early 1820s John Cook took over an old potash works. He then founded an Oxalic Acid works on Bow Common, calling it the Phoenix. It was on an important location, at the point at which the junction of Bow Common Lane and Poplar North Street cross the Limehouse Cut. Cook ran the works into the 1860s. It then passed to Frederick Allen in 1863. He made a range of domestic insecticides and fertilisers and the works closed only in 1984. In the 1990s the buildings had become the Phoenix Business Centre. Now in 2020 it is identikit, overbearing flats – but they are called 'Phoenix Works'.

Phoenix was not the only Bow Common work to endure. Moore and Pearce bought ammoniacal liquor from South Metropolitan Gas Company in 1839. William Pearce is listed as a sulphuric acid manufacturer from the early 1830s. The works were at 1 Bow Common Lane, opposite the Phoenix Works. They remained on site and in production until the 1920s.

HACKNEY WICK AND GREENWICH

A number of manufacturers set up in new areas from the middle of the century. They went predominately to East Greenwich, Rainham and Hackney Wick. James Forbes is a good example. He patented a new way of making sulphate of ammonia in 1865 and this was adopted at his chemical works at Iceland Wharf, Old Ford where he was in partnership with Abbott and Lennard. The company later moved to the Greenwich peninsula where their sites were eventually taken over by South Metropolitan Gas Company, from whom they had bought liquor for many years.

WATER TRANSPORT

The one common feature of all the sites used by purchasers of salts is that they were generally on or near to navigable water: the Thames, Deptford Creek, the Bow Back Rivers, Limehouse Cut and Regents Canal are on established barge routes (Cotton via the Grand Junction Canal and Firmin via Brightlingsea). Transport by water may have been important for bulky, and liquid, ammoniacal liquor. The use by Beneke of a barge on the Regent's Canal, together with its blocking of wharf space, was noted above.

WHAT DID THEY MAKE?

In the 1870s, Edward Ballard, Medical Officer of Health at the Local Government Board, who was writing a book about pollution and working practices, visited and reported on several chemical companies in the area: Wallace, Forbes, and Hills as well as Blott and Percival Smith, both on Bow Common, and Crow at Barking Level. Ballard commented that all of these used gasworks' liquor as their main raw material.

There were many more manufacturers than those visited by Ballard. By the 1860s London companies could not supply enough liquor and additional supplies came from gasworks in many areas outside London. In some years the Colchester Gas Co. sold all their liquor to the Imperial Company who handled its sale on their behalf. At another time, Colchester Co. sold their liquor to Simpson of Millwall who made sulphate of ammonia. The accounts of Lawes Agricultural Manure Company at Barking in the early 1870s gives some idea of the amount they were taking – i.e. 20 tons of ammonia from Hills.

Considerable quantities of ammoniacal liquor were bought from the early gas industry. It must be significant that most of it was bought by manufacturing chemists. Some, perhaps all, of them made ammonia salts. Most of them had works in east London. Despite the lack of records from the chemists themselves, it must be presumed that their products were sold to great range of industries. Thus gas companies were suppliers of raw materials to the chemical industry well before the development of coal tar dyes. The chemical industry itself was a major supplier of raw materials in this area and beyond.

AMMONIA SALTS

GEORGE LOWE

In 1819 a letter was published in the scientific press from a George Lowe. It was written from Derby where Lowe was the son of a brewer. He had undertaken experiments on his father's premises there. The letter described experiments, which he had done on ammoniacal liquor "*to ascertain its constituents and the quantity of ammonia it contained*". In doing this he had obtained a number of substances that had aroused his curiosity. After adding muriatic (hydrochloric) acid he obtained "*a precipitate ... a compound of sulphur and carbon*", following evaporation a *'waxy'* precipitate that gave a *'permanent brown dye'*, and *'globules of a beautiful red, or rather lake colour'*. He wrote his letter in the hope that *'the foregoing hints... stir up others with more ability and opportunity than myself'*.

The main outcome of this letter was that Lowe soon found himself in the employment of the Chartered Gas Company from which base he enjoyed a distinguished career as an innovative and important gas engineer. There is, however, little evidence that the gas industry, or Lowe himself, developed any manufactures based on the experiments that he undertook on ammoniacal liquor in his father's Derby works. His research may well have been limited by a lack of knowledge of organic chemistry. In undertaking these experiments in his father's laboratory Lowe was typical of many young men who were excited by what they read in the scientific press and set about experimenting for themselves. This episode is well-known because the experimenter became well-known – there may well have been many, many more.

Lowe's experiments may appear to foreshadow the coal tar dye industry. Although he was not to be closely involved in the industry, he was nevertheless an early supporter of the Royal College of Chemistry at a time when the theoretical basis of coal tar dyes were being developed there. None of the attempts at experimentation with ammoniacal liquor seem to have come to anything. None of those who undertook the experiments are recorded as future purchasers of liquor. No more is minuted about direct sales to dyers and the company seems to have concentrated on turning the liquor into salts.

AMMONIA SALTS

Once again the names of things become confusing. *'Sal ammoniac'* became better known as *'ammonium chloride'*. It was also once known as *'muriate of ammonia'* - *'muriate'* once being the term which defined a chloride. All three names are used, apparently at random, in the gas company minute books in the early 19th century. It could be made by adding hydrochloric acid to the ammoniacal liquor.

In advertising the proposed gas company in 1809 the projectors had mentioned, in *Considerations "the manufacture of muriate of ammonia'.* Accum's evidence on this to the 1809 Enquiry had been the source of extensive criticisms by Henry Brougham, acting for Boulton and Watt. Brougham questioned the methods used to make the sal ammoniac in tests set up for the Enquiry. He had pointed out that *"no one denied"* its usefulness and reminded the Enquiry that sal ammoniac had been made for many centuries. Dundonald made it as a by-product of tar manufacture.

Brougham was right, of course. There had been a number of sal ammoniac manufacturers in Whitechapel and Bermondsey in the late 18th Century; some are mentioned by A. & N. Clow. They were perhaps supplying the growing paper industry, like Koops' Neckinger paper mill in Southwark.

Sal ammoniac was used in medicine, by dyers and by tinplate workers. There were a number of these in London – like John and Thomas Bore, tinplate workers of Commercial Road who were subscribers to the scheme to light Mile End Road and perhaps hoped for cheap supplies.

Before the gas industry came along sal ammoniac was the best known ammonia salt, and there was one other in common use. This other principal ammonia salt, which Accum had advertised before 1810, was *'sal volatile'* or *'ammonium carbonate'* sometimes, commonly, called *'smelling salts'* or *'carbonate of ammonia'* – once again the early 19th century gas industry used all four terms indiscriminately. This particular salt was one which Accum had claimed in his evidence to the enquiry, could be made and sold for *'16 guineas a hundred weight".*

MORE EXPERIMENTS

With Accum's words in mind the Chartered's Court of Governors commissioned experiments on ammonia salts as well as on the use of the liquor itself. Another Chartered Director, Benjamin Newton, a notary, arranged these, in May 1814. Strangely however, the brief for the work appeared to be for something completely different to either sal ammoniac or sal volatile. Newton commissioned a Mr. McCormack to undertake tests on liquor. These were to be *'one without addition and one with addition of oil of vitriol.* A fortnight later McCormack was paid off and no results were noted. There the matter seems to have rested for two years.

In 1816 a David Richards did another set of tests. Soon after Clegg recommended to the Board that *'sulphate of ammonia be made with the surplus liquor'. 'Sulphate of ammonia'* had no common name, and is always known by the more modern idiom of 'sulphate of...' rather than 'sal'. It was a salt which Accum had hardly mentioned in his lists of chemicals which could be profitably made from gas industry wastes. It was however the beginning of a new and enduring manufacturing venture.

SULPHATE OF AMMONIA

The manufacture of sulphate of ammonia, it was said, in Hughes' *Treatise 'needs no skill'*. It was done by saturating the ammoniacal liquor with sulphuric acid. Then, as Peckston says in his *Theory and Practice of Gas Lighting*, the cask should be '*rolled around for a few minutes and the salt evaporated to crystallisation by heat.*

It thus became the first ammonia salt made by the early gas industry. Before that references to it are not easily found. Its lack of a common name perhaps indicates a lack of familiarity. Even after the early gas industry had begun to make sulphate of ammonia Rees' *Cyclopaedia* described it in terms of laboratory rather than industrial production and listed no uses. Even Dundonald, who detailed so much about the potential uses of coal based by products, made only passing references to it in his *Treatise*.

DAVID RICHARDS

David Richards, who carried out the first tests, seems to have been a contractor who was employed to manufacture items like ammonia salts by the Chartered. His status is not clear – and becomes less clear as his range of activities becomes apparent.

His address was Fieldgate Street, Whitechapel, where many small chemical manufacturers were sited. It is only a matter of a few hundred yards away from the one (or two) works of the Aldgate Gas Company. In its versatility Richards' career is very similar to many young men from the East End, happy to try anything.

In 1813 Richards was an employee of the Chartered. He worked as a foreman and was sacked when he upset some visiting shareholders. He was reinstated at the insistence of some of the directors but was sacked again having '*quarrelled with Clegg's assistant'*. From outside the company he offered them a cheap '*gasometer'*. This offer was made in partnership with Richard Torr – later of Knackers Lane, Deptford, a future contractor for the removal of ammoniacal liquor and a specialist in '*animal charcoal'*.

Four years later Richards was a foreman contractor for the construction of the Imperial Gas Company's new works at Haggerston and St.Pancras. He was then to be found discussing engineering drawings and purification methods with the Imperial's Works Superintendent, George Holworthy Palmer

JOSEPH JEWELL

In 1816 Richards arranged to buy ammoniacal liquor from the Chartered on the guarantee of a Mr. Jewell. This liaison connects the early gas industry with a member of

231

one of the most successful and progressive partnerships of the contemporary chemical industry.

William Allen, the Quaker philanthropist, had taken over a pharmacy which dated back to 1715, at Plough Court off Lombard Street in the City of London but in 1806 his partnership had split up. An entry in *Archives of the Chemical Industry* by Morris and Russell tells us that Allen remained in the City where his company evolved into Hanbury and Allen, and ultimately, in the 20th century, Glaxo. The other partner, Luke Howard moved to Plaistow where he began to make heavier chemicals. His company evolved into Howard and Sons, moved to Ilford, and, in 1961, became part of Laporte Industries.

William Allen had employed Joseph Jewell as a laboratory assistant, in the Plough Court pharmacy but Jewell had gone, as foreman, to the new factory at Plaistow where he eventually became a partner with Luke Howard.

It might be noted that Howard had experimented with ammonia salts in 1808 and that these were made at Plaistow and detailed in Howard's notebook. It seems very likely therefore that Howard and Jewell would have been interested in experimenting with gasworks' liquor. Perhaps Jewell developed the process that was used for making sulphate of ammonia for the Chartered. The minuted text of the Chartered company is ambiguous but it seems that Jewell either employed Richards directly, or underwrote the manufacturing process, which Richards then undertook for Chartered. Richards was however still in some sort of contractual arrangement with Chartered because there are records of some regular payments.

PROFESSOR WILLIAM BRANDE

The manufacture of sulphate of ammonia seems to have aroused some interest beyond Millwall within the scientific community. Richards reported to the Chartered that he had received an order for sulphate of ammonia from Apothecaries' Hall.

It seems very likely that this order originated from William Brande, who held a professorial appointment there. Brande's other appointment was at the Royal Institution, where he undertook research and had fulfilled a number of consultancies on the chemical nature of coal and oil gas. One of the Institution's main interests was in agriculture and Humphrey Davy had undertaken research on agricultural science there. Brande deputised for Davy on the Board of Agriculture.

The Apothecaries' Company sponsored research on current scientific developments but a trawl of their minutes for this period has revealed nothing about sulphate of ammonia. These minutes are, however, not detailed on points of this sort and merely record notice of lectures and reports from Brande, but not the content of them. It could be speculated however that Brande and his associates thought that sulphate of ammonia might have an agricultural use and that the request from the Apothecaries' Company was in some way to further research on this.

Brande himself was heavily involved in research into coal gas and had published a number of papers in the contemporary scientific press.

MR. COTTON

Samples of sulphate of ammonia were also sent, on request, to *'Messrs. Cotton of Kennelworth'*. Attempts to find out who they were have not proved easy.

The Warwickshire town of Kenilworth seems a very great distance from Westminster. However in 1816 it had the promise of a through canal link to London that might be attractive to a local entrepreneur. There are other instances where new canal links led to new customers – for example, a lime tenderer from Sussex who enquired at the time the Wey and Arun Canal was being built.

Cotton himself has not been identified but he seems to fit the description of a Thomas Cotton who was at work making *'blue'* in Hogg Lane, Kenilworth fifteen years after this date.

If it was this Mr. Cotton who enquired, it would be interesting to know why. Was there someone local to Kenilworth with a particular interest in ammonia? However, working on the hypothesis that sulphate of ammonia was being investigated for agricultural use, it has not been possible to connect Kenilworth with any improving agriculturalists of the period. Earl Spencer, a member of the Board of Agriculture was based a few miles from Kenilworth, at Althorpe House, but no connection seems to exist. Stoneleigh, the present Royal Agricultural Society building at Kenilworth was in other ownership until the 20th century, so is not a factor in this.

The reason for Cotton's interest in sulphate remains unknown. He seems to have expected a bulk use for the sulphate of ammonia because he asked how much it would cost per ton. Having examined it however, he wrote back to say that it was *'unfit for use of any description'*.

As a result of Cotton's comments Chartered said that Richards' operations ought to be *'immediately suspended'*, leading to the conclusion that Cotton's opinions were valued and that he must have been someone of more consequence than an obscure Midlands' chemical manufacturer.

233

DAVID RICHARDS, AGAIN

As Richards' work on sulphate was ended 'Mr. Boogg of Furnival's Inn' was sent '15-20 casks of ammoniacal liquor'. Everard, in his *History of the Gas Light and Coke Company*, suggested that Mr. Boogg was a new contractor, but he is not listed in relevant directories for Furnival's Inn although, perhaps 'Boogg' is a misspelling. It does, however, seems unlikely that chemical manufacture would take place in this medieval Inn of Chancery

Despite the apparent cancellation of contract, David Richards continued to buy liquor from the Chartered. In July 1817 he was told that he could not have more than 2,000 gallons a week, later he could have as much as he liked *'as long as he pays for it first'*. Throughout Richards' dealings with the Chartered Company there is a suggestion of unsteady finances. In 1818 they *'decided to delay any proceedings against him providing he pays 4/-a butt'* plus *'arrears at 2d. a week'*.

Richards also agreed with the City of London Gas Company to take all the *'volatile liquor for six months at 2s 2d a gallon (beer measure)'*. They allowed him to pay *'by bill of 3 months'*. By that time he must have been making sulphate of ammonia independently – probably in Fieldgate Street.

MANUFACTURE OF SALTS AT THE CHARTERED

The Chartered Company had apparently given up manufacture of sulphate of ammonia for themselves. Nevertheless an ammonia salt had been found which was easy to make and which seemed to be useful – ironically it was the one, which no one had thought about before 1810. In the course of experimentation, the gas industry had secured the attention of one of the foremost manufacturing chemists of the day. It was the first intimation that these new gasworks might produce something of interest to outside industry.

The Chartered Company recorded very little about the manufacture of ammonia salts, apart from sulphate of ammonia. There is no indication why other salts were not made. A clue might come from a minute that records a purchase of sal ammoniac from the large Bermondsey manufacturing chemist, Brandram. Perhaps other manufacturers of this salt would have been hostile to a competitor.

THE IMPERIAL GAS COMPANY

The Imperial Gas Company was from its beginning more enthusiastic about the manufacture of ammonia salts than the Chartered.

At St. Pancras they had employed George Holworthy Palmer as a *'draughtsman'*. Palmer, mentioned above in connection with David Richards, was still at the start of a long and colourful career in the gas industry which I have covered in detail in the *Journal of the History of Engineering and Technology*. Before gas production began at St. Pancras he had been directed to *'furnish plans and elevations of an elabotary as works and apparatus to be employed for the manufacture of carbonate, muriate and sulphate of ammonia* and a few months later he was required to provide apparatus for the ammonia laboratory. At the 'Shoreditch works' he was told to site the *'new purifying engine ...... alongside Scott's Pond.'* This was to be used for the evaporation and preparation of the ammoniacal liquor. As well as providing apparatus, Palmer was asked to run tests on the chemicals themselves. He was to *'take one gallon of ammoniacal liquor and saturate it with sulphuric acid'*

Imperial resolved *'to continue experimental works for conversion [of ammoniacal liquor] into a more suitable form for sale'* and set up its own products works at Millwall in 1823. Manufacture of these salts did not take place there until 1825, two years later. Everard implies that the delay in opening was through inefficiency, connected with the financial scandals current in the company.

The Millwall works was set up on land leased from the Mellish Estate – a site that later became known as Nelson Wharf. The Imperial, which never did anything by halves, erected buildings designed by their architect Francis Edwards, consisting of an open-sided, part-weather boarded shed for boiler and vats.

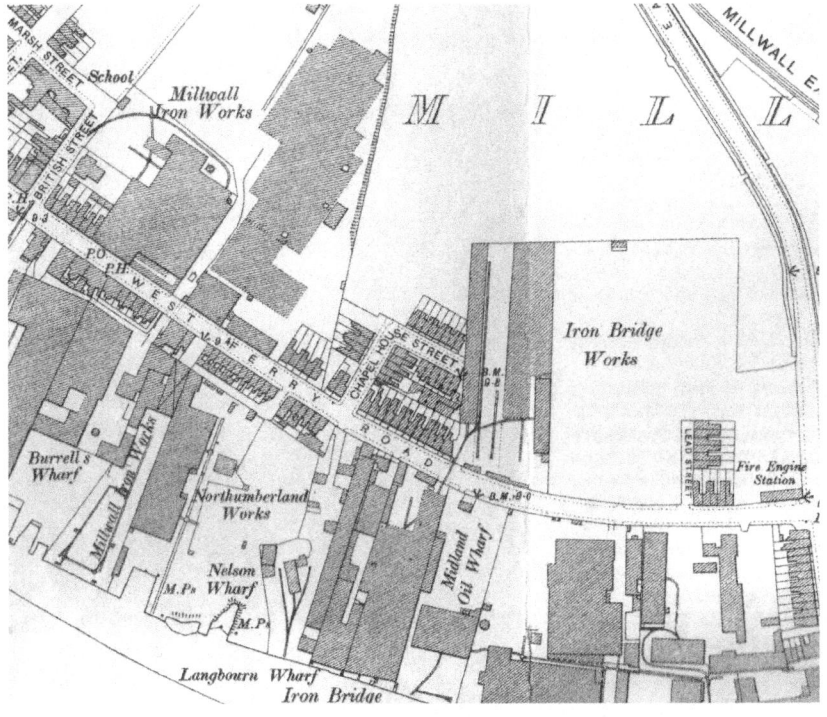

By building this works Imperial hoped that *'a considerable advantage will accrue the proprietors'*. In that they were mistaken. In 1829 the Millwall works was put up for auction and bought by the only bidder, George Elliott, a chemist and druggist of Fenchurch Street in the City. Elliott was also the leader of a group of shareholders who hoped to put an end to corrupt practice on the Imperial Board. His activities as a chemical manufacturer will be described later.

The Imperial's ammonia works had gone the same way as the tar works owned by the Chartered and the City of London. It appeared that it was only chemists from outside the gas industry who could make the manufacture of items from by-products pay.

CHEMICAL MANUFACTURERS UNDER CONTRACT

In the early London Gas industry a system seems to have evolved where individuals or companies working as sub-contractors made ammonia salts. There were a number keen to try – in 1824 Imperial, for instance, had received an offer from an otherwise unknown, Mr. Maples *'to manufacture ammoniacal liquor into saleable products'*. This offer was not taken up.

In June 1828 Imperial sold some sulphate of ammonia to a Mr. Sergeant and the next January received a report from him on the future manufacture of ammonia salts. In the meantime Sergeant had approached Chartered with the results of his tests on sulphate and they allowed him to set up ammonia works on site in their Brick Lane and Westminster works. He was allowed to do this as long as the apparatus, which was kept in the yard, was *'in tune with present arrangements'* and he was also allowed to make use of the *'waste heat'*.

Soon Chartered became *'very dissatisfied'* with Mr. Sergeant's sulphate of ammonia and they decided to employ a Mr. Greenhalgh. He was asked to make sal ammoniac for the company so that they could *'keep the vessels in use'*. Next, they decided to manufacture their own ammonia products at Brick Lane without the help of either Greenhalgh or Sergeant.

Sergeant meanwhile had returned to Imperial with a sample of his sulphate. At the same time he went to the South London based Phoenix Company with the same samples and offered to make ammonia salts for them. Phoenix instructed their engineer Munro to make them himself.

It is very unlikely that the other East London Companies, except those in the City, made salts. Smaller gas companies, like Ratcliffe and the Independent never seem to have started on chemical manufacture but disposed of liquor by selling it raw. The experimental work undertaken by the early companies themselves seems to have come, very largely, to nothing.

Chemical manufacturers from outside the gas industry, such as Frank Hills seemed more able to manufacture the salts and make money from it than the gas companies themselves. Perhaps they were more able to cultivate their market than the gas companies, whose business was, after all, to sell gas.

SALES

Prices quoted for these salts by the gas companies are often so vague as to be meaningless. For example, *'carbonate will be £52 in casks and £56 in jars'* quoted by Chartered is not specific as to either sizes or quality. It sometimes appears that the prices quoted are special ones and the price paid by ordinary customers is never given.

Transactions sometimes involved barter deals . Thus, *'Mr. Malades has 100 carboys of acid muriatic and will barter for sulphate of ammonia at 25/6 or muriate of ammonia at 25/--cwt'*. Or *'Mr. Elliott offered to take sulphur made by the company at 14/-..... and supply the company with brown vitriol at 2/8'* but Phoenix Company were *"not inclined to accept the offer"*.

What emerges is that the main purchasers were local manufacturing chemists.

A major chemical manufacturer who bought all three salts was Richard Farmer, whose vitriol factory was founded in 1778 on Kennington Common. Later St. Agnes Place covered the area. His son, Thomas, who was commemorated in Thomas Road (now gone), succeeded him. In 1839 Farmer became the first industrial chemist to use pyrites on a large scale as part of the process for sulphuric acid manufacture. Thomas Farmer held an 1840 patent for the process which is described in Morris & Russell, *Archives of the Chemical Industry*. The company dealt with the early Chartered providing *'sulphuric and muriatic'* acids in barter 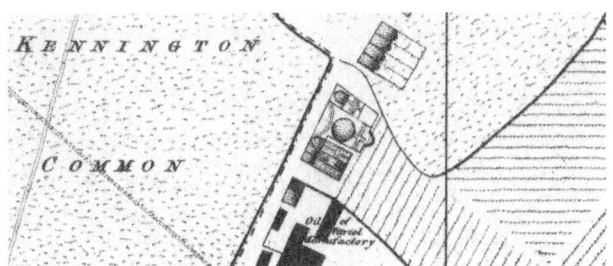 arrangements for coke. They provided other chemicals and took all three salts from the Chartered in a variety of arrangements.

'Learmouth' was another company that bought all three salts and all from Phoenix. They were either drysalters or, perhaps more likely, the large Bermondsey tanning company. They bought salts over a period of only eighteen months in 1832-3 – but, of course, could have been one of the regular customers, records of whose transactions have not survived.

Farmer clearly dealt in a very wide range of chemicals and it is no surprise that his firm should have bought an equally large range, perhaps to be sold on elsewhere. Learmouth, as a dry-salter, would have sold chemicals and, equally, had a need of a wide range. However they are also likely to be Learmouth and Roberts of Page's Walk, Bermondsey who employed 290 tanners and dyers and processed 350,000 skins a year.

If the Learmouth of the minute books was in fact the leather merchant then the purchase of this range of salts is particularly relevant. A clue to this is can be found in Winsor's pamphlets –*'The most ingenious ...national discovery'*, written thirty years earlier. He had suggested that ammoniacal liquor could be used by tanners and made a claim that it was 'one of the strongest lyes for tanning skin, cheaper and quicker and superior than what can be done by bark'. In the traditional tanning process, skins were treated with

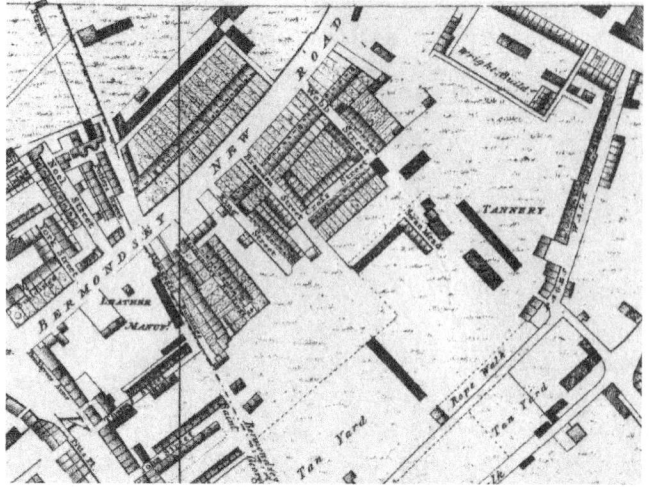

lime and dung, and then steeped in a solution of oak bark. Research was then in progress on many aspects of tanning and ammonia compounds were among the substances, thought likely to be useful.

Carbonate of ammonia was purchased by a Mr. Huskisson, from Chartered. He was one of the most prominent London makers of fine chemicals and described by Morris & Russell,. based in Clerkenwell. Samuel Huskisson had gone into business around 1768 and became associated with Tower & Co, of Warner Street off Saffron Hill. Correspondence with Boulton and Watt in 1802, and preserved in the Birmingham archive, might imply that the company was large enough to consider a steam engine. John Huskisson had works at Haggerston and Smith Street, Clerkenwell, in 1824. He was also involved in property development in the Barnsbury area of Islington (some detail of this in Mary Cash's *Squares of Islington*). Henry Huskisson was for many years based at Swinton Works in Swinton Street, just south of Kings Cross, as well as in the Grays Inn Road. John and Henry Huskisson exhibited ammonia *'for use in pharmacy'* at the 1851 Great Exhibition. The company eventually moved to Telford as F.L. Cox and were still there into the late 1970s.

Purchasers of sal ammoniac and sulphate of ammonia included George Elliot - who had taken over the City's Gas Co's Millwall products; Frank Hills who will be described in a great deal of detail later; Charles Pearson, the Deptford copperas manufacturer; Thomas Groves, a vitriol and aqua fortis manufacturer with a works on the Battersea riverside and John Jones, a vitriol manufacturer from Limehouse.. *'Merry'* who applied for *'rough muriate'* and *'sulphate in hogsheads'*. may have been a Whitechapel Gunsmith. Sal ammoniac was used in the gunsmith's trade to make the metal a brown colour.

Others include:

A *'Mr. Tomalin of College Hill'* who bought the salt in 1830. Was he the Obadiah Tomalin working as a drysalter and hatter here and in Pentonville. He had begun as a dissenting minister at the Northampton Academy but became involved with London druggists. By the mid 1830s he was insolvent.

'Arthur Lewis' made an offer for sal ammoniac in 1834. Lewis is a very common name -

but perhaps he was the druggist of Martin Lane in the City.
Parsons, who was a regular customer for sal ammoniac in the early 1830s. It is very tempting to identify him with the West Ham paint manufacturer of the same name. In the 1830s his works were at Belle Isle, near Battlebridge, an area in which several customers of Brick Lane Gas Works were located.
'Pickering' tendered for sal ammoniac in February 1832. There were several Pickerings in the London chemical trade in this period, any one of whom could be the customer concerned. They included a dyer in Finsbury, a varnish manufacturer at Snow Hill, a drug broker at Great St. Helens.
'Curtis' was probably a manufacturing chemist because he offered muriatic acid in exchange for sal ammoniac in February 1831. Alternatively he could be Curtis of Curtis and Harvey the gunpowder manufacturers. William Curtis, who was probably one of the first proprietors of the Imperial Gas Co, had founded the company.
'Fell' enquired about sal ammoniac in 1836. The Fell family was from south London and were Quakers in the leather trade.
'Price and Gifford', asked for the sal ammoniac to be *'inssisipated'.* They were 'commercial brokers', which probably meant that they were dealers in chemicals.
'Mr. Ditchburn', could be the shipbuilder, Thomas Ditchburn. He was a partner in the first iron shipbuilding yard at Blackwall in 1834 and involved in a shipyard at Rotherhithe.
'MacMurdo' with his sometime partner, John Pitchford, who had a turpentine manufactory in Stratford.
'Parkes', who probably had a chemical manufacturing business on Bow Common. He was, however, not the author of *Chemical Catechism,* as W.Parks suggested in his thesis on the *Chemical Industry of West Ham.*
'Visiger' who bought sulphate in the 1830s.
'Watson & Creed' who bought eight tons of sulphate in 1830;
'Malades' who bartered sulphate for acid in April 1830;
'Maddick' who tendered for sulphate in March 1839. William Maddick was a manufacturing chemist and dry-salter with outlets in Manchester and elsewhere. In London he was at Waterside in Wandsworth, and The Grove in Kentish Town and in Cheapside

239

'Firmin' came from Colchester where he was involved with Philip Taylor and with Colchester Gas Works and who is detailed above
'Costill', a manufacturing chemist in Stratford;
'Macdonald' a Southwark-based saltpetre manufacturer;
'Sandell' a manufacturer of pharmaceutical chemicals
'Tucker', who might be the dye manufacturer, who was soon to buy the Littler dye works at Stratford.

Also – and with more detail:

'Charles Papillon', who had his request to exchange muriatic acid for half cash and half sal ammoniac refused by Chartered. Papillon was, despite its foreign sound, not an unusual name in business circles in 19th Century London. Charles was probably the son of Pierre Jacques Papillon who had come to Britain from Rouen where he worked under the name of Cigale. He had formerly been in Turkey where he had learnt the 'Turkey Red' dyeing process. He had gone to Manchester and then to Glasgow where he had worked with Charles Mackintosh in the 1770s and 1780s. The process was revolutionary but Papillon and Mackintosh were unable to get on with each other. In 1790 Papillon had given his dye recipe to Dr. Black who found the process impossible and suspected him of duplicity. P.J. & C. Papillon had a cotton dyeing business at Neckinger, Bermondsey in 1817.

'Torr' who also bought tar and ammoniacal liquor. Torr, was an animal-charcoal manufacturer, already well-known to the Chartered and Phoenix companies. Together with David Richards he had tried to sell Chartered a cheap gasometer in 1815. In 1819 he gave his address as Man's Row, Bow Common and was apparently living in the Mile End Road. From there he bought ammoniacal liquor from Chartered together with complicated instructions for returning the casks. At the Enquiry into the explosion at the Severn and King sugar works he gave an address of *'Boney Court'* – this address has not been traced, but Torr continued to have addresses with similarly dead body related resonances. He opened an animal-charcoal (burnt bone) works in Trundley's Road,

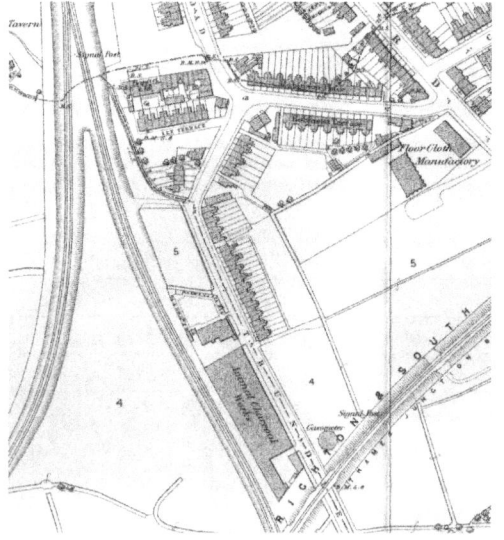

Deptford – an address also variously given as Black Horse Lane (the Black Horse pub and bridge are nearby) and Knacker's Lane. The works was at the north end of Trundley's Road in the area known until around 1990 as Surrey Docks, and since then Surrey Quays. His site has since successively been an LCC tram depot, Molins's art deco cigarette machinery factory, and latterly a Macdonald's burger bar. In Rotherhithe, Torr became well-known and Torr's field was one where children played and galas were held.

With prosperity Richard Torr moved to Bromley Common, Kent. In 1858 the family went on holiday to Worthing. A boat, carrying the five Torr children and some friends was overturned. Only George, aged five was saved. In 1852 another, older, George Torr had taken out a patent to make charcoal from bones. Young George must have lived to take the company over because Torr's site in Trundley's Road is still shown in 1880 on Bacon's Street Atlas, with houses marked as 'R. Torr Terrace'. Beside the houses is an otherwise unrecorded and totally unexplained 'gasholder'. Did Mr. Torr have his own private gasworks?

Probably they acted as brokers and sold them to their own customers. What emerges is a distribution network, spreading gasworks chemicals, throughout industry – locally and beyond. If these are typical, the gas industry supplied raw materials to industry on a large scale.

COPPERAS AND LIQUOR
ON
DEPTFORD CREEK

One customer in particular bought large amounts of ammoniacal liquor from most of the London gas companies. He was active over a period of seven years in the 1820s and early 1830s. If the number of entries in the gas minute books are a measure, he was easily be the biggest customer. Beneke of Deptford bought only ammoniacal liquor.

Deptford Creek is the mouth of the River Ravensbourne flowing into the Thames between Deptford and Greenwich. It has long been an industrial waterway. The mills on its length from Keston to Lewisham processed cutlery, leather, and silk as well as gun barrels for the Napoleonic Wars. Throughout Britain industrial museums give an important place to their local fire brigade equipment, almost always made on Deptford Creek by Merryweather. One major industry there was the manufacture of copperas. In operation since the 14th century, the best known works were at Queenborough and Whitstable in Kent. There were also works at Rotherhithe and Blackwall. There are a number of articles and essays on this – i.e. R.H.Goodsall, *Whitstable Copperas Industry*, in *Archeaologia Cantiana*. More recently the *Canterbury Archaeological Trust* has undertaken investigations and published a number of works.

COPPERAS

Copperas is 'ferrous sulphate heptahydrate', made from the oxidation of iron pyrites. Pyrites was known as 'copperas stone' and collected from the Kent and Essex shoreline. 'Pickers' gathered the stones along the estuary on behalf of landowners. The 17th century account books of Sir John Hayward record the amounts of stone sent to Deptford from the Isle of Sheppey. Copperas was used as a black dye for woollen cloth, inks, marking material and as a 'facing' for green tea. Its real importance can be deduced from its other name "green vitriol" – that is to say 'green' or "raw" sulphuric acid. Before 1800, copperas was a vital raw material for this important commodity.

The Deptford copperas works appears on a plan of 1674. The site was part of the Evelyn estate, although, strangely, John Evelyn never mentions it. The works were owned by a Royalist entrepreneur called Nicholas Crispe. Crispe, and those like him, had many economic interests in the period after the Restoration – Greenwich was full of such men.

Daniel Colwell, a friend of Crispe, described the Deptford works to the Royal Society in 1688. The copperas 'beds' were trenches of about a hundred by fifteen feet and twelve feet deep. The stones were put in these and covered with rain water. After several years the liquid would dissolve a boiled egg in three minutes! The liquid, crystallised, produced 'oil of vitriol', leaving a residue also used as a dye – Venetian red. Crispe's was not the only copperas works in the area. In 1695 another copperas works was owned by a Sir Samuel Thompson at Lamb Lane in Greenwich. For the next hundred years copperas was the basis of chemical manufacture carried out on Deptford Creek. These works passed through a number of owners, including a consortium which owned works throughout the Thamesside area.

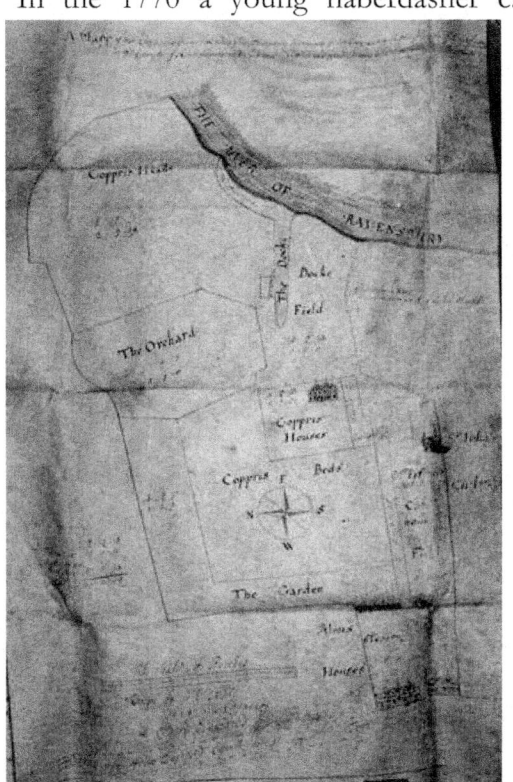

In the 1770 a young haberdasher called Charles Pearson bought the Greenwich copperas works with Ravensbourne House, took over the Deptford works and, married the heiress to one of the Whitstable works. He soon controlled the industry along the Thames and the estuary. Charles and Elizabeth Pearson had a son, also Charles, was to take over the business and a daughter, Elizabeth, who, usefully for the historian, kept a diary (the current whereabouts of which I do not know). She described how the family split their time between Greenwich, Whitstable and the family's main home at Ludgate Circus. Travelling to Greenwich by the 'Bromley Stage to Deptford' they walked down the Creek to the ferry. Her brother travelled between Greenwich and Ramsgate '*by majestic steam yacht*' – the London Engineer. By 1800 the Deptford works included '*three pieces of land, garden and wharf*' as well as '*tenements, manufactory and cottages*'. In Greenwich there were '*two coach houses, settling stills, warehouse, crane house, wharf, as well as a large chemical works, there since the end of the 17th century*'. In 1797, Ravensbourne House was destroyed in a fire and then rebuilt, despite the fact that insurance documents had not been completed. Elizabeth recorded replacement of the '*eagles*' and '*old fashioned glass*' despite '*great opposition*'. Later, as noted earlier, Charles Jnr. experimented on the woodwork with Mr. Kyan's, highly poisonous, sublimate preservative.

Charles Pearson Jnr. was closely involved with the local gas industry. He was an original Board member of the Bankside based South London Gas Company and became their auditor. He was on friendly social terms with its originator, George Munro. In 1822 an accident at the gasworks – which must have been at Bankside – kept young Charles and his wife Amelia in town for the night. This does not seem to have continued when they were taken over by the Phoenix Gas Company in 1824. In the early 1820s the Greenwich vestry had subsidised a Mr. Gosling to build a gasworks on the Greenwich bank of the Creek. As described above this was taken over and a new works opened in Thames Street by the Phoenix Company. By the time that Phoenix came to Greenwich Pearson had changed sides and acted for the local authority rather than the gas company. He continued with these connections as a chemical manufacturer and himself bought ammoniacal liquor from the gas industry. In 1833 he enquired about prices from the Imperial Gas Company and bought ammonia salts from Chartered.

JOHANN BENEKE

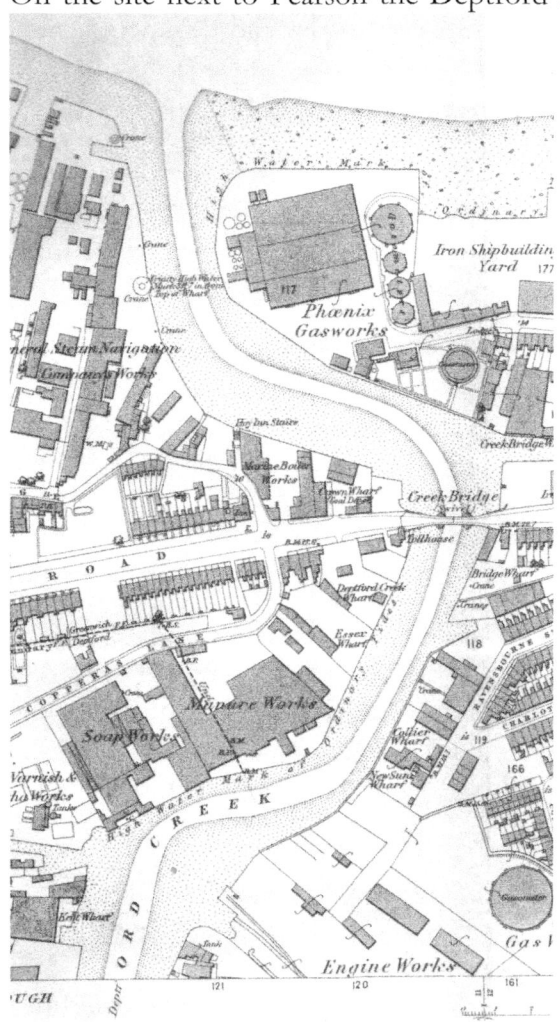

On the site next to Pearson the Deptford rate books for 1825 record an entry under William Beneke. Johann Beneke was a metallurgist who had extended the family business in Hamburg through an interest in dyes. Caught up in the French wars, he had been imprisoned and escaped from the fortress at Dinan. Discharged from the army he came to Deptford in 1814 to found a verdigris works. With him came William, described as a verdigris and colour manufacturer, and Frederick, who later patented the manufacture of spelter of zinc. 'Verdigris', also called 'blue vitriol' and 'copper sulphate', was made by interleaving rags soaked in pyroligneous acid between sheets of copper. At Deptford there was no ready supply of wood or copper available, but perhaps a clue to Beneke's interest in the area can be found in that he also made sulphuric acid from *'pyrites which was thrown in the river'*. According to his obituary in *Neuer Nekrolog der Deustsche*. Maybe he was attracted to Deptford by the copperas works.

In 1828 Johann Beneke left England, leaving William at the Deptford works. Johann went to Germany to continue a distinguished career as a chemist and

244

metallurgist. He died in 1841. He may well have been a member of the Silesian Jewish family who became bankers in Hamburg and who were associated through marriage with the family of the composer, Felix Bartholdy Mendelssohn. In 1842 the composer stayed at the Beneke family home in Denmark Hill and his daughter married one of their sons. Mendelssohn's son, Paul, became one of the founders of the German colour company, AGFA, set up in the Berlin suburb of Rammelsburg. This is the same district in which Johann Beneke had gone to install his sulphuric acid process in 1828.

When Beneke left England he seems to have left his business partly in the hands of Charles Pearson. This can be deduced because in 1833 Pearson offered to settle Beneke's account with the, Hackney-based, Imperial Gas Co. and took over his contract for ammoniacal liquor. It is far from clear what Pearson and Beneke did with the gasworks' liquor. It was not suitable for any of the manufactures which they are known to have undertaken: sulphuric acid, colour manufacture, verdigris. They may well have attempted to develop some new processes which used ammoniacal liquor for alkali.

Campbell in *The Chemical Industry* outlined investigations by chemists in this period into a *'direct route to soda'* through the use of brine and ammonium carbonate. A factory for this was opened in Whitechapel in 1838 by the patent holders, Harrison Grey, Dyar and John Hemming. No connections between Dyar and Hemming and the gas industry or other chemists listed here have been traced. Dyar seems to have other engineering and chemical interests evidenced by patents in a wide field from tunnelling to manufacture of white lead and zinc.

The Deptford and Greenwich copperas works seem to have continued until the mid-1830s when the sites were gradually taken up by other users. The new Creek Bridge was built through part of the site and when Mr. Huck, the Greenwich Miser, died having fallen in the beds, he was pulled out by the bridge workers. By 1840 copperas beds were technology marginal to the needs of industrial chemists. Old Charles Pearson had died in 1828 worth £27,000 having already left the industry. Charles Pearson Jnr, although leading a more 'gentlemanly' existence, tried very hard to diversify. Following downfall, and eventual bankruptcy he died in 1850 apparently leaving nothing.

THE GREENWICH RAILWAY

In the 1830s a number of things happened on Deptford Creek. First, in 1836, the Greenwich Railway was built, with a bridge across the Creek. Between the Creek and Beneke's works was built the Greenwich Railway Gasworks which became, in due course, the Deptford and Rotherhithe gasworks. Beneke's works was rented by Frank Hills. Frank Hills has already haunted these pages and will, I am afraid, haunt them for rather longer. What he did at the Deptford chemical works will be explained later — it involved rather more than the mere purchases of ammoniacal liquor.

245

This episode on Deptford Creek shows that there was something going on which was important to a well-connected industrial chemist with international contacts. Whatever it was there was something worthwhile for him to exploit and take back to Germany and, perhaps, elsewhere. He was able to work with a technology developed in the sixteenth century and turn it into something else. Frank Hills, as we will see, developed it further. These two technologies are divided geographically by the Greenwich Railway – the copperas beds on one site, and – something else on the other.

MR. ANGUS CROLL

For ever in the gaseous war,
May Crollious General be
And when again he leads his men
May I be there to see
Verse: The dauntless stern Dakinensii.

This quotation comes from an 1875 poetic account of 'The Battle of Bow Bridge', a pitched battle between workmen employed by two different east London gas companies. The leading figure in both battle and poem was 'Colonel' Alexander Angus Croll.

The gas trade press in the middle years of the 19th Century is never dull. Like *Mechanics Magazine*, it has a sharp Cockney humour. Frequently details appear about the more flamboyant of the gas engineers. None was more outrageous than Angus Croll. It is sometimes hard to remember that he was not a Londoner1875 Croll was a Scot and retained close Scottish links to the end of an extremely successful, if slightly ridiculous, life.

Croll is a very good example of a chemical manufacturer in a close relationship with the gas industry – or was he a gas industry worker with close links to other industries?. He had energy and ideas which allowed him to diversify into all sorts of different fields which he thought would be useful and profitable. The basis from which he worked was always his knowledge of gas industry residuals. It seems good idea have a short account of his work, since his main interest was in ammonia compounds (which precedes this chapter) and purification (which will come next). He was also poised in time and technological development between the earliest days of the gas industry, and the more sophisticated world of Frank Hills, whose rival he was for a short while. Croll was eventually to follow technological advances in a different field.

THE YOUNG CROLL

Gasworks, as we have seen, produced ammonia as a waste product. Manufacturing chemists hoped to find ways to use it profitably. Croll was in the forefront of this. He was one of the second generation in the gas industry. Expertise born out of youthful fanaticism is common in the early 21st Century when everyone knows young people unable to leave their computer screens. Gas manufacture was once no different and many of these lads grew up to be gas engineers.

Croll came from Perth, in Scotland, the youngest child of a septuagenarian father. He claimed, rather improbably, that he had had to make bird cages to pay for his schooling. He then became a weaver's reed-maker apprenticed to an older brother. In his early twenties he came to London and set up as a chemical manufacturer on a site in Millwall. This seems a strange thing for a poor boy to do and the source of his capital was never explained. The Millwall site has not been traced, and he could, in fact, have been an employee in someone else's works.

In 1838 he patented a method of making *'gas for affording light'* but then turned his attention to chemicals. In 1839 he patented a way of *'reconverting salts used in purifying gas and manufacture of ammoniacal salts'* from an address in Greenwich. A career in ammonia salts was launched.

CROLL THE CHEMICAL MANUFACTURER

Croll claimed to be a chemical manufacturer in Greenwich. In 1836 a request to buy ammoniacal liquor from the Ratcliffe Company came from 'Croll and Jones'. Jones is intermittently listed between 1810 and 1838 in the Rate Books. He made vitriol at the chemical works which had once been associated with the Greenwich copperas works. There is no sign of Croll in either rate books or directories. Perhaps his ammonia business was actually just a job in Jones' vitriol works.

Croll's chemical 'business' did badly. He then took a job as second engineer with the Chartered Gas Company at Brick Lane. It seems unlikely that the Chartered would have taken someone on in this senior post without experience of gas manufacture or supervision in a similar business. It rather leads to the suspicion that Croll's background was not quite what he later claimed. He was *'a young man .... full of ideas'* as *King's Treatise* explained. He was said to have been very effective, and happy, at Brick Lane. He had become a total abstainer and temperance beverages were provided in the works. Workmen were signed up to the cause. When he resigned after only five years work he was presented with a silver snuff box.

During the next ten years Croll took out eight patents, all but one concerned with the chemistry of coal gas and ammonia salts.

In this period it had become increasingly clear that gas purification methods ought to be improved in inner city gasworks. The smell was insupportable and disposal methods difficult. There were numerous attempts to find a better, cleaner, way and most London gasworks had tested several such. Some of those who formulated new methods of purification were chemists whose real aim was to recover ammonia.

In 1839, while employed at Brick Lane, Croll approached the Imperial Gas Company, together with a Mr. Bevington. They had a new scheme for *'removing the ammonia and sulphuretted hydrogen from the gas'*. For £1,000 they would supply a salt which *'could be applied to the gas making machine'*. The Imperial's Board were delighted by a suggestion that meant an improvement in purification. In the deal Croll would get the waste products to use in his chemical works and *'make a profit selling the muriate of ammonia'*.

Mr. Bevington, Croll's partner, was a member of the Bermondsey leather working family. The Bermondsey leather industry was well known and very large. In the 1850s a third of the country's leather was processed there. The grand buildings of the Leather Market and a Leather Hide and Wool Exchange can still be seen today. Colonel Samuel Bevington was to be the first Mayor of Bermondsey and his statue stands at the junction of Tower Bridge Road and Tooley Street. Croll's partner was one of the three brothers who owned Neckinger Mills, which, built as a paper mill, stand where the Neckinger river once crossed Abbey Street. In 1836 the Greenwich Railway was built

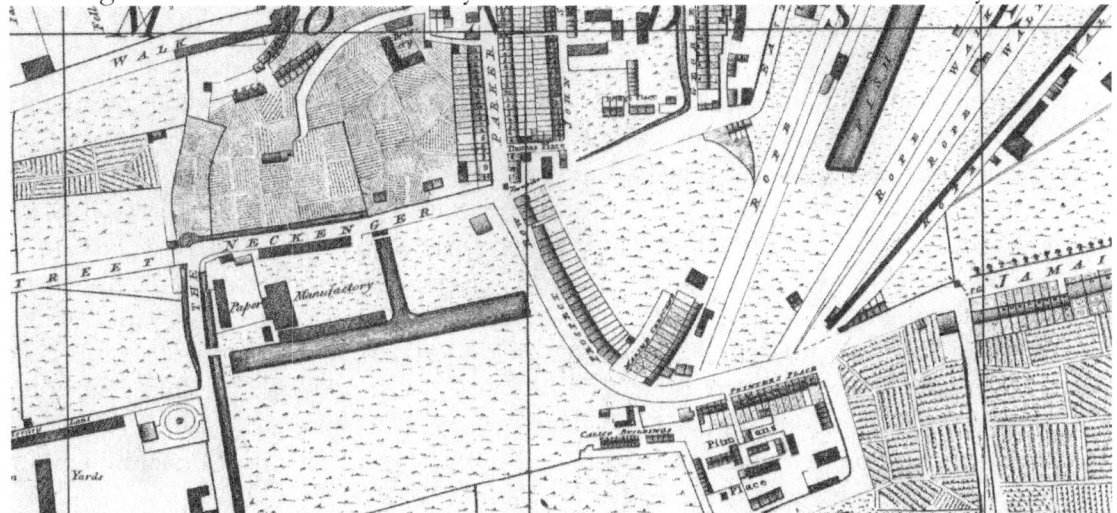

still provides workshops and homes long after the Bevingtons have gone. In the later 19th century they expanded into the fringes of the chemical industry to build a glue works on the Erith marshes described by Ballard as *'remarkably offensive'*. Why were they interested in Angus Croll?

Thirty years earlier, Frederick Albert Winsor had suggested in *Account of the most ingenious'* that tanners might have a use for ammoniacal liquor. He said that it was *'one of the strongest lyes for tanning skin ... cheaper and quicker and superior than bark'*. In the 19th century it was thought that ammonia compounds might be suitable substitutes. Alum, which Croll was to manufacture, was used in a different process called 'tawing' to make white, non-waterproof, leather.

Imperial bought Croll's new purification scheme but it had been formulated to please everyone and never really worked. It was not cheap for the gas company to run, lime was still used and the hydrochloric acid caused problems with machinery. It was *'troublesome and expensive'* and soon abandoned.

249

AGRICULTURAL CHEMICALS

In 1844 Croll read a paper to the Institution of Civil Engineers about a new method of making sulphate of ammonia. He suggested passing coal gas, which had been through the ordinary lime purifiers, and then through sulphuric acid. The resulting sulphate of ammonia was described, by Croll, as *'of remarkable purity'*. It would provide the double benefit of clean gas and a high quality ammonia salt. It seems a pity that members of the Institution who listened to Croll's paper asked no questions about it, and preferred to discuss the porosity of pipes afterwards. Perhaps they did not understand it.

Croll's paper also described tests made on his sulphate of ammonia and its use for agricultural purposes. A subject on which, he said, *'men of science, education and capital have for several years bestowed much attention'*.

Croll was right, the use of ammonia in agriculture had been given considerable attention for many years. It is very likely that much of the sulphate of ammonia that the gas industry made went for agricultural use. Ammonia was probably first used like this around 1800, which would have put the gas industry in a good position to become suppliers. A Mr. Cox had submitted a paper on this to the 1809 Parliamentary Enquiry into the Gas Light & Coke Co. The Board of Agriculture was also interested and in 1814 Sir Humphrey Davy had carried out some relevant experiments. Again, there are no details. Sir John Russell, commenting on this said that the sulphate of ammonia which Chartered Co. made in 1815 was intended for agricultural use but that it was *'unsatisfactory until further research'* had taken place. In the early 1840s numerous experiments with potential fertilisers were made. These included the pioneering work of Baron Von Leibeig as well as that of John Bennett Lawes. Croll's paper was part of this movement: in fact he embellished it with quotations from Leibeig, the leading current authority.

The experiments on sulphate of ammonia for fertiliser, which Croll described, had been undertaken at Manor Farm, Havering Atte Bower, at the back end of Romford. This was remarkably near to a future address of Croll's — he later lived at Haroldswood Lodge only a mile or so from Manor Farm. There is just a suspicion that it might have been his farm — another possible indicator of Croll's wealth. The report omits to say who supervised the experiments — perhaps it was Croll himself. He said that the sulphate was applied as a *'top dressing'* rather than by watering as with Davy's experiments. Croll however mentioned no other research or findings on the subject, despite the work done by Davy and others.

Croll had a commitment to research and education and was a founder supporter of the Royal College of Chemistry. He must also have known John Bennett Lawes, the best-known agricultural chemist of his generation. Lawes' first fertiliser works was on Deptford Creek and he later moved to Atlas Works, Millwall. Thirty years later, the

250

Lawes Manure Company, by then at Barking and without Lawes himself, bought 'patent ammonia' from Croll's Alum and Ammonia Company.

CROLL'S PURIFIER

Several manufacturing chemists tried to persuade the gas industry to take on their purification schemes. Richard Laming and Frank Hills were two leaders in this and, along with Croll, became enmeshed in rival processes and interminable litigation. An attempt to outline some of this saga will be made in another chapter. The whole process of patents, claims, counter-claims and legal cases went on for many years. Many volumes would be necessary to analyse and document exactly what was going on. If there were any winners then Frank Hills came out best while Richard Laming went out of his mind. Croll kept on for a while but eventually withdrew to pursue his many other interests.

CROLL'S GASW0RKS

One of Croll's other interests was a gas meter which he had patented. He set up a factory to make it just south of the Canal Bridge in the Kingsland Road, Hackney. Even this was not particularly straightforward and in 1869 Croll's report as Chairman included the news that large amounts of the company's money were missing. An event which *Journal of Gas Lighting* was only too happy to report. In the 1860s he was also Chairman of the Gas Engine Company.

Croll also took on the management and ownership of several gasworks. In the mid-1840s he took over the Tottenham and Edmonton Gas Works. The business had a majority of Scottish shareholders – associates of Croll.

He also leased gasworks in Coventry and Winchester. Most importantly he became involved with Charles Pearson, the City of London solicitor (this is a different Charles Pearson to the copperas manufacturer in the last chapter) and with him set up a '*consumer*' gasworks for the City of London. The background to '*consumer*' works has never adequately been explained. They were a common feature of the middle part of the 20th century and usually involved interests who wanted a say in the management of their local gas company. The City of London's works was one of the earliest and the story is told in some detail in Everard's *History of the Gas Light and Coke Company*. There was some dispute at the time as to Croll's exact role. Pearson had many ideas about the City's infrastructure. It is through him that that the City had such an early underground transport system and he wanted to integrate this with sewage, markets and the postal system. His plans for gas were part of this system.

To cut a very long story short: in the 1850s the Great Central Gas Works was opened on Bow Common in the presence of the Lord Mayor and with a great deal of ceremony. The main buildings stood into the 21st century. The idea was to have an out-of-town works which supplied the City of London and in which the City had a large financial stake. It also meant that the existing City of London Company works, on an undesirable inner city site at Blackfriars, could be persuaded to close.

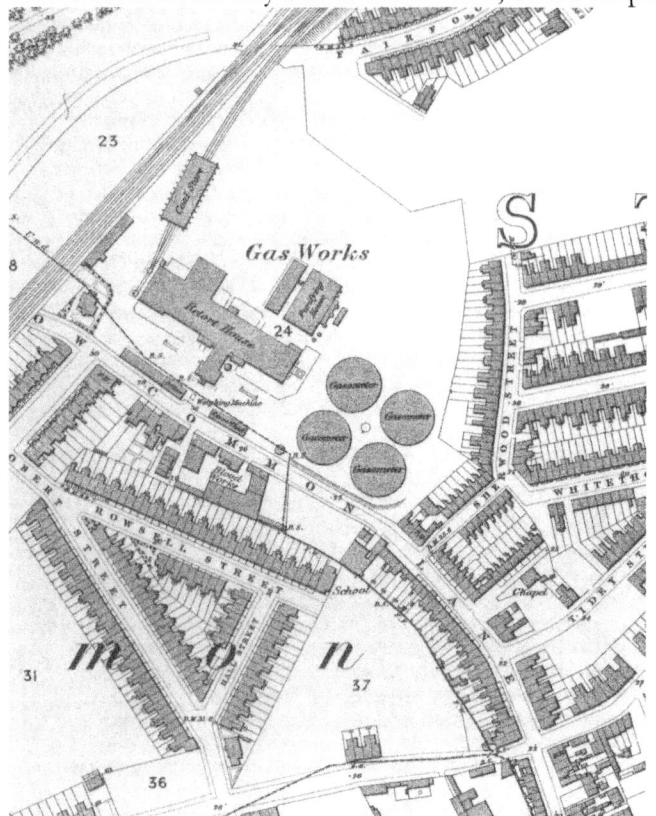

During the laying of gas mains for the Great Central the incident mentioned at the start of this chapter took place. The Great Central Company wanted to lay mains across Bow Bridge but were opposed by other gas companies, while supported by the local authority. In the early hours of the morning the Secretary of the Commercial Gas Company committed a technical assault on the Beadle by touching his shoulder. Barricades were built, and manned by 200 workmen, in order that the Commercial Company's mains could remain in place for the three days required to make them permanent under the law. A contingent of Great Central workmen stormed the barricades and tore down the pipes. Great Central and Croll were declared the winners. Regrettably Croll's management skills were not of the same order and the Great Central Gas Works quickly became a by word for chaos and bad practice. There were a number of prosecutions for nuisance.

Croll had considerable military pretensions. He was closely connected with the volunteer movement – his title of Colonel came from his involvement with the Tower Hamlets Volunteer Engineers. In later years this body had its training ground close to the place where Beckton gasworks was built in the late 1860s. It must have been co-incidental that a major dispute, eventually settled by the War Office, arose over this ground. Bullets, it appeared, from Volunteer rifles were flying over the heads of those building the new works. Perhaps it was just an echo of the Battle of Bow Bridge.

ROTHERHITHE

Following the foundation of the Great Central, Croll took over the failing Rotherhithe Gas Works. This had been built by Stephen Hutchinson and falling down ever since.

On Christmas Eve 1851 Croll led a sort of task force to Rotherhithe Gas Works and having been refused entrance laid siege to it. One of his men climbed over the back fence and let the others in, which allowed them to overcome the existing workforce. They then proceeded to rig up a sort of makeshift chimney to *"to get up the heat and give you something like comfort this same Christmas'*.

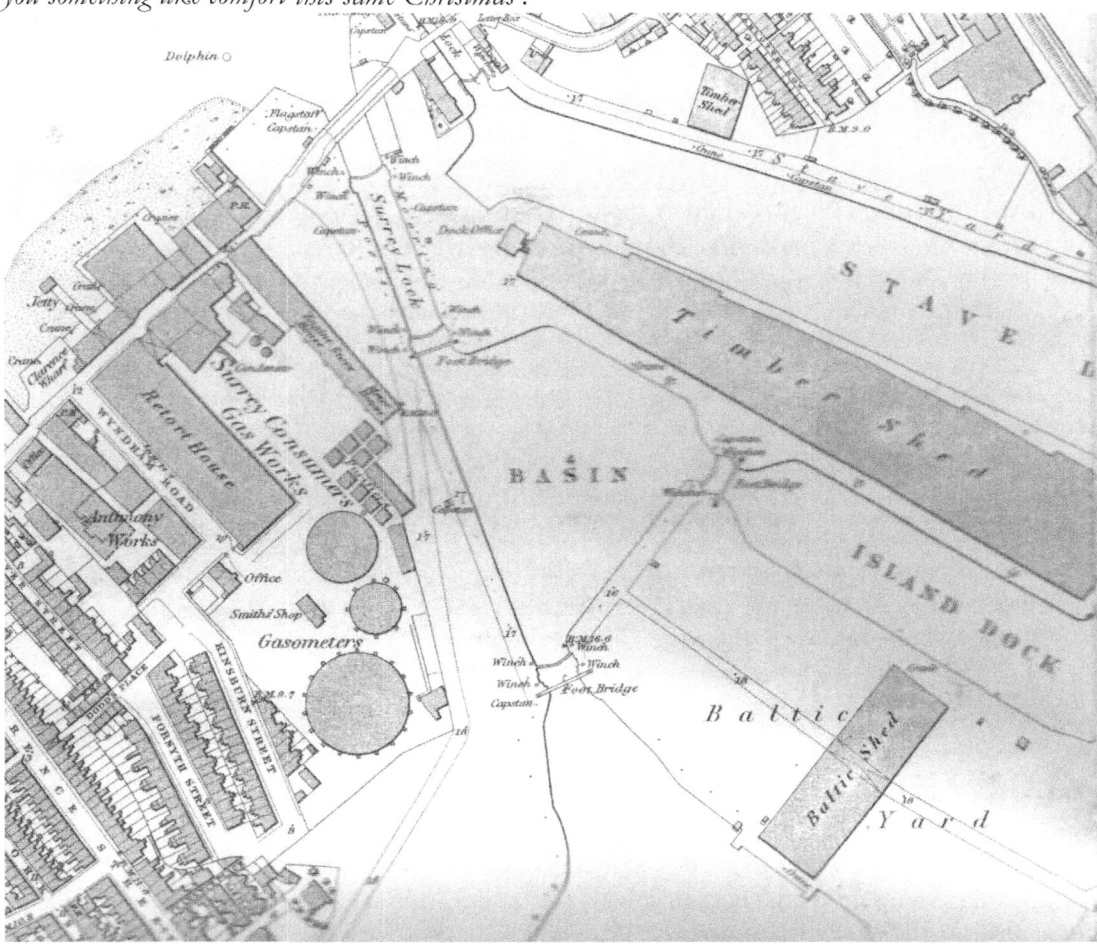

The Rotherhithe works became the Surrey Consumers Company and remained independent until taken over by South Met in the 1880s. A holder (although not an early one) still stands in Brunel Road although, like everything else, in 2021 it is time-limited.

Croll was to claim that the idea of a Surrey Consumers Company had been his and that he had persuaded the relevant Board of Works members to back him. He also claimed

253

to have to have set up the '*districting*' scheme whereby South London was divided into exclusive areas of supply.

TELEGRAPHS

Another project was the United Kingdom Telegraph Company. It was said that, when Croll opened the Great Central Gas Works at Bow and the mains were laid to the City of London, telegraph cables were also run through them for instant communication. The UKTC was formed in 1851 to develop telegraphs over public highways. Croll was a director, described in their prospectus as a '*contractor*' who held 3,000 shares. What he contracted for is not clear. Was it gas supply? The telegraph system was developed along canal tow paths and, despite great opposition, began work in 1860 using an early type of printing telegraph.

In 1871 the company gave a great banquet for Croll in the City Guildhall at which they presented him with a vast and extremely ornate silver object. Croll, it was, claimed had made the company financially secure through his negotiations in Scotland and Denmark, involving his personal friends.

By the 1850s he was living in some style in the East End of London: at Howrah House (now a convent) in the East India Dock Road. He was clearly a rich man. He claimed to have been supported in all these efforts by James Wyld, the younger, geographer and Liberal MP. His political connections and social position were considerable. He was a Sheriff of London and Middlesex, and later a Magistrate for the City of London and for Reigate in Surrey. Croll seems to have had a social conscience and is said to have written a pamphlet on prison reform as the result of seeing Danish prisons in the 1870s, although copies of this have not been traced.

ALUM AND AMMONIA

Croll remained, however predominately a chemical manufacturer. The Alum and Ammonia Company had been set up in the mid-1860s taking over from a predecessor Gas Products Utilising Company. Croll said that the company had works in Hurlet, a tiny hamlet near Paisley, and in West Street Glasgow, buying liquor from Glasgow Gas Works, and also at Nine Elms in London. It certainly had a works on Bow Common, where, in 1859, Croll was prosecuted for nuisance.

This site appears to have been on the north bank of the Limehouse Cut, west of Poplar North Street. It can be deduced that sulphuric acid was made there because, as Croll reported to a shareholders' meeting, '*the floor of the vitriol chamber had given way*' and '*a crowbar had been forced into the lid of the large vitriol chamber*'. In addition the 'secretary *had falsified the accounts*' and '*there was an action for libel against him*'. The shareholders wanted

254

Croll to resign on this occasion but he refused. He also refused to publish the company accounts, claiming 'commercial confidentiality'.

The Alum and Ammonia Company made 'ammoniacal alum'. 'Alum' is another chemical with a changing definition. It is a modern everyday name for 'a hydrated double salt of aluminium and potassium'; a modern chemist means 'a class of salts that crystallise with twenty-four molecules of water'. Its ancient use meant 'astringent salts'. Alum had been used since the middle ages as a mordant for fixing colours in dyeing and for 'tawing' leather (a tanning method not requiring tannin). The manufacture of alum is tied to that of copperas but it is also made on the Yorkshire coast, where a local aluminous shale was used as a raw material. In the 1790s Charles Mackintosh had begun the manufacture of alum from the waste of coal workings around Hurlet. Frederick Albert Winsor might have known of this process when he said, in 1804, that ammoniacal liquor could be used to make alum.

The development of a successful process for ammoniacal alum has been ascribed to Peter Spence who, in 1834, came to London and researched the use of waste lime from the gasworks. Later, finding the process unsuccessful, Spence left Limehouse and went north to research alum and copperas. He set up a works in the Manchester area to make alum using ammoniacal liquor from the gasworks, patenting the process in 1845.

There is no obvious sign of Spence in the gas company minute books. The nearest source of gas lime for him would have been the East London Company's Wapping works at Prusom's Island (a few minutes away by barge). There are no minute books for the East London Gas Company so he 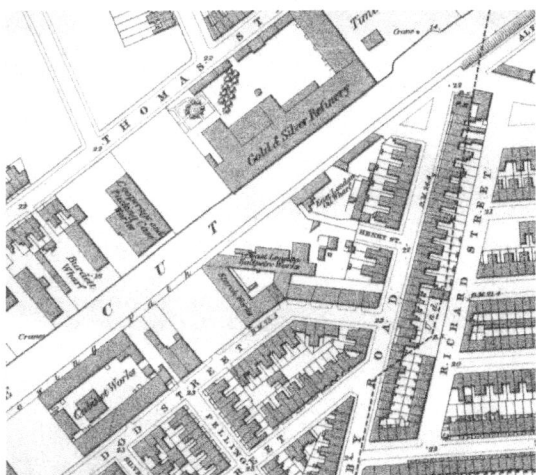 cannot be traced through them. Spence is said to have worked at Henry Street, Commercial Road. There are however two Henry Streets on the 1870 street map. One, an address on the Limehouse Cut, which could roughly be described as being on Bow Common was a turning from Stainsby Road going the distance of the depth of a suburban house to works backing onto the Limehouse Cut. Today it sites a block of flats. In the 1870s the East London Saltpetre Warehouse was at the end of it. It would have been roughly opposite Croll's works, on the other side of the Cut. The other Henry Street is today Clemence Street and appears, even in 1870, to be residential.

Ammoniacal alum was being investigated elsewhere in the area. In 1851, a James Wilson of Stratford registered a patent. James Thompson Wilson was not the same as James Pillans Wilson then managing Price's Candles. There is however a connection between this London company and alum. Prices had been set up by William Wilson, of

255

the Scottish ironworking family. John Wilson, Lanarkshire ironmaster, alum manufacturer, ex-partner of Charles Mackintosh and father in law of Charles Tennant, obtained the entire liquor production of Tradeston & Partick gasworks in 1851 — another tangle of relationships between these industrialists.

Previously alum had been imported into London. One importer was Thomas Farncombe, Chairman of South Met. Gas Co. in the 1840s. Farncombe is described as *'Agent to the Boulby Alum Works'* at Freshfield Wharf. Boulby, on the Cleveland coast, was a 'traditional' alum works dating from 1650, and closed around 1870.

By the 1870s Croll was not the only manufacturer. Both Frank Hills and Bethel were making alum at works in East Greenwich. At Old Ford, Ellis was also active in this field. Why were these works in London? Farncombe's imports may have been destined for the Bermondsey leather industry; where Croll, as we have seen, had contacts. Some alum might have gone to the growing paper industry in the east end of London and in north Kent. A number of paper mills were started in this period in Bow and Bromley by Bow. Alum was used as a size to make paper more water-resistant. A third destination might be the cement industry now growing in London and north Kent. A number of new processes in cement manufacture used alum.

CROLL, THE CIVIL ENGINEER

In the 1860s Croll described himself as a 'civil engineer' from an address at 10 Coleman Street. Perhaps this was the contracting which he did for the telegraph companies. He is said to have built the Wool Exchange in Basinghall Street but actually on the site of 10 Coleman Street in 1873. Pevsner says that it was built by John Gordon of Glasgow of *'Aberdeen Marble'*. The connection with Croll — apart from the Scottish one, is not clear. In the 1870s he began to write about his experiences, beginning with a history of the Great Central Company. *Journal of Gas Lighting* was to review this publication as *'a romance of which Mr. Croll is the hero'*.

In his later years Croll lived at Beechwood, in Reigate, with his wife, Sophia. They had no children. He died in Dunblane in 1886. It is perhaps fitting that, given his contribution to the exploitation of ammonia salts, he died while experimenting with sulphate of ammonia.

Croll was not typical either as a gas engineer or a chemical manufacturer. Despite his pretensions and undoubted skills, he always cut a figure of fun. He fell into vats of tar and remained totally impervious to criticism. He never seems to have been short of money despite the financial irregularities with which he was surrounded. Neither does he seem short of bright ideas. He was however very influential in moving the chemical industry on in its relationship with the gas industry and its by products.

There is something else which is very important. A young man was growing up in the back streets of east London while Croll was mismanaging his gas and chemical works on Bow Common. The Great Central Gas Works is said to have been at the end of his street but a blue plaque in Cable Street says "*Sir William Henry Perkin, FRS, discovered the first aniline dyestuff, March 1856, while working in his home laboratory on this site and went on to found science-based industry. 1838 - 1907.* The gas works nearest to that street was the Ratcliffe's old works, by then a holder station – but, as we have seen there were other gas works all around for him to learn from. William Perkin has been seen as the founder of the coal tar dye industry but who knows how much he learnt from his youth surrounded by the experimenters of the East End.

THE PURIFICATION SAGA

This account of early gasworks and chemists must now go right back to the beginning and look at another problem: how to prevent coal gas smelling so bad. In the course of this we will meet many of the same people again.

WET LIME PURIFICATION

Soon after coal gas began to be made for public use another, and very unpleasant, waste product began to make its presence felt. This was the refuse from the *'purification'* of the new gas — the residue from the cleaning up process designed to make it more acceptable for everyday use. Initially the problems were ones of disposal but as time went on those problems became a series of challenges for chemists to solve.

Some of the most formidable obstacles' to the introduction of gas for lighting involved the nature of the raw, washed, coal gas', to quote David Brownlie in his *'Early History of the Coal Gas Process'*, in the *Newcomen Society Transactions* as long ago as 1924. In the first gas-making plants of Boulton and Watt the gas may not have been cleaned at all Matthews says in his *'Historical Sketch* that people talked about the *'Soho Stink'*. The gas was washed with water but nothing more, despite hints about purification in the paper given to the Royal Society and attributed to Murdoch in 1808.

London publicists for the Chartered Company described in the *'Considerations'* pamphlet, *'the flame'* of the new gas which Mr. Winsor was advertising in 1808 as *'entirely free from smell'*. However, they had to admit the audience had noticed *'a disagreeable odour in Mr. W.'s old lecture room'*. Winsor washed the gas which he made by bubbling it through a solution of lime.

Chemists of the time knew that lime could be used in this way as a test for *'fixed air'* as described by Austerfield in his thesis on *The Development of Large Scale Production & Utilisation of Lighter than Air Gases*. Accum in *A System of Theoretical & Practical Chemistry* had suggested the method as a way of removing carbon dioxide from gas which had been made from distilled wood. William Henry, the Manchester chemist who had acted as consultant to Boulton and Watt on gas for lighting , also pointed out in 1819 in his *Experiments on the Gas from Coal* to the *Literary & Phil.Soc. of Manchester,* that *'sulphuretted hydrogen'* (hydrogen sulphide which gives a characteristic smell of rotten eggs) was the cause of the *'offensive smell'* from coal gas which *'resembled bilge water or the washings of a gun barrel'*. He described the way to remove it using lime. Lime was used as the earliest means of cleaning up the smell from coal gas.

Matthews in *Historical Sketch* quotes Winsor's as describing his assistants as '*bungling smiths and low tinkers*' but one of them was to claim the invention of lime purification for himself. This was Stephen Hutchinson who, during the late 1830s, made an astonishing range of claims in *Mechanics Magazine* about his role in the invention of gasmaking equipment. He said that, in this instance, slaked lime (Calcium hydroxide) was used '*accidentally*' during some experiments which he carried out for Winsor at the Rhedarium in Green Street. This was a big demonstration of gasmaking with many important people present. As a result of the lack of smell, Hutchinson claimed, seven people present subscribed a fund of 70 guineas to start the company. How this accident is supposed to have happened was not explained.

The bad smell of gas very quickly became a problem for the new Chartered Company. As early as 1812 the Committee for Chemistry raised the subject with Frederick Accum. He advised them to use lime water. Samuel Clegg had already used this method this in the gas-making plant he had set up 1811 to light Stoneyhurst College. As A.S.Bennet describes, at Stoneyhurst Clegg had '*used the scientific facilities at the College to experiment*' with different purification methods. He had then devised a '*lime machine*' that allowed the newly-made gas to be passed '*through lime water*'. Clegg's next private installation was in London, at Ackerman's Strand bookshop. There he met with what was to become a major problem with '*wet lime*' purification: complaints about the waste effluent from his lime machine, which had been allowed to run into the public drains.

Once in London, and in the employment of the Chartered Company, Clegg continued to add mechanical refinements to his lime purification system. He began to use a semi-solid process in which the gas bubbled up through the lime itself. So that residues would not build up and clog the mechanism he included '*a shaft ... furnished with teeth*' to scrape out the openings. In 1818, John Malam, one of Clegg's 'young men', improved the design of this equipment. For the next twenty-five years Malam and Clegg's system remained as standard practice for purification in most gasworks. The gas might have been cleaner but disposal of the smelly waste water remained a big problem.

BLUE BILLY

The foul effluent became known as 'blue billy', mention of which awakened in 'old *engineers ..... recollections of troubles and prosecutions*' as Stewart described in '*Town Gas*'. It was a waste product but could not be sold, unlike tar and liquor. The available means of disposal were all undesirable and led to constant complaints. Attempts were made to use it as a source of useful products. As early as 1816 one of the Chartered Directors, Mr. Warren, collaborated with Clegg on sulphur reclamation from spent lime through a special kiln described by Rev. Bowditch in *The Analysis... and use of Coal Gas*.

This liaison with 'outsiders' continued: in 1842 the Imperial Company made a contract with Frank Hills to remove blue billy '*for the purposes of his trade*'. Frank Hills was a resourceful industrial chemist who had once again found a means to make an economical product while not being prepared to make its details public.

In the early years blue billy seems to have been stored in tanks on site. All three of the Chartered's works were land locked and everything had to be transferred in and out by road – coal, chemicals, and blue billy. In 1810 sewers were managed on an individual basis by individual areas' Commissioners of Sewers set up in 1531, which were able to levy a rate on the area in which access to their sewer was available. The Consolidated Commission of Sewers dates from 1848 and Commissioners of Sewers took action to prevent gas industry wastes using their systems without approval. Generally, such wastes were not allowed to enter the sewage system.

Prevented from using the sewers, the Chartered Company decided to put liquid waste directly into the Thames. They had to get permission for this from the relevant Committee which oversaw Navigation on the Thames. In return for a fee, permission was given for a pipe to be laid into the Thames from the Peter Street, Westminster, works. The company also considered buying land from which a ditch ran to the Thames and where liquid waste could be dumped.

A number of complaints began to come from local businesses and residents. In 1817 the Chartered received a complaint from a Mr. Winter who had a japanned leather works in Peter Street. This was accompanied by another from a Mr. Cooper whose wife was enduring the smell while nursing a new baby. Michael Faraday was called in as a consultant to examine the seepage and described the problems to the Oil Gas Enquiry. Complaints continued for many years: in 1822 lime water was still getting into neighbouring premises, and Mr. Minton, a patent oil silk manufacturer complained about it.

As the industry increased and other gasworks were opened, so did the problem. The effect on the water systems was soon apparent. Many sewers were old natural watercourses into which domestic effluent ran, and from there into the Thames. While the waste was domestic and on a small scale it was acceptable, but the rise of large-scale industries – like gas – caused immediate problems. The Thames became seriously polluted. By the early 1820s the river was unfit *'for culinary purposes'* as eels and fish died and was described in articles including one in *Gentleman's Magazine* in October 1821.

This had an immediate and serious effect on the Thames fishing industry. In 1815 there were many fishermen between Dartford and Richmond who had expected to catch around 10,000 salmon in season and 50,000 smelts each year. Within five years of the gas industry opening only half of the smelts were left and the salmon had all gone. Dead fish were found which smelled strongly of gas: *'The residue of the gasworks .... floats on the surface in patches like oil'*. Press coverage included 'The Water Question" which appeared in *London Journal* in 1827. It is in this period that Thames fishing as a major industry collapsed.

260

In 1822 the City of London successfully prosecuted the Chartered Co. *'on account of the communication between the works in Peter Street and the river Thames'*. Indicative of the mood of the early 1820s is a Parliamentary Bill *'to prevent washings of substances from making of gas being conveyed into rivers'*, presented in 1822, but never passed, .

The history of London's water/sewage system has been covered in a number of works, some written for a popular audience. These have often appeared as either engineering or local government problems. Both have concentrated on the solutions rather than the continuing problem.

Two popular works both of which briefly cover a wider field have been Barton's, *The Lost Rivers of London* and Trench & Hillman *Underground London*. Histories have tended to highlight successive cholera epidemics and the achievements of the Metropolitan Board of Works in the 1850s. Public discussion of London's water supply and disposal system had begun long before this and was gathering momentum as time went on.

A number of water supply companies had been set up in London in the early years of the 19th century. Their establishment in many ways parallels that of the gas industry. Many of the same factors which affected the rise of the early gas industry in London influenced the water supply industry. Legislative, financial and technical developments are all important and sometimes complementary. A study which compares the two industries would illuminate both.

The first cholera epidemic of 1827 provided a focus for continuing disquiet on the provision and disposal of water. Initially, attention was focused on the sources from which water was drawn for distribution to the public. A *Royal Commission into Drinking Water* was set up: "*Enquiring into the Supply of Water in certain parts of the Metropolis*" in 1828. To them, however, the gas industry effluent was just one of many concerns.

Much later in the century these concerns were to come together with the engineering solutions of the Metropolitan Board of Works. Before this could take place, the tools for the analysis of water pollutants were developed. The story of Dr. Snow and the Broad Street pump is well-known. However these two famous episodes in the history of the London cholera outbreaks and water supply are usually told today with the benefit of hindsight. The development of ways of defining where infection arose is part of the solution to the perceived problem, as were ways found of analysing polluted water. In 1827 the problems were not so clear. Cholera was one problem, for which neither the cause nor the solution was known. Increasing pollution of water supply was another, different, problem but one that caused disquiet and in which the new gas industry was seen to be a major player.

OIL GAS AND POLLUTION

'Gas and Water' has become a cliché as part of the history of the growth of urban areas. They nevertheless provided a very real basis for urban growth at the same time as they caused problems. The early gas industry was being criticised for putting its effluent into the water system while it was simultaneously being asked about the cleanliness of the gas it was selling. A number of suggestions were made to solve these interrelated problems.

One suggested solution was in the promotion of companies selling gas made from oil rather than coal. Oil gasworks were designed, promoted and sold by Taylor and Martineau as we have seen.

One of the selling points for oil gas was its comparative *'purity'*. Witness after witness to the Oil Gas Enquiry to this. Oil gas was advertised as being without noxious effluent or dangerous vapours. At the Enquiry a long procession of local traders testified to the damage, or otherwise, done to their stock by coal gas used for lighting in their premises. The coal gas industry fought back and presented evidence on the efforts made to solve the problem. This included a contribution made by scientists working from outside the industry.

The failure of the London & Westminster Oil Gas Bill has been attributed to the *'extraordinarily lucid evidence'* given on behalf of the coal gas interests by George Lowe. Lowe was able to demonstrate by *'exhaustive comparative tests'* differences between oil gas and coal gas; his work was endorsed by John Dalton who described him to the Enquiry as *'competent as much as any person could be'*.

As described above in the section on oil gas, Lowe had come to the attention of the London gas industry following his letters to the scientific press *"on some singular products obtained from the ammoniacal liquor"* and *"On purifying coal gas, & increasing the quantity produced from a given weight of coals"*, both in *Philosophic Magazine* in 1818/19. He had demonstrated to the Chartered company a means of purifying foul effluent with charcoal and evaporating it in pans under the retorts. As a result he had been taken on as superintendent at Curtain Road. Evaporation did not prove the complete answer but it helped cut down the amount to be disposed of elsewhere. The description of Lowe as a 'gas engineer' is significant. It demonstrates that the gas industry now had a name for those it employed with technical expertise, albeit self-educated.

DRY LIME

The most telling point made by Lowe to the Oil Gas Enquiry was his account of the considerable efforts made by the coal gas companies to clean the gas before it was supplied to customers. One of the processes, new in 1826 was 'dry lime'. An outline of the history of gas purification by dry lime processes and some early processes using metallic oxides can be found in writers such as Bowditch and Stewart.

There were also continuing problems of refuse disposal although some experiments were carried out on the use of lime as an agricultural fertiliser. Gas companies were sometimes approached with requests such as *'a barge load of refuse gas lime for ... a farmer at Southall'* and this subject was intermittently discussed in detail over the next years. It was, however, said that if the lime was not used as a fertiliser it could, alternatively, be a weed-killer. An article of 1851 by Edward Taylor, *"The Use and Value of Gas Lime as a fertiliser for Agricultural Purposes"* describes the problems.

FRANK CLARKE HILLS,
HIS RELATIONS
AND
THE PURIFICATION OF TOWN GAS

Some of the most important by-products were those which arose from the waste products of various purification processes. Lime-based purification had caused many problems. As the gas industry developed, manufacturing chemists began to look at it as a source of raw materials. The career of Frank Hills and other members of his family is closely bound up with the gas industry in London and beyond. Biography and gas industry history are inextricably mixed in the ensuing pages.

This is about a big business made out of gas industry by-products – a business which spread around Britain and Europe and into industries not usually connected to gas or chemicals.

THE KENTISH GENTLEMAN

For a Kentish parish church, that of St. Luke, Chiddingstone Causeway is exceptionally modern. It dates from only 1898 and is a memorial to Frank Clarke Hills. He was one of many London industrialists who, having made their fortune on the London riverside, retired to the Kent countryside. His home was Redleaf, on the hill above Penshurst Place. In the 2000s only the elegant gateposts and lodge remain, designed by the prestigious gardener, J.C.Loudon, they had been commissioned by Frank's predecessor at Redleaf, William Wells, the shipbuilder. The families of Wells and Hills had been around Penshurst a long time: in 1700 a Richard Hills of Underriver rented a field in Kemsing to a William Wells. The Wells family were shipbuilders, industrialists and politicians. When Frank Hills came to live at Redleaf in the 1880s he had also become a builder of battleships.

When Frank Hills died in May 1893 his death was not reported beyond notes of two or three lines in local papers. It was not until 29th July of that year that The Times carried a report of his will, which had been copied from the Illustrated London News. It had been discovered that this unnoticed south London chemical manufacturer had left a personal fortune £1,942,836, 11s. 11d. When W.D.Rubenstein analysed rich men of the Victorian era in 1977 he listed only forty between 1809 and 1914 who left over £2m. Frank Hills was very close to being included in this list. In the period of 1880-99, sixty-nine British millionaires died but only three of these were chemical manufacturers.

Frank Hills is not known to have inherited great wealth– no will has been traced for his father, Thomas. His elder brother, another Thomas, who died in comfortable circumstances, left only £3,657; another brother left £20,909. Frank's accumulation of wealth must indicate some remarkable individual enterprise. The discovery three years after his death that the buildings and site of his main factory were not his to leave, removed only £1,583, their current value, from the total.

Piecing together Frank Hills' life has been a difficult exercise – and I am certain there is a vast amount more to unearth. He was only one prominent member of a family. There were many brothers, sons, daughters and nephews. Their father was a Thomas Hills. In 1811 a Thomas Hills moved into the Bromley by Bow Steam Mills on the River Lea in east London. It can be deduced that this is the right man because of a letter written in careful large lettering on squared paper and addressed to Bromley Steam Mills. Frank must have been about eight when he wrote it in 1815 and an adult has added a note at the bottom where Frank had run out of paper.

LYME REGIS

Although the roots of the Hills family seem to have been Kentish, it is far from clear what Thomas Hills had done before his arrival at Bromley by Bow. Frank's eldest brother was born in Lyme Regis, while another brother was to marry a girl from Lyme. Perhaps, their mother, Sara, came from there– she had been a Miss Clarke and the Clarkes are a Lyme family that goes back many centuries.   In the 18th century Lyme was not only a romantic naval seaport and holiday resort. It had a considerable chemical industry and was the source of the clay used for Coade stone - the terra cotta used all over London, the recipe for which was said to be 'secret'. Was Lyme the place where Thomas Hills got his training as an industrial chemist?

ROBERT HILLS

Thomas Hills had a brother, Robert – another very common name. Although he has not been identified, co-incidental evidence points to a Robert Hills who was a City of London based merchant with some connections to the world of South American metal mining – full of European fortune hunters and sleazy finances. There is even some

265

suggestion that he might have been in South America himself. The evidence for this is circumstantial and is based on a book written by a Robert Hills in 1827, *A Ray of Light* and another *"The Causes of the High Price of Coals."*

Robert Hills address was *'St. Michael's Alley, Cornhill'*; an area where many buildings were used for accommodation addresses. It may be co-incidental then that this address appears on Thomas Hills, Jnr's 1833 patent and is also the address which Frank used as his City office up to the 1880s. The Hills family had a continuing interest in metal mining and they also had enough capital to buy a substantial property in the 1820s. Was there a family member with experience in the Mexican copper mines that became a source of capital, expertise and support? Many years later South American guano was used by Frank Hills at Deptford.

BROMLEY BY BOW

Mr. Beneke of Deptford has been referred to earlier as perhaps the largest buyer of ammoniacal liquor from the early gas industry. The second largest was probably Thomas Hills. He once refused to buy liquor from the South London Gas Company because he had *'got enough from a country works'*, which indicates that he was buying from a much wider source area than just the London gasworks.

Thomas Hills appears to have moved to Bromley just before 1810. An account of his work written in 1827 mistakenly said that his factory was at 'Bromley, Kent' and this mistake has been repeated. Thomas Hills' address was at Bromley, as the St. Leonard, Bromley, Rate Books show. The confusion is easily made by those who know Bromley, Kent, as a town in the London outskirts but have never heard of the smaller industrial village of Bromley by Bow on the edge of Metropolitan Middlesex and sited on the River Lea.

In the early 1800s Bromley by Bow was a busy industrial area where Mr. Currie had the biggest alcohol distillery in the country. Bromley was, and is, full of mills: Three Mills still stand in the 2020s, while Four Mills has gone. They were tide mills but Thomas Hills's mill was 'Bromley Steam Mill'. An annotation in the Boulton and Watt Papers indicates that a steam engine had been erected for millers, C. & J. Milward, in Bromley by Bow. It was taken over by Thomas Hills in 1811. He used it for chemical manufacture as well as grinding corn. An 1827 inventory lists *'a kiln house with reverbatory furnace, tartaric acid and boiling house, coke ovens, drying houses, colour mill and machinery, laboratory...'* On some records the address is given as 'West Ham' in which case the mill would have been on the east bank of the Lea, as indeed the Three Mills complex is today. Horwood – like other maps of London and Middlesex would have found it totally impossible to include any buildings in Essex –and, to be fair, Essex maps cannot include any vestige of anything in Middlesex. Today the Blackwall Tunnel Approach Road thunders its congestion down through what was once Bromley by Bow. At the

266

point at which Gillender Street rejoins the motorway stands –miraculously – Bromley Hall, the oldest house in Tower Hamlets. Bromley Steam Mill would have been in this area, but on the other side of the Lea

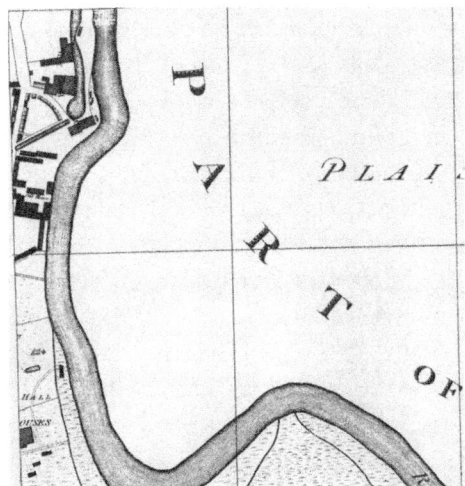

Philip Taylor, the chemist and inventor of oil gas, was also in Bromley in this period. He lived in rather more style at the local manor house, where the mulberry tree from his garden is said to survive. The site of the Taylors' Stratford chemical works has not been identified, despite the numerous chemical works in the Stratford area and the considerable research done on the industry there. Taylor's experimental oil gasworks were built only a short distance to the north, alongside Bow Bridge.

It has been suggested by Roger Burt in his biography of John Taylor that Philip Taylor manufactured vitriol using imported pyrites before 1819 at his chemical works at Stratford. This is a process which was to be identified with Bromley through the work of Thomas Hills. On a contemporary map of the area Bromley is shown next to land held by Philip Taylor. The distance from Stratford at this point is only the width of the River Lea. No connection has been traced between Hills and Taylor but the use of a similar process twice in such a small geographical area seems remarkable. This is only one of a number of similarities in their work.

Thomas Hills' patent of 1818 on the manufacture of sulphuric acid was a joint one with a Uriah Haddock. The patent was submitted from an address at City Terrace, City Road, on the Islington borders. It is probably co-incidental that a Dr. Robert Hills lived there in the 1850s. This is another area where many chemical manufacturers had their works. It was also very near the site of Taylor & Martineau's Winsor Iron Works where their oil gas machinery was made.

Very little has been traced about Uriah Haddock. In 1816 he was described as a 'chemist of Holloway' who was considering the registration of a patent for paint. He registered another patent in 1819 for making *'inflammable gas from pit coal'* – a patent described, by the gas engineer, Thomas Peckston as being of *'some importance'*. Haddock's address on this occasion was given as Saville Place, Mile End – a terrace through which the Regents Canal was being built. Haddock notified his intention to register another patent of gas manufacture in 1824, but did not do so.

The Hills and Haddock patent of 1818 was the first which covered for the use of pyrites instead of brimstone to make sulphuric acid and is described as so revolutionary and so important that it is described in almost every history of the chemical industry – as for example Campbell's *'The Chemical Industry'*. At the time the exact nature of the

267

process was the source of a great deal of speculation. Eventually there was a court case for infringement of patent by the Liverpool company of Thompson and Hill in which the Hills and Haddock patent was upheld. However, a letter in *Repertory of Patents* in 1826 by an Irish vitriol maker, J.C Gamble, threw some doubt on the process described in it. J.C. Gamble was the forerunner of the Gamble and Sons chemical empire and ultimately of United Alkali, but a propensity to become involved in court cases about patents seems to have been inherited by Frank.

It must not be forgotten that Thomas Hills was using the gas industry as a source of raw materials for his chemical works. What he manufactured from the waste materials of the early gas industry that he bought is not known. He bought liquor in considerable quantities between 1824 and 1827 when he seems to have left Bromley by Bow, possibly because of bankruptcy.

DEPTFORD CHEMICAL WORKS

Thomas left the Bromley mill in about 1827. Nothing more has been discovered about the family until Frank Hills began to contact the London gas companies from the Deptford Chemical Works in the early 1830s. This is the works that was owned by Beneke described above.

By the mid-1830s several of the London gas companies were minuting approaches from Frank Hills, who offered to sell acids, buy tar or ammoniacal liquor and to manufacture ammonia salts for them. The range of these offers seems to show that he saw the gas industry as a fruitful source for exploitation. Gas companies, immersed in the problems of manufacture and distribution, were probably happy to leave chemical investigation to others. It was a niche into which several chemists tried to put themselves, none more assiduously than Frank.

Notes of neighbouring frontagers compiled for the London & Greenwich Railway indicate that Frank Hills rented the Deptford Chemical Works from Frederick Beneke but how far Frank Hills took over his chemical business can be only be speculated. Perhaps it is also notable that, while the Beneke family lived in Denmark Hill, in Camberwell, Frank lived not too far away in North Terrace, Camberwell.

In 1836 the London and Greenwich Railway was built across Deptford Creek, and included a gasworks which lay alongside the line on its north side. On its south side was Deptford Chemical Works. When the gasworks became independent of the railway it was said in *Journal of Gas Lighting* that Frank had provided a mortgage on it. He was later to say that it was in this gasworks that he experimented on gas industry wastes.

268

Frank undertook a great deal of research at his Deptford works. Family sources told me that he was *'always experimenting in the laboratories and the engineering workshops'*. He claimed to have experimented on gasworks wastes there with a Rev. Dale. A correspondent to South Met. Gas Company's 'Co-partnership Journal in 1916 said that a German chemist, a Mr. Baume, worked for him there. While testing the impurities of a batch of guano, he discovered a means of extracting iodine. Henceforth the firm manufactured this industrially. He refined saltpetre by double decomposition– by using nitrate of soda and muriate of potash.

Sulphur was also refined at Deptford and sold to Kentish hop growers, where it was used to prevent mould and microbial growths in the fields and storage. Sulphate of ammonia was sold in large quantities to West Indian sugar growers.

As we have seen from the 1820s the manufacture of chemicals from gas industry wastes was often taken over by independent industrial chemists who made arrangements with the gas companies to do so. There were also elaborate arrangements made between the chemists. For example, a legal action of 1845 was reported in the Times, in which it emerged that Angus Croll had agreed to buy from Frank Hills only those acids he needed for which he held patents in order to make ammonia salts. He would then sell the salts back to Hills who would sell them on to the gas companies who would then sell them again to other chemists. Croll and Hills had agreed to issue licences to any other chemist or gas company who wanted to make the salts and these licensees would be required to buy the necessary acids from Hills at a higher price than that paid by Croll. Hills and Croll soon fell out and each accused the other of reneging on the agreement. Injunctions were issued, but were dismissed by the court. Then appeals were made. This pattern of constant litigation was to become only too familiar.

The Hills Brothers were to specialise in ammonia salts and won prizes at the 1851 Great Exhibition for them. Their carbonate of ammonia was said to be *'known all over the world'*. Family history sources say that sulphate of ammonia was exported to the West Indies to be used as manure for sugar cane.

WORKS AND BROTHERS

Frank Hills is often described as 'The Deptford Chemist' and I have come across him described as such in local histories and other relevant works. His business is often described as 'F.C. Hills' sometimes with a note which implies that this was a small and obscure chemical works. In fact there was a network of factories around the country and abroad which were owned or managed by Frank Hills's brothers and eventually their sons. Many of these works dealt with gasworks' wastes of various sorts. There were also considerable interests in Spain and maybe elsewhere. I am sure that much else remains to be discovered and, as with the steam cars mentioned below, it is perfectly possible that the network included non-chemical manufactures and interests.

STEAM CARS

Frank Hills did not confine his business interests to the chemical industry. In the early 1840s he became known for the development of steam road vehicles. He should not be confused with John Hill, a slightly earlier inventor in this field. The best known promoter of steam road vehicles was Stratford based Walter Hancock and in 1839 Frank travelled on a Hancock vehicle to Cambridge while, as *Mechanics Magazine* commented *'taking a lesson on steam carriage construction during the journey'*. He later patented a gearing system, although Fletcher, in *'Steam Locomotion on Common Roads'* suggests that this gearing had originally been developed by Roberts of Manchester. The cars appear to have been made by the General Steam Carriage Co. of East Greenwich. This was almost certainly Joshua Taylor Beale, who has been mentioned earlier here before in connection with naphtha lighting. Col. Francis Maceroni, mentioned above in connection with Joshua Taylor Beale, may also have been involved.

Some well-publicised trips were taken over particularly steep and difficult hills in the area and reported in *Mechanics Magazine* and elsewhere but the venture seems to have been unsuccessful. Sixty years later Frank's son, Arnold, as Chair of Thames Ironworks was to take up road vehicle manufacture in the 'Thames' line of coaches and cars.

THE PURIFICATION OF COAL GAS

Frank Hills and a group of other industrial chemists became immersed in the problems of coal gas purification. Early lime-based purification methods left a noxious residue and the industry was faced with how to clean gas without incurring legal action for the pollution resulting from waste disposal. Industrial chemists began to search for a means of cleaning the gas which would also leave a residue that could be processed and sold on and thus profitably exploited.

Throughout the 1840s and early 1850s these manufacturing chemists approached the gas companies with offers of various purifying schemes. An account of Angus Croll's offers to the Imperial Gas Company, together with Bevington, has already been described. The chemists offered deals with the gas companies and then only too often

270

took legal action against each other. In one example, taken at random, in 1846 Angus Croll, asked the Patent Office to rule that Frank Hills was infringing one of his patents. He told the Phoenix Gas Company directors that the Imperial Gas Company was no longer using Hills' process because there were complaints about infringement. He offered to indemnify Phoenix against any legal action which Hills, or anyone else, might take against them. A few days later Frank Hills met the Phoenix Board and told them the same story but in reverse and also offered to indemnify them against legal action by Croll.

The visits, the threats and the offers went on for more than twenty years. A number of chemists were involved but Hills and Croll were the most active, along with Richard Laming. The progress of invention and discovery is almost impossible to follow since all of them told the gas companies at various times about new processes, sometimes giving details of completely different discoveries to different companies on concurrent days. A complete analysis of who said what to each gas company might make an interesting, if extremely voluminous, story but one that bore little relation to what was really going on. The most impressive thing is that they seem to have kept track of these convoluted dealings themselves.

One particular process, using metallic oxides, seems to have been developed in France by Richard Laming. He was an English doctor who went to France for unspecified reasons. In France he developed and patented a process which involved the 'revivification' of a purifying mixture with air, and this was to become crucial during successive legal challenges. Once 'exhausted' the mixture contained a residue of chemicals that could be reclaimed.

An aggressive campaign to sell this process to the gas industry was pursued by Laming, Croll and Hills. All this had to be heard by judges and juries, who almost certainly had not the faintest idea what they were talking about. Frank Hills held the key patent and if a decision went against him, he appealed and probably confused the judge in the process.

THE OXIDE PROCESS

Lewis Thompson in *The Nature & Chemical Properties of Coal Gas* said that Angus Croll was the first to use oxide of iron for purification but that he that he failed to discover the revivification process which was later developed by Richard Laming and F.J. Evans. Thompson was a doctor who had worked in Paris with Richard Laming. In London he had set up as a consultant testing gas purity and wrote extensively about the issues surrounding the chemistry of gas lighting.

What he said about Croll was not quite true; the origins of the process for which Frank Hills held the patent went back many years before Croll's entry into the gas industry.

271

In the Institution of Gas Engineers' Library is a collection of letters dating from around 1816. The correspondents include a Mr. Johnson, who lived in Ireland and was later to come to England with purification process of his own. They also include Aaron Manby the Shropshire Ironmaster who also manufactured equipment and could supply a whole readymade gasworks, and a Daniel Wilson. It emerges that Wilson had just come to London from Dublin with a purification process that he wanted to sell to the gas industry. Johnson was his friend and confidant. In Dublin they had been backed by a Major Taylor. Taylor was clearly an important man and the letters suggest he was a trustee of Dunleary harbour. It is not impossible that he was related to John Taylor the engineer, who had an uncle in Ireland. The letters describe Wilson's attempts to lobby the nascent gas industry and his eventual liaison with Aaron Manby. Those between Johnson and Wilson are clearly between close friends and sometimes, in almost evangelistic tones, describe their hopes of successful careers. It is what happened to Daniel Wilson and his process which is significant.

In 1856 a letter from George Holworthy Palmer appeared in Journal of Gas Lighting. He pointed out that he held an old patent – by then expired – which covered the 'oxide' process which had by then patented by Frank Hills. In 1818, after being sacked by the Chartered Company, Palmer had gone to Macclesfield where he had set up an experimental purification plant. James Hargreaves, was the first Deputy Governor of the Chartered which he had left in unexplained circumstances. He had then set up gasworks in Liverpool and Macclesfield. It might therefore be speculated that Palmer had gone to Macclesfield under his patronage. Palmer's process consisted of *'a purifying machine and a small condenser'*. The gas went through *'fragments of sheet iron or any oxide of iron'*. A party from London came to view the installation and reported with some derision *'the effects of the process upon the gas was imperfect and inefficient'*. Palmer's patent seems have been abandoned at this point but its importance, recognised later, was that it embodied the principle of revivification. Fifty years later, Lewis Thompson, who wrote an account of this, said there was 'no *resemblance between [it and the oxide process as] ... chalk and cheese or egg of Columbus*".

Back in 1817 *Philosophic Magazine* had noted that Palmer's method of purification was similar to one currently being exhibited in London by Aaron Manby of the Horsley Iron Works. It was announced that Manby was employing as a chemist, Daniel Wilson, who had devised and patented the purification process. One of Wilson's purifying systems was installed at the Chartered's Brick Lane works where it *'proved useless'* and was removed. Sadly the Institution of Gas Engineers' letter collection does not record this setback which cannot have been helped by Wilson's operation for fistula. Although Johnson sympathised with him for *'setbacks'*, Wilson only described negotiations with *'friend Livesey'* together with the useful information that Clegg had left before he was sacked and that a director has *'bolted'* with £50,000 of the public's money.

In 1819 a fire devastated the sugar works of Severn, King and Company in Whitechapel as noted above in the section on oil gas. A series of complicated insurance claims subsequently came to court. This was described by J.Z. Filmer in an article in *Technology and Culture* in 1980. It emerged that the apparatus responsible for the fire had been supplied by Aaron Manby and designed for him by Daniel Wilson. The final decision on blame was inconclusive but some witnesses, such as Philip Taylor, described Wilson's process as '*hazardous*'. Was this tragedy the reason for Wilson's departure to France where he stayed for the rest of his life?

In France Wilson worked with Frederick Albert Winsor, and together they set up the first Paris gasworks which Wilson managed. Manby, Wilson et Cie became a major force in French industry even owning the great Le Creusot ironworks for a while.

A few years later two young chemists came to France – Lewis Thompson and Richard Laming. They sought out Wilson having heard of his reputation, met him in Paris and discussed his old purification process. Richard Laming undertook research on Wilson's process and patented it in England in 1847. He subsequently discovered that, if the used iron mixture was left to stand in the open air, then the iron salts were reconverted and could be used again. For reasons that have never been clear he did not include this in his English patent.

When French king Louis Phillipe was dethroned in 1848, Thompson and Laming returned to England. Thompson went to work for Hawes soap manufactory. Details of his work there are known because of evidence given in a court case concerning a woman who claimed to be Thompson's unsupported wife and which was reported in Journal of Gas Lighting. Hawes have an importance in this saga, partly because the company had a long standing interest in oil gas with their own small gas-making plant, promoted by the Taylors.

Richard Laming, returned to London and set up as a manufacturing chemist in Millwall, specialising in ammonia salts. An appeal by him against his rate assessment has left a detailed description of works and equipment in the All Saints, Poplar, Rate Assessments Register.

RICHARD LAMING, FRANK HILLS
AND
THE CONVOLUTIONS OF THE DISCOVERY OF THE OXIDE PROCESS

The tangle of patents and processes held by Croll, Laming and Hills are very complex. The details were followed in the gas press and have since been briefly outlined by W.V.Farrar in an article about Richard Laming in *Annals of Science* in 1969. The following, drastically abbreviated, account illustrates the ruthlessness with which these chemical manufacturers were prepared to act to get valuable by-products.

In 1848 Laming entered into a partnership with Frank Hills to exploit an, unspecified, process for purification that he had developed in Paris. This process was offered to the City, Phoenix and the Chartered gas companies. Laming explained that *'his material consisted of muriate of lime and carbonate of manganese evaporated to dryness in combination with sawdust'*. *'Half a bushel of this material'* he said *'would purify the same quantity of gas as a bushel of lime'*. He also told them that the *'resulting dry powder'* should be exposed to the air to absorb *'a further portion of oxygen'*. Unfortunately for Laming this statement, which might have proved his case for priority of invention, lay forgotten in the Phoenix Company minute books.

Laming returned to Paris in 1849. Before he went he lodged a caveat against any other patent being granted which involved revivification. In February 1849 he finally patented the revivification process in France but not in England. What is not clear is what had happened to the tests he had undertaken for the Phoenix Company nor to the fate of his partnership with Frank Hills.

The Chartered Gas Company agreed to test the new process at Westminster in August 1849, having reminded Laming that *'it was an experiment and therefore at his own expense'*. He was given facilities and the assistance of F.J. Evans, the Westminster superintendent.

It must be said that, considering Laming's ex-partnership with Hills and his account of revivification to the Phoenix Company, it might be thought that, in narrating the following series of events, the truth seems to have bent by some, or even all, of the parties involved. The incidents were related by Lewis Thompson and have been repeated often. Thompson was however clearly an interested party himself. Even more significantly, his employers, Hawes, may also have been interested parties. Within a year of this incident, Benjamin Hawes, Snr., already in his late 80s, became Governor of the Chartered Company. William Hawes (son of Benjamin senior and patentee of soap-making processes) was a partner in the brewery next door to the Westminster Gas Works and had numerous other industrial interests. His brother, Benjamin Jnr., married to Sophie Brunel, was to become Under-Secretary for War. Their sister Caroline was married to Bryan Donkin Jnr, who was also involved with Frank Hills.

During the tests at Westminster Gas Works, Evans emptied the purifiers and noticed the change of colour as the material 'revivified'. This it was said, was the moment of discovery.

Lewis Thompson's account also suggested that Evans knew well what he was doing and that he had run the same process in Berlin while working for the Imperial Continental Gas Association. ICGA, in Berlin, had close connections with the Beneke family of bankers and ran the European gas industry on behalf of British interests many of whom were also involved in the British gas and chemical industries. A description of their other connections with English business and the British chemical industry would make this account even more complicated than it is already.

As Laming ran his experiments, or rather demonstration, at Westminster, various interested parties came to see what was going on. One of these, of course, was Lewis Thompson. Thompson publicly warned Evans not to tell Frank Hills –who they could see out in the gasworks yard - about their discovery of the 'revivification' part of the process because '*he will put it in his patent*'.

There are several versions of this story in transcripts of the trial and articles in the gas press. In essence they are all the same – the circumstances differ slightly. Hills, of course, put in a patent application which he registered in November 1849. Evans and Laming took out a joint patent in April 1850 but Frank Hills had got there first.

CLAIM AND COUNTER CLAIM

Throughout the 1840s and early 1850s the gas companies were besieged by manufacturing chemists with variations on these purifying schemes, all complaining about numerous patent infringements, both before and after 1849. Chemists visited the gas companies, threatened legal action and offered deals. Some examples have been given above. The visits, the threats and the offers went on for more than twenty years. It is hard to believe that the gas company directors were not confused. The potential profits to Croll, Laming and Hills must have been enormous.

After 1849 the gas companies began to prefer to use the oxide process which Laming had demonstrated at the Westminster Gas Works. Frank Hills ruthlessly insisted that this was his patent. Any gas company that wanted to use it had to have a licence from him to do so. If they did not have his licence, he simply sued them. A sequence from the South Met. Minute Books demonstrates his methods: -

In February 1852 Frank Hills approached South Met. and asked for £400 a year for permission to use his method of purification. Following discussions he raised the price to £425. Laming then approached them with an offer of a licence for £400 a year and so the South Met. Directors chose the Laming offer. Three weeks later Hills complained to them that his patent was being infringed and said that South Met. must have a guarantee of no claims from him. In June South Met they received a letter from his solicitor, Shield and Co., '*about inclination to take action for infringement of his patent*'. In July they agreed to pay Hills what he wanted.

The financial arrangements for the use of the purification process were usually complicated and subject to much haggling. Gas companies were sometimes supplied with the purifying mixture to put in their machines for which they had to pay per ton of coal carbonised. For example, in 1853 Laming asked the Chartered, which had been paying 4 1/2d. per ton, to pay 5 1/2d. and to backdate this rise by three months. The

Company agreed '*provided the Company now be provided with the purifying material they require'.* Laming did not supply the material until he had received this backdated sum.

The chemical manufacturers removed the spent oxide when it could no longer be revivified and took it to be used in their chemical works. Frank Hills processed vast amounts at his Deptford and Greenwich works. He himself designed the furnace in which this was done. Lunge estimated that 2,180 tons of spent oxide were used a year at a works at Barking Creek to make sulphuric acid. This works at Barking was probably Lawes' Creekmouth works, which had opened in 1857 and so Lunge's comment refers to amounts used after that date. In addition, ammonia and sulphur were recovered from the mixture, giving more sources of profit to the chemists.

In the later 1850s a series of legal actions were started between the chemists and the gas companies and also between individual manufacturing chemists. In 1858 in Frank Hills v. the London Gas Company, a battery of lawyers heard a series of complicated statements on patent law and chemistry and, as Farrar commented: '*arguments which were almost certainly beyond the understanding of the jury, and, one suspects, of counsel and judge as well'.* Deliberate clouding of the details probably suited all parties very well. In one case, which involved an agreement between Hills and Laming and claims for '*liquidated damages',* the judge commented that the matters were '*monstrously absurd.'*

Frank Hills finally established his right to the patent. Rev. Bowditch commented that this was what '*the majority of lawyers and chemists think he was most justly entitled to'.*

Exasperation on the part of the gas companies is reflected in the minute books. On one occasion Hills' conditions on ammoniacal liquor included special conditions should the canal freeze. Underlining of this in the minute book clearly indicates the Chartered Directors' attitude.

The gas companies began to get together about the situation. They circulated information to each other: 'a letter was read from the directors of other companies with information at some degree of variance with statements made by Mr. Hills before this Court' reported the Chartered Company. As the time drew nearer for his 1849 patent to expire, Frank Hills announced that he was going to apply for an extension of it. He began to include in his contracts with the gas companies a condition that the gas companies would not oppose his application for an extension — for example he offered Chartered the process at 5d. per ton provided that they would not oppose an extension.

Eventually an appeal from a consortium of gas companies went to the Privy Council. The younger Thomas Livesey, Secretary of South Met. Board reported to them '*he* [Frank Hills] *had received £107377 0s. 9d. for sales and royalties. His expenses rated £16,942 only, but his other expenses included £6,450 for his own salary after paying the same sum to his brother, Thomas, and some large sums to some other brothers...'.* As a comparison, it should be noted that Thomas Livesey, a well-respected and well-paid manager, received a salary as

South Met's engineer and company secretary of £1,000 a year. This Thomas Livesey was the nephew of the Chartered's Mr. Livesey, and the father of George Livesey.

Laming had lost the legal battles but the mixture used in the oxide process was always known in the future as 'Laming's mixture'. He continued to work in Millwall on processes for the *'manufacture of ammonia and preparations for the purification of gas'*. It was said of his sulphate of ammonia *'nothing can exceed the beauty and purity of the article he thus manufactures'*. He appeared less and less in the gas industry minute books and retired in the mid-1860s. He had been involved, before 1865, with a journal, *The Electrician*, in which he put forward *'views on electricity and matter until they grew less and less comprehensible'*. He died in 1879, having been bedridden and demented for fourteen years.

Frank Hills continued to flourish, supported by his family, in particular his brothers and their sons.

THE HILLS BROTHERS

THOMAS HILLS. One of Frank Hills' brothers was Thomas — it might be assumed he was the eldest and named after his father, but this may not be so. He had been born in Lyme Regis in 1804. His early work is not known. In 1833 he patented a boiler grate and gave his address as St.Michael's Alley, Cornhill — perhaps the address of Robert Hills' City office. Thirteen years later he was looking for a job and in 1846 he applied for the post of Deputy Superintendent at the Phoenix Gas Works in Greenwich. He said he was *'a good practical chemist and accustomed to the control of workmen'* who would want a salary of £300 a year. Phoenix turned him down because he was *'too experienced'*. After that he worked for Frank, *'dealing with the commercial business at the works'* both at Deptford and East Greenwich. In the early 1870s he joined Frank on the Board of Thames Ironworks. As an old man he lived at 8 The Grove on Blackheath with his second wife and their young son. This son, Thomas Herbert, described in 1891 as a *'student of chemistry'* seems to have inherited the Deptford Chemical Works. Thomas' family of four daughters — the eldest in her mid-thirties — still lived with him in the 1880s. He died in 1885.

GEORGE HILLS. Frank also had a brother George, about whom little has been discovered: no will and no address. He seems to have worked for Frank at Deptford, and held joint patents with Frank on the manufacture of both sulphuric acid and sugar. On both patents the address is given as the 'Deptford Chemical Works'. George seems to have been active in dealing with these patents, because the record says that he *'swore it in Chancery'*. Does this mean that George was a sugar manufacturer? It was a very common business in London in the last century. In the 1820s some inventors, like Daniel Wilson, developed equipment for heating inflammable liquids that were useful for both tar and sugar. We have already noted that Frank's ammonia products were specially aimed at the West Indian sugar plantations. George was still alive when Frank

277

made his will in 1890. He did not leave money to George, as he did to his other brothers and sons but left instead a sum to be used *'for his benefit'*. That seems to imply that George was not able to make his own decisions and perhaps he needed to be looked after.

ARTHUR HILLS. Arthur Hills has remained elusive despite indications that he was a very important family member. He gave his address as 'Norwood' when he witnessed Frank's marriage agreement in 1847, but there is no presence on census records or a will, or indeed anything else. It may be that he managed the chemical works, which the family owned at Nine Elms and another in Wandsworth..   He could be the Arthur Hills of 18 Bedford Row, Clapham in 1851 — an address on the same social level as Thomas Hills' house in the Grove but Clapham is not Norwood by any stretch. This Arthur Hills was born in 1803, making him older than Thomas. He is described as a *'wholesale drug merchant'*. Arthur also had a chemical works on the Isle of Dogs at Millwall in the 1850s called, significantly, 'Anglesey' Works.' This was a sulphuric acid and colour works immediately across the river from East Greenwich. It was in an area known as 'Folly Wall' where, in the 1990s, housing was built. He also rented a plot of land at Deptford Creek next to the Deptford Chemical Works for nearly 30 years — did the brothers arrange things so that each held small parcels of land on which their works stood? He must have died in 1891, since he was alive when Frank made his will in 1890, but dead by the time of Frank's death in 1892.

HENRY HILLS. Anglesey is a long way from Blackheath and it is amazing that the fourth brother, Henry, managed to commute between the two. Henry lived in the comfort and affluence of Blackheath Paragon while his chemical works were in the strange industrial village of Amlwch on the northern tip of Anglesey. Henry was younger than Thomas and Arthur and was born after the family had moved to Bromley by Bow. His wife, Charlotte, came from Lyme Regis.

There is some vague indication that Henry might have had some connections with Birmingham since his eldest child, Alice, was born in Edgbaston in the late 1830s. *The Times*, in 1859, recorded a partnership in a Bromsgrove salt works which involved a Henry Hills. Salt is something we will come to in a few pages time.

Henry must have lived in Anglesey much of the time because he had a farm nearby and several of his large family of children were born there. He seems to gone to Amlwch in 1840 and established a fertiliser factory at Llam Carw, the exposed headland overlooking the tiny harbour. It is now open cliff top where walkers enjoy sea views and the clinker of Henry's works remains underfoot. In 1860 he made agreement with the Mona Mine Company to calcine copper ore for them. There is in indication that he had been making salt cake, since he was warned not to do so in the future. The agreement with Mona involved the erection of a sulphuric acid making plant at the works on the headland. Henry became active in the small business community in Almwch and was elected to the harbour board, no doubt reflecting his dependence on shipping in and out. Harbour records show shipments of Spanish sulphur and ground phosphate from Antwerp. In 1889 they advertised the fiftieth anniversary of the company in Amlwch and gave details of their products: nitro phosphate, bone manure and super phosphate. At some time before 1897 Hills had taken over a former smelting complex on the other side of the harbour, which is now the site of a housing estate. It continued to be run by a Lewis Hughes, and seems to have prospered. Much of what we know about Hills works in Anglesey can be found in Bryan Hope's book *A Curious Place'*.

Henry clearly spent a lot of time away from Anglesey and always seems to have had addresses in London. In 1863 he acted as executor to the will of his sister Jane. His address then was 282 Old Kent Road – one of a row of undistinguished shops among working class housing.

It is unclear how far Henry's activities were independent of Frank's although the indications are that they worked together. Henry ended his days described as a *'chemist of Deptford'* although clearly the Anglesey business was still thriving. Like Thomas he became a member of the Thames Ironworks Board in the 1870s. He died in 1897 at 6 Northbrook Road, Lee, a smaller and less affluent address than the Paragon. His son, Charles Henry, was later to fulfil an important role in the family business.

MORE AND MORE WORKS

MORFA DHU. Above Amlwch stands Parys Mountain where copper has been mined for centuries in a dramatic landscape. About a mile to west of the Parys Mine at Morfa Dhu, *'Messrs Hills and Sons of Amlwch'* worked a bluestone mine. This needed *'careful chemical operations'* to break it down into constituent parts of copper, lead, zinc, silver and other elements in smaller proportions. This information comes *Metalliferous Minerals and Mining* by D.C.Davies, a mining agent. This is the only mine identified by Davies as belonging to the Hills but other mines which he described were almost certainly theirs too. If so, their mining interests in Wales were extremely extensive.

BERWYN. D.C.Davies managed a phosphate mine at Berwyn in North Wales on behalf of Frank Hills. Phosphate, used for fertiliser, has already been noted as arriving at Amlwch from Antwerp but from what original source has not been discovered. The Berwyn mine was worked between 1872 and 1884 by Davies but does not seem to have been successful.

SPAIN. D.C.Davies also described the Hills' copper mines in Spain. The area is now within the Rio Tinto area which has been recently studied and visits arranged. There are some descriptions in Willies, *Industrial Landscape of Rio Tinto, Huelva, Spain* in *Industrial Archaeology Review*. Frank Hills owned the Ponderosa Mine in Huelva from 1876. In 1889 he acquired the Buitron Mines and in 1891 the Buitron and Huelva Co's assets which included a railway line. This meant that the family controlled the Buitron,

279

Zalonea, Ponderosa and Conception Copper Mines. They were managed for them by a James Bull and there were some '*inconsistencies*' in the way the mines were run.

It is very likely that the family had other foreign interests. I was told by family members that letters and a diary exist which indicate considerable travel abroad on business by Frank.

CHARLES HENRY HILLS AND NEWCASTLE. Henry's son, Charles Henry, seems to have had a home in Tynemouth, although he too seems to have spent much of his time in Blackheath and died in Bromley, Kent. In Newcastle he appears to have managed the Low Walker copper works. Although the Newcastle copper industry has been studied in some detail elsewhere, these studies have not included this works. Hills' works was called the '*Anglesey Copper Company*' and sited on the Tyne with a smelter at Low Walker. Charles Henry lived in Tynemouth. It is this Newcastle connection which has proved most elusive.

The Newcastle works must have smelted copper from Spain. but why should they have brought copper from Anglesey which could have been dealt with by the existing smelter on site there? Why then was the Newcastle Works, or indeed the one in Millwall, called 'Anglesey Works? The 'mixture' supplied by Hills for the oxide purification process is said, by Hughes in *Treatise on Manufacturing and Distributing Coal Gas*, to have included a by-product of copper smelting. Was some of this waste shipped down to London?

The modern Hills family believe that Frank Hills used waste slag from Bessemer's steel works in his chemical works. Bessemer lived close to Frank Hills in Denmark Hill and they certainly knew each other. *Thames Ironworks Gazette* tells how Bessemer visited Thames Ironworks and made a speech in which he introduced himself as a neighbour of the family. In the 1860s Bessemer opened a small steel works in Greenwich, near the Hills' East Greenwich works, but not adjacent to it. While this may be relevant, neither Frank Hills nor any of his associates are mentioned in Bessemer's autobiography in this, nor any other, context. Slag produced as scum in the Bessemer converter could have been used in the oxide process; like so much else with Frank Hills, or indeed Henry Bessemer, it is difficult to know the truth.

STRATFORD. Stratford, East London, had, and has, a very large concentration of chemical works. Frank Hills had a large site in Stratford High Street where oxalic and tartaric acids were made. The site, not yet identified, was sold to a soap company. It was said that once when the Stratford manager was away because of an attack of asthma, a large batch of tartaric acid was accidentally thrown down the drain - it was expensive and big loss to the company.

EAST GREENWICH. Frank Hills did not only operate from the Deptford Chemical Works. In the 1840s he acquired a large site at East Greenwich as part the settlement of his marriage to Ellen Rawlings. This was a tide mill built in 1804, used for corn milling. It had excellent wharfage facilities for a business which depended on water transport.

It seems likely that corn continued to be ground at the East Greenwich mill under Hills' ownership but it is not clear if the tide mill continued to work. From 1845 it was described as *'a steam flour mill'* and perhaps the tide mill itself was replaced by a 25 horse power steam engine, made by William Joyce whose steam engine factory was alongside Deptford Creek in Greenwich. Beneath the site was an artesian well.

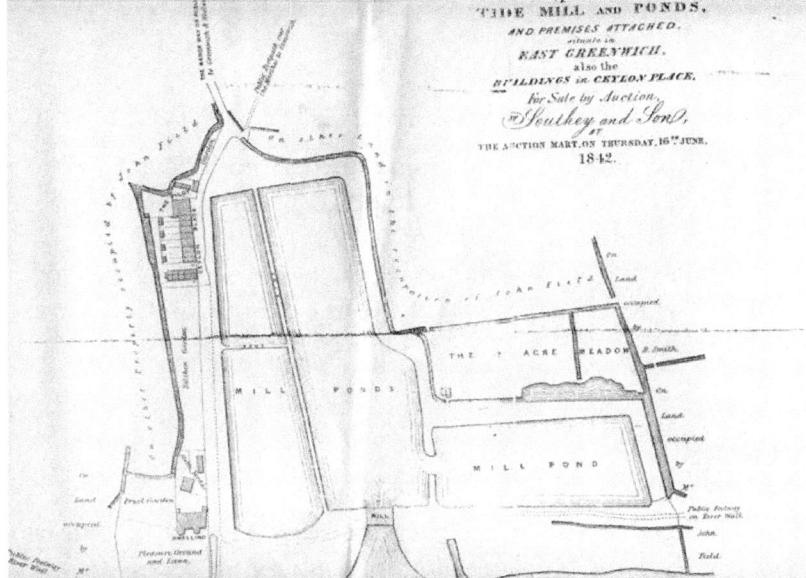

On the riverbank to the north of the mill Frank Hills erected a chemical works. This was gradually extended, for instance in 1869 an ammonia plant was built. Complaints from local people multiplied, in particular about a smell of *'an acid and sickening character'*. This could be discerned not only in Greenwich and Charlton but *'appeared to annoy the garrison at Woolwich'* three miles away. The works were investigated for the Local Government Board by Edward Ballard.

In 1865 special tanks were installed to make sulphuric acid. Other acids were made on site: nitric, tartaric and oxalic, as well as dyes. There is a story told by the present day family of a special and very profitable mauve dye. There was also a manure manufactory and for this there were two 30-ft long steam boilers with a chimney as well as an *'Archimedean screw'* and a bone crusher. The manure was made from 'shoddy', waste leather, dry bones, bone ash and refuse from sugar bakers, that is whatever organic rubbish could be bought cheaply. It was then piled up and mixed with sulphuric acid. In 1871 Mr. Pink, the Medical Officer of Health for Greenwich, gave advice for *'abatement of the nuisance which these works could scarcely have failed to occasion'*.

There was a fatal accident at the East Greenwich Mill. In 1846, Francis Levers, Thomas Darby and Richard Middleton died when they climbed into a giant mixing bowl to clean it. The bottom of the bowl was full of fumes which suffocated them. They were just three more to add to the death toll on this site.

In the 1840s housing was built near the mill in Riverway for Hills' workers. It was called River Terrace and added to the existing Ceylon Place built at the same time as the mill.

281

There was a big house on the riverside, and here lived Hills' works manager, Thomas Davies from Oswestry. Thomas Davies had a family of four daughters who produced a lively family magazine, much of it dealing with their holidays in Anglesey. Was Thomas Davies a connection of D.C.Davies who managed the mines in Wales? They both came from Oswestry and were about the same age. No connection has been traced despite extensive family history research by a descendant of Thomas Davies.

SALT

Frank Hills appears to have had interests and some ownership of salt works in Droitwich and possibly elsewhere. He bought the Imperial Salt and Alkali works in 1857 and later leased them, and eventually sold them to 'salt king', John Corbett. A partnership with this, or another works, involving Frank's brother, Henry, led to litigation on payment of debts which went eventually to the House of Lords with a statement from the Lord Chancellor.

THAMES IRONWORKS

The profits of the chemical business appear to have been invested in heavy engineering. In 1871 Thames Ironworks was, in the words of Philip Banbury in 'Shipbuilders of the Thames and Medway', 'the greatest shipyard of all'. It had been established following the bankruptcy of C.J.Mare in 1856 and had been launched with a capital of £100,000 in £5,000 shares, all sold on the first day of issue to 'local engineering companies'. Frank Hills

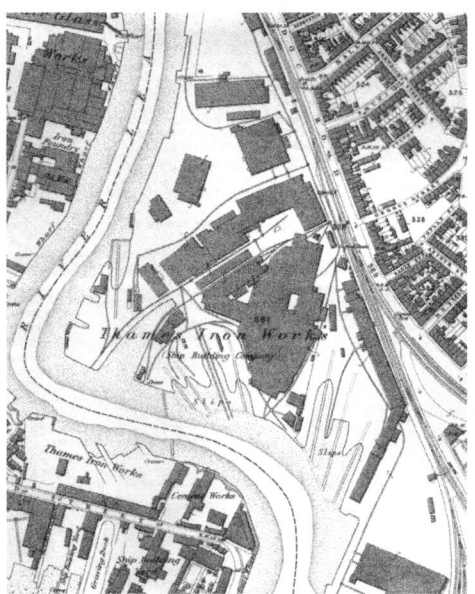

joined the board sometime before 1864 and first appears in the list of board members for a new share issue. at a time when he was at the peak of his activity with the gas companies. He acquired a controlling interest in the company in 1871 and was Chairman of the Board until his death. Thames Ironworks is best known for the construction of HMS Warrior but this, the largest warship in the world when built, was constructed before Frank's Chairmanship and is now berthed as a 'historic ship' at Portsmouth. She was only one of many important, and often glamorous, ships built at the yard. Thames Ironworks also produced the structural ironwork for many important pieces of civil engineering: Hammersmith Bridge, Menai Bridge, the roofs of Alexandra Palace and Fenchurch Street Station are only a few of the high profile projects in which they were involved. In 1898, after Frank's death, the company took over John Penn and Sons, engine builders of

Greenwich, and went on to expand that business. It was this expansion which led to the manufacture of road vehicles at Greenwich and Vauxhall.

The company appears to have embodied revolutionary methods of workplace management and, under Frank's son Arnold, was to embrace Labour Co-partnership. Arnold Hills wrote extensively on the Christian and temperance duties of employers.

Frank Hills' involvement with Thames Ironworks paralleled the period of their greatest success: 'by the early 1870s they were pre-eminent. Perhaps their golden age was in the 1890s when they specialised in quality work. The impetus from this period of excellence carried them, alone, over into the next century'. Frank loved being Chairman of Thames Ironworks. There are stories in Thames Ironworks Gazette, the company house journal, about him excitedly running round each new battleship as it set out on its first journey down the Thames. He was not to know that these was the last moments of Thames shipbuilding and that his son, Arnold, would fight the Government and see the ironworks closed down together with the skills which had made it famous along with the once pre-eminent Thames ship building industry.

FRANK'S DEATH

Frank returned to Kent in his old age and lived at the grand house which William Wells had built – Redleaf – with his 'zoophytes' and a new gramophone. He had made a very great deal of money. He was a very remarkable man, one of the great Victorian industrialists, and almost unknown.

A document exists in the Kent Country Archive by which Frank agreed to give power of attorney to his sons. It is signed in a sadly frail hand and witnessed by his butler. He died in 1895, and this was closely followed the deaths by his two eldest sons. The Deptford Chemical Works was put into the hands of Thomas Herbert Hills, perhaps his brother, Thomas's, son. It was administered from a distance by the husbands of Frank's two daughters, Constance and Annie. Within a few years it was bankrupt. The works at East Greenwich were sold to the gas industry and the old tide mill site was partly sold to South Met Gas while the rest became home to a electricity generating station. The Anglesey works closed in the 1890s and the Spanish mines were taken over by United Alkali.

Thames Ironworks was put in the hands of Frank's third son, Arnold. Successive volumes of Thames Ironworks Gazette chronicle Arnold's favourite causes, vegetarianism, total abstinence, West Ham football club and Labour co-partnership. In the next century his bravery in the face of ridicule and defeat can be seen as he addressed massed rallies in Trafalgar Square while paralysed from the neck down and supported in a specially made invalid basket. He argued the case for warship contracts to continue to be placed with London shipyards but on 21st December 1912 a notice was pinned to Thames Ironworks' main gate: '*Our extremity is God's opportunity and I do not doubt there is still in store for us a Happy New Year'.* Thames Ironworks closed two years before the Great War which would have ensured their future and perhaps the survival of large scale shipbuilding on the Thames.

Perhaps nothing illustrates the difference between Frank and Arnold than family stories of how, after Frank's death, Arnold poured a cellar full of prize claret down the drain. Arnold, talented, honest, brave and idealistic, ultimately failed but 'Elusive' Frank had made the money.

FRANK

It is very likely that many more of the enterprises of Frank Hills and his brothers remain to be discovered. Frank found a niche in the exploitation of gas industry wastes and was prepared to use the patent system to ruthlessly exploit what he could. His success rested on resourcefulness, tenacity, luck and relentless energy.

Gas company directors, in minuting their dealings with Frank Hills, sometimes allow what seems very much like exasperation to creep into the records. He seems to have been very difficult to pin down, and he has been very very difficult to research. Although secrecy is understandable in a world full of rivals, how was it that someone so successful could be so ignored at his death? Even the gas industry, from which he had taken so much money, never gave him an obituary. Perhaps secrecy had grown to be a habit with him, perhaps he was hated. He was devoted to his family, he always looks cheerful in his portraits, and, until the day of his death, he could recite the whole of Paradise Lost from memory.

This saga has come a very long way from the first hesitant ideas about the use of gas industry tar and liquor. Someone like Frank Hills was bound to have come along and find a way to exploitation these 'wastes' into a multi-national corporation.

284

CONCLUSION

At the end of this saga we may conclude that the he London gas industry established the idea of a 'gas factory' as a centralised works from which inflammable gas was distributed to whoever wanted to buy it, and for whatever purpose.

There were a number of successful and important gas companies, some surviving as nationalised boards into the 1980s, and their successors remain with us. The early industry was set up and served, not only by honest British businessmen, but also by chancers, conmen, fraudsters, dodgy dealers. There were also those who came from Continental Europe, some of whom were scientists and some just thought they were.

The industry provided raw materials for other surrounding industries, and some people made a lot of money out of it. It can be assumed that it created impetus for other industries.

The position of the early gas industry as a source for raw materials to other industries is one which needs to be studied in more detail, perhaps on an area basis.

The gas industry has never been shown to have a key role in the industrial revolution but a closer examination might reveal it as a driving force.

WHAT HAS BEEN MISSED OUT HERE?

This book is about some early works in east and east central London. There are a number of sites still around with large and prominent gasholders still on them — in 2021 most being relentlessly demolished. Their stories will need to be told elsewhere.

285

BIBLIOGRAPHY

A to Z of Georgian London, Harry Margary, Lympne Castle, 1981.

A to Z of Victorian London, Harry Margary, Lympne Castle, 1987.

A to Z of Regency London, Harry Margary, Lympne Castle, 1985.

A Century of Gas in South London, SMGC, 709 Old Kent Rd, SE15, 1924.

Accum, Frederick C., A System of theoretical & practical chemistry. Printed for the author, London, 1803.

Accum, Frederick C., Practical treatise on gas-light, 2nd ed., R.Ackerman, London, 1815.

Accum, Frederick C., Description of the process of manufacturing coal-gas now employed at the Gas Works in London, Thomas Boys, London, 1819.

Act for granting certain powers and authorities to a company to be incorporated by Charter, to be called The Gas Light and Coke Company, for making inflammable air for the lighting of the streets of the Metropolis, and for procuring coke, oil, tar, pitch, asphaltum, ammoniacal liquor, and essential oil, from coal and for other purposes relating thereto, June 9th 1810, 50G.III, c.clxiii.

Act for enlarging the powers of an act of his present Majesty, for granting certain powers and authorities to The Gas Light and Coke Company, 1814, 54G.III, c.clvi.

Act to Improve Mile End Old Town (Lighting etc.), 1821, 1&2G.IV, c.lxxii.

Act to Incorporate the British Gas Light Company, 1929, 10G.IV, c.cxxvii

Act to Incorporate the City of London Gas Light and Coke Company, 57G.III, c.xxiii.

Act to Incorporate the Imperial Gas Light and Coke Co., 1&2G.IV., c.cxvii.

Act to Incorporate the Independent Gas Light & Coke Company, 1829, 10G.IV, c.cxviii.

Act to Incorporate Phoenix Gas Light & Coke Company, 1824, 5G.IV, c.lxxviii.

Act to Incorporate the Poplar Gas Light Company, 1821, 1&2G.IV, c.lxxiv.

Act to Incorporate Ratcliffe Gas Light & Coke Company, 1823. 4G.IV, c.xcviii.

Act to Incorporate South London Gas Light & Coke Company, 1821, 1&2G.IV, c.li.

Act to Incorporate South Metropolitan Gas Light & Coke Co, 1842, 5&6V., c.lxxiv.

Act to Incorporate the Surrey Consumers Gas Light & Coke Company, 1854, 17&18V. c.xciv.

Act to Incorporate Woolwich Gas Light Company, 1823, 4G.IV, c.lxxvii.

Act to Light Whitechapel Road with Gas, 1821, 1&2G.IV, c.lii.

Aikin, Arthur & Aikin, Charles, Dictionary of Chemistry & Mineralogy, Hill & Phillips, London, 1804.

Allen, J.S., "History of the Horsley Company to 1865", TNS, V.58, 1986-7, pp.113-138.

Allen, John Fenwick, Some founders of the Chemical industry. Men to be Remembered, Sherratt & Hughes, London, 1906.

Almond, Dr.J.K., " Technical Aspects of Alum making", The Cleveland Industrial Archaeologist. The Alum Industry in North Yorkshire No.2, 1975, pp.11-20.

An Associated Proprietor, An account of the society denominated The Associated Proprietors of the Gas Light & Coke Company, London, 1817.

An Heroic epistle to Mr. Winsor the patentee of the carbonic gas lights & founder of the National Light & Heat Company, R.Spencer, Great Ormond Street, London, 1808.

An address to the proprietors of the intended Gas Light & Coke Company. To which is annexed an epitome of the evidence taken before the Committee of the House of Commons, London, 1809.

Anderson, G., "Manufacture of Sulphate of Ammonia", JGL, 18th July 1871.

Anderson, G., " Extraction of ammonia from gas & the exploitation of the Product", JGL, 12th July 1867, pp.177.

Andom, R., Industrial Exploring in & about London, Clarke & Co., 1895.

Annals of the Barber Surgeons of London compiled from their records and other sources by Sidney Young, one of the Court of Assistants, London, 1890.

Antisell, Thomas, The Manufacture of Photogenic & Hydro-carbon oils from coal & other bituminous substances, New York, 1860, Appleton & Co.

Armstrong, E.F.D.Sc., F.R.S., Murdoch Centenary Lecture. Delivered to the IGE at their 73rd Annual General Meeting in June 1939, London, 1939.

Ashdown, John, Bussell, Michael, & Carter, Paul, A Survey of Industrial Monuments of Greater London, Thames Basin Archaeological Observers Group, London, 1969.

Ashton, T.S., The Industrial Revolution 1760-1830, Oxford, OUP, 1948.

Athol, John, Duke of., Observations on Larch, 1817.

Atkins, G., "Origin & Progress of Gas Lighting", Repertory of Patent Inventions, XIV August 1826, pp.84-92; XV September 1826 pp.157-165; XVI October 1826 226-234; XVII November 1826 pp.272-277.

Austerfield, P.J., The Development of Large Scale Production & Utilisation of Lighter than Air Gases in France Britain & the Low Countries 1783-1821 with special reference to Aeronautics & the Coal Gas Industry, PhD Thesis, London, 1981.

Averley, Gwen, "The Social Composition of Engineering & chemical societies in the 18th & early 19th Centuries", Ambix, V.33, 1986, pp.99-129.

Baker, W., A Letter addressed to His Majesty's Justices of the Peace for the County of Middlesex on the subject of the increases in inquests, Homfray, London, 1839.

Ballard, Edward, Report of the Effluvium Nuisance arising in connection with various manufacturing & other industry, HMSO, London, 1882.

Ballard, Edward, Report on the alleged nuisance from noxious trades carried on the shores of the River Thames from Blackwall Reach to Erith Reach, Local Government Board, nd,

Banbury, P., Shipbuilders of Thames & Medway, David & Charles, Newton Abbot, 1971.

Barlow, Thomas G., A letter to the Right Hon. Sir George C. Lewis Bart, the Principal Secretary of State for the Home Department on the supply of gas in the Metropolis, W.B.King, London, 1859.

Barr, Jim, "Sun Flour Mills, St. Leonard's Road, Bromley by Bow", A London IA Miscellany, GLIAS, 1983.

Barty-King, Hugh, New Flame, Graphmitre, Tavistock, 1988.

Bayliss, Derek, Industries of Wandsworth, LB Wandsworth, 1983.

Beck, E.J., Memorials to serve for a History the Parish of St.Mary, Rotherhithe in the County of Surrey & the administrative area of London, CUP, 1907.

Bennett, A.S., A Brief account of the Early Career of Samuel Clegg & his gas installation at Stoneyhurst College & the subsequent History of Gas at the College, NW Gas Historical Society, 1986.

Berger, Thomas B., A Century & Half of the House of Berger. Being a Brief History of 150 Years of Trading of Lewis Berger & Sons. Manufacturers of Fine Dry Colours, Paints & Varnishes, Homerton, Waterlow & Sons Ltd., 1910.

Berman, Morris, Social Change & Scientific Organisation 1799-1844, Heinemann Educational, London, 1978.

Bessemer, Sir Henry, FRS, An Autobiography. With a concluding chapter, London Offices of 'Engineering', 1905.

Bick, David, The Old Metal Mines of Mid-Wales. Parts 4 & 5, West Montgomeryshire, Aberdovy, Dinas Mawddy, & Llangyno, The Pound House, Newent, Glos., 1990.

Bill for enabling his Majesty to incorporate by Charter a company to be called 'The Gas Light and Coke Company' for making inflammable air for lighting of the streets of the Metropolis, and for procuring coke, oil, tar and pitch, asphaltum, ammoniacal liquor, and essential oil from coal, and for other purposes, 1810, G111, c.50.

Bill to incorporate certain persons for procuring coke, oil, tar, pitch, essential oil and inflammable air form coal and for other purposes, 1809, G.111, c.49.,

Birch, J.G., Limehouse through Five Centuries, Sheldon Press, London, 1930.

Blanch, William., Ye Parish of Camberwell. A plain account of the Parish of Camberwell, its History & Antiquities, E.W.Allen, London, 1875.

Blochmann, Georg Sigismund, Beitrage zur Geschichte Gasbeleuchtung, Dresden, 1871.

Blundell, Spence & Company, 1811-1951, The Company, Hull, 1951.

Boase, Frederic, Modern English Biography, Frank Cass & Co., 1965

Booker, John. Essex as it Was, Essex CC, 1974.

Bowen,F.C. "Thames Ironworks", Shipbuilding and Shipping Record, 18th October 1945,

Bowditch, Rev.W.R., The Analysis Technical Valuation & Purification & use of Coal Gas, E.& F.N.Spon., London, 1867.

Brande, William, "Account of Mr. Clegg's Improvement of the Apparatus Employed in Gas Illumination", QJS, VI, 1816, pp.378-387.

Brande, William, "Observations on the Production of coal gas for the Purposes of illumination", QJS, VI, 1816, pp.71-80.

Brande, William, "On the Composition & Analysis of the Inflammable Gaseous Compounds resulting from the Destructive Distillation of Coal & Oil with some Remarks on their Relative Heating & Illuminating Powers", Phil.Trans., VII, 1820, pp.11-20.

British Tar Co., Description of the directions for using coal tar & varnish description of the works for use of different kinds of coal tar & varnish prepared by the British Tar Co at its works in Shropshire, Staffordshire & Scotland, George Glenny, Broseley, 1789.

Browne, C.A, "The Life & Chemical Services of Frederick Accum", J'nal Chemical Education, (Easton, Pa), 1925. Nos. 10, 11, 12.

Brownlie, David, "Early History of the Coal Gas Process", TNS, 6th June 1924, V.XLIII, pp.601-2.

Bud, Robert Franklin The Discipline of Chemistry: The Origins and Early Years of the Chemical Society of London A dissertation in History and Sociology of Science, Pennsylvania, 1980.

Bud, Robert & Roberts, Gerrylyn, Science versus Practice. Chemistry in Victorian Britain, Manchester MUP, 1984.

Burkitt, June, "Greenwich at the end of the 17th Century", TGLA, 1978, V.III/6, pp.223-234.

Burkitt, June, "The Town of Greenwich 1848', TGLA, 1979, V.IX\1, pp.7-21.

Burt Boulton& Haywood, A Century of Progress. 1848-1948, The Firm, London, 1948.

Burt, Roger, John Taylor, Moorland Publications, Buxton, 1977.

Butterfield, W.J.Atkinson, The Chemistry of Gas Manufacture. A Practical Handbook on the Production, purification & testing of illuminating & fuel gas & on the Bye-products of gas manufacture, Griffin & Co. London, 1907.

Campbell, W.A., "A Century of Chemistry on Tyneside", Society of the Chemical Industry, Newcastle Section, Harlow, Longman, 1968.

Campbell, W.A., The Chemical Industry, Longman, London, 1971.

Campbell, W.A., "A Synoptic View of the Early Chemical Industry in the North East", Cleveland IA, 4, 1975, pp.1-6.

Candidus, Observations on Gas Lights: being an impartial inquiry concerning the injurious effects of the health of the community, from the use of coal-gas for lighting the Metropolis, Underwood, London, 1817.

Carpenter, Charles, The purification of gas by heat. A Century's progress & its lessons, SMGC, London, 1914.

Cassell, J.H., Treatise on Roads & Streets, where the advantages of a Patent Invention for the Paving of Streets & the Making of Roads are fully explained, Dean & Munday, London, 1853.

Cawthorne, W.A. & Fuller, J.G.C.M., "James Mitchell's Brickmaking - an early 19th century study in economic geology", The London Naturalist, No.74, 1994, pp.31-35.

Centenary of the British Gas Light Co. 1824-1924, The Co., 1924,

Chandler, D & Lacey, A.Douglas, The Rise of the Gas Industry in Britain, British Gas Council, London, 1949.

Chandler, Dean, The Gas Industry: from light to heat, Leighton Buzzard, Avon Press Technical Publications, No.5, nd.

Chandler, Dean, Outline of the history of lighting by gas, Chancery House Print Works, London, 1936.

Chantler, P., The British Gas Industry. An Economic study, Victoria Univ. Dept. Economics & Commerce, Manchester, 1939.

Chapman-Huston, Desmond & Cripps, Ernest.C., Through an Archway. The Story of Allen & Hanburys 1715-1954, John Murray, London, 1954.

Chapman, R.Calvert, "An account of the manufacture of copper on the Tyne", Chemical News, 20/1/1870, V.XXIII/581, pp.26-27.

Chatterton, D.A., "State control of public utilities in the 19th Century: the London Gas Industry", Business History, 1972, V.XIV, pp.166-78.

Checkland, S.G., The Mines of Tharsis, Allen & Unwin, London, 1967.

Chester, W.R., Bibliography of Coal Gas. A subject Index of interesting matters published in connection with manufacture of coal gas to end of year 1891, Jones Bell, Nottingham, 1892.

Clark, E.T., Bermondsey: Historic Memories & Associations, Eliot Stock, London, 1907.

Clark, Sylvia, "Chorlton Mills & their Neighbours", IAR, V.II. No.3. 1978, pp.207-239.

Clarke, Benjamin, Glimpses of Ancient Hackney & Stoke Newington, LB Hackney & Hackney Society. Reprint 1894 (1986).

Clayton, Rev.John, "Part of a letter to the Hon.Rob. Boyle. Esq., from the late Rev.John Clayton D.D.", Phil.Trans, 1739, XLI, pp.60-1.

Clegg, Samuel, "Apparatus for making Carburetted Hydrogen Gas from Pit Coal & Lighting Factories therewith", Soc.Arts, 1808, V.XXVI, pp.202-6.

Clegg, Samuel, Jnr., A Practical Treatise on the Manufacture & Distribution of Coal Gas, London, Weale, 1841.

Clift, J.E., "Preservation of Timber by Creosote", JGL, 10th December 1851, p.236.

Clow, A.& Clow, N., The Chemical Revolution, Blatchworth, London, 1952.

Clow, A.& N., "Lord Dundonald", Econ.Hist.Rev., V.III 1&2, 1942, pp.47-59.

Coal the Basis of 19th Century Technology, Colin Russell for the Course Team, Open Univ. Press, Bletchley, 1973.

Cochrane, Alexander, [with the Earl of Dundonald], The Fighting Cochranes, Quiller Press, London, 1983.

Cochrane, Archibald, Account of the qualities & uses of Coal Tar & Coal Varnish, William Sadler, Edinburgh 1784.

Cochrane, Archibald, A treatise showing the intimate connection that subsists between agriculture & chemistry, J. Murray & S.Highley, London, 1795.

Cochrane, Archibald, Directions for extracting gum from lichen or tree moss, Chapman & Long, Glasgow, 1801.

Cochrane, Archibald, Introduction & Contents of a Proposed Publication, Thomas Barton, London, 1806.

Cochrane, Thomas, Autobiography of a Seaman, Richard Bentley, London, 1860.

Cochrane, Thomas, Demonstration of the superiority of the newly invented street lamps filled with a uniform succession of pure air following continuous to the flame & uniting other important advantages, London, 1814.

Cohen, J.M., The Life of Ludwig Mond, Methuen, London, 1956.

Colburn, Zeriah, The Gasworks of London, Regents Park, London, 1865.

Coleby, L.J.M, "The History of Prussian Blue", Ann Sci., V.4, 1939, pp. 206-211.

Cole, R.J., "Friedrich Accum. A Biographical Study", Ann.Sci., 1951, V.7/2, pp.128-144.

"Commercial Value of Gas Residuals", JGL 1st April 1856, p.181-2.

Considerations on the Nature & Objects of the Intended Light & Heat Company, Published by Authority of the Committee, London, 1808.

Cook, Rev. S.H., BA, Northfleet & its' Parish, Rev.Cook, London, nd.

Cook, B., "Methods of Producing Heat, Light & various useful articles from Pit Coal", Trans.Soc.Arts, 1810, V. XXVIII, p.73 &, Phil.Mag. 3/1810, pp.332-339.

Cooper, Susan & Pitt, Peter "The Pitt family of Dudley", The Blackcountryman, October, 1983.

Cooper, Thomas, Information concerning gas lights, Philadelphia, 1816.

Copeland, John, Roads & their Traffic, David & Charles, Newton Abbot, 1986.

"Coppermill" Monograph 18, Walthamstow Antiquarian Society.

Cotterill, M.S., "The Development of Scottish Gas Technology 1817- 1914; An inspiration & motivation", IAR V/1. Winter 1980-81, pp.19-40.

Cotterill, M.S., The Scottish Gas Industry to 1914, PhD, Stathclyde, 1976.

Cotton, William, FRS, A brief memoir of the late Captain Joseph Huddart FRS & an account of his inventions in the manufacture of cordage as contained in a letter to James Walker President ICE, School Press, London, 1885.

County of Kent in 1801, Harry Margary, Lympne Castle, 1990.

Coutts, A., "William Cruickshank of Woolwich", Ann.Sci., 1959, 15/2, pp.121-133.

Cowper, B.H., A Description Historical & Statistical of Millwall, commonly called the Isle of Dogs, Gladding, London, 1853.

Cowpox & gas lights contra malice & ignorance; or life, health & fortune against death, disease & poverty. A simple dialogue between Messrs. Life & Co & Death & Co. Published by a friend for truth for the uninformed, London, nd.

Cox, William, "On the fertilizing properties of manures which contain ammonia", Phil.Mag., 5/09, pp.438-442.

Co-partners Magazine, Gas Light & Coke Co., Monthly from 1911.

Co-partnership Herald, Commercial Gas Co., Monthly from 1908.

Co-partnership Journal, South Met. Gas Light & Coke Co., Monthly from 1906.

Crips, F.Southwell, Gas Literature, William Clownes, London, 1895.

Crips, F.Southwell, The Earliest Works on Gas Lighting, London, 1907.

Crips, Ernest C., Plough Court. The Story of a Notable Pharmacy, Allen & Hanburys Ltd., London, 1927.

Crocker, Alan, "The Paper Mills of Surrey", Surrey History, 4/1, Surrey LHC, 1989.

Croll, Archibald Angus, "On the Purification of coal gas & the application of the products thereby obtained to agriculture & other purposes", Trans.ICE, 1844 III, pp.290-308.

Croll,A.Angus, The Great Central Gas Co. It's History, Harris, London, 1875.

Crory, W.V., East London Industries, Longman, London, 1876.

Crouch, A.P., Silvertown & Neighbourhood -A Retrospect, Thomas Batch, London, 1900.

Cruden, R.P., The History of the Town of Gravesend, William Pickering, London, 1843.

Dalrymple, Sir John, Address on the Proposals from Sir John Dalrymple on the Subject of the Coal Tar & Iron Branches of Trade, Pearson & Rollason, Edinburgh & Birmingham, 1784.

Davies, D.C., Metalliferous Minerals & Mining, London, 1892.

Davis, J.W, "A few hints Concerning the Benefits that may be expected from the Nature of Coal Gas", Phil.Mag., V.5., 1809, pp.432-438.

Davy, Sir.H., Elements of Agricultural Chemistry, Campbell & Co., London, 1813.

Davy,H., "On the Firedamp in Mines", Phil. Trans, Read 9th November 1815.

Day, Joan, Bristol Brass, David & Charles, Newton Abbot, 1973.

Deane, Phyllis, The First Industrial Revolution, CUP, Cambridge, 1965.

Derry, T.K. & Williams, Trevor, I., A Short History of Technology from the Earliest Times to AD 1900, OUP, London, 1960.

Devereaux, R., John Loudon MacAdam, OUP, London, 1936.

Dews, Nathan, History of Deptford, J.D.Smith, Deptford, 1883.

Diary of John Evelyn Esq.FRS, ed. William Barry, London, nd.

Dickinson, H.W., "Condensed History of Rope Making", TNS, V. 23, 1942-45, pp.71-95.

Dickinson, H.W. & Stracker, C., "Charcoal & pyroligneous acid making in Sussex", TNS, V.XXVIII, 1937-8, pp.439-445.

Dickinson, H.W.& Jenkins, R., James Watt & the Steam Engine, London, 1927.

Dickinson, H.W., "History of vitriol manufacture in England', TNS, V.XVIII, 1937-8, pp.438-460.

Digging in the City, Museum of London, Dept. Urban Archaeology Annual Review, 1988.

Dockland. An Illustrated Historical Survey of Life & Work in East London, ed. R.J.M.Carr, NELP & GLC, 1986.

Dodd, George, Days at the Factories, London, 1843.

Donkin, Harry J., History of Bryan Donkin & Company, Evans, Chesterfield, 1925.

Downs, John, "History of Chemical Manufacture", JSoc.Chem.Ind. 3rd March 1890, pp.283-5.

Dummelow, John, The Wax Chandlers of London, Phillimore, Chichester, 1973.

Economics of the Industrial Revolution Mokyr, Joel, ed., George Allen & Unwin, London, 1985.

Elwell, Charles J.L., Aspects of the Black Country, Black Country Soc., Halesowen, 1991.

Essays in the Economic and Social History of South Yorkshire, South Yorkshire County Council, 1976.

Esson, W.,"Manufacture of Sulphate of Ammonia", JGL, V.XVI, 12th October 1866, p.74.

Everard, Sterling, The History of the Gas Light & Coke Company 1812- 1949, Benn.Bros., London, 1949.

"Facts respecting the increased volatility & inflammability which fish oil & its vapours acquire by continued or renewed exposure to certain high temperatures; elicited by the examination of evidence in a late trial in the Court of Common Pleas (Severn King & Co, versus Drew of the Imperial Insurance Office) before the Lord Chief Justice Dallas & a Special Jury", Phil.Mag., V.55, No.264, 4/1820, pp.252-289.

Fairlie, Susan, "Dyestyffs in the 18th Century", Economic History Review, V.XV 11, No.3, 1965, pp.488-492.

Fancy, Harry, Coal Mining at Whitehaven, Whitehaven Museum, nd.

Farrar, W.V., "Richard Laming & the Coal Gas Industry. With his Views on the Structure of Matter", Ann.Sci., 1969, V.25, pp.243-253.

Farrar, W.V., Farrar, Kathleen R. & Scott E.L., "The Henrys of Manchester. Thomas Henry", Ambix, 1973 No.3., pp.183-205; "William Henry & John Dalton", 1974 No.4, pp. 208-229; "Thomas Henry's sons", 1974 No.4, pp.179-208;"William Henry. Hydrocarbons & the Gas industry", 11/1975, V.22, pp.186-228.

Faulkus, M.E., "The British Gas Industry before 1850", Econ.History Review, 2nd Series, 1967, V.XX, pp.494-508.

Faulkus, M.E., "Early development of the British Gas Industry 1790-1815", Econ.History Review, 2nd Series, 1982, V.XIX, pp. 217-234.

Faulkus, M.E., "The development of Municipal Trading in the 19th Century", Business History, 1977, V. XIX, pp.108-124.

Fayol, Amédée, Phillipe Lebon inventeur au gaz d'éclairage, Publications Techniques, Paris, 1943.

Forbes, Prof.I.R.H., "Roots in the Past. The Past of the Petroleum Industry", TNS, V.XXXII, 1959-60, pp.111-123.

Fortescue, J.W., Dundonald, English, London, 1895.

Francis, A.K., The Cement Industry 1796-1914, David & Charles, Newton Abbott, 1977.

Frederick Allen & Sons, Helping Mother Nature, The Co., nd.

French, Alfred, "The Story of Limehouse", ELR, No.5, 1982, pp.22-30.

French, Alfred, "Money for Old Rope", ELHS Newsl'r, Spring, 1981, p.8.

Fry, Katherine, History of the parishes of East & West Ham, 1888, Printed for private consumption by Siegle.

Fullmer, June, Z., "Technology, Chemistry & the Law in Early 19th Century England", Technology & Culture, V.21, No.1, January, 1980, pp. 1-28

Gale, W.K.V.,Boulton, Watt and the Soho Undertakings, Birmingham Museum of Science and Industry, 1952.

Gamble, J.C. "Remarks on the Hills and Haddock Patent" Repertory of Patent Inventions, April 1826, X, pp.236-241.

Gander, Mr, "The Old Sugar Refiners of St. George's in the East", ELHS Newsletter, 1/1989, pp.6-7.

Gardner, W.M., The British Coal Tar Industry, Williams & Norgate, London, 1915.

Garton, W.F.D., "History of the South Metropolitan Gas Co.", Gas World, 2/1952 et seq.

Gas Light & Coke Co., An Account of the Progress of the Company from its' Incorporation by Royal Charter in the year 1812 to the Present Time, Watson & Layton, London, 1912.

Gas Light & Coke Company Bill. A Criticism, Galabin & Marchant, London, 1809.

Gas Engineer, Birmingham from 1877 (19 vols.).

Gas Gazette, London, from 1847.

George, William H, "A short account of the Copperas Industry of the Isle of Sheppey", Tertiary Res, Leiden, 3/1984 5(4), pp. 169-172.

Gibbs, F.W., Some studies in the history of soap manufacture. MSc, Univ. College, London, 1937.

Gibbs, F.W., "History of the Japanning Trade", Ann.Sci., V.7, 1957, pp.407-416;, V.9, 1958, pp.88-95; 187-213; 214-252.

Gibbs, F.W., "History of the Manufacture of Soap", Ann.Sci., 1851, V.4 p.169-174.

Gillespie, Charles.C., Dictionary of Scientific Biography, Charles Scriber & Sons, New York, 1976.

Gittings, L., "Manufacture of alkali in GB 1779-1789", Ann.Sci., 1965, V.22, pp.175-196.

GLIAS Gas Man, "Early years at the Old Kent Road Gas Works", GLIAS Newsletter No.85 April, 1983, pp.4-5.

Golisti, Ken & Wilkinson, Barry, A New Light Dawning. Gas Engineering in the first half century of the industry, Presented to the Yorkshire Gas Assoc. April, 1992.

Goodsall, R.H., "The Whitstable Copperas Industry", Archaeologia Cantiana, 1957, V.LXX, pp.142-159.

Goodyear, Charles, Gum Elastic & its origins Newhaven 1855.

Gordon, Alexander, The Fitness of Turnpike Roads & Highways for the most Expeditious, Convenient & Economical method of Travel, London, 1835.

Gordon, Alexander, A Historical & Practical Treatise Upon Elemental Locomotion by way of steam on Common Roads, London, 1832.

Grant, J.L., The report of James Ludovic Grant, Esq. Chairman, & the other acting trustees of the fund for assisting Mr. Winsor in his experiments: to the subscribers of that fund, at a meeting convened by public advertisements, at the Crown & Anchor Tavern in the Strand, on the 26th May, 1808 Printed by T.Davison, Whitefriars, London, 1808.

Gray, Michael, "Joseph Priestley in Clapton 1791-1794", ELR, 1983 No.6, pp.32-41.

Green, Henry & Wigram, Robert, Chronicles of Blackwall Yard Whitehead, Morris & Bone, London, 1881.

Griffiths, John, The Third Man. The Life & Times of William Murdoch, Andre Deutsch, London, 1992.

Gurney, W.B., A Report of the Trial of Severn & King v. Phoenix Insurance Co. Taken in Shorthand, Gurney, London, 1820.

Haber, L.F., Chemical industry during the 19th Century, Oxford Clarendon, 1958.

Hales, S., Statical Essays: Containing Vegitible Statics or an account of some statistical experiments on the sap in vegetables Innys, London, 1769.

Halstead, D.E., "The Early History of Portland Cement", TNS, V. 34., 1962, pp.87-94.

Hamilton, J., The English Brass & Copper industries, Blond & Briggs, London, 1926.

Hancock, T., Personal Narrative of the Origin & Progress of the Caoutchouc or India Rubber Manufacture in England, James Lyne Hancock Ltd., London, 1857 .

Hardie, D.W.F.& Pratt, J.Davidson, History of the Modern British Chemical Industry, Pergammon Press, London, 1966.

Harris,S., Development of Gas on North Merseyside 1815-1949, NW.Gas Liverpool, 1956.

Hassan, J.A., "Relationship between coal, gas & oil production", IAR Summer, 1978, V.II/3, pp.277-289.

Hautala, Kustaa, Svomalisen Tiedeakatemian Toimitskia, Ann. Academie Scialfer Fennicae Helsinki, 1964. Helsinki, 1970.

Hedley, Joseph, Letter to the Rt. Hon the Lord Mayor On the Supply of Gas to the City of London Containing the official documents laid before the Commissions of Sewers an Epitome of a statement submitted to the Secretary of State for the Home Department & an Account of the Proceedings before a Committee of the House of Commons on the Application of the Chartered Gas Light & Coke Co. for the Act of Incorporation, Richardson, London, 1828.

Henry, William, A general view of the nature of chemistry, Manchester, 1799.

Henry, William, An epitome of chemistry, London, 1803.

Henry, William, "Experiments on the gases obtained by the destructive distillation of wood, peat, pit-coal, oil, wax", JNat.Phil, 1805, V. XI, pp.65-74.

Henry, William, "Description of an apparatus for the analysis of the compound inflammable gases by slow combustion; with experiments on the gas from coal, explaining its application", Phil.Trans., 1808, pp.281-295 &, Phil.Mag., 1808, V.32, pp.277-294.

Henry, William, The Elements of experimental chemistry Barlow Crawford & Son, London, 1810.

Henry, William, "Experiments on the Gas from Coal, chiefly with a view to its Practical Application", Memoirs of the Literary & Philosophical Society of Manchester, V. III (2nd series), 1819, pp.391_429 &, Phil.Mag., V.XXII, pp.117-126;, pp.164- 172. Also published as a pamphlet, Manchester, 1819.

Henry, W., "On the Aeriform compounds of charcoal & hydrogen with an account of some additional experiments on the gases from oil & coal", Monthly Magazine, 1821, V.LVIII &, Phil.Mag., V.58 No.281 9/1821, pp.90-98 &, pp.169-177.

Henry, William Charles, Biographical Account of the late Dr. William Henry MD FRS GSD., Manchester, 1837.

Hills, R.L., Paper Making in Britain 1488-1988, Athlone Press NJ, 1988.

Hodgkin, J., "James Sadler of Oxford", TNS, V.8, pp.27-28.

Hughes, S, A Treatise on Gas Legislation, London, 1861.

Hughes, S, A Treatise on the Practice of Manufacturing & Distributing coal gas, Weale, London, 1853.

Hughes, S., London & Its Gas Companies, London, 1863.

Hughes, S., Metropolis Gas F.Phipps, London, 1859.

Hughes, A.C., Tar Roads E.Arnold & Co., London, 1938 .

Humber, Sean, Gas Works in London. An investigation into Contaminated Land Friends of the Earth, London, 1991.

Hunt, Charles, A history of the introduction of gas lighting, Walter King, London, 1907.

Ibbetson, John Holt, Treatise on the manufacture of gas illustrative of the theory & practice of certain improvements in the system which the author has made the subject of a patent, The author, London, 1826.

Imperial Continental Gas Association 1824-1974, Published privately, 1974.

In Parliament. Remarks on the Bill for incorporating the Gas Light & Coke Company, London, 1809.

In Parliament, Gas Light Bill. An observation in opposition to the bill now descending in Parliament. Printed Galabin & Marchant, Ingram Court, London, 1809.

In the Exchequer Court of Pleas, 1855 Hills v. The London Gas Co at Guildford before Baron Bramwell, 1858.

Inkster, Ian, "Science & Society in the Metropolis. A Preliminary examination of the social & historical context of the Askesian

Society in London 1796-1807", Ann.Sci., 1977 34, pp.1-32.

James, Mary, The History of Chemistry in Essex & East London, Essex Section of the Royal Society of Chemistry, 1991.

James. Frank A.J.L., Davy in the Dockyard, Firenze, MCMXCII.

Jenson & Nicholson Co.Ltd., Story of an English firm, London, 1948

Jones, Yvonne, Georgian & Victorian Japanned Wares of the West Midlands. Catalogue of the permanent collection & a temporary exhibition, Wolverhampton Art Galley & Museums, 24th October- 17th November, 1982.

Jones, M, History of gas production in Wales, Wales Gas Printing Centre, 1978.

Kargon, Robert H.,Science in Victorian Manchester. Enterprise and Expertise, MUP, Manchester, 1977.

Kaufman, M., The First Century of Plastics. Celluloid & its Sequel The Plastics & Rubber Institute, 1963.

Kimber, Harry, Wilfred Nicholson. A record of his work. Privately published, 1960.

King, W., Treatise on the science & practice of the manufacture & distribution of coal gas, London, 1878-1882., Ed. T.Newbigging & W.T. Fewtrell, 3 vols.

Industrie du gaz en France, 1824-1924, Paris nd.

Laming, Richard, "The purification of coal gas", JGL, 10th May 1850, p.207.

Layton, W.T., The Discoverer of Gas Lighting, Walter King, London, 1926.

Layton, W.T., Early years of the South Metropolitan Gas Company 1835-7, Spottiswood Ballantyne & Co., 1920.

Leaback, David, "Discovery in the East End. A personal account of discovery against a seemingly very ordinary East End background"., ELR, No.12, 1989, pp.2-16.

"Les Mines d'Asphalt", Revue Suisse, 7/1991, pp.19-22.

Letheby, Dr.H. "On the Utilisation of the Waste Products of the Making of Coal Gas", JGL, V.XVI, 1867, p.574.

Lewis, F., Essex & Sugar, Phillimore, London, 1976.

Liveing, Edward, Pioneers in Petrol. A Centenary History of Carless, Capel & Leonard, London, 1959.

Livesey, George, "Gas Purification", Engineering, 14th September, 1866, pp.195-6.

Livesey, George, "On the Practical Working of the Liquor system of Purification", JGL, V.XVI, 1867, p.571.

LL, "Materials for a Memoir of Mr. Samuel Clegg & Authentic History of the Art of Gas Lighting", Mechs Mag., 1835, XXII, pp.470-2.

Lloyd, Christopher, Lord Cochrane. Seaman - Radical - Liberator, Longmans Green & Co., London, 1947.

Loadman, J. & James, F The Hancocks of Marlborough, OUP 2010

Lowe, George 'Remarks on an article entitled 'A Few Facts Relating to Gas Illumination', Phil.Mag., 1820, V.18, p.37.

Lowe, George, "On the purifying of coal gas; on the ammoniacal liquor of coal gas & on some singular products obtained from the ammoniacal liquor", Phil.Mag., 3/1819, pp.262-266.

Lowe, George, "On purifying coal gas, & increasing the quantity produced from a given weight of coals", Phil.Mag., 11/1818, pp.371-3.

Lowther, Sir J., "An account of damp air", Phil.Trans., 1733, V.XXXVIII, pp.109-13.

Lunge, G., Manufacture of Sulphuric Acid & Alkali, Gurney & Jackson, London, 1886.

Lunge, G., A Treatise on Coal tar & ammonia Gurney & Jackson, London, 1909.

Macadam, John Loudon, Remarks on the Present System of Road Making & Observations deduced from the Practice & Experience of the Introduction in Improvements in the Methods of Making, Repairing & Preserving Roads & Defending the Road Funds from Misapplication, Longman, Hurst, Orme, Rees & Brown, London, 1821.

Macculloch, J., "On certain products obtained in the distillation of wood, with some Account of bituminous substances & remarks on coal", Phil.Mag., 3/1815, pp.203-218; 269-274.

MacDougall, Philip "The Isle of Sheppey and 'Roman' Cement', Bygone Kent, Vol 11, No.5, pp.293-298.

Maceroni, Francis, Memoirs of the Life & Adventures of Col.Maceroni, London, 1838.

Maceroni, Francis, A Few Facts concerning Elementary Locomotion, London, 1834.

Macfarlan, J., "The discoverer of gas light", TNS, 1924/5, V, pp.53-55.

Macfie, William, "An account of a lecture on W.M. with Samuel Smiles in the chair, the Royal Aquarium, Westminster, on September 14th", Gas Engineer, 1883, V.XI, p.2.

Macintosh, Geo, A memoir of Charles Mackintosh FRS of Campsie & Dunchattan, Privately printed, Glasgow, 1847.

MacKenzie, Compton, The Vital Flame, London Gas Council, 1947.

Mathias, Peter, The Brewing Industry in England 1700-1830, London, CUP, 1959.

Mathias, Peter, Science & Society 1600-1906, CUP, 1972.

Matthews, Derek, "Rogues, Speculators & Competing Monopolies: the London Gas Companies 1812-60", London Journal, 1985 XI, pp.39-50.

Matthews, Derek, The London Gas Industry: a Technical, Labour & Commercial History to 1914. PhD Thesis, Hull, 1986.

Matthews, Derek, "Laissez faire & the London Gas Industry in the 19th century, another look", Economic History Review, 1986, V.XXXIX, pp.244-63.

Matthews, M.H., "Development of the synthetic alkali industry in Great Britain", Ann.Sci., 1976, V 22, pp.271-382.

Matthews, William. An Historical sketch of the origin, progress & present state of Gas-Lighting, London, 1827.

Matthews, William, Letter to the Honourable Lord Mayor of London in reply to the letter lately addressed to him from Mr. Jos Hedley with remarks upon the prospectus recently issued to form a west London gas company & also upon the elusive nature of many of the projects for gas lighting, London, nd.

Matthews, William, A compendium of gas lighting, Simpson & Maskell, London, 1827.

McTear, J., "History of the Technology of Sulphuric Acid", 1900, Proc.Phil.Soc., Glasgow, 1881, pp.701.

Messham, Susan E., Gas. An Energy Industry, A Science Museum Book, HMSO, 1976.

Merle, G. Traite sur le Gaz et Tout les Appareil Necessaire a sa Fabricant, Paris, 1837

Miall, S, A History of the British Chemical Industry, Benn, London, 1931.

Millington, John 'On Street illumination?', QJS, V. V., 1818, pp.277.

Mills, Mary 'George Livesey', London's IA, No.4., GLIAS, p.41-49.

Minutes of Evidence taken before a Committee of the House of Commons on the London and Westminster Oil Gas Bill, Sessions 1824 and 1825.

Minutes of evidence taken before the Committee to whom the Bill to incorporate certain persons for procuring coke, oil, tar, pitch, ammoniacal liquor, essential oil, and inflammable air, from coal; and for other purposes was committed, London, 1809.

Mirror of Literature, Amusement & Instruction. J.Limbord, Strand, London, from 1816.

Mokyr, Joel, The Lever of Riches, Oxford, OUP, 1990.

Morris, Peter J.T. & Russell, Colin A., Archives of the British Chemical Industry 1750-1914, BHSS, Faringdon, 1988.

Mott, R.A., History of Coke Making & the Coke Oven Managers' Association, Coke Oven Managers Assoc., Cambridge, 1939.

Mr. Barlow's proposals for establishing with or without an Act of Parliament a company to light the County of Surrey from end of Blackfriars Bridge to the Obelisk Borough, and public buildings and every establishment in the neighbourhood. Gentlemen of the first respectability have sent. Mr. Barlow's new carbonising stove for the production of hydro_carbonated gas, etc. nd.

Multhauf, Robert P., "Sal ammoniac. History of an industry", Technology & Culture, 6/5/1969.

Murdock, William 'An account of the application of the gas from coal to economical purposes', Phil.Trans., 1808., V. LXXXXVIII, pp.124-32 & Phil.Mag., XXI, pp.113.

Murdock, William, Letter to a Member of Parliament from Mr. William Murdock in vindication of his claims in reply to a recent publication by the committee for conducting through Parliament a Bill for incorporating a Gas-Light & Coke Company, Galabin & Marchant, London, May 4th.

Muspratt, J.S, Chemistry, Theoretical, Practical & Analytical as applied to Arts & Manufactures, London, Edinburgh, Glasgow & New York, 1853-61.

Musson, A.E., Growth of British Industry Batsford, London, 1981.

Musson, A.E.& Robinson, Eric,. Science & technology in the Industrial Revolution, MUP, 1969

Musson, A.E., Enterprise in soap & chemicals, MUP, 1965.

Nabb, Harold, The Bristol Gas Industry 1815-1949 Bristol Branch Historical Assoc., 1987.

Natural Dyes, Wandle Industrial Museum, nd.

Neuer Nekrolog der Deustschen Ilmemn Weimar JG, 1841 (1843).

Newbigging, Thomas, The Gas Managers Handbook, W.B.King, London, 1870.

Nicholls, Mr., Pontypool & Usk Japan Ware, Mr. Nicholls, nd.

Nicholson, William, "Remarks on a pamphlet by Winsor", Phil.Mag., 1807 X, VI, pp.308.

Non di Ricordo, Metallic influence of gas upon the dark of the lampposts. Being the substance of a Report to the Committee upon the Gas Co. Greenwich, 1824.

Nowell-Smith, Simon House of Cassell, Cassell & Co., Curwen Press, Plaistow, 1958.

P, H.L. & B., An Account of the Parish of Bermondsey & the Course of its Boundaries, Brixton, 1868.

Palgrave, D.A., "Some precursors of Modern Liquid Fertiliser Technology", IAR, V.1. No.2. Summer, 1977.

Parkes, Samuel, Treatise on the Chemical Industry, J.Chidley, 1839.

Parkes, Samuel, Chemical Catechism. For the Use of Young People, Printed for the Author, London, 1806.

Parkes, Samuel, Chemical Essays, For the author, London, 1815.

Parkes, Samuel, Observations on the Chemical Part of the Evidence Given upon the Late Trial of the Action brought by Messrs. Severn, King & Co. Against the of Imperial Insurance Co., London, 1821 & QJS, V.X, 1821, pp.316-54.

Parks, W.A., An Analytical Survey of the Influence of the Development of Chemical Theory, during the 19th Century upon the Evolution of the Chemical Industry with Particular Reference to East London: the Development of the Heavy Chemical Industry of West Ham and District, MSc.Thesis, Univ. London, 1950.

Partington, J.M., A Short History of Chemistry, Randall, London, 1937.

Peckston, Mr. of the Westminster, Gas Light & Coke Co., Cursory Observations on Different Processes for the Distillation of Coal. For Mr Crawford a Member of the Committee, I. Hebler. Southampton, 1819.

Peckston, T.S., Practical Treatise on Gas Lighting, London, 1841.

Peckston, T.S., The Theory & Practice of Gas Lighting, London, 1819

Peebles, Malcolm, W.H., Evolution of the Gas Industry, Macmillan, London, 1980.

Phillips, G.W., History & Antiquities of the Parish of Bermondsey, London, 1841.

Phillips, Richard, Remarks & Comments given in the XXth Number of the Journal of the Institution of Science & Art on the Observations on the Chemical Part of the Evidence Given upon the Late Trial of the Action brought by Messrs. Severn, King & Co. Against the of Imperial Insurance Co. by Samuel Parkes, Esq., R.Phillips, London, 1821.

Pickles, Roger L., "A brief history of the Alum industry in North Yorkshire", The Cleveland Industrial Archaeologist. The Alum Industry in North Yorkshire No.2., 1975, pp.1-10.

Pitt, W., "On converting the smoke arising from steam engines, etc. into Tar. Dundonald's coke ovens near Birmingham", Trans.Soc. Arts, 1791, V.8, pp.31-40.

Ponting, K.G., "Important Natural Dyes of History', IAR, V.II No.2., 1978, pp.154-159.

Read Holliday & Sons. Ltd., The Company, Huddersfield, 1914.

Reader, W.J., Imperial Chemical Industries. A History, OUP, London, 1970.

Rees, Abraham, The New Cyclopedia or Universal Dictionary, London, 1819. ed Neil Cossons, David & Charles, Newton Abbott, 1982.

Remarks Upon a Bill for Incorporating the Gas Light & Coke Company, G.Sidney, London, 1809.

Report of the Committee Appointed on the 1st day of March last for Lighting & Watching this Town & Parish. Greenwich Printed by Order of the Vestry 22/6/1824, Greenwich, 1824.

Report from the Select Committee on gaslight establishments. Ordered, by the House of Commons, to be printed 7th July 1823. Gaslight establishments. Copy of the Report of the Royal Society [drawn up in 1814] .. on the subject of gaslights; and copies of two reports of the person [Sir William Congreve] appointed ... to inspect the gaslight establishments existing in the Metropolis. Ordered by the House of Commons, to be printed, 26th March 1823.

Richardson, J.B., Metal Mining, Allen Lane, London, 1974.

Richards, William, A Practical treatise on the Manufacture & Distribution of coal gas, Weale, 1877.

Richards, William, Richards Gas Consumers Guide, Spon, London, 1866.

Roberts,G.K. The Royal College of Chemistry (1845-1853): A Social History of Chemistry in the early Victorian period, John Hopkins Univ., PhD Dissertation, 1973.

Robertson,J.C., Practical Instructions for the Improvement of the Carriage Pavement Appendix: Hints to Paviours by Colonel Maceroni, London, 1838.

Rostron, L.W.S., Powers of Charge of the Metropolitan Gas Cos., Benn, London, 1927.

Rowlinson, P.J., Regulation of the Gas Industry in the early 19th Century, 1800-1860, D.Phil. Thesis, Oxford, 1984.

Russell, Colin, Roberts, Gerrylyn & Coley, Noel, Chemists by Profession, Open Univ. Press, Milton Keynes, 1977.

Russell-Wood, "Scientific Work of William Brownrigg, MD FRS, 1711-1800", Ann.Sci., 1949, V6/2, pp.181-196, V.7/1., pp.877- 100, V7/3, pp.199-106 7/1, pp.77-95, 1951, 2 7/2 199-207.

Russell, Sir E.John., History of agricultural science in Great Britain 1620-1955, George Allen & Unwin, London, 1966.

Rutter, J.O.N., Street Lights, London, 1853.

Rutter, J.O.N., The Price of Gas, London, 1851.

Rutter, J.O.N., Practical Observations on gas lighting, London, 1833.

Rutter, J.O.N., Gas Lighting its Progress & its Prospects, London, 1849.

Rutter, J.O.N., Ventilation of Gas Lights, London, 1844.

Science & Technology & Economic Growth in the 18th Century ed, Musson, A.E., Methuen, London, 1972.

Shurer, H., "The Mackintosh. The Paternity of an Invention", TNS, 1952, V.28, pp.77-87.

Shirley, Thomas, "Description of a well & earth in Lancashire", Phil.Trans, 1667, V.2, pp.482-4.

Simmonds, Henry S., All about Battersea, Ashford, London, 1880.

Simms, F.W., Practical Observations on Asphaltic Mastic. London, 1835.

Singer, Charles, The Earliest Chemical Industry, Folio Soc., London, 1948.

Skempton, A.W., British Civil Engineering 1640-1840 Mansell, London, 1987.

Smith, J.Walker, Dustless Roads, Tar Macadam, Charles Griffin, London, 1909.

Smith, Norman, Gas Manufacture & utilisation, British Gas Council, 1945.

Smith, Raymond, Sea Coal for London, Longmans, London, 1961.

Speech Delivered before a very numerous & respectable meeting of the proprietors on Thursday, 6th July 1809., London, 1809.

Speeches of Henry Brougham Esq. delivered before a Committee of the Honourable House of Commons, in opposition to a Bill, for incorporating certain persons by the name of the Gas Light & Coke Company, Straharn & Preston, London, 1809.

Spiers, C.H., "William Thomas Brande, Leather Expert", Ann.Sci., 1969/9, V.25,3., pp.179-201.

Standing, S, History of the pharmaceutical industry with particular reference to Allen & Hanbury 1775-1843, Thesis. MSc, London,

Stewart, E.G., A Historical index of gasworks past & present in the area now served by North Thames Gas board, NTGas, 1958; Supplement NTGas, 1959.

Stewart, E.G., Town Gas its manufacture & distribution, Science Museum, HMSO, 1958.

Stockhardt, Julius A., Agricultural Chemistry, Henry G. Bohn, London, 1855.

Stokes, A., East Ham. Village to Corporate Town, Wilson & Williams, Stratford, 1935.

Sturt, Brian, "Early Years at the Old Kent Road Gas Works", Ind.Heritage Autumn 1990.

Sturt, Brian, "Low pressure gas storage", London IA, 1980/2, pp.13- 24.

Sturt, Brian, "The London & Greenwich Railway Gas Cos", GLIAS Newsletter 99, June 1986, pp.8-9.

Sturt, Brian, "A Brief History of the Wandsworth & District Gas Company", GLIAS Newsletter 99, Summer 1985, pp.10-13.

Sugden, John, Lord Cochrane. Naval Commander & Inventor. 1775-1860. A Study of his Later Career, PhD Sheffield, 1981.

Taylor, Edward, "The Use & Value of Ammoniacal Liquor for Agricultural Purposes", JGL 6th October 1851, pp.321.

Taylor, Edward, "The Use & Value of Gas Lime as a fertiliser for Agricultural Purposes", JGL, 10th July 1851, pp.26-7.

Taylor, F., Sherwood, A History of industrial chemistry Heinemann, London, 1957.

Taylor G.L. FRS MRIBA, The Introduction of Cannel Coal Gas Thoroughly Purified into the Metropolis, London, 1848.

Thames Ironworks Gazette, London, 1895-1911.

Thomas Parsons & Sons. 150 Years of Paint & Varnish. Parsons, London, 1857.

Thompson, Lewis, Nature & chemical Properties of Coal Gas. Published from Surplus Funds by the Committee for the Exhibition of Gas Apparatus at the Royal Polytechnic Institution in the Year 1851, London, 1851 & "Chemistry of Gas Lighting", JGL, V.III.,

1853-4, pp.24, 35, 76, 104, 170, 125, 239, 351, 388, 378, 551.

Thomson, T. 'On Coal Gas', Proc.Phil.Soc.Glasgow, 1843, V.1, pp. 165-175.

Threlfall, R.E., 100 years of phosphorous making, Albright & Wilson, Oldbury, 1952.

To be sanctioned by an Act of Parliament. A National Light & Heat Company for providing our streets & houses with light & heat, on similar principles, as they are now supplied with water, demonstrated, with the patentee's authority & instructions, by Professor Hardie at Theatre of Sciences, 98 Pall Mall, London, nd.

Tomory, Leslie. Progressive Enlightenment. MIT 2012

Tomory, Leslie. Let it Burn: Distinguishing Inflammable Airs 1766–1790. Ambix 2009

Tomory, Leslie The environmental history of the early British gas industry, 1812–1830 Environmental History 17

Tomory, Leslie Building the First Gas Network, 1812—1820

Technology and culture 52 2011

Tomory, Leslie Fostering a new industry in the Industrial Revolution: Boulton & Watt and gaslight 1800–1812. British Journal for the History of Science 46 (2), 2013

Tomory, Leslie Gaslight, distillation, and the industrial revolution

History of science 49 2011

Tomory, Leslie Competition and regulation in the early history of the London gas industry, 1800–1830. The London Journal 39 (2), 2014

Tomory, Leslie Science and the arts in William Henry's research into inflammable air during the Early 19th Century. Annals of Science 71 (1)

Trinder, Barrie, Industrial Revolution in Shropshire, Phillimore, London, 1981

Turner, G.L., "James Sadler, Oxford Engineer, Chemist & Aeronaut", Oxfordshire Roundabout, V.1/1 June 1965, pp.1- 6.

Tute, W.S., Cochrane, the life of Admiral Cochrane, Earl of Dundonald, London, 1965.

UK Electric Telegraph, Proceedings of the banquet & testimonial to the Chairman, The Company, London, 1872.

Van Voorst, John, The Gas Light & Coke Company. An Address to the Proprietors of the Intended Company, London, 1809.

Voelcker, August, "On the Composition & Use of Gas Lime in Agriculture", JGL 14th April 1865, p.210.

Walker, M.C., History of the Manufacture of Sulphuric Acid up to 1860, Thesis MSc Univ. London, 1933.

Ward, Edward, "The Death of Charles Blachford Mansfield (1819-1855)", Ambix, 7/1984, July 31, Pt.2, pp.68-9.

Warren, C.M., "Researches in the volatile hydrocarbons", JGL 3rd Oct 1865, pp.726-728.

Warren, K., Chemical Foundations The Alkali Industry in Britain to 1926, Rees, Oxford, 1980.

Watson Smith, W., "The earliest methods of the coking of coal, coke ovens for metallurgical purposes & the recovery of tar& ammonia"., JSocChemI, III 29th Dec 1884, pp.661-606.

Watson, Richard, Chemical Essays, Jackson, London, 1800.

Watts, J.I., First fifty years of Brunner Mond 1873-1922, The Company, Nantwich, 1923.

W, F.A., Description of the Thermolampe invented by Lebon of Paris, Published with remarks by F.A.W. of London, Braunschweig, 1802.

Whitton, E.W., The Oilman's Vade Mecum & Useful Assistant, Sherwood, Neeley & Jones, London, 1809.

Williams, R.A., Old Mines of the Llangynog District, Northern Mine Research Soc., 1985.

Williams, Trevor I., History of the British Gas Industry, OUP, London, 1981.

Williams, Trevor I., The Chemical Industry, Pelican, London, 1953.

Willies, Lyn, "Industrial Landscape of Rio Tinto, Huelva, Spain", IAR, V. XII,1. 1989.Wilson, Charles, The history of Unilever, Cassell, London, 1954.

Wilson, J.F., "Ownership, management & strategy in early NW Gas Companies 1815-30", Business Hist., 4/1991, V.33/2., pp.203- 221.

Wilson, G., The old days of Price's Candles, 1876.

Wilson, John, Lighting the Town. A Study in Management in the North West Gas Industry 1805-1880, Paul Chapman for British Gas North West, 1991.

Winsor, F. A., Plain questions & answers refuting every possible objection against the beneficial introduction of coke & gas lights, London, 1807.

Winsor, F.A., National Deposit bank; or the bulwark of British security, credit & commerce, in all times of difficulty changes & revolutions, London, 1807.

Winsor, F.A., The superiority of the new patent coke, over the use of coals, in all family concerns, displayed every evening, at the large theatre, Lyceum, Strand. Addressed to all the enlightened inhabitants of London & the British Empire, London, nd.

Winsor, F.A., Analogy between animal & vegetable life. Demonstrating the beneficial application of the patent light stoves, to all green & hot houses, London, 1807.

Winsor, F.A., Notice Historique sur L'utilisation du Gaz Hydrogene pour l'Eclairage avec un Extrait du Proces Verbal d'Enquete faite par le Parlement d'Angleterre sur Cette Eclairage, Paris, 1816.

Winsor, F.A., Mr.W. Nicholson's attack in his Philosophical Journal on Mr. Winsor & the National Light & Heat Company; with Mr. Winsor's defence, London, 1807.

Winsor, F.A., Account of the most ingenious & important national discovery for some ages. British Imperial patent light ovens & stoves, by which above 1, 000 per cent are saved & gained in light, heat, & some valuable products for British manufactures, commerce & navigation, London, 1804.

Winsor, F.A., The New Patriotic Imperial & National Patent Company, for establishing sundry manufactories to make & extract for home consumption & exportation, coke, charcoal, ammonia, acids, oil, tar, chemical salts, &c. From all the combustibles in nature; & for applying the inflammable air obtained from the raw fuel to the purposes of heating, boiling, smelting, lighting, illuminating, &c., London, nd.

Winsor, F.A., Ludicrous debate among the Gods & Goddesses in a Grand Council assembled on the proposed destruction of the notorious London smoke by the use of gaslights. By 'Obadiah Prim, M.D., B.A., F.R.S., F.A.S., London, 1807.

Winsor, F.A.Jnr, A short sketch on the benefits resulting from gas lights, London, nd.

Winsor, F.A.Jnr, A concise tract on the production of gas lights., London, nd.

Winzer, F.A., Prosperity of England midst the clamours of ruin., London, 1799.

Wooder, L.G., Paint & Varnish Industry in GB, Thesis MSc (Econ) Univ.London, 1955.

THE FOLLOWING INDIVIDUALS AND INSTITUTIONS HAVE PROVIDED INFORMATION IN VERBAL, LETTER AND UNPUBLISHED MANUSCRIPT FORM.

Andrew Alexander, Tallow Chandler's Company [notes on Hawes family]

Bob Barnes, Brunel Engine House [info. on Rotherhithe industry]

David Bick, Glos. [info. on Welsh mines]

Howard Bloch, Local History Librarian, LB Newham [info. on West Ham]

E.J.Burford, NW8 [info. on Hatchard]

Dr.R.J.M. Carr, N4 [MS on Thames Shipbuilding and misc.info.]

Chatham Historic Dockyard Trust [info.on ropemaking]

Julia Elton, Elton Engineering Books [MS notes on Elton collection]

Dr.Keith Fairclough [MS notes on Limehouse Cut]

Mrs. Sue Haytor, Farnborough, Kent [Translation from German]

Patrick Hills, Penshurst, Kent [papers on Hills family]

Mr. Humpheries, Aberdeenshire [papers on Hills family]

Mrs. Barbara Ludlow (ex-staff LB Greenwich Local History Dept.) [info. on Greenwich industries]

Philip MacDougall, Rochester [info. on Royal Dockyards]

Dr. Peter Morris [print out of extracts from Kelly's Directories]

Dr. Margaret Mullins, Farnborough [Info. on Farnborough Hill]

Neil Rhind, SE3 [info. on Blackheath residents]

Tom Ridge, Ragged School Museum [info. on canal side industry]

Dr.G.Roberts, Open University [trans. from German plus info.]

Prof. C.Russell, Open University [info. on Hills]

Stanley Shoop, Elstree [info. on Margate Pier

Dr.C.Schmitz, University of St.Andrews [info. on Taylor family]

John Smith, East Grinstead [sight of MS on Congreve]

Tim Smith, Berkhamstead [sight of MS on coke, plus much misc. info.]

Brian and Nigel Sturt, SE13 (Nigel, ex-staff London Gas Museum). [misc. info. on gas industry]

David Thomas, SE1 [info. on Brandram]

James Thorburn, Aberystwyth [info. on Hills Spanish mines]

Ray Vickers, Huddersfield [info. on London soapmakers]

Mrs. Walsh, Oxford [info. on Pearson family]

Mrs. Wagstaffe, Dorchester [info. on Davies family]

Tom Wareham, Drapers Company [info. on members of Drapers Co.]

'Tosher' Wilskowski, LB Tower Hamlets, Polluted Sites Officer [info. on chemical works in LBTH]

MANUSCRIPT SOURCES

BRITISH LIBRARY

Bennet Woodcroft Collection (at Science Reference Library)

Crips,F.Southwell annotated copy of The Earliest Works on Gas Lighting, London, 1907

Greenwich Scrapbooks

Letter from John Taylor, 1819, add MS 34612, ct 5/1819

Prospectus collection

CITY OF LONDON GUILDHALL LIBRARY

City of London Gas Light and Coke CoDirectors Minutes.

Great Central Gas Light and Coke Co. Directors Minutes.

Hill, N.K. The History of the Imperial Continental Gas Association 1824-1900.

Imperial Continental Gas Association, (misc. collection).

Imperial Continental Gas Association, Directors Minutes.

A.E.E.Jones, Daniel Bennett and Co.

Apothecaries' Company, Minute Books.

CITY OF WESTMINSTER LOCAL HISTORY DEPARTMENT

St. John, Westminster, Poor Rate Books.

St. Margaret, Westminster, Poor Rate Books.

Westminster, Sewer rate books.

CITY OF BIRMINGHAM PUBLIC LIBRARIES

The Boulton and Watt collection consists of a mass of MS material and includes:

Assay House Collection;

Doldowled Papers;

Muirhead Collection;

Matthew Boulton papers, etc.

DENBIGH COUNTY LIBRARY

Deeds of Woodlands, Denbigh

DUDLEY, METROPOLITAN DISTRICT, LOCAL HISTORY LIBRARY

Dudley Parish Rating Records

Lord Dudley's Estate collection.

GRAVESHAM BOROUGH LIBRARY

J.Barnes, Notes on Rosher Family, nd.

LONDON METROPOLITAN ARCHIVE

Commercial Gas Light and Coke Co., Director's Minutes.

Commissioners of Sewers, Greenwich, Records and Assessments.

Commissioners of Sewers, Hackney Level, Records.

Commissioners of Sewers, St. Anne's Level, Records

Equitable Gas Light and Coke Co., Directors Minutes.

Gas Light & Coke Company, Directors Minutes from June 1812.

Gas Light & Coke Company, Proprietors Minutes from June 1812.

Gas Light & Coke Company, Committee of Accounts from August 1812.

Gas Light & Coke Company, Committee of Works Minutes from February 1815.

Gas Light & Coke Company, Committee of Chemistry & Machinery. Minutes from August 1812-1813

Gas Light & Coke Company, Committee of Light & Experiment. Minutes Feb 1815-March 1815

Imperial Gas Light & Coke Company, Directors Minutes from July 1821

Imperial Gas Light and Coke Company, Shareholders Minutes, from 2nd July 1821

Imperial Gas Light and Coke Co. Committee for General Purposes, Minutes, from 16th June 1831

Imperial Gas Light & Coke Co., Committee for Works, Minutes, from June 1822

Independent Gas Light and Coke Co., Directors Minutes from March 1827 inc. packet of letters from Richard Laming

Independent Gas Light & Coke Co., Shareholders Minutes from July 1829.

Luke Howard's Notebook & items relating to Luke Howard & James Jewell.

Map collection

Metropolitan Commissioner of Sewer. Records and rate books

Metropolitan Board of Works, Reports Collection

North Thames Gas Collection; Misc. documents

Phoenix Gas Light and Coke Company, Proprietors Minutes from January 1853

Phoenix Gas Light and Coke Company, Directors Meetings, Minutes from August 1824

Ratcliffe Gas Light and Coke Co. Minutes

Shoreditch Independent Gas Light and Coke Co. Minutes

South London Gas Light and Coke Co, Committee of Management, Signed Minutes, June 1823-Aug 1824
South Metropolitan Gas Light and Coke Co., Deed of Settlement, 20th February 1834
South Metropolitan Gas Light and Coke Co., Proprietors Minutes from Oct 1834
South Metropolitan Gas Light and Coke Co., Directors Minutes from February 1834
Sydenham Gas Light & Coke Co., Directors Minutes
Thames Ironworks, Minutes, 1871.

HOUSE OF LORDS RECORD OFFICE
Evidence to House of Lords Enquiry on Gas Light & Coke Co.

INSTITUTION OF GAS ENGINEERS, LIBRARY
Arthur Elton, Rise of the Gas Industry in England & France
E.G. Stewart, Samuel Clegg, 1962.
E.G. Stewart, Calendar of events in the gas industry, nd.

Sir Arthur Elton, The Triumph of Gas Lights
Items of Elton gas collection cf: The Arthur Elton Gas Collection with some related works on Heating and Ventilation. Part I. Books]
{Julia Elton. [majority of collection is at Ironbridge Gorge Museum]

LONDON BOROUGH OF TOWER HAMLETS LOCAL HISTORY LIBRARY
All Saints, Poplar, Health Committee Report, 1833.
All Saints, Poplar, Rating Assessements and Approvals.
Bethnal Green, Land Tax Assessments.
Deed collection.
M.Gladon, History of the Antiquities of Bromley, St.Leonards, Middlesex, 1844.
Liberty of Norton Folgate, Minutes.
Sydney Maddocks, Historical notes relating to the formation of the Commercial Gas Light and Coke Co.
St Mary, Bow, Poor Rate Books.
St.Leonard, Bromley, Land Tax Assessments.

St.Leonard, Bromley, Poor Rate Books.
St.Mary, Bow, Vestry Minutes.

LONDON BOROUGH OF NEWHAM LOCAL HISTORY LIBRARY
West Ham, Abbey Lands, Rate Books
All Saints, West Ham, Nuisance Records
All Saints, West Ham, Poor Rate Books
Commissioners of Sewers, West Ham, Rate Book

LONDON GAS MUSEUM (Collection dispersed, current whereabouts unknown)
Gas Light and Coke Co. Journal.
Minutes of Evidence of Oil Gas Enquiry (handwritten), 1825

LONDON BOROUGH OF LEWISHAM LOCAL HISTORY LIBRARY
Josephine Birchenough, 400 Years of Lee, 1971.
St.Paul, Deptford, Poor Rate Books.
Thankful Sturdy Collection
An ashtray which illustrates Lawes Deptford works.

LONDON BOROUGH OF LAMBETH LOCAL HISTORY DEPARTMENT
Christ Church, Blackfriars, Poor Rate book.
Deed collection.

LONDON BOROUGH OF GREENWICH LOCAL HISTORY DEPARTMENT
St.Alphage, Greenwich, Vestry Minutes
St. Alphage, Greenwich, Poor Rate book.
St. Alfage, Tithe Map and Records, 1843.
St. Margaret, Woolwich, Vestry Minutes.
St. Margaret, Woolwich, Poor Rate Book.
St. Nicholas, Deptford, Poor Rate book.
St. Nicholas, Plumstead, Poor Rate Book.
A number of subject based files containing family history records, letters etc. (file titles are referenced in footnotes).

LONDON BOROUGH OF HACKNEY LOCAL HISTORY DEPARTMENT
St.John, Hackney, Poor Rate Book.

LONDON BOROUGH OF SOUTHWARK LOCAL HISTORY COLLECTION
St John Horsleydown, Poor Rate Books.
St.Mary Magdalene, Bermondsey, Poor Rate Book.
St Mary, Rotherhithe, Poor Rate books.
St.Olave, Poor Rate Books.
St.Saviour, Poor Rate Book.

LONDON BOROUGH OF BARKING LOCAL HISTORY COLLECTION
Lawes Agricultural Manure Co., Minute Books and misc. papers.

LONDON DOCKLANDS DEVELOPMENT CORPORATION)
Travers Morgan & Co., Report, Planning Committee Papers, for meeting 17th October 1994.

MR. PATRICK HILLS
Misc. documents concerning Hills Family

MR. HUMPHERIES
Misc. documents concerning Hills Family

MRS. WALSH
Elizabeth Pearson, Diary

NATIONAL LIBRARY OF SCOTLAND
Misc. Letters Earl of Dundonald

ROYAL SOCIETY
Council Minutes.

ROYAL ARTILLERY LIBRARY
MS notes, Isaac Landmann

SCIENCE MUSEUM LIBRARY
Simon Goodrich Diary.
Farmer collection

TRINITY HOUSE ARCHIVE
Minute books of the Elder Brethren

UNIVERSITY COLLEGE, UNIVERSITY OF LONDON
Admission Registers.

WELCOME FOUNDATION LIBRARY
Proofs of evidence in case of Hancock v. Goodyear. (WMS 2583)
Misc. letters W.T. Brande.

The extracts from "The A to Z of Georgian London" are reproduced by kind permission of Harry Margary at www.harrymargary.com in association with the London Metropolitan Archives at 40 Northampton Road, Clerkenwell, London EC1R 0HB and at http:collage.cityoflondon.gov.uk.

Thanks to many many people over many many years – in particular the late Patrick Hills.

In producing this book thanks to R.J.M.Carr, Pam Carr, Jane Lawson, Rob Powell, Julian Watson, Nadeem Ahmad, and Nina Baker.

INDEX

312

The basis for this work was her PhD Thesis 'The Early Gas Industry and its residual products in East London' completed in the Department of History of Science and Technology at the Open University in 1995. This was supervised by Dr. Gerrylyn Roberts who is thanked for her support. She is aware that some of her research, part of the PhD, has subsequently appeared in works by another author.

This work uses a great deal of material which she published in the 1990s both from her PhD Thesis and in 'People and Places in the East London Gas Industry'. By bringing them together it is hoped to make a stronger argument for the pivotal role played by gas manufacture in industrial growth.

Mary lives in Greenwich and has worked in east London for many years, and is involved in a number of bodies promoting the industrial history of the area. She has written extensively in local and other publications.

Mary Mills

316

Printed in Great Britain
by Amazon

1

The Early East London Gas Industry.
How it began
and
How it helped London Industries to Grow

By

Mary Mills

2

3

FOREWORD

This is a history of the early gas industry in east London - primarily a story of bright ideas with a bit of fraud and some incompetence. It attempts to show its links to many other contemporary industrial enterprises. It is about the working east of the metropolis, with many impoverished residents, along with the astonishing wealth of the City of London. It was, and is, an area of great resilience – the whole tradition of dodgy geezers, doing the best they can.

I also hope to show how the early industry related to this intensely busy industrial area – including information on their sites and their shareholders. In particular how it became a source of raw materials as well as light and heat.

It is about London to the east of Westminster – the City itself and what we now call the East End, but which , beyond the City wall, was then part of Middlesex and, across the Lea, parts of Essex. South of the river was Surrey with the Kent boundary at the Earl Sluice. It was an important area for the early gas industry – as for much else. We hear a great deal about the wealthy elite in London's West End, as similarly we hear a great deal about the poverty, and exploitation of the poor. Both of these things are true and I would not want to devalue them but discussion of them, and only them, leaves out the vast majority of the population in an area of extraordinary dynamism.

Those who do not know London need to be aware that by 'The City' is meant the area governed by the Corporation of the City of London and enclosed within the Roman Wall – not the wider Metropolitan area. The ancient City has vast wealth and privileges, and has encompassed ventures as extraordinary and impactful as the East India Company. It has resources for research available from the ancient Livery Companies (has anyone studied the industrial innovations funded by the Apothecaries Company?).

Beyond the City and stretching east was a vast world of commerce. In the early 19th century there were the newly built docks receiving and processing the plunder of empire; an enormous and innovative ship building industry with all the ancillary trades involved, a whole riverside culture of small boats and diverse trades. Alongside them was a wealth of small businesses and manufacturers – and some huge breweries – and much, much else.

4